THE CULTURE OF
POVERTY

A CRITIQUE

EDITED BY

Eleanor Burke Leacock

SIMON AND SCHUSTER
NEW YORK

FIRST PRINTING
SBN 671-20845-4 Casebound edition
SBN 671-20846-2 Clarion paperback edition
Library of Congress Catalog Card Number: 75-139640
Designed by Irving Perkins
Manufactured in the United States of America

CONTENTS

PART II:
Theoretical and Methodological Problems with the "Culture of Poverty" Concept

PREFACE

The present book originated as a series of papers given in a critical symposium on the "culture of poverty" concept. The symposium, organized and chaired by myself, was held in Pittsburgh at the 1966 meetings of the American Anthropological Association. At that time it was already commonplace for people working in social welfare and education to refer to the "culture of poverty" as a supposed explanation for the myriad problems to be found among the poor, a practice which served to mask the crucial issue of social and economic injustice that our society must face. It seemed high time that anthropologists, along with other social scientists and with educators, should concern themselves with these circumstances and explore their implications.

The papers given at that time, and later rewritten for this book, are those by Estelle Fuchs, Stanley Newman, and Lisa Peattie, anthropologists, Vera John, psychologist, and Janet Castro, educator. When Charles Valentine, anthropologist, spoke from the floor to criticize us for not being hard-hitting enough, he was promptly asked to contribute a chapter to the book that was to come out of the symposium. Other authors who were unable to contribute to the original symposium due to pressure of time are Anthony Leeds, anthropologist, Hylan Lewis, sociologist, and Ernest Drucker, psychologist. Anthropologists Mildred Dickeman, Herbert Ellis, Murray Wax, Rosalie Wax, and Rolland Wright, and educator Jean Lester were subsequently invited to participate.

With one or two exceptions, the chapters were written expressly for the book, and many of them embody reports on the original research or direct experience of the writer. The authors vary in their emphases and interests; they certainly do not see eye to eye

7

on every particular point. All, however, share the concern that a too hastily conceived concept of a "poverty culture" has been widely applied and misused; and all share a professional commitment to making clear the scientific, political and ethical issues involved. Any number of papers have been written which point out difficulties with the "culture of poverty" concept, or which specifically criticize the theoretical viewpoint of Oscar Lewis as its originator and popularizer (although Lewis' contribution of data on life among poor Mexican families is generally respected). However, such papers are seldom readily available to the interested public. The purpose of the present book is to make critical material available to the many people working in education, health and welfare fields who know something is amiss but who are bemused by the scientific backing the "culture of poverty" notion seems to have.

Insofar as it was possible, the authors of the various chapters have met together both at anthropology meetings and elsewhere, to discuss problems relevant to the book and offer criticisms and suggestions on each other's chapters. Thus the book as a venture has strengthened both friendships and intellectual commitments. Many people have been helpful to me in the writing of my own introductory chapter, and I particularly wish to thank Anthony Leeds for his detailed suggestions, as well as colleagues whose works are not included here: Rosa Graham, Hyman Rodman and Constance Sutton. I am indebted to Ernest Drucker for seeing the book through some of its final production stages when I departed for field work in Zambia. I am also grateful to Martha Livingston, Lila Waldman and Maryon Fischetti for their help in preparing the manuscript for publication.

In this period, when the very life of mankind is at stake, and crisis itself has become institutionalized, it seems indeed to be fiddling for a group of professionals to contribute yet another to the mountain of books that exists. It is with something of an apology that I express the hope that this one adds a little to the understanding of our society's ills, and helps to undo some of the mischief that professionals themselves have done.

ELEANOR BURKE LEACOCK

INTRODUCTION

ELEANOR BURKE LEACOCK

The Culture Concept

The special contribution that the science of anthropology has made to the study of man has been to clarify the enormous significance of "enculturation," or socialization, as the process whereby a group's characteristic attitudes, behaviors, and talents are passed on to the young. The detailed study of man and his many lifeways has led to the recognition that it is the cultural—the historically developed and traditionally accepted—attitudes and standards for behavior of a society which are transmitted to children, rather than genetic determinants of such attitudes and behaviors. The study of human infants and of animal societies has shown that man's biological inheritance, his "human nature," involves not only a high degree of intelligence, but also a strong emphasis on *sociality,* or the predisposition to learn and accept the behaviors and share the concerns that make a person an accepted part of his group.

Sociologists and social psychologists have adopted the culture concept from anthropology as helpful in revealing the ways in which social conditions (instead of innate propensities) lead to differences in group behavior. It is a bitter irony, therefore, that the concept of culture is now being widely applied in such a form as to be almost as pernicious in its application as biological determinist and racist views have been in the past. As an extreme example, consider the use of the term "dregs-culture" in a book on *Social Issues in Public Education.* The author, John A. Bartky,

9

refers to the Chicago ghetto as "dregs areas" where Southern urban laborers or farm hands "contribute the worst of the cultural values they have brought with them to . . . dregs cultures, and soon acquire the most vicious of their values." Bartky continues with such statements as "The dregs-culture child, if he is old enough, is probably being cared for by his second father and third mother" and "is inculcated with a race consciousness that is likely to get him into difficulties." Crime is so rampant in "dregs-culture communities" that the law must work "fast and ruthlessly," and the "policeman must often be judge, prosecutor, and punisher." The storefront church, rather than being something of a fraternal organization and community center, is to Bartky a "wild cat church," which "is more of an amusement than . . . a moral influence." Teachers in the "Negro dregs-culture schools" are frustrated in their attempts to teach by such "cultural considerations." In sum:

In the dregs-culture community we find the Negro philosophy of life is quite different from that of the middle-class white man or Negro. He accepts, with or without resistance, the fact that he is barred from many material successes, and as a result material values are paramount for him. He refuses to encourage his children to study because the advantages to be gained from study are too remote. We call him improvident, but in reality he is merely a fatalist . . . [Bartky, 1963, pp. 135-41.]

Here the term "culture" is used as a thin veil for the expression of the most vulgar stereotypes about the experience of black Americans, the vast majority of whom are poor. (Bartky exonerates the "very few" Negroes in Chicago who are "well-to-do fugitives from the restrictions of Southern culture" from participation in "dregs-culture.") No anthropologist would countenance such views as even partially describing ghetto culture. However, some of the writings by anthropologists and other behavioral scientists, that deal with concepts as "lower-class culture," "cultural deprivation," and the popular "culture of poverty," have contributed to distorted characterizations of the poor, and especially the black poor. The fact is that, through the "culture of poverty" and similar notions, the nineteenth-century argument that the poor are poor through their own lack of ability and initiative, has reentered the scene in a new form, well decked out with scientific jargon. The concern of the social scientists and educators who discuss their own research and experience in the pages that follow is to correct the misconceptions that support such a view.

The major assumption made by many "culture of poverty" theorists is that a virtually autonomous subculture exists among the poor, one which is self-perpetuating and self-defeating. This subculture, it is argued, involves a sense of resignation or fatalism and an inability to put off the satisfaction of immediate desires in order to plan for the future. These characteristics are linked with low educational motivation and inadequate preparation for an occupation—factors that perpetuate unemployment, poverty and despair. For example, Oscar Lewis makes a statement to this effect:

The culture of poverty is not only an adaptation to a set of objective conditions of the larger society. Once it comes into existence it tends to perpetuate itself from generation to generation because of its effect on the children. By the time slum children are age six or seven they have usually absorbed the basic values and attitudes of their subculture and are not psychologically geared to take full advantage of changing conditions or increased opportunities which may occur in their lifetime. [Lewis, 1966, p. xlv.]

Along similar lines, the position taken by Daniel P. Moynihan in his report *The Negro Family: The Case for National Action* was that the "tangle of pathology" he described as characterizing the Negro community was "capable of perpetuating itself without assistance from the white world." Its basis was to be found in the Negro family, which, "once or twice removed, . . . will be found to be the principal source of most of the aberrant, inadequate, or antisocial behavior that did not establish, but now serves to perpetuate the cycle of poverty and deprivation" (Moynihan, 1965, pp. 30, 47).

Culturally established standards for behavior and goals for

achievement—often loosely referred to as "values"—can be remarkably persistent. For example, as we shall see in the pages that follow, Indian groups have for generations maintained their own attitudes about the proper and desirable way children should relate to adults. And in our cities we observe the sense of identity and cultural distinctiveness possessed by many national groups who refuse to be entirely "melted" away. Rolland Wright suggests in his chapter on the "stranger" mentality of the urbanized industrialized world that some of the attitudes ascribed to a so-called culture of poverty are attitudes which stem not from poverty, but from the more familial traditions of Mexican Americans, American Indians, American blacks, and rural Europeans.

On the whole, however, those cultural traditions that are valued and kept alive by precept and example are either distorted or ignored by culture of poverty theorists. Instead, there is a focus on traits that contribute to a failure to live up to presumed "middle-class" ideals. For instance, while culture-of-poverty theory stresses the "tangle of pathology" of the black ghetto and its relation to "lower-class values," black America has its own concept of its values, as connoted, for example, by the term "soul." "Soul is the essence of blackness," stated Professor C. Eric Lincoln in his address at the founding of a new Black Academy of Arts and Letters. "If black is beautiful, it is soul that makes it so." The term embodies a positive assertion of a common identity, history and tradition. It suggests, among other things, a sense of life and vitality and a feeling of distinctiveness from white society that is viewed as inhumanly cold and impersonal in its competitiveness and assertion of superiority.

Not only does poverty-culture theory focus on a negative, distorted and truncated view of a cultural whole, but it also implies an untenable view of the process whereby cultural traits are evolved and transmitted. At first glance, the passing down of a "poverty culture" along family lines may seem to involve a process similar to the preservation of somewhat separate traditions among different groups in the larger society. However, the papers by social scientists and educators that follow exemplify quite a different view of the culture process and of the relations among individual personality, culturally patterned belief systems, and historically evolving social and economic structures. These differences pertain to assumptions in three intricately related areas: (1) child development, (2) the effect of culture on individual personality, and (3) the effect in turn that individual personalities *in toto* have on the further development of culture.

1. Developmental Stages and the Culture of Poverty. Culture-of-poverty theory assumes a person's "value-attitude system" and response pattern to be virtually set by the age of six or seven. Discussions of the ill effects of poverty culture on children generally assume that what happens prior to school entry is more important than what happens later. Few would argue that some of what we refer to as an individual's "personality" takes shape in the early years, and even in the early months. And few would argue that the particular way each individual, with some given but vaguely defined propensities, organizes his life experience and internalizes it as a network of patterns for thinking about and relating to other people, to the world around him, and to himself becomes increasingly well established over time and increasingly more difficult to change. But to say or imply that *values* and *motivations* are set by six or seven flies in the face of findings in developmental psychology. For example, Jerome Kagan enumerates the profound developments which take place in our society between the ages of six and ten, and which involve the conscious definition by children of attitudes about relations with peers, about intellectual mastery and rational thought, and about sexual identification and sex-role behavior (Kagan and Moss, 1962).

2. The Effect of Culture on Individual Personality. Poverty-culture theory generally implies that culture is a mold which produces a uniform set of dominant characteristics in those growing up under its influence. The match between culturally prescribed behavior and individual personality is thereby exaggerated and an unwarranted homogeneity of both is assumed. To some extent this problem stems from early writings on culture and personality, such as Ruth Benedict's *Patterns of Culture.* The central point Benedict made was that cultures do not draw equally upon the wide arc of potential human behavior, but select different aspects for particular emphasis and elaboration. Benedict made an important contribution in demonstrating the plasticity of man's nature, and the variety of cultural courses mankind has taken. However, individual behavioral styles do not simply mirror dominant cultural goals. Cultural norms do not exist outside man's living history, and they involve conflicting and contradictory goals and values, from which people choose, and which allow for change and development.

Furthermore, individuals may either passively accept their cultural environment or actively seek to develop or change some part of it, and they will exhibit a wide variety of styles in the way they do either one. C. W. M. Hart commented on the variety of personalities to be found even within a small and culturally homogeneous band of Australian aborigines. He wrote that, while an individual will follow a cultural course, he will follow it "cheerfully or sourly, silently or garrulously, in a relaxed manner or a tense manner, like a leader or like a follower, with his eye on the gallery or regardless of the world's opinion" (Hart, 1954, p. 259). As a matter of fact, the earlier work of Oscar Lewis (1961) explicitly documented the diversity of responses to poverty that he found within a single Mexican family. In a critique of personality and culture writings, Anthony F. C. Wallace notes that the direction of much contemporary research in this area is away from a view of culture as producing motivational uniformity. Wallace proposes that a more productive approach to culture would be to view it "as a mechanism for the organization of a diversity of individual psychological differences within cultural boundaries," a diversity so great that "the analytical problem would be the elucidation of the processes of the organization of diversity rather than the mechanism of inducing a supposed uniformity" (Wallace, 1962, p. 4).

Perhaps an even more important drawback to poverty-culture theory than the variety of responses individuals make within a given cultural setting is the lack of internal consistency within any one person. The ambivalence of conflicting desires is constantly at play in the choices and decisions a person makes, the results of which then become incorporated into his ongoing development.

The powerlessness of the poor is clearly undermining, but contemporary events offer ample evidence of the new energy which can be released when steps are taken for a redress of grievance. Interviews with black high-school youths, some from extremely poor homes, who were taking part in a school boycott gave testimony of the exhilaration they experienced when doing something together toward improving the situation they had found so demoralizing (Fuchs, 1966).

3. The Effect of Individual Personalities on Culture. The third failing of poverty-culture theory lies in the closed-circle relationship between the individual and society that it implies. Often implicit, rather than explicitly stated, the assumption is that childhood experiences in the family, which have become encapsulated in the personality, are somehow projected into the institutional structures that pattern adult behavior and beliefs. Thus, social-economic organization, technological developments, and unresolved conflicts within and among institutional structures with which the individual must cope if he is to live are not taken into account as exerting a constant and pervasive influence on the culture patterns that define adult behavior. Shortcomings in this static view of culture as perpetuating itself through the medium of "group personality" were not quite so obvious when the concept was applied to self-contained primitive societies in which change appeared to be relatively slow and tradition strong. Furthermore, anthropologists studied such societies after their autonomy had been destroyed by Western colonialism, and it was difficult to reconstruct the internal processes of change that were evidenced by the archeological remains of their earlier histories. However, such a nondynamic and "psychological reductionist" view of the individual in society as the above is clearly absurd, given the contemporary world of accelerated change and conflict, and virtually instantaneous worldwide communication and cross-cultural influence.

The papers that follow document in various ways the dynamic interaction between individual and society. Anthony Leeds points out that many supposed "culture of poverty" traits are not of the type to be passed down as part of a world view. They are practical responses to adversity as it is structured within a particular social system. Lisa Peattie describes the "institutional press" that leads to the appearance of "poverty culture" traits among some of the migrants to a new Venezuelan city. Herbert Ellis and Stanley Newman describe several alternative modes of response to society among Chicago ghetto youth, who "play the system" with rare sophistication as they don and discard roles according to the situation.

In my own study of second- and fifth-grade classrooms in city schools, I observed the extent to which teacher attitudes and practices varied according to the children's home and backgrounds, black and white, middle and lower income, and I documented the active role the school plays in socializing the young for the occupational roles (including that of unemployment) they are expected to fill as adults (Leacock, 1969). This is obviously not a matter of conscious connivance. It follows from the way institutional structures in a society mesh and reinforce one another, and the way individuals learn the rationales that make sense of their behavior in given settings. It is true that all human behavior is in some sense adaptive, and when repeated over generations adaptive behaviors become institutionalized as cultural norms that may be internalized as "values." However, the process of adaptation continues actively throughout an individual's lifetime; individuals are not simply set in motion as children to respond automatically for the rest of their lives. Cultural norms and definitions of roles are constantly reinforced for an individual, or redirected, by the institutional structures within which he functions.

Urban school systems have a dual track, one for middle-income children who will for the most part go on to college and more or less professional occupations, and one for poor and minority children who will go into trades or service occupations if they do not fall into the categories of under- or unemployed. Every mother who fights to get her child into the fast class on a grade in a heterogeneous school, or who moves away from a "changing" neighborhood so that her child can go to a "good" school, knows this fact. The double-track system meshes in turn with patterns of urban demography and neighborhood segregation by race and income, and with the structure of employment, of decision-making political institutions, and so forth. The child from a poor family meets anew at each stage of his life difficulties parallel to those which he had to face when growing up. The complex intertwining of institutional structures and individual habits and expectations has been dramatically underlined by the intensity of the reaction to the recent movement for community control, which has threatened to upset existing status systems and redistribute decision-making powers.

Stereotyped Interpretation in Culture-of-Poverty Writings

When we turn from the definition of culture implied by culture-of-poverty theory to a consideration of the presumed content of poverty culture, we find an ethnocentric tendency to interpret behavioral patterns among lower-class people as isolated traits rather than in terms of their total context, and as shortcomings from some presumed "middle-class" ideal. As a comment on this, Janet Castro notes in her chapter that she has yet to find in her classrooms the well-organized and motivated middle-class youngsters implied by the discussions of deprived children. However, it is not too surprising if it is difficult for researchers to avoid misinterpreting and distorting "how the other half live," given certain deeply ingrained American attitudes toward class differences that follow from the particular history of this country.

The social history of the United States is usually presented in terms of poor people coming to these shores and working their way up toward security and success. Although studies suggest that upward mobility was not as great as it is commonly assumed, many family histories include parents or grandparents who came with very little and worked their way, if not that far "up," at least definitely "in." One might think that, as a result, Americans would feel more akin to those below them on the social scale than seems to be the case.

It appears, instead, that the closer a person's experience has been to that of his poorer brethren, the more strenuously he may argue that it takes will and ability to get ahead, and that the poor are poor out of laziness, stupidity, or lack of ambition. He thereby not only vindicates his own gains, and assuages, perhaps, a lingering guilt that he does not wish to cast behind a helping hand, but he also reassures himself. It is important to him that his position should follow from an intrinsically greater worthiness; this helps protect him from the threat of social vagaries like the rise and fall of unemployment, the greater insecurity that comes with age (apart from those in assured upper-status positions), the unpredictability of technological displacements, or the occurrence of serious accident or illness. Furthermore, the fact that the vast majority of black Americans have historically been relegated to a lower-class status means that traditionally learned and deeply held attitudes of white superiority contribute to the sense of distance middle-class white people feel in relation to their lower-class compatriots. In her book *Pickets at the Gates,* Estelle Fuchs documents how some of these middle-class attitudes influence a school principal of immigrant background who is at loggerheads with the black parents of his school (Fuchs, 1966, pp. 43ff.).

Social scientists aim to achieve an objective, detached, and truly scientific attitude toward society, free from subjective involvements in their own social position. Unfortunately, however, the findings of their own sciences constantly affirm the fact that, though they may constantly strive for the goal of objectivity, they should never assume that it can be completely attained. Social scientists are human beings, which means social and cultural beings whose needs, desires, fears and persuasions must impinge upon their work in various ways. By definition "middle-class," their scientific calling does not automatically make them immune to ethnocentrism when looking at members of the lower classes. Since the vast majority of social scientists are white, their attempts to achieve understanding across black–white lines are also subject to the chauvinism embedded in our culture. When viewing black members of the lower classes, we must examine their claim to objectivity with a particularly critical eye.

An anthropologist knows well that the faces he meets as an

outsider when he first enters an American Indian, African, or Polynesian community are far different from those he comes to know after living with a people and gaining some insight into their life from their own viewpoint and within the context of the objective conditions with which they must cope. Yet he too can fall into a trap and, along with his colleagues in sociology and psychology, can project his own biases as a middle-class person on members of the lower class, interpreting the latter's behaviors in terms of unstated assumptions about what is sensible and worthy. When we examine the literature on poverty culture, we find that this misinterpretation may be made in any of three ways: (1) through assuming that the behavior observed or attitudes tapped in the limited interaction situations in which a researcher often works with members of a low-status group represent the range of lower-class behavior and attitudes; (2) by working with a partial or biased sample of situations, groups, or individuals, and overgeneralizing from these to a major segment of some undefined "lower-class" group, or even to blue-collar workers as a whole; or (3) by interpreting lower-class behaviors in terms of single dimensions that are seen as the polar opposites of certain behaviors imputed to the middle class. To elaborate:

1. The Interaction Situation of the Research as Unrepresentative. It is axiomatic in the behavioral sciences that human behavior can be largely defined in terms of "role playing." A person does not simply "express himself," or even any considerable part of himself, in a given situation, but acts according to the patterns defined as appropriate to the situation and to his status within it. He expresses different aspects of himself as a teacher, as a husband, as a neighbor, as a warm friend, as a father, etc. Among the more restricted roles a person enacts—those in which he is most circumspect and controlled—are subordinate roles in formal situations. No matter what façade of easy informality one may adopt when meeting, say, a prospective employer, a department chairman, a supervisor, or a school principal, one is well aware that a proper reserve and deference is expected and one does not allow oneself to be unguardedly spontaneous. Obviously, behavior is the more wary the greater the distance between two people and the lower the status of the subordinate. Yet roles that are defined primarily in terms of clear superordinate and subordinate statuses are precisely those which have predominated in situations where data on lower-class behaviors are collected. Thus the social-service worker, or the social scientist, meets the unemployed worker, or welfare client, or delinquent youth under circumstances where the latter groups have to be extremely cautious and reserved. (Or, as an angry reaction, perhaps they may be assertively surly or hostile.) The "findings" resulting from such interactions have all too often been taken at face value, or the unwarranted assumption has been made that the restricted nature of the interaction btween the data collector and the subject has been taken into account.

When the partial view gained from the outside is replaced by some knowledge of total community life as seen from the inside, the results are altogether different. Years ago, in his pioneering study of an Italian slum neighborhood written up as *Street Corner Society,* William Foote White reported that a level of organization existed that was not reflected in the social-science literature of the time. In order to understand this organization, White stated, "the sociologist [must] become a participant observer of the most intimate activities in the social life of the slums." He continued, "Proceeding by this route, he will find many evidences of conflict and maladjustment, but he will not find the chaotic conditions once thought to exist throughout this area" (White, 1943, p. 39).

It seems each generation of social scientists makes and must correct the same mistakes when it comes to views of the poor. Some twenty-five years after White's work, Charles and Betty Lou Valentine write, as participant observers in a black and very poor community, that "it is proving difficult to find major community patterns that correspond to many of the subcultural traits often associated with poverty in learned writings about the poor." Instead the Valentines cite as common such practices as participation in organizations both inside and outside the community, the saving of money, and the planned acquisition of household appliances. They also note adherence to many goals and standards considered to be middle-class, that involve various aspects of style and behavior, as well as career orientations, commitment to education for children, and aspirations for community improvement. They write:

We see much energetic activity, great aesthetic and organizational variety, quite a number of highly patterned and well displayed behavior styles. Apathetic resignation does exist [as indeed it does in American society generally—E. L.], but it is by no means the dominant tone of the community. Social disorganization can be found, but it occurs only within a highly structured context. Individual pathology is certainly present, but adaptive coping with adversity is more common. Positive strengths (often ignored in the literature) include the ability to deal with misfortune through humor, the capacity to respond to defeat with renewed effort, recourse to widely varied sacred and secular ideologies for psychological strength, and resourceful devices to manipulate existing structures for maximum individual or group benefit. Perhaps least expectable from popular models is the capacity to mobilize initiatives for large-scale change like the movement for local control. [Valentine and Valentine, 1969, p. 412.]

Further examples of views "from the inside" are given in the pages that follow. Anthony Leeds reports similar impressions in his chapter where he describes life in urban slum areas in Brazil. The account by Herbert Ellis and Stanley Newman of adaptive roles assumed by ghetto youth reveals anything but attitudes of "resignation" and "fatalism." The chapters by Murray and Rosalie Wax and by Mildred Dickeman describe how one-sided is the view of Indian children held by teachers who know them only in the limited and formally structured school situation, when compared with the view of school as seen by the children and their parents.

In relation to misinterpretations of behavior based on observation of a very narrow behavioral range, Drucker discusses the distorted images yielded by techniques of testing and measurement. I.Q. tests have long been criticized for ignoring the rich diversity and range of human aptitudes and abilities. In the words of Irving Taylor, they show "how quickly people can solve relatively unimportant problems making as few errors as possible, rather than measuring how people grapple with relatively important problems, making as many productive errors as necessary with time no factor" (quoted in Frank Riessman, 1962, p. 49). Test scores are also known to measure educational experience rather than innate ability, and to be readily influenced by such things as a few hours of previous training and various modifications in the test-taking situation. A most dramatic instance of I.Q. modification is reported by Rosenthal and Jacobson (1968). As a result of their study-design, a Mexican-American boy was thought by his teacher to show promise of a jump in achievement. Indeed he did jump, moving from a retarded 61 to 106 during the course of the study year.

The citing of group test scores persists, however, and is accepted by those who would like to prove that there are differences in innate potentials along racial lines. Furthermore, since tests measure previous learning in a given school system, they are reasonably predictive of future learning in the same system, despite the fact that they yield a very restricted view of individual or group potentials. Anthropologists, who are on the whole skeptical of such data-collection techniques and who use them (when they do at all) with great reservations, are sometimes viewed as hopelessly idealistic and naïvely biased in favor of the people with whom they work—typically low status people from "backward" nations. Indeed, anthropologists do comprise the one academic group that gives virtual consensus to the conviction that inferior "intelligence" cannot be ascribed to any racially defined group. What is noteworthy is not only that anthropologists are the only social scientists to focus on the study of lifeways other than their own, but also that *they necessarily employ as their major technique of data collection a systematic learning from the people they study.* By putting themselves, however temporarily, in the subordinate position of pupils who wish to learn and understand something they do not already know, they come to know and respect the true measure of their subjects.

2. Sample Bias. Most discussions of poverty culture have been oriented toward seeking solutions for urban problems. In fact, however, there is a serious paucity of sound data on lifeways of the urban poor. The primary data upon which inferences have been based have been statistics drawn from records of people who are dependent upon or in trouble with the authorities in some way—welfare records, mental-hospital records, statistics on delinquency and crime, etc. The data focus on those who are demoralized, addicted, delinquent, etc., and do not concern those who manage to overcome the difficulties of poverty. Furthermore, statistics can easily be misused. Often figures are cited only in part. For example, reference may be made to the rising rate of divorce in black families, without referring to the rising rate nationally (or internationally, for that matter), or to the fact that the rate of increase happens to be higher at present among whites. Statistical materials can also give a skewed impression of what they are supposed to reveal. Moynihan cites rates of illegitimacy as an index of disorganization in the black community, but after analyzing the figures and what they indicate, the public-health psychologist William Ryan writes:

. . . the reported rates of illegitimacy among Negroes and whites tell us nothing at all about differences in family structure, historical forces, instability, or anything else about which the authors speculate [in the "Moynihan Report"]. From the known data, we can conclude only that Negro and white girls probably engage in premarital intercourse in about the same proportions, but that the white girl more often takes Enovid or uses a diaphragm; if she gets pregnant, she more often obtains an abortion; if she has the baby, first she is more often able to conceal it and, second, she has an infinitely greater opportunity to give it up for adoption. [Ryan, 1965, p. 381.]

Another example of how partial a view statistics can give is afforded by the figures showing a greater incidence of severe mental illness as one moves down the economic scale. An increase of mental illness is certainly not surprising, considering the stress that accompanies poverty. However, the statistics do not do justice to the strengths to be found among the poor. They reflect more than differences of occurrence of mental illness across classes, for they also include the effects of a differential access to treatment. A New Haven study of treatment for mental illness, both private and public, showed that the vast majority of the more wealthy and better-educated, 78 percent of the classes designated as I and II, were receiving psychotherapy by comparison with 53 percent of Class III, 31 percent of Class IV, and 16 percent of the lowest group, or Class V. Conversely, 51 percent at the lowest levels were receiving no treatment at all, but simply custodial care, with the proportion diminishing to 11 percent at the upper levels (Hollingshead and Redlich, 1958). A follow-up study of an outpatient clinic showed a marked bias in admission procedures, with the higher-status person standing a much better chance of being accepted for psychotherapy (Meyers and Schaffer, 1954, pp. 308-9). Thus, the lower his class status, the greater the chance for a person to become so sick as to reach the attention of the authorities through legal procedures, and to be committed to custodial care for the rest of his life. In short, statistics on the prevalence of mental illness say as much about the care available to people as about the variations of incidence across classes.

Studies which have gone beyond statistical materials and have followed up various populations have concentrated largely on "problem" groups that have been seen from the partial or "outside" viewpoint discussed above. Conclusions drawn from these studies have then been projected onto some large but ill-defined section of what may be called the "poor," or "lower class," or "working class." Thus bias in the sample, combined with bias in the situations studied, as discussed above, and bias in the interpretation of the material, to be discussed below, all reconfirm assumptions that the difficulties of the poor follow for the most part from their own failings.

3. *"Sociocentric" Interpretations of Data.*   The same attitudes that underlie the reluctance of therapists to accept lower-class applicants for outpatient treatment in the study reported above have been noted with relation to diagnostic procedures generally. As pointed out by William Haase, a number of studies show that the clinician influences "both the results that he will elicit from any given test and the significance assigned to them," and further research indicates that this influence takes the form of class bias

when lower-status patients are involved (Haase, 1964, p. 241, *passim*).

We have discussed the biased judgments about behavior across classes that follow from the nature of interclass relationships. These are so largely defined in terms of authority and control of resources, on the one hand, and dependence, servitude, or employee status, on the other, that the middle-class person experiences the lower-class person either as easygoing and not very "deep" or as hostile and guarded, or whatever the situation may dictate. The middle-class person tends not to become engaged with a lower-class person in relationships that involve such acts as a common sizing up and interpreting of situations and events or a mutual weighing of alternatives and consideration of means. The resulting assumption on the part of the middle-class person is that such behavior does not obtain in lower-status groups. Further, the researcher often forgets that his own analytic bent is not a standard "middle-class" characteristic—Babbitt has by no means suddenly disappeared from our national life—but is the concomitant of the specific training and type of occupation he has chosen. He does not recognize that the amount of introspective, contemplative, and analytic behavior indulged in varies enormously from individual to individual and that such behavior is by no means the property of any one group.

Instead the tendency in discussions of class differences in behavior is for them to become exaggerated by being stated in terms of polar opposites. Middle-class people plan; the poor do not. Middle-class people defer gratifications; the poor do not. Middle-class child-rearing modes are democratic; those of the poor are authoritarian. A middle-class person considers his life chances rationally; a poor person approaches them fatalistically. Middle-class families are patrifocal; poor families are matrifocal. Middle-class people think abstractly; the poor think concretely. And so on and on. When Lewis writes that "it would be . . . helpful to think of the subculture of poverty as the zero point on a continuum which leads to the working class and middle class," the focus is on quantitative differences along single dimensions, with the middle class as the norm (Lewis, 1969, p. 190).

However, both the middle and working, or lower, classes, while sharing certain universals of American culture, also manifest many subcultural variations according to the specific histories and circumstances of different regions, nationalities, religious groups, occupational groups, and residence styles (rural-urban). Such variations, either within or across cultures, cannot be adequately described or understood in terms of continua. Another distortion which results when thinking in terms of continua is that differences in trends can become magnified into unfounded contrasts. For example, that 23.2 percent of nonwhite families are matrifocal by comparison with 8.6 percent of white families means that *more* matrifocality exists in the nonwhite group. But it is quite a trick to say that the nonwhite population *is* matrifocal, when 76.8 percent of the families are not.[1] As to child-rearing modes, they vary so widely and change so rapidly—and are so imperfectly studied, to boot—that broad generalizations like the above cannot be made with any accuracy. Furthermore, it is not so easy to distinguish between such categories as "democratic" and "authoritarian" behavior. The use of corporal punishment is often considered *ipso facto* authoritarian, and the authoritarian component is ignored in presumed middle-class manipulative techniques of discipline such as threatened withdrawal of affection and denial of desired activities.

The conceptualization of behavior in terms of single dimensions obscures the fact that differences in group behaviors are more generally qualitative than quantitative. It is not that middle-class people plan and the poor do not, but that they necessarily plan about different things in different ways, as discussed in the chapter by Wright. For example, the strike is a characteristically lower-class form of planning and delayed gratification, one which

[1] In a review of discussions of "class culture," Hyman Rodman writes: "One important point that underlies all discussions of class culture revolves about the distinction that must be made between statistically significant class differences and characteristics of a class. There is a danger that the statistically significant differences—which may be represented by a finding that 25 per cent of lower-class adults are 'authoritarian' in comparison to 15 per cent of middle-class adults—will be converted into an unqualified statement that authoritarianism is a lower-class characteristic." (Rodman, 1968, p. 335.)

may be undertaken by the very poor even without benefit of union sanction and support.

Since the situations with which middle- and lower-class groups are dealing may differ widely, one cannot jump to the conclusion that one form of behavior is necessarily more effective than another. Hyman Rodman speaks of the "cross-eyed, middle-class view of lower-class behavior," and writes that lower-class behaviors which deviate from middle-class ideals (what middle-class *realities* may be is another question) "are frequently viewed in a gross manner as, simply, *problems* of the lower class." Rodman continues: "My own feeling is that it makes more sense to think of them as *solutions* of the lower class to problems that they face in the social, economic, and perhaps legal and political spheres of life" (Rodman, 1964, p. 65).

Culture-of-poverty theorists all too often talk about the "orality" of the poor and their inability to delay gratification, forgetting that the more affluent take for granted as necessities a good diet, comfortable surroundings, and the constant enjoyment of many other such gratifications that the poor must defer for their lives long, with at best, perhaps, some forlorn hope for gratification in an afterlife. Furthermore, the comments often made by culture-of-poverty theorists on the fatalism and resignation of the poor are strangely out of step with middle-class complaints about the impropriety of the means the black poor are using to express their anger with their situation and their demands for redress.

Life Style and Education

It has been widely assumed that the different atmospheres to be found in middle-income and lower-income schools follow from differences in the children's out-of-school experiences. The greater disciplinary problems, and what seems to be a lesser inclination to learn, are viewed as concomitants of "cultural deprivation," reinforced by the distance bteween the "middle-class" goals and orientation of the schools and the "lower-class values" of the children. From the standpoint of teachers who face bored and dispirited children, and who do not know how to arouse interest and awaken abilities, the "culture of poverty" explanation seems apt. Teachers commonly feel they are in conflict with something, and that it is their "middle-class values" versus those of the "lower class" is persuasive.

A strong counterposition has developed, following the Supreme Court decision on desegregation of schools and the exposure of the double-track system along class and race lines that exists in Northern cities. That the structure of the schools mirrors an existing status system and that there is greater financial expenditure per child in middle-income areas have become clear. Children in low-income areas, and particularly black low-income areas, go to poorer schools (or, in heterogeneous neighborhoods, into "slower" classes in a grade), which lead into slow classes in junior high, or poorer junior highs, and thence into catch-all commercial and industrial high schools where standards are low and dropouts high. By contrast, children from middle-income areas go to "good" schools, or "fast" classes which feed into "special" programs in the later elementary and junior-high years, and into specialized college preparatory high schools. The structuring of this double-track system and the expectations for children's performance which it presupposes dictate that economic and racial status, rather than ability, will determine for the most part who shall ascend the educational ladder and gain positions with prestige and security. The lower expectations for poor children are self-fulfilling.

Within this structure, teachers are both the victims and the villains, a position which has caused them great stress and confusion in the recent battles fought over the education of black and Puerto Rican children. Teachers, after all, daily face the children in the classroom, and have the responsibility of teaching them. However, as cogs in a machine so structured that teaching is well-nigh impossible in low-income schools, as Jean Lester's chapter so graphically illustrates, only the most gifted and insightful among them do not fail. Hence teachers both are and are not responsible, and hence the bitterness and anger surrounding attempts to restructure the educational system. (Hence, too, the perfect setting for "divide and rule" ploys by those in positions of real decision making and responsibility.) Teachers may ultimately be frustrated by a situation in which they have not been successful at their trade, but most of them have adapted to it either by accepting outright racist rationales for their failure with the poor and the black or by grasping at the "culture of poverty" rationale. Only a few have found ways to act on the understanding of how their failure is built into the very structure of the school system and from their own restricted position within it. Jonathan Kozol, author of *Death at an Early Age,* is an example, and he was expelled from the Boston school system as a consequence of his dissidence.

I have referred above to the active role the school plays in the socialization of children for their role in society. On the basis of observing classrooms in both black and white schools, in both middle- and lower-income neighborhoods, it became apparent to me that the projection of a middle-class orientation to life in general was not the major problem for poor and black children. It was rather that *a middle class attitude toward them and their inferior status as poor and black was being foisted upon them.* Tragically, this could be observed on the part of black as well as white teachers. This was before the assertion of black demands for some power over their own lives gave black teachers the moral support necessary for transcending the status quo. Expectations for the children's future subordinate status were expressed in various ways, particularly for black children from low-income homes: through the minimal goals for them expressed by the teachers in interviews and stated in the classroom; through the failure to structure the classroom in ways which would encourage the children to handle formal responsibility (although the children's classroom behavior indicated their readiness to do so); and through the negative ways in which teachers would respond to a child's proffered discussion and would evaluate the performance of a lesson.

The articles by Murray and Rosalie Wax and by Mildred Dickeman, although involving rural schools for Indian children, afford poignant illustrations of the process whereby attitudes founded in racist ideology are reinforced by experiences based on superordinate–subordinate relations with Indians and their children. The result is the inability of teachers to empathize with and respect the children, and the projection of teachers' expectations of failure upon the children. Janet Castro's chapter, on the other hand, is a dramatic example of what can happen when someone determined to *teach* children starts by first *listening* to them. Herbert Kohl relates a parallel experience as an elementary-school teacher in East Harlem, when he dropped a stilted and superficial lesson plan on "How We Became Modern Americans" and encouraged the children to write of their blocks, their lives, their experiences and concerns. Once their suspicion was allayed, the children wrote and wrote. "Everything I'd been told about the children's language was irrelevant," Kohl stated, and continued:

Yes, they were hip when they spoke, inarticulate and concrete. But their writing was something else, when they felt that no white man was judging their words, threatening their confidence and pride . . . Recently I have mentioned this to teachers who have accepted the current analysis of "the language" of the "disadvantaged." They asked their children to write and have been as surprised as I was, and shocked by the obvious fact that "disadvantaged" children will not speak in class because they cannot trust their audience. [Kohl, 1966, p. 27.]

Language and the Classroom[2]

Kohl's observation brings us to our next point, which concerns the presumed inadequacy of "working-class language" for conceptual development and expression. This is one of the more pernicious misconceptions that has resulted from the overinterpreta-

[2] Much of this section was originally incorporated into a paper on "Cultural Influences on Learning and Coping Behavior" presented at the Elementary School Guidance Work Conference of the Division of Guidance Services, Pennsylvania Dept. of Public Instruction, Oct. 16-18, 1967, Dr. Edwin L. Herr, chairman.

tion of scientific research and hypothesizing to conform to racist and sociocentric biases. One can read in educational literature such infelicitous statements as "working men . . . tend to think in the concrete rather than in the abstract and they find little meaning in verbal symbols" (Graham, 1963, pp. 317-18). All words, of course, are "verbal symbols," and only mental defectives do not respond to such common garden symbols as, for example, "if," "and" or "but"! Probably what is really meant here is that people who experience poverty and discrimination may be less swayed by such redoubtable symbols as "justice," "freedom," and the like, and wish to see their concrete expression.

One "middle-class value" is to revere "standard English" and to look down on the colloquial speech patterns found among various sections of the poor. The failure to speak standard English has long been a mark of low status, and teaching children "proper" and "correct" speech has always been a major purpose of the school. For the poor child, school experience seldom entails respect for *what* he has to say, but characteristically involves constant correction of *how* he chooses to say it.

As Ernest Drucker points out in his chapter, the abstract–concrete polarity now in vogue when speaking about learning difficulties of lower-class children has a long history in the search for differences between pre-urban or "primitive" patterns of language and thought, and those of post-urban or "civilized" peoples. Drucker and Vera John show how unwarranted it is to jump from the fact that language and thought are intricately related to the assumption that standard English is a better vehicle than other languages for abstract thought. Benjamin Lee Whorf, the anthropological linguist whose name is closely associated with the study of linguistic influences on thought, decried any assumption that some languages were "superior" to or more "abstract" than others. Instead, Whorf saw languages as varying *qualitatively* in the *types* of abstractions and relationships they emphasize.

As an example of a causal relation embedded in the grammatical construction of another language but masked in English, Whorf cites the English use of "that." When we say, "I see that it is red," and "I see that it is new," we confuse "two quite different types of relationship into a vague sort of connection expressed by 'that.' " The language of the Hopi Indians of the American Southwest, on the other hand, "indicates that in the first case seeing presents a sensation 'red,' and in the second that seeing presents unspecified evidence from which is drawn the inference of newness." In this instance, Whorf writes, English compared with Hopi

is like a bludgeon compared with a rapier. We even have to think and boggle over the question for some time, or have it explained to us, before we can see the difference in the relationships expressed by "that" in the above examples, whereas the Hopi discriminates these relationships with effortless ease, for the forms of speech have accustomed him to doing so. [Whorf, 1956, pp. 84-85.]

Whorf's insight has fascinated students of language, and one can readily see that different linguistic usages can make certain perceptions and causal assumptions either simpler and more automatic or somewhat more difficult. However, the case can be overstated. Once the conceptual implications embedded in verbal or grammatical constructions are made clear, one can consciously shift one's thinking. The performance in American schools and colleges of students whose mother tongues were not Indo-European, but who first spoke Japanese, Chinese, Hungarian, and so forth, indicate that people reared with one style of linguistic usage can readily handle concepts which may seem more congenial to another.

Returning to the hypothesis that characteristic differences in the handling of English by children from middle- as compared with low-income backgrounds impair the ability of the latter to conceptualize, it is clear that middle-class children come to school better prepared to handle the language skills that are part and parcel of education. Obviously the greater possibility for and attention to formal language training in the early years, the greater number of books, magazines, hobbies and educational games found in financially secure homes, provide a background for schooling upon which most teachers find they can readily build. However, to jump from this to the assumption that there are class differences in the ability to think is another example of middle-class bias.

A common type of psychological study shows that middle-class children respond to picture cards of a cat, a dog, a cow, etc., with the word "animal," while working-class children more often respond with statements like "They all have four legs." The first answer is considered "abstract," since the categorical word is used, the second "concrete" since an explicitly descriptive generalization is employed. Unquestionably the first answer is "correct" as a classroom response. What is missed in the analysis, however, is that the second answer follows from *abstracting* a feature common to all the objects. It is, in fact, closer to what is called in science an "operational definition"; and such definitions are sought as a prelude to finding out *what something actually is in terms of how it functions*. Knowing a right word may or may not entail mastering a concept. To test the conceptual skill of the middle-class child one would have to follow up his answer with "What is an animal?" Instead a value judgment is placed on the answer "animal," and it is considered *ipso facto* at a high conceptual level.

A similar interpretation is too often put upon idiomatic slang as compared with formal English. A free flow of idiomatic speech from a working-class child is often met with a rebuke, like "Stand straight when you talk and do not say 'ain't.' " The content of the statement is ignored, and the usage of a technically adequate but socially unacceptable negative is implicitly equated with inability to learn. Words which have found their way from the black idiom into informal English, like "cool," "square," and "hip," are ruled out in the classroom, although they are every bit as meaningful, and as "abstract" or "symbolic," as acceptable synonyms like "assured," "naïve," and "sophisticated." Indeed, the constant output of new words from the black community and the common use of metaphor (the very essence of abstraction) indicate a high level of linguistic interest and ability. A black man from rural Mississippi, who had received virtually no formal education in his life, recently characterized to me the position of his people by saying, "They clip your wings and tell you to fly." The terms are "concrete," but the metaphor is highly abstract.

The Conclusion

To sum up, differences between the poor and the nonpoor in our society stem from three sources. First, there are the different traditions of peoples with different histories; these are often reinforced by racial or religious segregation and discrimination. Second, there are realistic attempts to deal with objective conditions that vary from one class to another. In his chapter, Anthony Leeds shows how many so-called poverty-culture traits are of this type. There is no hard fast line between this order of behavior and the third, which are those adaptive acts and attitudes that become institutionalized, and incorporated into internalized values and norms appropriate for living in a given position in the social-economic system. It is, of course, the last—the subcultural variations along class lines—which come closest to what culture-of-poverty theory is supposedly documenting. However, as discussed above, sociocentric methods of data collection and analysis, plus a nonhistorical theory of culture and its relation to personality, have contributed to stereotypical and distorted views of these class-linked cultural variations.[3]

In writings intended for the use of educators and social workers, the culture of the poor is all too commonly described solely in terms of the grim and destructive results of poverty and discrimination. By this use of the culture concept, the effects of what is being done to people who are accorded a low status, in a highly acquisitive, competitive and discriminatory society, are somehow ascribed to the people themselves. The term "culture" is being inaccurately used when it thus implies that poor people perpetuate the condition of poverty in our society through their adherence to unhealthy or dysfunctional values; and that they need only turn to presumably healthy and functional middle-class values to enter the world of relative economic security. Poverty, as a structural feature of our society, cannot be changed by a change of attitudes only.

[3] For a review of the literature on class culture, see Rodman, 1968, pp. 332-37.

As used by anthropologists, "culture" refers to the totality of a group's learned norms for behavior and the manifestations of this behavior. This includes the technological and economic mechanisms through which a group adapts to its environment, its related social and political institutions, and the values, goals, definitions, prescriptions, and assumptions which define and rationalize individual motivation and participation. Social anthropology as a science is concerned with describing and analyzing four aspects of man's culture: (1) the variety of cultural forms which has existed, past and present; (2) cultural changes over time and the influence different cultures have had upon each other; (3) relationships among the various components of culture in general, and of specific cultures in particular; and (4) the relationship between cultural norms and individual personality and behavior. To the non-anthropologist, however, the term "culture" is often limited to its ideological and psychological aspects. It is these that are constantly and directly experienced in our heterogeneous nation, in which many different cultural traditions have been brought together within a common social-economic system. Emphasis on these dimensions of culture without some understanding of the whole has resulted in a lack of awareness that ideological aspects of culture develop and change in complex interaction with fundamental economic and social institutions.

Anthropologists vary in how they interpret the relation between the social-economic and the more ideological or psychological sides of culture. However, even those anthropologists who place strong emphasis in their studies on the psychological dimension do not in the last analysis accept the notion that social and economic structure are secondary to psychological mechanisms. In a recent debate with Charles Valentine, Oscar Lewis contradicts the implication of his earlier statement quoted in the beginning of this chapter when he writes:

The crucial question from both the scientific and the political point of view is: How much weight is to be given to the internal, self-perpetuating factors in the subculture of poverty as compared to the external, societal factors? My own position is that in the long run the self-perpetuating factors are relatively minor and unimportant as compared to the basic structure of the larger society. [Lewis, 1969, p. 192.]

And Lee Rainwater, who has elsewhere stressed the self-perpetuating psychological aspects of lower-class culture, states succinctly:

. . . one can hope that as a result of the social science efforts to date, "thinking people" will stop deluding themselves that the underclass is other than a product of an economic system so designed that it generates a destructive amount of income inequality, and face the fact that the only solution of the problem of underclass is to change that economic system accordingly. [Rainwater, 1969, p. 9.]

BIBLIOGRAPHY

Bartky, John A., *Social Issues in Public Education.* Boston: Houghton Mifflin, 1963.

Fuchs, Estelle, *Pickets at the Gates.* New York: Free Press, 1966.

Graham, Grace, *The Public School in the American Community.* New York: Harper and Row, 1963.

Haase, William, "The Role of Socioeconomic Class in Examiner Bias," in *Mental Health of the Poor: New Treatment Approaches for Low Income People,* ed. Frank Riessman, Jerome Cohen and Arthur Pearl (New York: Free Press, 1964).

Hart, C. W. M., "The Sons of Turimpi," *American Anthropologist,* Vol. 56 (1954), No. 2.

Hollingshead, A. B., and F. C. Redlich, *Social Class and Mental Illness: A Community Study.* New York: Wiley and Sons, 1958.

Kagan, Jerome, and Howard Moss, *Birth to Maturity.* New York: Wiley and Sons, 1962.

Kohl, Herbert, "Children Writing: The Story of an Experiment," *The New York Review of Books,* Nov. 17, 1966.

Leacock, Eleanor, *Teaching and Learning in City Schools: A Comparative Study.* New York: Basic Books, 1969.

Lewis, Oscar, *The Children of Sanchez.* New York: Random House, 1961.

————, *La Vida*. New York: Random House, 1966.

————, Review of Charles A. Valentine, *Culture and Poverty: Critique and Counter-Proposals,* in *Current Anthropology,* Vol. 10 (1969), No. 2-3.

Meyers, Jerome K., and Leslie Schaffer, "Social Stratification and Psychiatric Practice," *American Sociological Review,* Vol. 19 (1954), No. 3.

Moynihan, Daniel P., *The Negro Family: The Case for National Action*. Washington: U.S. Department of Labor, 1965.

Rainwater, Lee, "The American Underclass, Comment: Looking Back and Looking Up," *Trans-action,* Vol. 6 (1969), No. 4.

Riessman, Frank, *The Culturally Deprived Child*. New York: Harper and Brothers, 1962.

Rodman, Hyman, "Middle-Class Misconceptions about Lower-Class Families," in *Blue-Collar World: Studies of the American Worker,* ed. Arthur B. Shostak and William Gomberg (Englewood Cliffs, N.J.: Prentice-Hall, 1964).

————, "Stratification, Social: Class Culture," in *The International Encyclopedia of the Social Sciences* (New York: Macmillan, 1968).

Rosenthal, Robert, and Lenore Jacobson, *Pygmalion in the Classroom: Teacher Expectation and Pupils' Intellectual Development*. New York: Holt, Rinehart and Winston, 1968.

Ryan, William, "Savage Discovery: The Moynihan Report," *The Nation,* Nov. 22, 1965.

Valentine, Charles A., and Betty Lou Valentine, "Making the Scene, Digging the Action, and Telling It Like It Is: Anthropologists at Work in a Dark Ghetto," in *Afro-American Anthropology: Contemporary Perspectives,* ed. Norman Whitten and John Szwed (New York: Free Press, 1969).

Wallace, Anthony F. C., "The New Culture-and-Personality," in *Anthropology and Human Behavior* (Washington: Anthropological Society of Washington, 1962).

White, William Foote, "Social Organization in the Slums," *American Sociological Review,* Vol. 8, February 1943.

Whorf, Benjamin Lee, *Language, Thought and Reality*. Cambridge: Massachusetts Institute of Technology Press, 1956.

PART I

Language, Life Style and Education Among the Poor

COGNITIVE STYLES AND
CLASS STEREOTYPES

In their zealous search for the bases of differences between the children of middle- and lower-class background, many researchers and educators have asserted that the thought and language of the lower-class child is relatively "concrete," while that of the middle class child is "abstract" and of a higher developmental order. By "abstract" is usually meant a type of thought characterized as more "logical" and "symbolic," while "concrete" thought is seen as dominated by personal reference, sensory-motor qualities and a functional organization of events. Many social scientists have specified this difference as a basic consequence of growing up under the conditions of poverty and have asserted that the "culturally deprived child" is quickly put at a disadvantage in school by virtue of his deficient powers of "abstraction." Such a difference is today seen by many as a fundamental basis for the failure of primary education with *lower-class* children. The practical failures are well documented in terms of reading, grade-level achievement tests, successful completion of high school and entrance into professional vocations. It is commonly felt that these failures are causally related to the character of the *lower-class* social and family environment. This is the crux of the "cultural deprivation" approach.

To support claims of a "concrete–abstract" difference in the thought of lower-class and middle-class children, evidence of the following sort is usually offered: Presented with a pair of words such as *apple* and *peach,* the lower-class child will respond, "They're both round," or, more likely, "They're both good to eat," while the middle-class child will say, "They're both fruits." Presented with a problem like "What would you do if you lost the ball or doll of a friend?" the average middle-class child tells you he "would get another to replace it," while the lower-class child will often want to know "Whose ball was it?" or "How come it got lost?" or say, "I don't know, it depends on whose ball it is" and discuss some problem about being unable to easily replace it. In the first example, the quality of the two fruits which the sub- ject responds to is roundness. He might answer "Soft" for another pair such as *sweater* and *scarf;* or for *wine* and *beer* he might say, "They both get you drunk" (instead of "They're both alcoholic beverages"). This would be seen as evidence that the child's thought is organized primarily in terms of sensory features of the world. Motoric or functional responses are seen as representing a somewhat higher level of development of thought, since, in the timetable of child development, mobility, manipulation and usage come after sensations and perception. Symbolic thought disso- ciated from sensations and actions is viewed as the highest level in the schema, since it can be shown that such thought always de- velops later. In the lost-ball example the middle-class child gives you a "principle" supposedly incorporating what should be done and assuming personal responsibility for doing it. This type of re- sponse is rated highest in I.Q.–testing procedures and is therefore definitive of the way in which differences in level of intellectual development are inferred from children's verbal responses to test items.

In this paper I would like to present some history, theory and data which seem to me to suggest another way of seeing the matter. Specifically, I would like to argue that tests and data of the sort presented above do reflect differences but not differences in level of *conceptualizing* and *abstracting* ability or the capacity for the *adaptive use of thought*. Instead, I think they reflect an arbitrary dichotomy which has been imposed by a particular the- ory and a particular social system upon a mass of data which lends itself to many interpretations and differentiations. I plan to discuss material which questions the validity of the assumptions underlying the concrete–abstract model as a means of differentiating levels of intellectual development. This model can be shown to reflect classbound stereotypes of *both* middle- and lower-class life and to function in the service of realizing those stereotypes through the school system. By virtue of the considerable influence of certain developmental theories on education, the abstract–concrete model has made a lasting impact on education and educational-selection procedures. It is therefore appropriate to examine the roots of the theory and the data and assumptions underlying its foundation.

Myths about "Primitive" Thought

There is a long-standing and popularly held notion that the thought of primitive man functions at a lower level than that of Western man. A great deal of evidence has shown that this is simply not true, and modern anthropologists themselves hold no such notion today (e.g., Boas, 1938, and Radin, 1953). Thirty years ago the anthropologist Franz Boas saw the problem and identified it clearly:

. . . the differences between civilized man and primitive man are in many cases more apparent than real . . . social conditions, on account of their peculiar characteristics, easily convey the impression that the mind of primitive man acts in a way quite different from ours, while in reality the fundamental traits of mind are the same. [Boas, 1938, p. 130.]

But this does not seem to have affected the stereotype of generally held notions. Primitive man is still widely seen as having his thought processes dominated by magical operations despite the fact that the cultural contributions, poetry, traditions and well-developed social institutions of most preliterate peoples show unequivocally that logical symbolic processes figure prominently in both their history and their daily life. There is, however, resistance by many social scientists to facts which contradict deeply in-

grained prejudices. Theory and practice easily take a line determined by simplified stereotypes which in turn come to influence
the perception and interpretation of new phenomena. This has
been especially so in the case of some psychologists' treatment of
the thought and action of primitive man. Recently the "culture
of poverty" concept has led to consideration of lower-class life in
ways quite similar to early views of primitive culture. This has led
to the application of many of the same stereotypes which have been
applied to numerous preliterate peoples around the world to the
poor of this nation. It is not surprising, therefore, that one of the
most pernicious and misleading concepts about primitive peoples
has been applied wholesale to the "culture of poverty"—namely, a
belief that the thought processes of this group are qualitatively inferior and at a lower developmental level when compared with
middle-class groups. Some examples from this sort of treatment of
anthropological data may serve to illustrate the type of reasoning
that was often applied to the behavior of primitive peoples and is
now being tried with the poor.

The abstract–concrete distinction has been most seriously developed with cultural implications by the developmental psychologist Heinz Werner in his massive and influential work *Comparative Psychology of Mental Development,* first published in 1948.
Werner sets forth a comprehensive theory of cognitive development in which he asserts that the thought of primitive peoples,
children, brain-damaged patients and persons in psychopathologi-
cal states have certain common characteristics similar to those
described above as concrete thought. For Werner one of the features of the mind of primitive man is his hypersensitivity to and
recall of visual images. This is seen as evidence of the "sensory
dominance" of "primitive thought" and an index of lower developmental level (recalling the model in which sensory precedes conceptual). Thus Werner cites several examples of the amazing sensitivity to physical and topographic details in many native groups:

With no aid except his memory, this Eskimo drew a map of a territory whose shores he explored but once in his kayak. This strip of
country was 1,100 miles long as the crow flies, but the coast was six

times that length. A comparison of the Eskimo's map with an Admiralty chart revealed a most unexpected agreement . . . [and the Eskimo's map] was superior to any map he had seen drawn from memory by a white man.

Grey tells of an intelligent native, who, without the slightest hesitation, identified the three thieves who had stolen some potatoes, merely by glancing at the foot prints of the culprits.

An Australian Bushman makes a drawing by placing many seemingly unrelated dots on a board which showed no relationship or any trace of contour of any kind to the looker-on, but appeared like a picture of a group of stars. When he had convinced himself . . . of the sufficiency of this group of dots, he began to draw free, bold lines from one part of the field to another. As he did this there developed spontaneously the form of an animal. This was all done in freehand, and with such unerring precision of line, that not one stroke stood in need of erasure or improvement. [Werner, 1961, p. 147.]

Werner's conclusion from this is: "With primitive man, images and percepts are more nearly related and are less differentiated with respect to one another than is the case with the man of a more advanced culture" (*ibid.,* p. 148). Here the productions and imagery of the natives are actually seen as *too good* and *too close* to physical reality and not sufficiently differentiated from the sensory stimuli which compose them. Yet in the next paragraph comes the statement "In the primitive sphere there is a very close connection between emotion and memory image. *Reality, in retrospect, is shaped strongly by affective need.*" After documenting how incredibly accurate the perception and memory of primitive man can be, the author still insists that primitive man's perception is suffused with and distorted by emotions. The following example is intended to support such a view: "boastful revision of accounts of marital exploits [*i.e., boasting about sexual prowess*] found everywhere among primitive people are *evidence* of a mnemonic reality formed through affective influence" (*ibid.,* p. 148; emphasis mine).

This is not just naïveté on the part of the author, but is the systematic misapplication of a psychological-causal model to explain phenomena which have, above all else, social meaning. One might just as well conclude that the average American male develops a temporary visual disorder affecting size perception and a failure of numeric reasoning and recall every time he goes on a fishing trip and lies about the catch to his wife and friends. At every turn the behavior of the primitive is explained in some way which makes it first *different* and then developmentally *inferior,* with no regard for the contradictions within the argument, or for the contexts of the behaviors themselves.

While these examples may seem crass, they are representative of the dubious quality of the underpinnings of the belief in the lower developmental order of "primitive thought." The stereotype can best be seen in the following selection from Werner.

. . . *typical* European reflection is universal in nature, abstract; it functions more or less independently of the immediate concrete reality and is governed by an awareness of general laws. The thought of primitive man is pinned down to the reality of the thing-like world and is therefore pragmatic, concrete and individual. [*Ibid.,* p. 299.]

This is very close to the "culture of poverty" view of the thought, language and lifeways of the lower class.

As in all human pursuits, scientific inquiry into poverty is inevitably shot through with the bias and values of the investigator. But if one examines the sort of misinterpretation noted above in the anthropological material, one encounters not just ethnocentric bias but systematic distortion. The white-man's-burden view of primitive man has been clearly shown to be a function of the colonial period and all its implications for relations between different peoples and races. The inferiority-of-primitive-thought model functioned in the service of the fabric of colonial relationships. Much the same analysis may be made of the use of a model of intellectual evaluation based on an abstract—concrete dimension: it may serve the function of justifying the status quo.

In a recent article on the role of social sciences in social problems Benjamin Pasamanick commented: "As the lukewarm skirmish against poverty gives promise of turning into a hot war of rebellion for justice and equality, the fifth estate—science—rides precipitously into the fray, frequently to add confusion and to protect and give comfort to the establishment" (Pasamanick, 1969, p. 7). The notion that the scientific study of a problem might be biased to give comfort to the establishment is actually, in the case of the evaluation of intellectual functions in poor children, a benign interpretation. In fact the history of such evaluation *per se* via I.Q. tests is an unbroken record of the development of instruments which would not only "give comfort" but substantially and actively "aid" the establishment to propagate itself via its primary tool—the schools.

The Historical Role of Intelligence
Measures as Gatekeepers

Intelligence tests were developed in an atmosphere which was characterized by a belief in fixed, genetically determined intelligence not amenable to alteration through social experience. The founders of the intelligence test, Francis Galton and James McKeen Cattell, were closely linked to social-Darwinist notions popular at the time and saw their work as ultimately leading to a eugenics program. Needless to say, this was not a popular position and is seldom mentioned, but it forms the conceptual substrate and historical origin of a long line of scientists pursuing the study of intellect as a static single characteristic (see J. McVickers Hunt, 1964). This line of approach may be seen today in the 1969 article by Jensen which has received such wide publicity and indicates that these notions are not so *implicit* any more.

The other thrust of intellectual evaluation has been empirical selection for the qualities which correlate with success or failure in a particular situation. Binet, the French founder of the modern intelligence scale, was commissioned in 1905 by the Minister of Public Instruction in Paris to develop a test which would identify children who were likely to fail in school. From a wide range of testable qualities (all *a priori* related to some common-sense notion of intelligence), Binet narrowed down his battery to those few factors which correlated with school performance and teachers' expectations. The most important I.Q. tests in use today are descendants of Binet's, and all function the same way. The spectrum of consideration is narrowed down to those elements of mental activity which were originally selected because they correlated with school performance; *these, in turn, are called "intelligence."*

The use of intelligence evaluation procedures as a basis of differentiating individuals is a sort of cultural litmus test which serves the simple social function of screening and sorting for individuals who may adequately respond to a particular educational system with its particular views of what constitutes intelligence and general behavioral style. These measures serve the purpose of selecting and further shaping those individuals of any class level into a certain *style* of thought which is subsequently advocated as developmentally superior. In our society such evaluations are used to justify admission to the success-bound tracks in the educational system. Thus the predominant middle-class definition of intellectual style is fostered and preserved through systemic selection to fit a particular model. One can begin to perceive something of "the politics of intelligence" and gain appreciation of the power and leverage implicit in educational systems.

Quite a different view is promulgated for the public, however, and is implicit in the abstract—concrete view of class differences in intellectual functioning. A technique whose primary and intended function is to make a social discrimination is viewed as objectively measuring quantitative differences in basic dimensions of intellectual competence. The cycle of mystification becomes complete when this gatekeeper is called in as a witness to attest to the validity and superiority of the system it serves. Observations of failures (e.g., in school) are then attributed to "deprivation" in the life or cultural experience of those affected. Conversely, "success" is due to the enriched content and superior lifeways of the dominant group. There is, therefore, a strong tendency to develop simple, idealized stereotypes of class life styles which are then juggled about in an attempt to explain phenomena of school performance.

Stereotype as "Cause"

In most studies of lower-class children there is documentation of school failure, lower I.Q. scores and poorer concept-formation task performance, which seems to show "intellectual" deficits. Then there is a rapid and unwarranted assumption that this failure is reflective of *qualitative* intellectual differences in the lower-class individual based on deficiencies in his "culture" and "family experience." The most sweeping assertions are made about the outcome of lower-class existence. Its effects on the individual are typically explained in terms of the shortcomings of the "culture of poverty"—an environment supposedly characterized by emotional and intellectual malnutrition.

In a New York State Division of Youth report entitled *The American Lower-Class Family,* (Keller, 1968) the following remarks are representative of the attempts to develop a stereotype of lower-class life which might account for the observed deficit.

. . . there is a definite relationship between social class and language, verbal and *therefore* intellectual development.

. . . clearly shows the *paucity of verbal interaction* between lower class mother and child by comparison with middle class.

. . . they [working lower-class mothers] did not *typically* eat breakfast with their children, talk to them at meal times or often demonstrate their affection for children overtly.

. . . the lower class milieu does not foster interest in intellectual activities or in ideas for *their own sake.*" [Emphasis mine throughout.]

One could cite many more examples of such terribly oversimplified and downright foolish statements, for the most part questionable generalizations based on limited observations of behavior by investigators who are often quite naïve about the real life patterns of the people studied.

Think about these stereotypes of the poor and then think of the verbally "rich" interaction of the "typical" middle-class adolescent with his parents: "Where'd you go?" "Out." "What'd you do?" "Nothing." The emotionless milieu described as "typical" could well be a description of the upper-class English household, where, for example, "Mother" and "the boys" (who are away at boarding school nine months of the year) converse with all the warmth and spontaneity of a computer. And as far as "ideas for their own sake" is concerned, perhaps the author imagines that typical middle-class responses to the child's inquiries are fashioned after Walt Whitman's "A child said, 'What is the grass . . .'" In my experience, however, the pursuit of engineering, law and business administration are more likely to be fostered by middle-class parents than are poetry or philosophy, and the general foci of middle-class schools are the citywide tests, scholastic-aptitude scores and graduate record exams. These, not "ideas for their own sake," are the coin of our educational economy.

In addition to having little face validity, the stereotypes of "lower-class culture" are not borne out by studies which make a point of carefully controlling social interaction in the research itself. Many supposed "facts" about thought and learning potential of the lower-class child have been found to be artifacts of the middle-class-oriented research process itself. For example, Francis Palmer, at the City University of New York, has shown an absence of difference between middle- and lower-class children on a host of basic intellectual tasks *when prior preparation and familiarization with a test situation were provided*. In most studies, a researcher who must get many "subjects" run in a day's work will grind out data. The middle-class child is accustomed to accepting the arbitrary demands of adult strangers to engage in meaningless activity, while the lower-class child is often not. Many findings, therefore, really represent totally different situations to class-differentiated children. Palmer's findings show that when adequate time was spent with each child, all children could be engaged deeply in extensive testing and important preschool learning be clearly demonstrated. It is noteworthy that this study also found that lower-class mothers who accepted participation in the study, which involved frequent visits with the child to a neighborhood testing center, attended as well as or better than their middle-class counterparts and evidenced the same degree of interest in the test procedures themselves (re: "the disinterested lower-class parent" myth).

Another line of research which questions the use of culture differences as responsible for observed deficits in schoolwork is the relation between *specifiable and tangible* aspects of poverty and observed deficits in function due to the *physical conditions of poverty per se*. Benjamin Pasamanick has documented an unequivocal relation between a score of important physiological parameters related to nutritional deficits in lower-class diets. He has shown that these factors can strongly affect attention, alertness, attendance and a host of school-relevant variables; these show clear responsiveness to nutritional improvement. Of course, nutritional levels are strongly associated with class levels in our society, and upward mobility in one will usually accompany the other, but there is all the difference in the world between attributing functional deficiency to the state of health of the organism and attributing that same to the organized structures of a subculture on the basis of the cultural stereotypes and generalizations noted above.

There is actually little real evidence to support the conclusion that the deficits observed in the school performance of lower-class children can be accounted for by factors within the life space of the poor. At best, we can speculate about the interaction of two social orders in a setting usually dominated by one of those orders, who sits in judgment on the other. There is even less evidence for any clear extension of failures in the school setting to assertions about the level of mental development of lower-class children.

Just as the theoretical basis of the model is shaky, and the assertions about facets of the "deprived" environment responsible for deficit are highly questionable, so also the actual data supposedly demonstrating arrested development are suspect and should be examined critically.

The Interaction of Test Procedures and Personal/Cultural Style

The relation between typical research tasks (on which so many of the questionable conclusions mentioned above have been based) and a child's style of activity is critical to interpreting findings but is seldom discussed. In this section I would like to describe some experiences I have had in testing children on measures of "number conservation"—Piaget's term for the child's developing ability to realize that the number of objects in an array remains constant despite changes in the physical size or configuration of that array. The development of this concept is seen as critical to the development of mathematical reasoning and indicative of the developmental shift from perceptual to conceptual dominance. Once again, researchers have found deficits in lower-class "performance" in this area, but a close examination of the actual phenomena and behavior of the child in the test situation is revealing. It illustrates the highly individual as well as classbound differences in children's behavior and how important these differences are to the interpretation of findings.

The basic test of the presence of number conservation is to place several objects (e.g., checkers)in a row and ask the child, "How many are there?" Typically, the child aged four to six will count and give the correct answer. Then the objects are spread out to make a larger row and the question is repeated. Older children with "conservation" will respond, "The same" or "Same amount," while younger children will often recount or guess "More." Here are three brief "case studies" of the type of experience which always confronts researchers but is seldom expressed in the "data":

The first case example is a five-and-a-half-year-old Negro boy in a Harlem school who "failed" on the first conservation task (by recounting after the checkers were spread out). The experiment is repeated with some small toy dump trucks on the table. The checkers are put in a line and the child is asked, "How many trucks will you need to carry these checkers from here to there?" (The child is aware that each truck can hold one checker.) He counts and responds with the correct number. He is told to try it and see. Placing one checker in each truck, he moves the checkers from one end of the table to the other and "dumps" them there in a heap. He "parks" the trucks in a row and plays with one, inspecting the mechanism, as I put the same checkers in a row considerably longer than the first. "How many trucks do you need now?" He looks at the checkers, hesitates, and responds, "The same number." He is urged to try it and, of course, is found to be right. The process is repeated; the answer is offered with increasing expressive indications by the child that he believes the experimenter is mentally deficient.

The second case is a first-grade white child in a predominantly middle-class school, considered by his teachers as "bright and well motivated for school." The boy hovers over the checkers when they are being placed in a row initially. When asked how many are there, he pounces on them and quickly counts them, missing one in his haste. He gives the wrong number. I ask him to count them again. He does so correctly. I move them apart, forming a larger row. "How many now?" "The same!" he states triumphantly—then he counts them quickly, touching each one, and repeats, "Yep, still the same number." When the process is repeated, he behaves similarly, with the exception that he wants to know if I have more checkers in my hand or up my sleeve. By the fourth trial he counts quite carefully before asserting, "It's still the same."

The third case is a second-grade Yeshiva student who tensely inquires about the "tests" he has been told to take by his teacher, and despite my insistence that it is only a "game" to help us understand children better, he is clearly nervous. During the procedure he becomes increasingly disorganized and starts knocking some of the checkers off the table. After several trials the child is inexplicably crying. I ask, "What's the matter?" "You said it wasn't a test," he bawls, "but you're failing me!" I say, "No, I'm not failing you, it's just a game." He points at the pad where I'm drawing patterns of checkers (small circles) and whimpers, "You are too! You're giving me all zeroes!"

These three examples illustrate the enormous range of stylistic and deeply personal responses a child can have to a test situation. More significantly, they also underscore the fact that these styles are associated with certain classbound styles and that in some circumstances each can become maladaptive and lead to functional failure for quite different reasons. We should remember that typical school interactions will usually take the "test" form, in which the driven, competitive response of the middle-class child to adult demands will be rewarded. In "real life" the testing with the Negro boy would have been discontinued and his "failure" noted, while the anxiety of the middle-class child would have been sensitively handled by a psychologically minded teacher or researcher. In the examples given, however, it is the middle-class children whose behavior becomes infused with affect which paralyzes one and leads to the functional regression of the other, while the Negro boy is found capable of operating at a higher level in a situation which has some personal relevance and interest for him and in which he is motivated through his interest to succeed. In a recent radio talk Paul Goodman commented that "the important life performance is *to get by*—that's what school is all about." And when one examines the examples above, one can see that each child brings his own set of priorities to the test situation and tries his damnedest to "get by" within that framework.

While most developmental theorists admit that levels of development overlap, there is usually little attention paid to the factors which determine usage of a particular level in a given situation. The previous examples suggest that the child's needs and viewpoint should be taken quite seriously in interpreting test results, and that the true test of cognitive competence is the ability to get by in the real-life milieu of which the test situation may or may not be representative.

The child learning to walk suffers at first a setback in efficiency of mobility and gets a few bruises to boot, yet tries again and again to walk. However, if he needs to get somewhere rather urgently he may well revert to his prior level of functioning—crawling. This is "pseudoregression" and refers to a falling back to an older, *more perfected* mode of operation which serves the purpose adequately. Much the same case may be made for the child's operational definition of quantity in the number-conservation task. The developmental course, with its *emphasis* shifting from action to perception to cognition, often presents instances where consolidation at one level is necessary for the exploration of the next-higher level. But if concrete demands are made, the child will probably tend to operate in the best consolidated manner available. Good perceptual operation will displace poor conceptual operation. I say "displace" intentionally, for the higher level is often already present in nascent form. Its usage, however, depends on specific factors of the situation—e.g., ease of task, confidence in the higher level, demands for correct and/or careful operation and, most important, relation to the task itself. In the conservation situation, for example, "longer" and "bigger" are perfectly reasonable definitions of quantity, and "more" is not the same to the child and the adult. The gradual incorporation of the adult version (i.e., more = number) is at least as representative of imitative modeling of adult norms as it is of "higher" thought processes. My point is, then, that usage of a perceptual approach to a problem which *we* see as numerical, but which in reality has a dual interpretation, is evidence only of lower confidence level in the abstract mode, not absence of or inability to operate in that mode.

A single instance of unequivocally conceptual operation precludes any general statement about inability to operate in that mode. If a child operates conceptually in one situation, but does not do so in another (when given free rein), the place to look is the structure of the problem in relation to the needs of the child. We must ask what there is about this structure that makes the child who is capable of operating at a conceptual level operate at a "lower" one. We can show that a child who at first operates *perceptually* on a task may operate *conceptually* when the perceptual alternative is not available. The success or failure at this point will be a much truer index of level of development than the "free choice" which characterizes standard tests of conservation and so many other developmental tests. In short, we are talking about the difference between a *dominant mode* of functioning, with which a child is comfortable, and the *capacity* for some type of operation.

Within the conservation task itself, we can see this difference in the example of the Negro boy with the trucks. In the neutral situation, using checkers, he takes an approach which apparently does not mobilize resources he reserves for the relevant (meaningful *to him*) situation involving dumptrucks. This can be seen more dramatically in results of testing children who seem to waver at or near conservation—a transitional stage in which conservation is intermittently evident. If the experimenter simply covers the row of checkers after the child sees them spread out to form a longer line, the child is deprived of the legitimately compelling cues of size and is forced to deal with the task in the "abstract" numerical mode. Confronted with a situation where the spontaneous perceptual response to size is not available, most of these borderline cases will use the numerical mode.

Even in the area of verbal conceptualization, one must be hypersensitive to the difference between the expectations of the tester and those of the child. Children see problems in terms of their own needs and interests, and unless the adult has the ability to make what he expects *clear* and *acceptable* to the child there is no reason to assume that the child cannot function at a given level. Yet psychological-test manuals, in their instructions, call for the statement of a problem and, if the child does not seem to grasp the idea, repetition in *exactly the same way*. Encouragement and direction, for the sake of uniformity, are limited to "Yes," "Go ahead," "Please explain further," or "Tell me more about it."

The Similarities subtest of the Wechsler Intelligence Scale for Children (WISC) is one of the cornerstones for assertions about abstract–concrete differences in the level of cognitive development of children. Some examples of how instruction and procedure influence test results suggest that these assertions should be questioned.

The subject is a twelve-year-old Negro boy from a relatively poor family. "What is the same about a plum and a peach?" he is asked. He answers, "They're both good to eat." "That's true," says the questioner; "they're also both fruits." The child nods. "How are a dog and a cat alike?" "They both have fur." "How else are they alike?" "They're both animals," says the child. "How about a lake and a mountain—how are they alike?" "They both have water." "Does a mountain have water?" "Yes, in the winter it has snow—that's frozen water, and in the spring it melts and becomes streams and brooks on the side of the mountain." "How else are they alike?" "They're both in nature."

We may cast a problem in such a way that the child's response will be more or less in conformity with what an adult's might be.

In the covered-checkers example, we force a numerical response which has little meaning to the child but satisfies us, since it is responsive to *our* way of interpreting magnitude. In the verbal similarities, we can also demand that a specific level of categorical response be given and the child will comply. Initial response may follow the lines of need, interest or imagination, and *this is appropriate* to the situation from the child's viewpoint. But we typically demand that a child should treat each new situation as a *test* and understand immediately what *we* expect of him. What is really sad is that so many children do see things this way and thus sacrifice an opportunity for creative responses to new situations in favor of an empty stereotype to which we drive them.

Indeed, *cognitive conformity* and not level of cognitive development may be what we are actually seeing when we look at the differences between middle- and lower-class children in school. This view has been implicit in much of what has been written criticizing the typology of intelligence as ranging from abstract to concrete. In the final section of this paper, I would like to present data which complements this criticism by supplying research data in support of an alternative construction—a unified model of individual differences.

Cognitive Styles

Herman Witkin and his associates at the psychological laboratories at Downstate Medical Center in New York have, over the course of two decades, amassed impressive evidence that individual differences in *verbal style* (not quantitatively different levels of intelligence, abstracting ability, or degree of cognitive development) may lie at the root of class distinctions in the educational system (Witkin, 1965, 1967; Witkin *et al.,* 1962, 1966, 1967; Dyk and Witkin, 1965). In his research Witkin has investigated individual differences in *"cognitive styles"* and found this to be the most meaningful dimension of difference for the assessment of cognitive development. By "cognitive style" is meant characteristic, self-consistent ways of functioning in perceptual and intellectual activities which apply across a wide range of situations and are based on the quality of perceptual performance in real problems—not just verbal proficiency.

Witkin has described two basic types of cognitive style: "field-dependent" and "field-independent." The *field-dependent* person is characterized by more global, poorly differentiated and poorly articulated cognitive and perceptual processes. His figure drawing (reflecting the development of body image) is more simple, with fewer discrete parts and less attention to the proportion and organization of these parts. In tasks involving the abstraction of some part from a confusing background ("hidden figures"), he has more difficulty. In situations where feedback from his own senses conflicts with a visual input he tends to deny the data from within himself. The *field-independent* person, on the other hand, seems to have a greater sense of the separateness of his body from the external world and is better able to integrate that data with external cues. His productions are more differentiated and better organized, with more attention to discriminating factors. Perceptually, he is better able to isolate (i.e., abstract) some important part of a picture or situation; in this sense *his perception is analytical*.

This differentiation is not limited to perceptual processes but manifests itself in intellectual activities as well. "Thus persons whose perception is field-dependent do less well at solving problems which require isolating essential elements (i.e. abstracting) from the context in which they are presented and using them in a different context" (Witkin, 1965, p. 319). These stylistic differences have been found to relate reliably to important differences in personality such as sense of identity, the use of more or less mature defenses and even to the forms of psychopathology. Finally, there is great consistency in the stability of the measure within an individual over the course of his development. This factor provides a powerful tool for the analysis of individual differences from the broadest possible perspective. Furthermore, it relates these differences to a continuum which is genuinely reflective of psychological/cognitive development and directly predictive of important behaviors relevant to real-life functioning.

The application of this "stylistic" analysis to the problems of this paper reveals some startling information. First of all, *there are no significant differences in field-dependence/independence as a function of socioeconomic class.* Analysis of intelligence-test data does reveal that middle-class children do better on the verbal and *social-comprehension* parts of the test (the most middle-class "culturebound"), but these parts show *absolutely no correlation with cognitive style.* The sections which reflect *"analytic ability"* (Cohen, 1959) in cognitive functioning are the only parts that correlate with Witkin's measures—and they correlate extremely well. *This factor is evenly distributed over all classes and is the I.Q. test factor which comes closest to predicting genuine differences in cognitive style.* Now, it should be remembered that it is the verbal-comprehension "factor" which has been found to be class-correlated, and it is, of course, this factor which also correlates with success in school. "The answer may lie," Witkin suggests, "in the heavy emphasis placed upon verbal skills . . . to the relative disregard of other kinds of ability (Witkin *et al.,* 1966, p. 312). I would substitute "verbal styles" for "verbal skills," for even in this area, as several papers in this book point out, the attribution of superior verbal development to class differences in language is highly questionable.

In addition to specifying discrete factors in intellectual style and their relation to and meaning for school performance, the cognitive-style typology provides important data on the personal and social matrix for development of a particular style and clearly shows its importance for school behavior. Witkin and his associates have noted that many children who succeed in school seem to do so on the basis of acute attention to and perception of adult feedback via expressions and other nonverbal cues that serve to shape behavior in a powerful way. "Field-dependent" children are not only hypersensitive to adult cues indicative of reaction to the child's performance, but are also the children who develop precocious use of adult speech patterns. "We know from our studies that field-dependent children, low in analytic ability, are often conforming to adult authority. This characteristic, together with their ability to 'talk nicely,' is apt to be particularly pleasing to teachers" (Witkin *et al.*, 1966, p. 313). Often, however, these same children are markedly deficient in performance areas based on the need for analytic ability, and get to higher grade levels on the strength of the "good impression" they make, only to fail miserably in substantive tasks and subjects requiring action rather than empty words and facile verbal responses.

We may also examine the social and family experience and its relation to cognitive styles. Here it is especially important to differentiate between verbal and cognitive styles, for while the former is closely linked to culturally specific experiences, the latter is linked to early experience with the family.

The possibility arises from these findings that cultural stimulation, as commonly provided by schools and other social media, may work most of all on behalf of verbal comprehension and social communication skills. On the other hand, development of the cluster of characteristics which includes an articulated cognitive style, as well as an articulated body concept and a developed sense of separate identity (together signifying self-differentiation), is more under the influence of the quality of relations with critical persons (as in the family) early in life. Given the necessary interpersonal relations, *these important attributes of any autonomous person may apparently develop even under conditions of so-called cultural deprivation*. The observation in our own studies and in studies by others that socioeconomic status does not relate to field dependence, but is significantly related to level of verbal comprehension abilities, is consistent with these views. [Witkin, 1967, p. 248.]

In their paper "Family Experiences Related to the Development of Differentiation in Children," Dyk and Witkin (1965) spell out some of the family characteristics which seem to affect the development of cognitive style. They have found that many of the qualities of the stereotypical middle-class mother (such as overprotectiveness) stress a verbal responsiveness, conformity and imposition of certain middle-class styles and values on the child which may interefere with the development of field-independence but foster a verbal stylistic development conducive to success in school. Thus, there are data to suggest that inappropriate development in the verbal sphere (the pre-mature use of middle-class adult language patterns) may reflect and foster an overly dependent child–parent relationship which in turn inhibits the development of analytic intelligence.

In sum, the particular formula embodied in the abstract–concrete model of class differences in intellectual functioning turns out to be an artifact of subcultural differences in verbal style. The history of the conceptual framework on which it and most other current intelligence measures rests is the history of attempts to justify the superior or inferior position of a particular group by looking *within* that group for causal factors. The assumption that dominance or greater privilege and power are due to greater intellect or any other endogenous factor is to deny the reality of the cultural matrix as a whole. The function of the "culture of poverty" approach may very well be to distract attention from the culture of affluence and privilege. While this and other elaborate systems of rationalization may assuage guilt, they cannot forever delay confrontation with reality.

Trying to explain cultural phenomena by recourse to the quality of life in a subculture is a deception. Just as we deceive the lower-class child with our promises of success and adaptation to the "good life" in America, we deceive ourselves when we seize upon the "culture of poverty" to explain massive school and social failure within our society. Poverty is an integral part of this culture of ours, and the consequences of life in poverty are hardship. There is, however, a wide range of individual response to hardship. If there is degradation, there is also pride; if there is fragmentation, there is also cohesion; and if there is failure, there is also success against overwhelming odds. Any genuine desire to rectify inequities in our society should focus on the distortions and prejudices which insulate us from perceiving the realities of our culture, and should avoid developing stereotypes of a "culture of poverty."

BIBLIOGRAPHY

Boas, Franz, *The Mind of Primitive Man,* revised edition. New York: Free Press, 1963.

Cohen, J., "The Factorial Structure of the WISC at ages 7-6, 10-6, and 13-6," *Journal of Consulting Psychology,* Vol. 23 (1959).

Dyk, Ruth B., and H. A. Witkin, "Family Experiences Related to the Development of Differentiation in Children," *Child Development,* Vol. 30 (1965), No. 1.

Hunt, J. McVickers, "The Psychological Basis for Using Pre-School Enrichment as an Antidote for Cultural Deprivation," *Merrill-Palmer Quarterly,* Vol. 10 (1964), No. 3.

Jensen, A., "How Much Can We Boost I.Q. and Scholastic Achievement?" *Harvard Educational Review,* Vol. 39 (1969), No. 1.

Keller, Suzanne, *The American Lower Class Family: A Survey of Selected Facts and Their Applications.* Albany, N.Y.: New York State Division for Youth, 1968.

Pasamanick, Benjamin, "A Tract for the Times: Some Sociobiologic Aspects of Science, Race, and Racism," *American Journal of Orthopsychiatry,* Vol. 39 (1969), No. 1.

Radin, Paul, *The World of Primitive Man.* New York: Grove Press, 1953.

Werner, Heinz, *Comparative Psychology of Mental Development.* New York: Science Editions, 1961.

Witkin, H. A., "Psychological Differentiation and Forms of Pathology," *Journal of Abnormal Psychology,* Vol. 70 (1965), No. 5.

———, "A Cognitive-Style Approach to Cross-Cultural Research," *International Journal of Psychology,* Vol. 2 (1967), No. 4.

———, R. B. Dyk, H. F. Faterson, D. R. Goodenough and S. A. Karp, *Psychological Differentiation.* New York: Wiley, 1962.

———, H. F. Faterson, D. R. Goodenough and J. Birnbaum, "Cognitive Patterning in Mildly Retarded Boys," *Child Development,* Vol. 37, No. 2 (June 1966).

———, D. R. Goodenough and S. A. Karp, "Stability of Cognitive Styles from Childhood to Young Adulthood," *Journal of Personality and Social Psychology,* Vol. 7 (1967), No. 3.

LANGUAGE AND EDUCABILITY

VERA P. JOHN

Although the children of the poor are the focus of much public and academic attention, they are still but gross statistics to most university scholars. The statistics most often emphasized in the press as well as in research applications and reports relate to the dropout rate among minority youth, the "achievement gap," youth unemployment, and the much discussed "family instability" syndrome. Recently the Berkeley psychologist Jensen has questioned the potential for learning of nonwhite children in the midst of a national debate on compensatory education. He ascribes the failure of such programs to a lower genetic potential for abstract learning in Negro children when compared with white children. Stale and often erroneous statistics serve as the point of familiarization to the sizable group of university workers and educators now involved in antipoverty and related programs, in lieu of their having some form of prolonged and direct experience with the poor.

Perhaps an equally serious problem confronting these workers is that they are bereft of *theories* pertinent to the children of the poor. The social Darwinism of the past (and in some limited circles of the present) is expressed in psychological studies in the form of hereditary theories of intelligence and educability.[1] This approach is rejected by the majority of contemporary workers, though Jensen's article in the Winter 1968 issue of *The Harvard Review* has created much confusion on this subject. Many social

[1] For an excellent discussion of this topic, see Schwebel, 1968.

63

scientists were impressed by the scope of his presentation and could not pinpoint, by themselves, the statistical, biological and other fallacies in his argument. Unfortunately, the rejection of genetic theories of class and race differences is not frequently accompanied by the choice of an alternative theoretical system.

I submit that the behavioral consequences of living in poverty cannot be adequately studied without reliance upon a *generalized theory of the social environment*. The impact of the social setting has been generally acknowledged as having crucial significance upon the growing child. However, the social scientists of poverty have approached this realization either via a Freudian emphasis upon an intact family, as illustrated by the well-known Moynihan Report on the Negro family, or by the equally questionable one of comparisons of social class, in which deprivation is stressed as an explanatory variable. Lacking a theoretical framework, salient class differences, as viewed from the vantage point of middle-class existence, are selected by these research workers to form the basis of their investigations. These attempts, then, can be best characterized as post-hoc explanations of statistical findings. They are not theories.

To generate a comprehensive theory of the social environment as it affects behavior is a big order. Part of the problem arises from the discomfort American scientists and educators experience when confronted with the challenge of social turmoil and class-related phenomena. Generally, they have argued, studies of face-to-face small groups are more manageable. Indeed, the complexities of the relationship between class and consciousness are enormous, and thus, regrettably and understandably, we all look for shortcuts.

The many attempts at interdisciplinary approaches to complex social phenomena also suffer from weaknesses. Even with goals of unity of focus and search for a common method, interdisciplinary studies have often been overambitious and devoid of a shared content. However, in the case of language, the distinguishing attribute of the human species, attempts by social scientists to conduct integrated interdisciplinary studies appear promising. An examination of the uses of language has led a number of thinkers to attempt a broader theory of the social environment.

I. The Study of Language

Traditionally, psychologists approached language as sequentially organized behavior, the acquisition of which results in a smooth and socially appropriate behavior. This definition of language, particularly favored by behavioristically oriented psychologists, has been criticized in recent years. My own concern with this simplistic approach to language is with its outcome: if the motivational roots of language are a single, direct process, then the overt structure of language is also single and direct.

Descriptively, language could be thought of as a walk along a moving stream of water, at times reflecting tranquillity, at times turbulence. Whether the questions one poses concerning the role of language are abstract (how verbal are our thoughts?) or concrete (what is good timing in the teaching of reading to the bilingual child?), the study of language inevitably leads to some of the most significant social and individual processes of contemporary life.

In conceptualizing language theoretically, my basic hypothesis has been as follows: that although the final act of stringing words into phrases in the presence of an audience may appear smooth, it is the result of many contradictory processes. To speak is to unite, *temporarily,* the intrapersonal and interpersonal forces which simultaneously affect the speaker.[2] This process is a varying function of situational, cognitive, experiential and social variables.

This approach to language is not a new one. It is based on the obvious but complex notion that language is the product of the

[2] Illustrations of this interplay are shown in speech studies by Frieda Goldman-Eisler and others, where distinctions have been made between short pauses preceding automatic or overlearned phrases and longer pauses preceding newly elaborated messages requiring time to think and plan (Goldman-Eisler, 1964). In our own work with young children, we found a similar trend in correlations between pauses and sentence types of different cognitive complexity (John and Berney, 1967). Beven describes the fluctuating of attention during speech perception; he differentiates between outward, *social* attention and *inward* attention. In some instances these processes of outward or inward attention may be contradictory and thus limit the character and volume of productive and receptive language.

interplay of both the external, objective components of communicative situations (setting, task, and nature and size of the audience) and the internal, subjective components of communicative situations (thoughts, wishes and fantasies), as well as a reflection of the structural features of language. The British philosopher Caudwell described this antagonism between object and subject as the "creative source of knowledge" and wrote that "the private thoughts of an individual are inaccessible, the desires of a man to do something invisible. But as soon as man's thoughts issue in language, in concepts, in a coherent system, they become social. They have adopted social forms: language and ideas evolved in the process of society." (Caudwell, 1950, p. 248).

One of the challenges confronting the present-day psychologist of language is the examination of this interplay between subjective thought and objective expression. In the past, a statement phrased this way would have been considered antithetical to science. But "representations," "schemas," even thoughts, are being examined anew. The developmental approaches of the Harvard psychologist Bruner and the world-renowned Swiss scholar Jean Piaget offer a particularly fruitful avenue of investigation concerning the objective and subjective aspects of language.

Some of the most significant work on the interrelations of language and thought has been done by the Russian psychologist Vygotsky. Vygotsky sees word meaning as basic to this process. He identifies a prelinguistic phase in thought and a pre-intellectual phase in speech and posits that in the course of development the child moves through several stages; ultimately, thought and speech coincide like two intersecting circles to produce "verbal thought," which Vygotsky sees not as an innate form of behavior but as "determined by a historical-cultural process" (Vygotsky, 1962, p. 51).

The development of the speaker and thinker in all of us emerges in the communicative and instructional settings of our childhood. The study of the variety of these settings and their impact upon the growing individual has been approached by researchers drawn from several disciplines. (Some of the research illustrating the impact of widely differing social environments will be described below.) But most psychologists and anthropologists still tend to look at language as a unitary, well-integrated process which develops as a function of age. Even Vygotsky, who excelled in describing the intricate, often fleeting character of language in the young child, minimized, in his discussions, the continually developing flux of adult language.

But through the new discipline of sociolinguistics a more differentiated view of language is emerging. Of particular significance are the theoretical writings of Dell Hymes, the anthropological linguist. In our own work we have attempted to apply his concept of "communicative competence," a knowledge of the forms and uses of language to the young child learning to speak. In addition, we are working toward a theory of language development by looking at language at different levels of structure (syntactical and semantic) and varied functions (cognitive, communicative, emotive).[3]

While work in the theoretical aspects of language is attracting an increasing number of scholars, it is difficult, at this stage of our knowledge, to see how to apply what is being learned. Nevertheless, the demands for applied knowledge are enormous. In this discussion of language and educability, I have chosen to explore two variables only. This choice is dictated by a recognition of the difficulties of a premature application of generalized theories of language to learning in school.

One variable is the *audience,* which is of particular importance in the development and inhibition of language forms and use in the home and school. The second variable is an elusive, subjective one, the internal pressure on the individual to express his feelings and ideas in language, particularly at a time of stress and change. The speech produced at these times of stress is a striking example of communicative competence. We see this use of language dramatically illustrated today by speakers arising amongst the minority groups in all parts of the country.

[3] We note Cazden's suggestion that while direct tutoring may be of critical importance in the acquisition of *vocabulary,* it may be of little importance in the acquisition of syntax (Cazden, 1968).

II. Language Socialization in the Home

The physical and social setting in which the child first enjoys play and learns to talk and think creates in him a particular hierarchy of skills and preferences; this is the process called language socialization.

Much of our knowledge about variations in daily routines of family life is still based on hunches. Techniques for recording and analyzing long sequences of ordinary events are just being developed. There are a few studies, however, of relevance to the socialization of language. The sociological pioneer in the study of family life Bossard has analyzed mealtime conversations and has found consistent social-class differences, in measures such as variations in child-centered versus adult-centered talk, in different social environments.

Two studies of very young children will serve to illustrate the dynamics of the different roles mothers play in their responses to their children's earliest verbalizations. In one well-known study of two- to three-year-old children of Harvard graduate students, the social psychologist Roger Brown and his co-workers recorded mother–child interactions in their homes. Brown's samples reveal that while many of the children's utterances were simple, playful monologues without a clear-cut focus, the mother responded to them with great seriousness. For instance, one sample goes as follows:

CHILD: O.K. I get that brush, that brush. Hi, bunny rabbit. My screwdriver. Hi, bunny rabbit. Adam Carter.
MOTHER: "Adam Carter"? Is that the bunny rabbit's name?
CHILD: O.K., kitto.
MOTHER: "O.K., kitto" what?
CHILD: Oh, Adam fall. Toy. Adam fall toy.
MOTHER: "Adam fall toy." You did not fall that time. You just sat down.
CHILD: Adam fall toy. Oh, Adam belt. How are you, belt? . . .

The directive-, tutorial-type responses of the mother to the child reveal what social critics describe as the middle-class mother's tendency to "push" her child toward intellectual achievement. An additional feature of middle-class life may also be at work in these types of interactions. Many educated young women find the social confinement of life with their young children trying, and in their need for companionship they develop in their toddlers a skill and a desire for talkative exchanges. Consequently, their children learn at a very young age the technique of conversing with adults. In the context of this intensive one-to-one relationship, the dialogue serves to transform the child's playful speech into speech for social use.

In contrast to Brown's study at Harvard, a somewhat different picture emerges from a study of young children in the Negro ghetto of Rochester, New York, recently completed by the linguist Vivian Horner. Horner's work, based on taped verbal interactions, reveals a complex network of speakers and listeners surrounding the three-year-old low-income child. (The taped communicative exchanges were obtained from transistorized equipment sewn into the young children's clothes, with the consent of the parents.)

While in their homes these very young children address most of their talk to their mothers, though they spend a great deal of their time in the company of their age peers. They go in and out of the house by themselves, talking, playing, fighting, and occasionally assuming responsibility for even younger children. The low-income mother lives in an environment where many children and adults come to speak to her, entering and leaving in rapid succession. She does not spend many consecutive hours alone with one child, or with two children; she has neither the need nor the opportunity to shape her child's verbal utterances with the intensity recorded in the Harvard samples. Following is an example of an exchange among three-year-old John, his five-year-old brother, Roddy, and their mother:

MOTHER: Count.
JOHN: One . . . two . . .
MOTHER: (Responding to someone who called) Yeah? (To John) Wait. (To caller) Yeah?

JOHN: . . . three . . . four . . .

RODDY: That's four, Boo-Boo.

JOHN: Huh?

RODDY: That's four.

JOHN: (Unintelligible)

MOTHER: Count, Boo. Come on. Count my fingers.

JOHN: One . . . two . . . three . . .

   (Mother's attention turns to something else)

JOHN: Two . . .

MOTHER: Count my toes. (Pause) Count. (Pause) Here. Count yours.

RODDY: (Butting in) One . . . two . . . three . . .

JOHN: One . . . two . . . three . . . four . . . five . . .

MOTHER: Good! Five little toes! All the toes there.

[Horner, p. 155.]

In correlative studies of young children the availability of the mother as a significant factor affecting language growth has been stressed. In research on the verbal superiority of the firstborn (as measured by vocabulary tests), the mothers often report that they were more involved with and spent more time stimulating the verbal development of their firstborn than their later children. However, it is well to note that while the firstborn may show language proficiency, they often lose out in other ways, such as social maturity, and they perform less well than later-born on nonverbal tasks.

While some of these findings are intriguing, our current knowledge of language socialization and its consequences to the growing child are still hardly understood. Ease with words cannot be assessed effectively outside the social context in which language is actually used. According to the psycholinguist Susan Ervin-Tripp, in a review article, *"the basis of the child's most important and complex achievement still remains unknown"* (Ervin-Tripp, 1966, p. 81).

Despite the lack of a widely agreed-upon explanatory model of language acquisition, many practitioners have chosen to look at the speech of low-income children as inadequate and "restricted." The latter term is adopted from the British sociologist Basil Bernstein, whose theories have been adopted as an answer to those searching for a theoretical handle. Indeed, vulgarized forms of his theory can be found by perusing many of the current publications dealing with the language of the so-called "culturally deprived." For instance, Bereiter writes: "Our estimation of the language of the culturally deprived children agrees, however, with that of Bernstein, who maintains that this language is not merely an underdeveloped version of Standard English but that it is basically a *nonlogical* mode of expressive behavior which *lacks the formal properties necessary for the organization of thought*" (Bereiter, 1966, pp. 112-13; emphasis mine).

The assumption that the mastery of standard English is a prerequisite for the development of abstract thought in low-income children was criticized by Basil Bernstein as a misrepresentation of his theory. Indeed, there is little justification in equating *any* form of overt language with the process of conceptualization. We are, as yet, profoundly ignorant about the precise characteristics of *conceptual language* (both in its overt forms, when appearing spontaneously in the context of everyday problem solving, and in its covert forms, the process Vygotsky has called "inner speech").

Thus, it appears that basic to the theoretical and practical dilemma of the "interventionists" is their lack of differentiation between *language as a communicative process* and *language as an intellective (intrapersonal) process,* a confusion which reflects the lack of detailed scientific information concerning the latter phenomenon. As our knowledge of the nature and development of conceptual, or intrapersonal, language unfolds, specialized forms of teaching, aimed at all children, will be perfected.

III. Language Socialization in the Schools

In the school, language is a primary means of *instruction* and *control*. The children who are attuned to the verbal world of the adult, and socialized by its complex speech patterns, are at an advantage here. What happens, though, to children whose language forms, skills, preferences, or even mother tongue are at variance with that of the teacher? Let me quote Facundo Valdez, Office of Economic Opportunity director in northern New Mexico:

It is sad but true that the way the educational philosophy and educational concepts of our country have evolved, they have always tended to do away with, and replace, any language system a minority group might have. To this day and age that is true in New Mexico. Educators still preach that the value system of our language system— Spanish—has little value, and it is of no benefit to speak this language.

Conscientious efforts have been made by the public institutions of education to urge people to forget who they are. It is common knowledge that in many schools in the area, though native teachers may be teaching, punishment is administered because kids insist on speaking Spanish.

You can imagine the kind of ambivalence that this creates in the child, at an early stage of his development. In effect, many of the problems the Spanish-speaking youth have, with regard to their heritage, are due to the fact that they have been robbed of their birthright. They find themselves in a state of limbo, in a state of nowhere.

I have quoted at length from Valdez because he expresses so well, from the viewpoint of the Spanish-speaking of the Southwest, the sorrow and frustration of parents, community leaders, educators and social scientists with the state of contemporary public education. The message that emerges is: *the schools have failed the poor.* We hear this message when we listen to parents demand community control of the schools; we see this message when we scan the new titles in the bookstores: *Our Children Are Dying, Death at an Early Age, The Way It Spozed to Be, 36 Children.*

But even a broader observation can be made about the schools, and that is that they are not educating *anyone* adequately. "The hidden curriculum" of the middle-class home offers, for the children raised in it, a substantial compensatory program to the school. But the school's failure here is merely less visible among the college-educated, white-collar adults who motivate, prepare, and tutor their children (often unintentionally) in the skills they themselves use in their daily jobs.

I would like to note, parenthetically, that the teaching of their own children by parents of a family of what they themselves have learned, directly and indirectly, has been the *rule* rather than the exception in human history. It is only in the last hundred years, in industrialized societies, that most children are taught much of what they are expected to know by strangers.

In its evolution, the public-school system in this country has developed three basic functions: (1) *citizenship training* or the transmission of the work ethos—children are trained to be punctual, thrifty, and politely competitive; (2) *education for literacy and/or vocational skills*—this is the minimal instructional content often described as the 3 R's; and (3) *selecting individuals for specialized intellectual and occupational roles.*[4]

The public-school system can claim the highest record of achievement in its first function of citizenship training. The effective dissemination of the so-called Protestant ethic among a "nation of immigrants" and indigenous people is no small achievement. Though seldom recognized as such, much of the school experience consists of *training,* not *teaching.*

In its second function of educating for literacy, the school system has had a high casualty rate, even by its own criteria. We need only recall the large number of illiterates identified by the armed forces in twentieth-century wars.

Society could tolerate these large-scale educational failures because, until recently, there was a plentiful supply of jobs which did not require academically taught skills. However, there is now widespread dissatisfaction with the limited quality and effectiveness of academic instruction in the schools. Some ascribe the outcry for better schools to Sputnik, others to the Supreme Court decision of 1954.[5]

[4] Many writers have identified school functions in this or related ways. See Eleanor Leacock's 1967 paper, or Talcott Parsons' classic essay on this subject (1961).
[5] While a detailed description of the social evolution which led to unprecedented congressional appropriations for education and to heated debates about school reform are outside the scope of this paper, one development cannot be bypassed in this discussion of language and education. I refer to the panacea of automated teaching, which is favored by many educational technologists. These educators, who insist on the one hand that the mastery of a rich, flexible, and abstract language is crucial to the ac-

The role of language in education, though recognized, is still scarcely understood by most practitioners. There are many indications that fluent and socially accepted speech is the outcome of habitual thought and language, while the verbal expression of new ideas is accompanied by unevenness in speech production.[6] Nevertheless, teachers pay close attention to the prestigious forms and grammatical "correctness" of their pupils' language, and spend many tedious hours correcting their speech. Later, when the teachers have tired of the effort, they will isolate or withhold attention from children whose speech patterns offend their ears. In this way they silence the very children who are most in need of an *attentive* and *rewarding audience* for their developing speech "repertoire." Kohl summarized this development by saying that disadvantaged children will not speak in class because they cannot trust their audience (Kohl, 1967).

No child from any background is immune to the effects of a flawed educational system. But it is among the children of the poor that the most crippling features of the school's language program are found, a program basically aimed at remaking children into a single, favored image. By replacing, or attempting to replace, the child's currently spoken language forms with those spoken by "mainstream" children, the teacher tampers with the very act of speech itself, which the child creates out of the interplay of forces in his internal and external worlds. To quote Valdez again, "The identity built up during a child's formative years is destroyed . . . they have not killed the children, but they have killed their spirit." Recognizing the damage of forcing children into a rigid linguistic mold has led to new approaches in developing the language of the minority child. Bilingual instruction programs for the non-English-

---

quisition of academic skills, fail to recognize the paradox of recommending a language-based curriculum taught by machines. *Language is socially acquired and practiced.* A heavy dose of automated teaching will not insure its acquisition; on the contrary, automated teaching is bound to weaken a meaningful language curriculum.

[6] Of interest here is research of a decade ago, when, in the taping of the flow of language of two adults in a vacation setting, utterances scored as "thinking aloud" were found to be preponderantly sentence fragments. These findings were in line with the concept that inner speech is *telegraphic* (Soskin and John, 1963).

speaking child constitute one attempt at modifying the school instead of trying to remake the child. In working with black children, linguists and teachers are developing a new awareness about the rule-governed regularities of black English. In some schools, readers which are specifically devised for Negro children and which recognize the integrity of his home language are used.

IV. Communicative Competence and Low-Income Speakers

The first variable of language socialization in the home and in school is the audience. I now turn to the second variable—the internal pressure on the individual to express his feelings and ideas in language, particularly in times of stress and change.

I have already noted that speech produced at these times of stress is a striking example of communicative competence. As defined by Dell Hymes, communicative competence aims at specifying how "each social relationship entails the selection and/or creation of communicative means considered specific and appropriate to it by its participants" (Hymes, 1966, p. 9).

We are now witnessing dramatic examples of communicative competence in the untapped reservoirs of cultural diversity and language richness of low-income communities throughout the country. Of striking immediacy is the power and eloquence of the language used by the spokesmen of the poor. These self-taught spokesmen, like Cesar Chavez of California, Fannie Lou Hamer of Mississippi, Reies Tijerina of New Mexico, and the late Malcolm X, have articulated in their speeches the experience of living in the communities of the poor.

It is primarily through the spoken work that these leaders express some of the conflicts of the poor today: Will they be subjected to cultural extermination as people, or will they survive and develop communities with institutions reflecting their own cultural traditions?

Some have questioned this way of presenting the choices confronting this society in its relation to the minority communities. Is it not the lack of preparation in coping with a highly developed technological society which is the essential problem confronting the poor today? An interesting answer is given to this dilemma by an anonymous writer contributing to the American Indian publication *The Sentinel:*

Granted that assimilation has not and will not work, we still have a serious problem of making sufficient progress with, for and by Indians so that they are not made obsolete by the onrushing technology of today. We would suggest that new Indian policy be formed to take into account the differences in culture and outlook that Indians have with the rest of American society. And we would not suggest that we begin with a group of anthropologists talking about beads, braids and dances. When we advocate the recognition of cultural differences we are thinking primarily of the ways that people act and react to situations, the way they view the world, and the values they consider most important. For example, profit, while dearly worshipped by the rest of the society, is not particularly dear to tribal hearts. Tribal enterprises are operated more to provide employment and opportunity than to create dividends. The rest of society has a mania for "giving" to every noble cause . . . Indians would rather share daily than give weekly, monthly at income tax time, or by fund raising appeals. Indians truly believe that the gift without the giver is bare and with the giver it is sharing, not giving.

We would advocate, therefore, a program of acculturation rather than a temporary patchwork of assimilationist programs. Acculturation is, we feel, a program by which tribes can be encouraged to change behavior patterns by giving them the opportunity to develop programs by incorporating their present values with new opportunities for human resource administration. . . .

There is continual emphasis on bringing the poor into the "mainstream" of American society. Quite often this means the ridiculous assumption that poor, and especially rural, people must assume a value system that will always be foreign to them. There is not that much stability in the "mainstream" that a certain set of values will prove to be universally valid. And the "mainstream" itself must inevitably give way to innovations demanded by the poor to fit their needs.[7]

[7] Quoted in S. Steiner, 1967, pp. 302-3.

Unaccustomed as we are to listening to the articulate among the poor, we are surprised by the emotional drive and clarity of these expressions. There are "speakers" among tribal people, and speechmakers among the industrialized. But unless speech acts are analyzed in terms of a comprehensive theory of communicative competence, the literature will continue to abound in the type of distortions illustrated by the above quote from Bereiter.

As Whorf, Vygotsky, and Bernstein, pioneers in the study of language, have stressed, language acts as a filter to what is perceived. Consequently, the language forms spoken by members of a social group can *hasten* or *delay* the clarity with which they confront their social reality at a particular time. Low-income speakers often lack receptive audiences in their formulations of significant problems of their existence, but, once they are given such an opportunity for social amplification of their objectives, their language gains shape and individuality.

The central question, thus far neglected by most theorists, is: What is the underlying language model used in assessing communicative competence in low-income individuals? The model, it seems, is that of standard English represented by the mass media. This is a bland version of contemporary speech whereby a smattering of knowledge is communicated to a heterogeneous group of listeners; but the mastery of the "code" is considered a necessary prerequisite for educational success and social mobility. This expectation leads to a failure to recognize the stylistic and functional diversity of language of speakers of disparate backgrounds.

The meaning and significance of the language resources of the communities of the poor have not been grasped by educators. No widespread programs have been developed to draw on indigenous speech resources; to fulfill ghetto youth's need and capacity to articulate their experiences; or to appreciate the deep eloquence of the leaders of the poor. On the contrary, educators, for example, ignore these possibilities and continue to teach by pattern drills in standard English and new automated devices.

How can we reshape our educational methods to cope with and develop this urgent and universal need for self-expression? In his pamphlet *Teaching the "Unteachable,"* Herbert Kohl describes his experience in a Harlem ghetto school:

Nothing the school offered was relevant, so I read the class novels, stories, poems, brought my library to class and let them know that many people have suffered throughout history and that some were articulate enough to create literature from their lives. They did not believe me, but they were hungry to know what had been written about and what could be written about. . . . The class began a romance with words and language that lasted all year. [Kohl, 1967, pp. 17, 21.]

More than one hundred years ago the scholar and philosopher of the "American Renaissance," Ralph Waldo Emerson, noted the dichotomy between the richness of the language of the people and the paleness of the language of scholarship. He suggested that if the scholars wished to enrich their language they ought to "frequent the public square" and listen, attentively and appreciatively. Educators might be similarly advised to go into the ghetto classrooms and listen, attentively and appreciatively.

BIBLIOGRAPHY

Bereiter, Carl, S. Engelman, J. Osborn and P. A. Reidford, "An Academically Oriented Preschool for Culturally Deprived Children," in *Preschool Education Today,* ed. Fred M. Hechinger (Garden City, N. Y.: Doubleday, 1966), pp. 105-137.

Bernstein, Basil, "Social Structure, Language and Learning," in *The Psychology of Language, Thought and Instruction,* ed. John P. De Cecco (New York: Holt, Rinehart and Winston, 1967).

Beven, T., Untitled paper presented at Psycholinguistic Circle of New York, Fall, 1967.

Bossard, J. H. S., "Family Table Talk, an Area for Sociological Study," *American Sociological Review,* Vol. 8 (1943), pp. 295-301.

Brown, Roger, *et al.,* mimeographed copies of original transcripts, work done at Harvard University under Public Health Service Research Grant MH 7088, 1963.

Caudwell, C., *Further Studies in a Dying Culture.* London, Bodley & Head, 1950.

Cazden, Courtney, "Some Implications of Research on Language Development for Preschool Education," in *Early Education,* ed. Robert D. Hess and Roberta Meyer Bear (Chicago: Aldine Press, 1968).

Ervin-Tripp, S., "Language Development," in *Review of Child Development Research,* Vol. 2, ed. Hoffman and Hoffman (New York: Russell Sage Foundation, 1966).

Goldman-Eisler, Frieda, "Discussion and Further Comments," in *New Directions in the Study of Language,* ed. E. H. Lenneberg (Cambridge: Massachusetts Institute of Technology Press, 1964), pp. 109-130.

Horner, Vivian, mimeographed transcription of tapes obtained for Ph.D. dissertation, *The Verbal World of a Low-Class Three-Year-Old: Pilot Study in Linguistic Ecology,* 1969.

Hymes, Dell, "On Communicative Competence," presented at Research Planning Conference on Language Development in Disadvantaged Children, June 7–8, 1966, Yeshiva University.

John, Vera P., "Children and Language Acquisition," in *The New Elementary School,* ed. Alexander Frazier (National Education Association, Association for Supervision and Curriculum Development), Washington, 1968.

————, and Berney, T., *Analysis of Story Retelling as a Measure of the Effects of Ethnic Content in Stories,* final report, OEO grant No. 577 (1967).

Koch, H., "The Relation of Primary Mental Abilities in Five- and Six-Year-Olds to Sex of Children and Characteristics of His Siblings," *Child Development,* Vol. 25, September 1954, pp. 209-23.

Kohl, Herbert, *Teaching the "Unteachable"* (pamphlet). *New York Review of Books,* 1967.

Leacock, Eleanor, "Cultural Influences on Language and Coping Behavior," paper delivered at the Elementary School Guidance Workshop Conference sponsored by the Bureau of Guidance Services, Pennsylvania Department of Public Instruction, Oct. 16–18, 1967.

Parsons, Talcott, "The School Class as a Social System: Some of Its Functions in American Society," in *Education, Economy and Society: A Reader in the Sociology of Education,* ed. A. H. Halsey, J. Floud and C. A. Anderson (New York: Free Press, 1961).

Schachter, A., "Birth Order, Eminence and Higher Education," *American Sociological Review,* Vol. 28, No. 5 (October 1963), 757-68.

Schwebel, Milton, *Who Shall Be Educated?* New York: Grove Press, 1968.

Slobin, D. (ed.), *A Field Manual for Cross-cultural Study of the Acquisition of Communicative Competence* (mimeographed). Berkeley: University of California, 1967.

Soskin, W. F., and V. P. John, "The Study of Spontaneous Talk," in *The Stream of Behavior,* ed. R. Barker (New York: Appleton-Century-Crofts, 1963).

Steiner, S., *The New Indians.* New York: Harper and Row, 1967.

Valdez, Facundo, excerpt from interview taped by S. Steiner.

Vygotsky, L., *Thought and Language,* ed. and transl. E. Hanfmann and G. Vakar. Cambridge: Massachusetts Institute of Technology Press, 1962.

UNTAPPED VERBAL FLUENCY OF BLACK SCHOOLCHILDREN

JANET CASTRO

This is the story of a most unusual school festival production, and what it has meant to me as an educator. Some background information about the school and about myself will be necessary.

In September of 1965 I came to a newly created position in a "More Effective School" in the Farragut community of Brooklyn. The More Effective Schools program existed in twenty-one public schools in New York City. It was conceived by the United Federation of Teachers and implemented through the combined efforts of the United Federation of Teachers and the New York City Board of Education. Basically, the characteristics of the program included small classes, team and cluster teachers, resource and demonstration teachers, heterogeneous grouping with small group and individualized reading, and an abundance of teaching aids and audio-visual equipment. There was little difficulty in getting and keeping teachers, because they were attracted by the small classes, the pleasant atmosphere, the absence of tedious patrols and extra duties, and the remarkable amount of new equipment.

I was assigned to the Farragut school by the Bureau for Speech Improvement to fill a newly created position made possible through federal funds. Unfortunately, by September of 1967 the Board of Education had begun its characteristic watering down of experiments in education and as a result, my position, along with several others, no longer exists in the More Effective Schools program. However, I was fortunate enough to have been involved in this extraordinary experiment for two years. I functioned as a resource and demonstration teacher of speech improvement and speech arts, working with the children and assisting the classroom teacher.

I had been on maternity leave for five years. My attitude toward my job and the black children I was to teach was very much influenced by literature on the "culturally deprived." For example, I believed Frank Riessman when he told me my job would be harder because culturally deprived children view education differently from the middle-class child. In his book *The Culturally Deprived Child* he comments:

What does education mean to the culturally deprived? It is easier to state what it does not mean . . . There is practically no interest in knowledge for its own sake; quite the contrary, a pragmatic intellectualism prevails. Nor is education seen as an opportunity for the development of self-expression, self-realization, growth, and the like; consequently, progressive approaches are opposed.[1]

So impressed was I by Riessman and others that it did not occur to me to ask myself where in middle-class America was one going to find this abstractly intellectual bourgeois student interested only in self-expression, self-realization, and knowledge for its own sake? I viewed the children as being verbally destitute (Riessman said nonsymbolic), and as lacking the ability to express themselves in an organized manner with an adequate vocabulary. I had been told there was no conversation in the home, no emphasis on reading or "experiences," that speech and listening attitudes were poor, that the children all spoke in a Southern Negro dialect, and so on.

Well, I was going to "enrich" them. I would teach them that dialect was wrong, would correct their improper usage, show them how to produce sounds correctly, and enrich their vocabulary. In other words, I would make it clear that only middle-class standards of oral communication can ever be acceptable. My lessons were highly structured. I would teach a language skill (*st* endings,

[1] Riessman, *The Culturally Deprived Child* (New York: Harper, 1962), p. 12.

for example) and then have the children use the new skill in role play, creative dramatics, poetry, or some other speech art.

My lessons seemed successful, because the children appeared to be listening attentively. Later I discovered that they were waiting patiently for the end of my lesson, which they knew would provide them with an opportunity to express themselves through games or role play. Correct use of the new skill was often ignored in their highly imaginative play-acting.

That fall a friend who was doing research on children's games asked me to help her find out about games played in the Farragut community. I decided to drop my carefully planned lessons in some classes for a few days and interview the children. At first they described games I already knew—"Ring-a-leevio," "Red Light, Green Light," "Statues," and so on. Then some children began to volunteer information about games I did not know. I found myself listening to unfamiliar and highly intriguing material. The classroom teachers who were present were equally fascinated. In response to my eager questions the children volunteered more and more information about tag and clapping games. I asked them to demonstrate. The Farragut children displayed a fantastic repertoire of singing, chanting, clapping and dancing games. The chants were highly ritualistic and the words were very important to the children. They wanted to be sure I recorded every syllable correctly. The chanting and clapping games are incredibly rhythmic and musical. They require intricate hand movements; they incorporate gestures, body movement, and language. My enthusiasm and admiration for the children's games and the way they performed them established a new kind of rapport between us. It was evident that there was a wealth of vocabulary, descriptive phrases, ideas and fluency here.

The children were eager to show me the games and talk about them. They seemed amazed at the interest and enthusiasm I displayed. The implication here, I think, is this: in a conventional teaching situation, the teacher is following his own lesson plan, and is, therefore, listening for expected and anticipated answers. On the other hand, when the children describe and demonstrate something from their own experience which is unfamiliar to the teacher, the teacher becomes the listener and the learner. When an adult is the eager listener, the children become the eager communicators. When a teacher not only listens and observes, but also approves and admires a given activity, the children feel rewarded. They experience not only the gratification of teacher interest but also the strengthening of their own identity.

Early-childhood educators are aware that children at play are really children at work. It is generally known that their playing of games helps them to understand and to cope with reality. As the *Encyclopaedia Britannica* indicates:

Games are the child's first joining in group activity. One can almost say in the human race. In the effortless, exhilarating act of playing with other children, he learns social interaction with his fellow beings and begins the first step toward civilization and self-control. Games provide a natural outlet not only for his excess energy but also for tensions, aggressions and emotions. As he grows older and takes part in more organized games and sports, he learns the principles of fair play and courtesy, of abiding by pre-arranged rules, and he·learns to accept defeat as well as success with some degree of equanimity. . . . He unconsciously learns to join others in moving toward a common goal; his childhood ability to play with others will become his adult ability to work with others. . . . A child is not playing but working toward becoming an adult.[2]

And Erik Erikson states in *Childhood and Society*,[3] "To play it out is the most natural self-healing method childhood affords."

Although early-childhood teachers recognize the value of children's games, I found generally that upper-grade teachers appear to rely on "school-taught" games. I therefore began to explore the educational, social and psychological implications of indigenous game-playing for older elementary children.

Their own games provide an unusual opportunity to act out anxieties; adjust to new situations; experiment with winning and losing; learn to take turns, develop standards of fair play, and learn to abide by rules and realize that rules can be changed by mutual consent.

[2] *Encyclopaedia Britannica* (1963), vol. 5, p. 480.
[3] *Childhood and Society* (New York: Norton, 1963), p. 211.

For example, "Hide and Seek," a game common to children everywhere, can be seen as symbolizing the lost-child-searching-for-a-parent situation. In acting out, the child gets to play the various roles: he is the lost child who is never really lost, because the game is so constructed that he is either found or gets home free; as "it" he can experience the anxiety felt by the surrogate parent searching for the lost child.

Another example (this time from the Farragut children) is "Old Mother Witch," which provides an opportunity to experiment with self-imposed time schedules and then to set them for other children. Think of the anxiety that must accompany a beginning school child's first encounter with rigid time schedules: suddenly to have to go to school at a certain time, eat at a certain time, go to the bathroom at a certain time, respond and adjust to electronically timed bells all day long.

Some of the Farragut children's games deal with attitudes about race, marriage and family. "When I Was a Baby" describes an attitude toward each of the important life stages with a characteristic gesture. For "When my husband dies," they clap their hands above their heads in a gesture of triumph, first to one side, then the other.

In "Winston Tastes Good" there is a line, "The bull's too black, I want my money back." "Amos and Andy" describes a situation in which the singer is accepted by a white boy and then rejects him:

> Amos and Andy,
> Black as tar,
> Tried to get to heaven
> On a candy bar.
> I like coffee
> I like tea
> I like a white boy
> And he likes me.
> Step back, white boy,
> You don't shine.
> I'll get a colored boy
> To kick your behind.

One game comments on life on the welfare rolls:

> I like bread and butter,
> I like bread and jam.
> I like bread and butter,
> But I hate that Welfare Spam.

The most exciting game of all to the children is "Who Stole the Cookie from the Cookie Jar?" One girl stands in the center of the circle and chants the accusing lines, her finger pointing up and down at each person in turn, her hips swaying back and forth. The responder takes a position that combines defiance and shame, one foot perpendicular to the other, head turned sideways, eyes downcast. And so that chant goes around until everyone has denied having stolen the cookie and all together they accuse the accuser.

While I was in the midst of this games research project, the principal asked me to produce a spring festival. I suggested a production based on the street games of Farragut children. It would be titled "Springtime Is for Growing" because games are for growing and springtime is for growing *and* street games. One assistant principal thought it was a novel idea, and he was tremendously supportive throughout the rehearsal period. We received support from a guidance counselor, a kindergarten teacher and a young third-grade teacher. These people volunteered free time to work with the various aspects of rehearsal. Some members of the staff, however, felt we should produce something more standard. One black teacher told me she felt I was encouraging "typically Negro" behavior which should be discouraged and replaced by more acceptable middle-class decorum. My employer and supervisor, the director of the Bureau for Speech Improvement, was most enthusiastic in supporting me. She understood and appreciated the value of this unique language experience.

I began to get support from people outside the school. A young poet-songwriter composed opening and closing songs very much in the spirit of the games, and a professional dancer choreographed several tag games into a dance number.

The children were delighted with the plan for a big production. They enjoyed all the adult interest and were undoubtedly ready for the appreciation and recognition of performance. They felt it was their show; it belonged to them.

We rehearsed in a creative-dramatics style. Different children played different games, with no interruptions from me. Toward the end we selected a few children for each game. However, none of the original group of children was left out. I did not tamper with the games themselves, with the words or any part of them. Several tag games were choreographed and a script was written to tie the games together.

Of the five most severe discipline problems in the school, three were in the festival and were usually no trouble at rehearsals. Once, however, a sixth-grade girl caused an upheaval. This girl hated herself, she hated being black. She hated all whites; she could not stand praise. One day she threw the whole group into an uproar by inserting the word "mother" into "Cookie Jar" ("who stole the mother from the mother jar?"). The other children became very upset and turned the rehearsal into a lampoon of the games. This girl is now in junior high school. The guidance counselor told me she made a fairly good adjustment at her new school. The counselor at her new school saw the show and greeted her with "Oh, yes, you're the girl who stole the cookie from the cookie jar." This instant rapport was gratifying to both student and counselor.

Another girl, who was constantly being disciplined for "acting out" in class, was cooperative at all rehearsals, a leader who helped other children with games and dance steps. She displayed an extraordinary amount of acting, singing and dancing ability. I find it difficult to describe this girl's special talents and the joy she experienced in movement; her naturally adept delivery of lines was sheer pleasure to beholders. She learned dance steps and stage business faster than the teachers involved, and she was very helpful in instructing the other children.

Many of the sixty children selected for the production couldn't believe that they would actually be in the final performance. They were always testing for insincerity. They constantly anticipated rejection, or ejection. If every child was not included in every rehearsal (if I called for only the girls or the boys, or for younger

children), the "excluded ones" besieged me with tearful accusations: "You've kicked me out, haven't you, Mrs. Castro?" No
matter how many times I assured them to the contrary, they
jumped to the same conclusion the next time, and I had to reas-
sure them all over again.

Opening night was undoubtedly one of the most exciting events
of the children's lives. Their performances sparkled with vitality
and enthusiasm. The audience was ecstatic—teachers, parents,
children, and visitors alike.

When the festival was repeated for an assembly of the entire
student body, the principal introduced me as the director. The
children rose and showed their appreciation with extended ap-
plause. We all knew that this ovation was really for everyone who
participated. Many adults who had been skeptical of the value
of this program in the beginning were now liberal with praise for
the children and their performance.

The sharing of this experience with the children has established
a rapport between us that has helped me enormously in classroom
teaching situations. As Riessman said, "It would seem essential
that the method of teaching formal language to the culturally deprived child takes advantage of their communication style by employing teaching techniques that stress the visual, the physical, the
active, as much as possible."[4] I cannot argue with Dr. Riessman's
pedagogical wisdom, except to say that it was said a long time ago
by John Dewey—and he included *all* children. School curricula
must come from the children and be based on their needs, regardless of cultural background. "Learning by doing" means essentially that one brings one's own experience to new situations and
learns by reasoning and application. Stressing the visual, the
physical and the active is necessary in *every* classroom.

As far as verbal fluency is concerned, James Olsen, in an article published in the March 1965 issue of *The Educational Forum,*
states (p. 281):

While it's true that many of the children of the poor do not have
any apparent verbal ability in formal learning situations like the classroom, most culturally different children are no more verbally destitute

4 Riessman, *op. cit.,* p. 80.

than their middle-class peers. And more than that, these children have a great deal of untapped verbal ability of a highly imaginative nature which remains latent because the institutions, the arrangements of our schools militate against direct and meaningful discussion.

There may, as Olsen suggests, be many reasons why children choose to be silent in the classroom.

My experience with these children, both in the classroom and at rehearsal, bears out what Mr. Olsen has said about "untapped verbal ability." My approach to teaching oral language improvement changed considerably as a result of this experience. I learned to respect the children's ability to communicate and use descriptive words meaningfully. I used role play, creative dramatics and movement about the room in all parts of the lessons. A reading teacher, the guidance counselor and I collaborated on a series of lessons based on the game "When I Was a Baby." Because the game deals with attitudes and behavior at various stages of life, it proved to be ideal for a reading lesson on sequence and organization. Similarly, since the game dealt with changing attitudes, it served as a springboard for discussions in guidance sessions on the children's attitudes toward themselves, the school and their families. The children, of course, were both flabbergasted and pleased to find us drawing upon their own games for lessons like this.

One of my official tasks as a speech teacher in the school was to "teach" standard English. My admiration of the "richness" of the language of the games enabled me to alter my approach to these lessons. I tried to make it clear that we were learning a *different* way to use language, not the only way that was acceptable. I discovered that introducing black children to standard English usage posed many problems. It implies a rejection, not only of the child's language, but of the child himself, his family, and his background. Ralph Ellison, in an address at Bank Street, spoke of poor achievement in language skills on the part of black schoolchildren. He said that Southern Negro dialect, vital, rich, and perfectly relevant to life in the South, becomes a handicap when the black comes North. Northern life dispossesses him of language, because it dispossesses him of his sense of reality. He concluded his address with the following plea to educators: "Let me cling to what is real to me, and at the same time teach me a way into a larger society."[5]

This plea of Ellison's, made several years ago, would now be considered extremely controversial. In the struggle for black identity, some members of the black community are demanding a cessation of instruction of mainstream English to black children. They insist that their own language is rich in vocabulary and adheres to different and perfectly logical rules of grammar. Studies by linguists indicate that this is indeed true. For example, some forms of the verb "to be" are not used in dialect speech because they are really not necessary. The sentence "She in the kitchen" is perfectly clear. The verb form "is" is really not needed for greater clarity. The infinitive form "be" is used only to describe a state of being which lasts over a long period of time. If a black child sees a classmate throw up on the floor, he might say, "She sick." If he is referring to a classmate who has been home ill for several weeks, he would say, "She be sick." Without question, teachers working with black children should know that black children speak their language with logical grammatical consistency. This kind of knowledge might put an end to the sporadic, uninformed and totally useless correction of dialect usage which occurs daily in ghetto classrooms across the country. Dr. Beryl Bailey, a leading linguistic expert in dialect speech, addressed herself to this problem recently in an article published in the May 1968 issue of *Elementary English Magazine*. She asks teacher-training institutions to provide prospective teachers with a course of study in the structure and function of language. She states that only teachers with a workable knowledge of both standard English grammar and dialect grammar can be effective teachers for children who speak a nonstandard dialect.

As a teacher and as a human being, I must express some personal feeling about this whole issue. When I was a teacher at P.S. 307 in Brooklyn, my experience with the children's games taught

[5] Bank Street Seminar on the Education of the Deprived and Segregated, *Education for Culturally Different Youth* (New Haven, 1963), p. 2.

me to respect the richness of the language of black children. I did not know very much about the grammatical structure of Negro dialect, but I sensed that there was a logical consistency to it. I did not anticipate the current controversy over the teaching of standard dialect in the classroom; but I did know that the books children must learn to read are written in standard English.

I felt, and still do feel, that in order to read well, black children must know how to speak standard dialect. So I devised a series of language usage games. The rules of the games I used incorporate the rules of standard English. In order to "win," the children had to use a standard language pattern. Riddle games and games involving the five senses proved especially valuable. (I.e.: It looks like . . . , it smells like . . . Is it a book? No, it's not a book.)

This game approach to standard English patterning was entirely acceptable to the children. In fact, they loved it. A period of time each day was devoted to this kind of practice. The rest of the day, in other subject areas and in school activities, children could speak dialect freely without fear of constant interruption and correction. However, although I introduced standard English through games, I told the children flatly that they needed to know it for reading, for learning, for jobs, and for college.

As a teacher of speech arts, I had already used creative dramatics as a teaching technique extensively. The children's enthusiasm at festival rehearsals, their ability to move creatively, the ease with which they improvised connecting dialogue confirmed my belief that drama techniques should be basic teaching tools in every classroom. Role playing and improvisation in the classroom are often considered "enrichment frills" by the educational establishment. In fact creative dramatics provides the kind of language involvement vital to the reading process. Participants in the Bank Street Seminar on urban education problems in 1963 understood the necessity for this kind of language experience. The report issued by the seminar stated:

Children do not learn to read unless and until reading becomes for them a meaningful extension and expansion of their lives. They do not learn to read unless they know and enjoy the uses of language—to deposit and recover and cherish, as something that connects them to a world beyond the immediate and the transient. . . . To teach reading without full exposure to essential experiential prerequisites is to stay on the surface, not to dig under.[6]

Children need to get excited about language. They need to experience the pleasure and satisfaction that successful communication can give them. Creative dramatics provides this very special kind of language involvement. Certainly this particular speech art has tremendous contributions to make to the education of the urban poor. No other language art involves the child so completely, giving him a chance to "try on life"—affording him an opportunity to use his own experience and his own language in a new language dimension—thereby extending and expanding his language, his ability to listen, think and learn.

My work at P.S. 307 was appreciated and supported by the director of the Speech Bureau at the Board of Education. She subsequently asked me to write curriculum material in collaboration with other speech teachers. The final result was a teachers' guide for oral-communication activities in urban schools. The use of children's games, language pattern games, creative dramatics, movement, new and relevant books and audio-visual material were included. Teachers using the manual during its first trial year report that the activities for the most part were extremely successful in the classrooms. A television teacher-training series to implement this manual was produced this year. Its purpose was to introduce these techniques to classroom teachers.

However, all of the speech teachers and supervisors dedicated to revising the language arts curriculum find that there are a number of obstacles. In the first place, it is very hard to convince teachers and supervisors in elementary schools that there is any connection between having fun with language and learning to read. When I was demonstrating dramatic techniques in the classrooms of P.S. 307 I was always infuriated by the assumptions of some teachers and supervisors that since the children were "having such a good time" they couldn't possibly be doing any serious

[6] *Ibid.,* p. 2.

learning. In addition, recent attendance at local school board meetings left me with the distinct impression that parents are equally conservative about the educational process and the teaching techniques that lead to successful reading.

Finally, and perhaps most importantly, our teacher-training institutions do not train teachers in drama techniques. Few colleges have courses in creative dramatics. Often, if there is such a course, it requires only that the students read several books on the subject and write a term paper. Improvisational techniques cannot be learned in this manner. The only way prospective teachers can learn about dramatic techniques is through active participation in improvisations, pantomime and role play. This, of course, must be followed by dramatic work with children in a teachers' laboratory course.

Because teachers' colleges do not prepare them for this kind of classroom activity, many teachers are afraid to try it—and one cannot blame them. Many of the classroom teachers at P.S. 307 who worked with me while I demonstrated creative dramatics in their classrooms are still using this technique extensively in all subject areas. Math, social studies, vocabulary, economics and literature can be taught through role play. Children never forget what they have dramatized, because they have related to it in a highly personal manner. The teachers continue to use these techniques because they saw them demonstrated in their own classrooms and they had ample opportunity to try drama techniques themselves in follow-up lessons.

In order to be ready for learning, children must feel good about themselves in the classroom situation. Effective teaching recognizes, appreciates, and draws from the child's interests, experience and background. Successful teaching techniques stress combined movement and language, involving the child and his total self. The good teacher listens, she learns, she approves, and she communicates her approval.

I would like to close with a description of an incident which took place during a fifth-grade creative-dramatics session. We were preparing to act out a scene from "Hansel and Gretel." We talked about the story and the characters, setting the scene. I asked the children what Hansel and Gretel might find in the gingerbread house to make them suspect that a bad witch lived there. A number of imaginative suggestions were forthcoming, among them a recipe book entitled *How to Cook Children*. When the time came to act out, the girl playing Gretel said, "Oh, look, there's a book that says *How to Cook Chitlins*," and then with a horrified gasp she said, "Oh, no, it doesn't say that, it says *How to Cook Children*." The children were just as stimulated by this kind of language perception as I was. They were using language in another dimension—their own experience had been involved in something other than their own experience.

Isn't this, after all, the essence of language and thought in action?

SPRINGTIME IS FOR GROWING

Part I

NARRATOR *appears alone on stage and addresses audience:*

NARRATOR. This is a play about growing. Since this is spring, our title is "Springtime Is for Growing."

Everything we do helps us to grow. One of the nicest ways to grow, especially in the spring, is to play games.

The games we play in the street, in the playground, in the schoolyard, and in the halls of our buildings (before someone chases us, that is) help us to grow.

Some games make friends for us.

Some games teach us about justice, injustice and playing fair.

Some games help us to overcome fear and violence.

Some games make us laugh and sing.

In other words, games are one way to bud, blossom and reach for the sky, like spring flowers.

So here is our story about spring, growing and games.

(*Orchestra plays overture. Then* CHORUS *appears and sings* "Springtime Is for Growing.")

CHORUS.
Springtime is for growing,
That's what our games are showing.

We hope you'll soon be knowing,
Just what we all can do, do, do.
Springtime, springtime, grow, grow, grow;
Singtime, singtime, go, go, go;
Daytime, daytime, ha, ha, ha;
It's playtime, playtime, rah, rah, rah.
Now we are displaying
The games that we like playing,
And we have all been praying
That you will like them too, too, too.
Nametime, nametime, fiddle-dee-dee!
Gametime, gametime, come play with me.
Schooltime, schooltime, ride a bus;
Fooltime, fooltime, play with us.
They teach us about living.
They teach us about giving.
This lesson should be driven right home,
Right home to all of you, you, you.

(*refrain*)

Springtime, springtime, grow, grow, grow.
Singtime, singtime, go, go, go.
Daytime, daytime, ha, ha, ha.
It's playtime, playtime, rah, rah, rah.

(CHORUS *joins hands and recites* "Little Sally Waters." *As they recite, they step in line, facing audience, toward left wing of stage, then step back to right wing and back again, ending the recitation in their starting places. A* LITTLE GIRL *with a little flower in a pot comes on stage behind the moving* CHORUS *when the audience's view is blocked. She moves to stage center behind the chorus and remains hidden until the middle of the recitation.*)

Little Sally Waters, sitting in the sun.
Crying and weeping for a young man.
Rise, Sally, rise, dry your weeping eyes.

(*Center of* CHORUS *steps back to reveal* LITTLE GIRL.)

> Turn to the east, Sally, turn to the west,
> Turn to the very one that you love the best.

(LITTLE GIRL *turns in the various directions. She hands the flower pot to a* CHORUS MEMBER *and on the last line she points to a* LITTLE BOY *who has been standing with the chorus.* LITTLE BOY *moves to* LITTLE GIRL, *who takes his hand.* CHORUS *disperses around stage. As they do this, the members take up casual poses and act as spectators of the games to follow. The person holding the flower pot goes to the rear of the stage and puts the pot down near the center of the stage. The* LITTLE BOY *sings* "Lily of the Valley.")

LITTLE BOY.

> Lily, lily of the valley,
> Lily, lily let's be palsy.
> Heads up, eyes all down on the floor,
> Left foot, right foot, back one, two, three, four.

(*Song and movement are repeated once.*)

(*As the* LITTLE GIRL *and* BOY *perform* "Lily of the Valley," *the younger* BOYS *and* GIRLS *enter singly but closely together from the wings. They all sit, ultimately forming a circle around the couple. When the song is finished,* LITTLE GIRL *sits in the circle and* LITTLE BOY *moves around the outside of the circle, choosing players with* "Old King Glory of the Valley.")

> Old King Glory of the valley,
> The valley was so high it nearly touched the sky,
> It touched the first, the second, the third, follow me.

(*This game is played to its conclusion. Players stand about and discuss what to do next.*

BOY. What'll we do now?

GIRL. Let's play another clapping game. (*She starts reciting and clapping.*)

ANOTHER BOY. Aw, no, who wants to do that.

(*A couple of other* GIRLS *have joined in the clapping.*)

ANOTHER GIRL (*clapping*). Yeah, let's do Miss Mary Mack.

(*Other* GIRLS *agree and join in clapping.*)

ANOTHER BOY. Oh, no!

(GIRLS *ignore* BOYS *and form up to play* "Miss Mary Mack." BOYS *show disgust and stalk off stage.*)

    Miss Mary Mack, Mack, Mack,
    All dressed in black, black, black,
    With silver buttons, buttons, buttons,
    All down her back, back, back.
    She ask her mother, mother, mother,
    For fifty cents, cents, cents,
    To see the elephant, elephant, elephant,
    Jump over the fence, fence, fence.
    He jump so high, high, high,
    He touch the sky, sky, sky,
    And never come back, back, back,
    Till the Fourth of July, ly, ly.
    Her mother got sick, sick, sick,
    So sick in bed, bed, bed,
    She scratch her head, head, head,
    With a piece of cornbread, bread, bread.

GIRL. Okay, "A Sailor Went to Sea, Sea, Sea!"

(GIRLS *go into next game.*)

GIRLS.
    A sailor went to sea, sea, sea,
    To see what he could see, see, see.
    But all that he could see, see, see,
    Was the bottom of the deep blue sea, sea, sea.

(GIRLS *continue with variations. During the final one, another* GIRL *enters, carrying a doll.* GIRLS *notice her at end of* "Sailor" *and immediately go into* "Miss Polly.")

Miss Polly had a dolly who was sick, sick, sick,
And she called for the doctor to come quick, quick, quick.
The doctor came with his bag and his hat,
And he came with a ratata-ratatat.
He looked at the dolly and he shook his head,
And he said, "Miss Polly, put her right to bed,"
He gave her some aspirins and some pills, pills, pills.
"And tomorrow I'll be back for the bills, bills, bills."

(GIRLS *all laugh and snicker at the end of game and go right into*
"Take Me Out to the Hospital.")

Take me out to the hospital,
Take me up to my room.
Give me some needles, for I don't care,
I'm in love with Dr. Kildare.
So it's boop, boop, boop for Ben Casey,
If he don't win it's a shame.
So it's one, two, three strikes you're out
At the old hospital, hospital.

(*A new, older* GIRL *enters, carrying a larger flower in a pot. She
is wearing the same costume as the little girl with the smaller
flower who opened the part. The* GIRL *also carries a rope. The
other* GIRLS *run to her; one takes the flower pot and carries it
to the rear center and leaves it with the first flower. The* GIRLS
start jumping-rope games. The first game is "Champagne.")

Champagne, follow me
To the bottom of the sea.
While you're there,
Wash your hair
And your dirty underwear.

(GIRLS *rearrange selves and go on to rope game of* "I like coffee.")

I like coffee, I like tea,
I like Cynthia to jump with me.
Angel, Devil, Fairy Queen,
Doctor, Lawyer, Indian Chief.

I like ice cream with chocolate on top.
A, B, C, D, E, F, G, H, I, J, K, L, M, N, O, P, Q, R . . .

(GIRLS *go right into* "Rattlesnake" *when their chanting reaches the letter "R."*)

R-A-T, T-L-E, S-N-A-K-E spells rattlesnake.

(*Repeat until line of* GIRLS *is wound into tight group.* BOYS *enter and tease* GIRLS *by mimicking* "Rattlesnake" *and interfering until some* GIRLS *leave in a huff. The* BOYS *and remaining* GIRLS *start playing competitive games. One of the* BOYS *enters, carrying a still larger flower in a pot, which is carried to rear of stage by one of departing* GIRLS *and placed with the other two flower pots.*)

BOY. Come on, I'll be "Red Devil."
BOY. No, you won't, I'll be "Red Devil."
GIRL. I wanna be "it"!
OTHERS. "Me!" "I'll be it!" "No, me!"
BOY WHO CARRIED FLOWER POT. Let's choose!

(ALL *agree and he chooses with* "Engine, Engine Number Nine.")

BOY WHO CARRIED FLOWER POT.

Engine Engine, Number Nine,
Going down Chicago line.
If the train go off the track,
Do you want your money back?
YES!
Y-E-S spells "yes" and out you may go.
OUT go the cat!
OUT go the rat!
OUT go the lady with the seesaw hat!

(*Choose the game leader and go into the game of* "Red Devil."
GIRL WHO PLAYS MOTHER *recites* "Someone Came Knocking"
as the GROUP *arranges itself for the game.*)

GIRL WHO PLAYS MOTHER.

Someone came knocking
At my wee small door.

Someone came knocking.
I'm sure, sure, sure.
I listened, I opened,
I looked to the left and right,
But naught there was a-stirring
In the still, dark night.

(*Then the game begins.*)

RED DEVIL. Knock, knock.
MOTHER. Who's there?
RED DEVIL. It's the Red Devil.
MOTHER. What have you come for?
RED DEVIL. I've come for a color.
MOTHER. What color?
RED DEVIL. I've come for green.

(*The game is played almost to conclusion, when the dialogue is:*

RED DEVIL. Knock, knock.
MOTHER. Who's there?
RED DEVIL. Red light . . . I mean . . .

(GROUP *laughs and some start repeating* "Red light" *and then* "Red light, green light," *and the* GROUP *starts to play that game. The first to reach the "it" person in this game says he wants to play* "Ring-a-Leevio." GIRLS *who left stage at start of this segment are "captured" by players and brought back, so that the whole group is now on stage again for the finale of* "Head and Shoulders." *This ensemble number takes place at the conclusion of* "Ring-a-Leevio.")

ALL.
　　　Head and shoulders, baby, one-two-three;
　　　Head and shoulders, baby, one-two-three;
　　　Head and shoulders, baby, one-two-three.
　　　Knee and ankle, baby, one-two-three;
　　　Knee and ankle, baby, one-two-three;
　　　Knee and ankle, baby, one-two-three.
　　　Press the button, baby, one-two-three;
　　　Press the button, baby, one-two-three;

Press the button, baby, one-two-three.
Milk the cow, baby, one-two-three;
Milk the cow, baby, one-two-three;
Milk the cow, baby, one-two-three.
That's all, baby, one-two-three;
That's all, baby, one-two-three;
That's all, baby, one-two-three.

END OF PART I

Part II

(CHORUS *comes on stage with another chorus of* "Springtime Is
for Growing." TWO GIRLS *enter, one carrying the largest flower
of all. She is wearing the same colors as the other three* FLOWER
CARRIERS. *They enter during the ending of the singing, so that
they have time to walk to the rear of the stage to deposit the
pot next to the other pots and then walk forward to the apron
as the* CHORUS *finishes and disperses.*)

FIRST GIRL. I'm going to be a nurse when I grow up. What are
you going to be when you grow up?

SECOND GIRL. Gee, I never figured I was going to get any older.

(*They go into clapping game of* "When I Was a Baby.")
When I was a baby,
When I was a baby, baby, baby,
When I was a baby,
This what I did.
I went umm (*pantomime thumb-sucking*) thisaway,
Umm thataway, umm thisaway,
That's what I did.
When I was a schoolgirl . . . (*each strokes her hair and
    wriggles*)
When I was a teen-ager . . . (*wiggles and walks*)
When I got married . . . (*hooks an arm*)
When I had a baby . . . (*rocks baby*)
When I had a fight . . . (*makes punching motions*)
When my husband died . . . (*hands in victory clasp over
    head*)

When my baby died . . . (*weeps into hands*)
When I died . . . (*waves goodbye*).

(TWO MORE GIRLS *enter and watch the last bit. When it's finished,
the* FIRST TWO GIRLS *wave them over and the four go into
another clapping game,* "Winston Tastes Good.")

FOUR GIRLS.
Winston taste good, like a
Ooh ah ah, I want a piece of pie.
The pie too sweet, I want a piece of meat.
The meat too tough, I want to ride a bus.
The bus too full, I want to ride a bull.
The bull too black, I want my money back.
Are you ready?
Yeah!
Are you sure?
Yeah!
Hawaiian eye, Hawaiian eye,
Hawaiian e-e-e, y-y-y, e-e-e (*They poke each other in eye.*)

(TWO MORE GIRLS *enter, and the six go into* "In Spain.")

SIX GIRLS
In Spain the tulips together,
I like the weather.
Bring back my love to me,
For that's the meaning
Of all the flowers.
They tell a story, a story
Of LOVE, LOVE, LOVE, LOVE.

(*Enter* TWO MORE GIRLS; they all do "Eena Meena.")

EIGHT GIRLS.
Eena meena, ipsaleena,
Ooh ah ah maleena.
Take a peach, take a plum,
Take a piece of bubble gum.
Saw your boy friend yesterday.
Yeah? What's his name?

You know who.
How you know?
Saw him through the peephole.
Nosy.
Give me some candy.
Greedy.
Help me wash the dishes.
Lazy.
Eena meena, ipsaleena,
Ooh ah ah maleena.

(BOYS *appear, dribbling a basketball. They stop and tease the* GIRLS *as the clapping game ends.*)

BOY. Hey! Why are you singing those little-kid songs instead of practicing cheers for our team?
GIRL. Oh, we know the cheers.

GIRLS (*going into cheerleader chant*).

Big apple, little apple, Susie Q!
If you want to be a Farragut, it's hard to do.
You got to walk up, run up, and that ain't all;
You got to learn how to play some basketball!
You got to shoot 'em high, you got to shoot 'em low.
So come on, girls, let's go, go, go!
Who're you yelling for?
Farragut!
A little louder; who're you yelling for?
Farragut!!!!!
A little softer, who're you yelling for?
Farragut.
Who're you yelling for?
FARRAGUT!!!!!

(*As the cheer gets to its climax, the* BASKETBALL PLAYERS *hop about almost as excitely as the* GIRLS *and join in the final* "Farragut!") (*In the flying about, one boy takes another by the wrist and swings him around. The* BOY *freezes into a statue and the game of* "Statue" *begins among the* BOYS *as the* GIRLS *sit and watch.*)

(*As the various players are made to laugh and are eliminated in* "Statue," *it is noticed that one of the last to go is frozen in the position of umbrella step from the game of* "Giant Step.")

BOY. Hey, you're in the wrong game, man.

(GIRLS rise.)

GIRL. Hey, take a giant step.
BOY IN UMBRELLA POSE. Can't. This is an umbrella step.

(*Form up for* "Giant Step," *showing umbrella, banana, gorilla and hopscotch steps. During the playing, car honking interrupts and* "Sidewalk Blues" *number begins. During the dancing,* CHILDREN *appear carrying protest signs such as* "CARS GET OUT," "GET A HELICOPTER," "KIDS, SI, CARS, NO!" "CARS GO HOME," "KEEP OUT!" "CHILDREN AT PLAY!" "GET A HORSE." *At the end,* SIGN CARRIERS *pursue a car off stage amid cheers and jeers of the* PLAYERS.)

BOY. That got rid of them!
GIRL. Good! Let's go back to the games.
BOY. Right! Let's show them!
GIRL. Grandma!
OTHERS (*agreeing*). Grandma, Grandma!!
SOME BOYS AND GIRLS.

> Grandma, Grandma sick in bed.
> Call the doctor and the doctor said,
> Grandma, Grandma, you ain't sick,
> All you need is a boogie-woogie stick.
> Hands up, shaky, shaky, shaky shake,
> Hands down, shaky, shaky, shaky shake.
> To the front, to the back, to the side, side, side,
> To the front, to the back, to the side, side, side.
> You never went to college, you never went to school,
> But I bet you five dollars you can shake it like a fool.
> Hands up, etc.
> Turn to the east, turn to the west,
> Turn to the very one that you love the best.

A COMPETING GROUP (*superimposes* "Telephone").

> Hey, Elijah
> Somebody calling my name.
> Hey, Elijah!
> They must be playing a game.
> You wanted on the telephone.
> If it ain't my girl/boy friend
> Tell 'em I'm not home
> From the city
> To the city
> Tick, tock, tick, tock, Du Wadda, Wadda,
> Tick, tock, tick, tock, Du Wadda, Wadda.

(*Game is repeated a few times, substituting other children's names.*
LARGER GROUP (*does* "Baltimore").

> I know a boy/girl from Baltimore, Baltimore, Baltimore,
> I know a boy/girl from Baltimore, let's see what he can do.
> He can frug (twist, jerk, Batman, duck swim, etc.),
> He can turn to the east, turn to the west
> Turn to the very one that he loves the best.

ALL CHILDREN ON STAGE (*join together to do* "Jackie Gleason Studio").

> Here we go to the Jackie Gleason Studio.
> Mr. Knickerbocker, Knickerbocker, boomelie boom,
> You sure look cute, like a boomelie boom.
> Now let's get together with the hands, one-two-three,
> We got the rhythm with the hands, one-two-three.
> Let's get together with the feet, one-two-three,
> We got the rhythm with the feet, one-two-three.
> Let's get together with the aaarrrmmms,
> We got the rhythm with the aaarrrmms.
> Let's get together with the hips, oh boy,
> We got the rhythm with the hips, oh boy.
> Let's get together with the eyes, eyes, eyes,
> We got the rhythm with the eyes, eyes, eyes.

> Let's get the rhythm with the counting by fives—five, ten,
> fifteen, twenty . . .

(*The game breaks up as the* GROUP *clusters around the* GIRL WITH
A COOKIE JAR *and the cookie jar is passed around. The* GIRL
*gets her cookie jar back and exclaims angrily on seeing that it's
empty.*)

COOKIE GIRL. Somebody took all my cookies! Who stole my
cookies?

(*The* GROUP *forms into a circle, and the game of* "Cookie Jar"
begins.)

GIRL. Who stole the cookie from the cookie jar?
NUMBER ONE. Not I stole the cookie from the cookie jar.
GIRL. Then who stole the cookie from the cookie jar?
NUMBER ONE. Number Two stole the cookie from the cookie jar.
GIRL. Did you stole the cookie from the cookie jar?
NUMBER TWO. Not I stole the cookie from the cookie jar.
GIRL. Then who stole the cookie from the cookie jar?
NUMBER TWO. Number Three stole the cookie from the cookie
jar.

(*The round robin continues until all in the circle have been
quizzed, whereupon they all ask the* GIRL:)

GROUP. Did you stole the cookie from the cookie jar?
GIRL. Yes. I stole the cookie from the cookie jar!
ANOTHER GIRL. Say, listen, it's getting dark and I've gotta go home.
BOY. Are you going to break up the game?
ANOTHER BOY. Yeah, I've gotta be going real soon, too.

GROUP (*goes into* "Willoughby").

> Here we go, Willoughby, Willoughby, Willoughby,
> Here we go, Willoughby, all night long.
> Step back, Sally, Sally, Sally,
> Step back, Sally, all night long.
> Here come Jane, Jane, Jane.

(*Repeat*)

BOY. Come on, one more game.

GIRL. It's getting dark.

BOY. Are you afraid of the dark?

GIRL. I'm not afraid of the dark!

ANOTHER BOY. Okay, anybody who's not afraid of the dark play one more game.

ANOTHER GIRL. "Old Mother Witch."

ANOTHER BOY. That's good for chicken kids.

(GROUP *forms up for* "Old Mother Witch.")

GIRL. Old Mother Witch, it's one o'clock. Are you ready?

WITCH. I'm just getting out of bed.

GIRL. Old Mother Witch, it's two o'clock. Are you ready?

WITCH. I'm just fixing my bed.

GIRL. Old Mother Witch, it's three o'clock. Are you ready?

WITCH. I'm just getting into the bathroom.

GIRL. Old Mother Witch, it's four o'clock. Are you ready?

WITCH. I'm just getting in the tub.

GIRL. Old Mother Witch, it's five o'clock. Are you ready?

WITCH. I'm just getting out of the tub.

GIRL. Old Mother Witch, it's six o'clock. Are you ready?

WITCH. I'm just going back in my room.

GIRL. Old Mother Witch, it's seven o'clock. Are you ready?

WITCH. I'm just cleaning up the kitchen.

GIRL. Old Mother Witch, it's eight o'clock. Are you ready?

WITCH. I'm just fixing my hair.

GIRL. Old Mother Witch, it's nine o'clock. Are you ready?

WITCH. I'm just washing the dishes.

GIRL. Old Mother Witch, it's ten o'clock. Are you ready?

WITCH. I'm just putting some bobby pins in my hair.

GIRL. Old Mother Witch, it's eleven o'clock. Are you ready?

WITCH. I'm just putting on my coat.

GIRL. Old Mother Witch, it's twelve o'clock. Are you ready?

WITCH. YES! And here I come!

(WITCH *chases children around stage.* MOTHER'S *voice breaks in.*)

MOTHER (*off stage*). Come on, children, it's time for bed. Do you want to be late for school tomorrow?

CHILDREN. Oh, nuts, I guess the time has come for leaving.

(CHORUS *sings* "The Time Has Come for Leaving" *while* CHIL-DREN *pantomime various games and call out characteristic chants.* ALL CHILDREN *join in finale song,* "The Time Has Come for Leaving," *and "leave" up the aisles.*)

ALL CHILDREN.
<blockquote>
The time has come for leaving,
The time has come to go,
But don't you do no grieving,
'Cause we sure enjoyed the show.
We have done some singing
And we have danced some, too.
We hope our voices ringing
Came swinging home to you.
    We have played our games and all,
    We find them lots of fun.
    All you people big or small,
    We've shown you everyone
    There's a time for laughing and
    There's a time to cry,
    There's a time for growing up
    And reaching for the sky.
There's a time for playing
And asking questions why,
There's a time for saying
So long but not goodbye.
</blockquote>

<blockquote>
We have played our games and all,
We find them lots of fun.
All you people big or small,
We've shown you everyone
There's a time for laughing and
There's a time to cry,
There's a time for growing up
And reaching for the sky.
</blockquote>

THE END

THE TEACHER IS ALSO A VICTIM

In September 1966 I took my first teaching assignment as an
English teacher in a New York City academic high school. This
paper is the result of my two years of experience in that school
and the frustrations which I met there in my efforts to do a good
job. It should not be construed as an apologia for poor and ineffective teaching; it is, rather, an exposition of the poverty of the
New York City teaching environment—an environment carefully
established and developed by the Board of Education—which not
only makes ineffective teaching possible, but also causes it to
flourish.

Much has been said about the deficiencies of both the New
York public-school students and their teachers, but comparatively
little has been stated about the deficiencies of the Board of Education. Unfortunately, the public has been slow to identify this
prime source of poor education in New York City; it is apparently
much easier to assail the more familiar and vulnerable pedagogue
and his pupil than it is to assail the unfamiliar and invulnerable
Board and its inscrutable methods. The Mayor's Advisory Committee on Decentralization has done a great deal to change this,
but thus far its recommendations have only been met by a largely
unresponsive public, a confused teachers' union and a resistant and
resilient Board of Education which has once again managed to
elude the forces which would change it for the better.

Critics of the teaching profession have essentially overlooked the teaching hardships created by poor working conditions, and they have been slow to recognize the multitude of pedagogical imperfections which these working conditions have created. Teachers themselves have been slow to protest these conditions, and so has the United Federation of Teachers, which has continually shown a reluctance to fight for the most minimal working standards and which has, moveover, neglected to enforce those few poor standards which it has obtained through its contracts.

This paper hopes to correct in some small way some of the misunderstanding which has been brought about by a paucity of research in this critical area. It also outlines for the reader some of the numerous obstacles which beset the teacher in the New York City school system, exhausting and exasperating him and thereby precluding the educative process for the hapless student.

When I began teaching, I was not wholly naïve about New York City education, for I had over the years met many teachers who in despair had abandoned the profession. Yet I was not at all prepared for the actual conditions which I subsequently encountered.

For one thing, I was disappointed to learn that the school to which I had been assigned provided no adequate working space for either teachers or students. Whether one wishes to believe it or not, the physical plant does not have an altogether minor bearing upon school morale; it is certainly not the most important defect of urban education, but it is much more detrimental than many people realize. The building to which I was assigned was overcrowded and inadequate, a factor which, I believe, contributed to a good deal of animosity on the part of both students and teachers. We have probably heard too many of the wrong things about crumbling walls, aging stairwells and broken toilets, and I do not intend to devote any time to that problem here, for the school which I entered in 1966 possessed none of these defects. It was, to be sure, shabby and unattractive, reflecting what one friend has termed the peculiarly bathroom atmosphere of *fin de siècle* school architecture. Our immediate problem was, rather, one of overcrowding, with all the psychological and authoritarian aspects which this entails.

It has somewhere been said that the overpopulated society is an over-regimented society, and I think the New York City school system offers a fair exposition of this point. The school in which I taught was on double session, and many other schools were, I was given to understand, on triple session. The immediate ramifications of this space shortage for the teacher are manifested in a critical lack of work space.

During my first semester, I was not assigned to an official class, a mixed blessing enjoyed by a small number of teachers every term. I therefore had no home room, nor did I have a desk anywhere in the building. I was forced to utilize the teachers' workroom, which was an impossible place to do any serious or contemplative work. When I was given a home room in subsequent semesters, I was chagrined to learn that my new desk was not my own—that it was, in fact, shared with at least two other teachers, one of whom worked on the opposite session from my own and the other of whom taught in the night school. This would perhaps not have created difficulties if all of one's classes were scheduled in one's official classroom, but, as the two school sessions overlapped, different classes were constantly entering and leaving, making it impossible to use one's desk or closet. I therefore found myself, like all of the other teachers in the school, hauling around bags of papers and briefcases full of books and spending the little preparation time I had in a useless endeavor to work in the teachers' workroom.

Working conditions of the morning session were superior to those of the afternoon session, I found. If one came into the building an hour before the school day began, one could have one's official classroom to oneself. The teachers on the afternoon shift rarely, if ever, had their rooms to themselves, since school policy dictated that everyone had to be out of the building within five minutes after the last bell rang. I do not think anyone was ever told the precise reason for this, although it was generally hinted that this policy had something to do with the lateness of the hour and the general shabbiness and hostility of the local community.

The morning session provided further advantages with regard

to the use of the teachers' cafeteria. For what must have been purely economic considerations, the cafeteria closed just before the end of the early session, although there were a full four periods to go before the late session concluded. (This was, incidentally, clearly against U.F.T. policy, but when the chapter chairman was approached he refused to act on the matter.) In a large number of cases, this meant that preparation periods would come and go without allowing one the benefit of any drink or snack. Had school rules not expressly forbidden leaving the building, this small discomfort could have been remedied. The availability of a hot plate or coffee pot, another possible remedy, was also clearly forbidden.

In addition to the crucial lack of work space, I was given neither the use of a telephone nor a minimal amount of clerical help. The building in which I worked had only two pay phones, one of which was shared by the entire student body of some thirty-five hundred. Furthermore, instead of being aided by the school, I was myself the object of several clerical assignments as a result of the school's desperate attempt to complete its voluminous records with a skeleton office staff. In the end, perhaps the only areas of the school which could be called one's own were a mailbox, which was open and hence subject to petty thievery, and a very small space in a crowded closet of one's official classroom, which was shared by at least one other teacher. As for the teachers' general work space, this was limited to two wretched and tiny workrooms filled with numerous dingy chairs, tables, washbasins, and coat racks which were supposed to accommodate a faculty of approximately two hundred. For reasons I was never able to learn, one of these rooms was occupied by the men and the other by the women members of the faculty. The rooms were always filled to the brim with teachers who were eating or smoking or playing cards or trying to work. It was an extremely difficult place to work, but in the end one felt lucky if one arrived in time to get a seat and could get off one's feet for a few minutes.

The ramifications of inadequate space for the students are somewhat similar, although the students enjoy none of the privileges of free passage which the teachers do. I confess I was personally stopped and challenged several times by both teachers and student aides over my two-year period in the school, despite the fact that I was nearing thirty. About a month before I left, I was stopped for the last time by a man I recognized to be a guidance counselor. "You are not allowed in the building," he said rather sternly. (No doubt his anxiety was the outgrowth of a recent faculty conference at which we were all admonished very severely to be on our guard against local community members who were walking into classrooms without authorization.) "But I'm a teacher," I said. "Don't you recognize me?" At that comment, a wave of recognition passed over his face, but it quickly vanished and he said very cruelly in his embarrassment, "Big deal! So you're a teacher. Who cares?" For a fleeting instant I understood very clearly what it meant to be a vulnerable and mistrusted student.

Just as the teachers had no real work area, the students also had no place to work. Most study periods were held in the school auditorium, the seats of which were not equipped with the folding desks which one finds in more modern structures. But studying would not have taken place in any event, since the auditorium also doubled as a practice room for the several school orchestras and bands.

Since our building lacked even the most essential educational equipment, I suppose it is foolish to question why the public schools do not have student unions where students might enjoy recreation, relaxation and the proper studying facilities that one finds in colleges. As a direct result of the limited space, high-school students in New York City are subject to a fierce sort of regimentation. Beyond the few minutes allotted to class changes, a student is not allowed in the halls without a pass; neither is he allowed into the cafeteria—the only somewhat social part of the school—without adequate proof that he has been programmed for lunch at that particular hour. As a result, violations of rules are flagrant. Students freely exchange program cards in order to get in and out of the cafeteria; teacher passes are stolen or manufactured, or else the student flies through the halls, sometimes pursued by teachers or aides, but, more often than not, unchallenged.

Such incidents do, I believe, play a direct role in the *Blackboard Jungle* type of literature that has become so ubiquitous.

The school administration had a gnawing fear that a full-blown riot would one day erupt in the cafeteria, the scene of all the small disturbances which occurred. Curiously enough, however, the administration never seemed to understand that most of the fights which had broken out were the direct result of the presence of a policeman in the school. What this policeman was doing in the school I do not know; his presence was clearly against school rules. Nevertheless, he came and went very freely, always passing through the student cafeteria on his way to the teachers' lunchroom, where he took all his meals. His appearance always seemed to anger the students, as indeed it angered me, for it only served to reinforce the growing penitential atmosphere of the school. Furthermore, he was constantly exchanging sharp words with the students, which he should not have done. These exchanges once sent him to the hospital and put a very fine boy in jail and were the catalyst in many other disturbances.

If the cafeteria was a fortress, so, too, were the bathrooms, which could not be entered without a pass. A teacher or aide is always stationed outside every lavatory. He collects the program cards of entering students, allowing only a certain number in at any one time. Under the circumstances, it is not difficult to understand why so many students react badly to school authority. If the student is not given any degree of free movement and if, in fact, the school does not provide a hospitable and suitable working and social environment, it does not seem likely that the student will view the system with any degree of charity. But, of course, some students do view the school with charity—the "achievers" who are successful in its environment and who have learned to bypass the harshest school laws. Who would deny an honor student a pass? Who would question the answer of an honor student when he is challenged at the cafeteria door? These students certainly have their own difficulties, but I venture to say that they are not nearly as insurmountable as those of the more ordinary, less trusted members of the student body.

To shed light on the hysteria with which the ordinary student is

met when he ventures forth into the inviolable halls, let me recount one small incident. I once gave a student a pass to the bathroom. She had hardly been gone a few minutes when the bell
rang. The chairman of the mathematics department, an extraordinary woman known for her highly emotional accounts of the
evil activities which she had observed in the school corridors
(though I confess that I never observed anything more untoward
than an occasional race through the halls) met me at the door.
"Who is that student?" she screamed, pointing to the girl to
whom I had given the pass. I told her. "Come into my office," she
bawled. "What did she do?" I inquired. "She was shuffling
through the halls." "What do you mean, shuffling?" I asked.
"Shuffling—shuffling, in a typically defiant Negro manner, and
she was looking into the classrooms as she passed the doors. What
is her official class? I want to fill out a dean's report." Feeling that
I was in the presence of a madwoman, I did not offer my protest,
though I was quite angry. I privately wondered how it happened
that so many distinctly antisocial people could have been en-
trusted with so much responsibility by the Board of Education.
As for the student, whether or not this incident was the proverbial
straw I do not know, but she disappeared from class after this
and I did not see her again for three weeks. She had missed every
test, and she was unable to pass a single subject as a result of her
inability to meet the minimal attendance requirements.

In the end, however, the paucity of space and the regimentation
which this inflicted upon the student populace was, for me, only
a minor problem in a day fraught with major catastrophes. It was
when my chairman handed me my program that I first began to
grasp the difficult nature of my new job. Having once worked as
a secretary in a college department where the academic community considered a teaching load of twelve hours to be substantial,
I was astonished to learn that I had been assigned to twenty-five
teaching hours—five periods or classes a day. I subsequently
learned that teachers in New York City once carried a teaching
load of twenty hours. The teaching load was increased to twenty-
five "temporarily" after World War II in order to accommodate
the returning veterans at a time when there was a critical teacher

shortage. This fact becomes doubly interesting when one realizes that the trend in all other jobs is now toward a shorter work day.

Besides an inordinate teaching load, I was given five so-called "assigned hours" of nonpedagogical labor, which involved such tasks as filing in the record room under the supervision of the office clerks and acting as lunchroom policeman, as substitute infirmary nurse to replace the nurse the school had never hired, and as height, weight and eye measurer for the school physician. Having been concomitantly and perhaps cavalierly granted a mere five periods of weekly preparation time to be spent on my own work, I wondered how on earth I was going to meet the heavy demands of my new "profession," which in all truth was beginning to look highly unprofessional. I soon found out, though by this time I was not completely unprepared for the avalanche of work which I was forced to take home with me. In any event, during my first few months I spent every spare minute in a desperate attempt to keep my head above water. After a while, I could not maintain the pace any longer and slacked off. At this point, my teaching effectiveness fell into a slow decline to which other corrosive factors in the school had now begun to contribute.

I had been temporarily spared the onus of an "official class," for I had come into the school to replace a retiring teacher a few weeks after the term had commenced. This teacher had, it appears, been mercifully saved from those tasks from which he could be reasonably relieved, so for a few months I benefited from his schedule. (Teachers are occasionally relieved from an official-class assignment because they are doing some more demanding task for the school.) The respite was, however, transitory, for at the beginning of the spring term I received an official class and thereupon took upon myself a new burden.

The official class in New York City can be compared to what other school systems have termed the "home room." Every day the teacher meets with his official class for ten minutes, and it is here, theoretically, that all of the school's clerical work is performed. I say "theoretically" since the teacher must in reality surrender much more time than ten minutes a day to this task. The official-class teacher keeps all of the records for approximately thirty-five students. He takes attendance, collects absence notes, fills out the program cards, enrollment cards, term sheets, makes announcements, receives complaints, collects monies for student activities, writes report cards and maintains the official school files for his official class in the general office. In short, the term "official class teacher" is really a euphemism for "school registrar." But no matter what the name, the job is exasperating and difficult, and I met at least two new teachers who told me that they would not teach another year because they found the clerical work so burdensome.

The tedium of this job can, in some measure, be alleviated if the teacher wishes to take advantage of student help, which many teachers do. As may be imagined, there are many students in every class who enjoy being singled out as teacher "secretaries." Such positions are looked upon as advantageous and are actively sought after. The school looks upon these posts with approbation and even encourages them by giving what they call "service credits" to those students who assist teachers in a secretarial capacity. It is perhaps not a bad method of relieving the teacher of some of the worst clerical functions which confront him. Yet, unfortunately, many students are falsely led to believe that a certain number of accumulated service credits are necessary to the achievement of a diploma; and still others are led to imagine that service credits on their permanent records are a necessary adjunct to the acquisition of a decent job after graduation. This notion does, as might be imagined, lead many poor students to believe that their service credits will somehow mitigate their poor grades. I do not mean to entirely denigrate a system which apparently satisfies both students and teachers, but I think it is unfortunate that the teacher has to be bothered with these tasks at all, and I further believe that student helpers should be paid for these jobs in currency rather than sham service credits.

To return briefly to the problem of the teaching load, let me say that it is impossible to prepare adequately for five classes a day. While a college professor will undoubtedly recognize the stress such a task involves, it is not easy for the layman to appreciate the demands which such a schedule places on the teacher.

Whenever the teacher complains of an inequitable schedule, the critic is altogether too anxious to point to the attractiveness of the six-hour-and-twenty-minute day. Yet how many critics are aware of the preparation which goes into the development of five lessons a day, to say nothing of the energy which the teacher expends during his actual time in the classroom? Many people unfairly believe that once a lesson is prepared it can be filed away for use over and over again. Naturally, old lessons can be utilized to some extent, but they must be constantly refurbished with an emphasis on new material; and since every class is truly different, every old lesson must be revamped with the new class in mind. Furthermore, there are approximately twenty-five to thirty different classes in each department. Since sooner or later nearly every teacher is programmed for every one of these classes and since there are approximately sixty teaching days in every semester, a rough estimate of the total number of lesson plans needed in a teaching career is approximately one thousand eight hundred. Even this figure is barely adequate when the problem of changes in textbooks and newly introduced courses is taken into account. Needless to say, I did not meet a single experienced teacher who was not constantly in the process of putting new lessons together.

The average high-school teacher has at least two different types of class; many teachers have three; too many have four. Three preparations are supposed to be the contractual limit, although the U.F.T. has never done anything to end the flagrant violations of this rule. This, then, necessitates the production of from two to four lessons per evening. These lessons are not easily developed. First, they require deep study and reflection. Often they require additional background reading. All too frequently, they require the preparation of such classroom materials as graphs, maps, charts or readings which must then be transferred to stencils and personally mimeographed by the teacher on the departmental machine (which usually worked poorly or not at all, since it was old and overused and, like all of the other equipment in the school, not a good make to begin with). Finally, they necessitate the extrapolation and collation of the most pertinent materials for classroom discussion and the development of appropriate homework and follow-up assignments, to say nothing of the grading of such assignments once they have become a reality in the form of student papers or tests.

The grading of compositions was one of my most difficult tasks. I graded about six hundred compositions a term, making individual comments on each paper. I pored over some sixteen hundred examinations, and tried to check some three thousand homework assignments. I confess that I found this last task impossible and finally merely checked to see whether or not the pupil had done the assignment.

The teaching load, the paucity of work space, the clerical responsibility of the official class, and the nonpedagogical assignments become insurmountable impediments between the teacher and the individual student—for as the teacher suffers, so suffers the student. If the teacher bears his burden with something less than equanimity, the student, whose young mind is far less equipped for such difficulties, bears it painfully and its ill-effects pursue him the rest of his life. No matter how one chooses to look at it, the teacher has little time to devote to either his lessons or his students. As a result of the demands of his rigorous schedule, the teacher is faced with a time/energy problem which has its effects in loss of morale and, finally, in a variety of shortcomings, most of which are eventually manifested in the classroom.

The most significant debility which every teacher suffers is the overuse of vital psychical energy. One can simply not prepare for and teach five classes a day, perform the school's clerical functions and participate in the assigned tasks without feeling totally depleted. It is a cruel and enervating process which results in the overtaxation and eventual usurpation of the most creative faculties as well as a concomitant loss of spirit and morale. As a result, one ceases to participate in the most vital professional activities. Let me emphasize that this dysfunction is *not* a result of any primary lack in the individual teacher. Its cause is, rather, to be located in the crippling effects of the work load with which the educational system has hobbled the teacher. I have spoken with intelligent and responsible English teachers who have found it impossible to read a novel in the course of a work year. I have similarly spoken with dedicated history teachers who had not read a single scholarly historical work since they obtained their master's degree. The demands of an ordinary teaching day do not allow for such professional activities, which must of necessity be looked upon by the overworked teacher as frivolous entertainments. This is a terrible loss for both teacher and student. If the teacher is not allowed adequate time in which to replenish the psychical and physical drain which he suffers daily, the quality of his teaching must be vitiated. This fact, I believe, largely accounts for the lack of scholarship in the public-school teaching community.

It may be assumed that winter and spring intersessions and summer vacation afford a sufficient panacea for this malady, but they do not. Daily energy consumption must be remedied by daily respite. We would not overwork an animal for several months, give him a recuperative break in the summer and expect him to return to normal vitality in the fall. Yet the teacher is driven madly for months at a time, set at pasture for a while (a time which is, incidentally, frequently spent in moonlighting, since the salary of public-school teachers leaves much to be desired) and expected to return refreshed. It would certainly be better if our teachers were given a sensible work load which would enable them to revitalize their energies daily. Then they might bring to their students something more stimulating than that which they are presently able to offer. It is not uninteresting to note that the teacher is the only member of the professional community who is asked to deal with thirty-five individuals every hour. Lawyers, doctors and psychiatrists always deal with their clients on a one-to-one basis, at fees which range considerably higher than the fifteen to twenty cents per hour per client which the teacher earns.

Indeed, time is so short and the atmosphere and work space so limited and incommodious that even effective professional relationships among colleagues cannot flourish in the school system; nor, for that matter, can any scholarly ambitions come to fruition. Such ambitions are shriveled on the vine as quickly as they emerge. There is no place for them, though they would surely prosper in a more amenable environment. While teaching methods are sometimes superficially touched upon, rare departmental and faculty conferences are too frequently devoted to clerical procedures. Commencing with an explication of the proper form to follow in filling out a particular record for either the state or the official class, they inevitably conclude with an admonishment concerning the time clock. The time clock is universally detested among teachers, for at best it is an irritation and at worst it is a serious imposition on both one's time and one's patience. Teachers who have first- or last-period preparation periods are, because of the time clock, forced to spend them in school, although, as I have indicated, the working conditions in the school are so abominable that time spent at home is infinitely more profitable. However, this is not the worst problem that arises in regard to the time clock. During Regents Week (when uniform state examinations are given) teachers who have only one- or two-hour proctoring assignments, or no assignments at all, are required to remain in school for the full six hours and twenty minutes. While many teachers follow these rules explicitly, many more make arrangements to punch each other in and out, and hence the constant warnings against such practices at faculty conferences.

A more prominent subject of faculty conferences during my second year was the local community and the administration's fear of community control. In discussing this subject, the administration usually did its utmost to elicit sympathy for its position, always pointing to the inherent dangers which community control posed for the teaching community. Many older teachers felt threatened by these "dangers" and genuinely believed that they would be fired by a hostile and capricious community. Yet many of these same teachers were some of the best teachers in the school, and their loss would have been keenly felt by any community. While I could at least appreciate the complaints of an incompetent administration which would undoubtedly have lost its post, I could never understand the unjustified fears of these teachers. I think, in the end, their fears had something to do with the racist nature of our society and the great barrier of bitterness and mistrust which this has raised between even people of good will but of different races.

As I have stated, it is ultimately the pupil who suffers from the myriad of maladies which beset the school system. Should a student have a problem, it must be solved within the first few minutes before or after class, or else it is not solved at all. Several times I gave over my lunch hour to student conferences, but this became an impractical and trying system and eventually I gave it up.

Since the teacher conducts five classes a day, this necessitates dealing with approximately 150 different youngsters every term. It is not easy to get to know 150 people every few months. Yet teachers do try and generally succeed in learning quite a bit about at least a dozen of the more vocal students. This is not good enough, for a teacher's friendship and encouragement are of vital importance to the futures of many children who must rely upon the school for guidance.

The teacher must ultimately take the easiest path out of the labyrinth. The most gifted youngsters receive the most attention, since they are so much easier to learn about and so much easier to deal with than those shy or recalcitrant children who would benefit so much from more personal attention. I personally encountered several very promising students who, because of their shyness or social backwardness, had been frightfully neglected by the school system. One of my finest students, a shy Puerto Rican girl, who, incidentally had a ninety-five average in all subjects, told me that she was in the commercial curriculum and that she was going to become a secretary. I spent a lunch hour with this girl convincing her that she could easily go to a city college on a scholarship. She was elated to learn this and subsequently told me that neither her guidance counselor nor any other teacher had encouraged her to pursue an academic curriculum. When I later discussed this with one of the school's guidance counselors, I was told that it was not the school's policy to recommend that underprivileged students go on to college; for, the counselor went on to explain, parents frequently prefer that their children acquire jobs instead in order that they may provide some financial assistance to their desperate families. Strangely enough, the student to whom I have just referred was not underprivileged. I therefore had to conclude that her counselor either had made an error or had automatically assumed that all minority-group students are under-privileged. I do not know which was the case, but I saw many other academically inclined students who seemed bent on secre-tarial careers precisely because no one had ever suggested that they might be wasting their talents. In all fairness, however, it must be admitted that the guidance counselors were as harried and overburdened as the teachers, and there is no reason to as-sume that their effectiveness was not similarly impaired.

Contrary to popular educational mythology, it is surprisingly easy to motivate the shy, the backward, the recalcitrant, the un-derprivileged or even the truant child. All it takes is a small dose of daily encouragement and a belief that the work that is being done is meaningful. I have often seen a small bit of faith in a child work great miracles. Children cannot resist a compliment, nor are they invulnerable to well-placed confidence in their intel-ligence. It fires their imaginations, expands their hopes and opens up possibilities for their futures that they had never before en-visaged or dreamed could be theirs. I once encouraged a student to read some of the better books and drew up a quick reading list for him which included some of the classics. This student, who was in the general curriculum, had a strong interest in school, though a poor background in verbal skills. I did not think about him again until I overheard another English teacher discussing the extraordinary literature which one of her students was read-ing. She went on to comment that it was this student's intention to go on to community college despite the fact that he would have to attend another year of high school in order to make up the courses which he had missed by being in the general curriculum.

There are many students in the general curriculum who, despite a lack of verbal sophistication, consistently achieve extraordinary marks on every test. These students are marveled at by their teachers and concomitantly dismissed as freaks who nonetheless would not do well in an academic program. Unfortunately, the teachers are generally correct about this, for students who lack verbal skills frequently do poorly in an academic curriculum, precisely, I believe, because they are not given the necessary encouragement (there is no time) and because they are not given intensive training in writing *before* they enter the academic program.

A small amount of time can have startling results, and if encouragement could be given frequently and freely it is possible that countless numbers of New York children could be saved from the despair which presently fills their lives. Unfortunately, the educational structure currently provided by the Board of Education militates against such behavior on the part of the teacher. As I have indicated, there is pitifully little time in the course of a day for student conferences or for the encouragement that a large percentage of our school population urgently needs. As a result, the school is an incredibly dwarfing environment for many children. A cheerless place where aspirations are too infrequently encouraged, the school is depressing and hopeless for all but the most privileged children.

New York City high schools have in the past offered three diplomas: academic, commercial and general. Upon entering high school, many underprivileged children are automatically assigned to the "general." This is a most peculiar curriculum, involving a melange of depressing courses, uniformly low in content. Granted, some students are just not able to do academic work. Still, that fact does not begin to account for the thousands of intelligent and pliable minds which are routinely assigned to suffer its crippling consequences. Since the content of the general-curriculum courses is so low, most teachers are ashamed to teach them—a fact which leads, as may be imagined, to the further impoverishment of the curriculum. I have heard the courses referred to by one perspicacious teacher as "applesauce," and I believe it is a fit description, indicating, as it does, fare for infants. From my own experience, I would venture to suggest that at least 75 percent of the children in this curriculum are capable, given the proper stimulation, of surviving a tough academic program. And if the elementary-school program were revitalized, even more children could be included in this figure. This is, of course, a highly subjective evaluation on my part, and few teachers would agree with me. Yet these same teachers have witnessed the successful operation of such educational programs as Higher Horizons and College Discovery—programs wherein the very same types of youngsters have been successfully embarked upon college-bound futures. (Strangely enough, the Board of Education has destroyed both of these programs. Higher Horizons has been dropped altogether and College Discovery has been considerably weakened and will, I assume, eventually be dropped.)

It was announced that the Board of Education, in response to a deluge of criticism, would soon begin to confer only one diploma on all of its high-school graduates. (As of the time of this book's going to press, this has not occurred.) This will, of course, end the stigma which has been attached to the general diploma, but it will do nothing to remedy the greater stigma which the general courses will continue to inflict upon the student, for the Board of Education does not intend to alter the content of these courses.

In conclusion, I would like to say for the record that the few good deeds which I somehow managed to accomplish occurred *during my first term in the school system.* It is important for me to note this, as by the time the second semester rolled around I felt completely debilitated and washed out and did not devote any spare time to student guidance, nor did I devote any time to either individual instruction or student conferences. I say this by way of emphasizing for the reader the change which the teacher undergoes as he labors against the clock and a woefully inadequate environment. It is virtually impossible to maintain some semblance of integrity and order in a life which constantly threatens to become a shambles as a result of the unnatural pressures to which it is subjected. Many teachers labored much more heroically than I did; I met several who consistently gave many hours of their personal time to their job and to their students. I was not able to do this. Like most teachers, I was finally forced to succumb and henceforth performed at that low energy and creativity level which enabled me to endure somehow the enormous pressures of an ordinary work day.

It is an unfortunate fact that the New York City schools have been declining over the past several years. They will, sadly, continue to decline until the Board of Education decides to create a healthful environment where both students and teachers will begin to prosper. If such burdens as the nonpedagogical assigned tasks are eliminated, if the teacher is relieved of clerical work and the number of classes is reduced, the teacher will at least be free to function as an educator. Certainly the student deserves the same break—which could conceivably be managed in the form of a stricter and more meaningful curriculum. Without a doubt, both students and teachers would profit greatly from increased space and from less transitory interpersonal contact.

Hopefully, the day is not far off when men will begin to expend the money and energy which is necessary to the proper organization and maintenance of a comfortable, attractive and effective school environment. Until then, we must look forward to a period of greater educational decline.

CULTURAL DEPRIVATION AS AN
EDUCATIONAL IDEOLOGY[1]

MURRAY L. WAX AND
ROSALIE H. WAX

In the summer of 1959, fresh from teaching in the College of the University of Chicago, we assumed the tasks of directing a workshop for American Indian college students. The first day of organized events went quietly; there were so many directorial and clerical duties to perform that we could barely manage some introductory statements to the students and the assignment of the initial chapter from their first week's reading, *Where Peoples Meet: Racial and Ethnic Frontiers,* by Everett C. and Helen M. Hughes. Murray had volunteered to lead a discussion, Chicago College style, about that reading, and so the next morning, after

[1] An initial version of this paper was delivered at the 62nd annual meeting of the American Anthropological Association, November 1963. The paper was subsequently revised and appeared as an article in the *Journal of American Indian Education,* Vol. III, No. 2 (January 1964); the present article is further revised and elaborated; however, passages from the previous article are used herein with the kind permission of the *Journal.* The data utilized in the various drafts of the article were gathered during a series of research projects sponsored first by Emory University (Atlanta) and then by the University of Kansas (Lawrence) under contracts with the U.S. Office of Education (particularly Cooperative Research Project Nos. 1361 and S-099). The report of CRP No. 1361, containing further detail about the educational problems of Sioux children, was published in 1964 by the Society for the Study of Social Problems, as a monograph of the society. The responsibility for the texts of the research reports and these papers belongs solely to the authors.

we had seated ourselves in the circle of discussion, he opened simply, "What happens when peoples meet?"

A profound silence ensued, such as one had not been prepared for after dealing with the loquacious, verbally aggressive Chicagoans. We began to feel restless, as whites usually do in the presence of conversational stillness.

Finally Ed Stalker, the senior male among the students, must have felt that the burden to respond was his. Ed was not the stereotypical college student, but a middle-aged Apache who was working as manager of the produce department of the co-op supermarket in the university neighborhood. Married and with children, he had nonetheless enrolled in night classes at a junior college level. His teachers had said of him that he was diligent and reliable but that he had great difficulties with the subject matter, and we had admitted him to the workshop because he sounded like a good man and we thought—correctly, so it proved—that a stable older man would be a useful member of this little community. Today, in our moment of conversational despair, Ed responded, quietly but with assurance, to the question "What happens when peoples meet?" with the laconic answer "Bad feelings."

He was right, of course, and he had subtly alluded to the very problem we were facing that morning. But we persevered, as did the students, and somehow we got through the short summer term, although not without conflicts with the dormitory supervisors about such matters as hours, drinking, and the shenanigans of healthy young people. Yet throughout the workshop sessions we never lost the feeling that we were dealing with another people—or, more precisely, with a selection from other peoples. It was not just the physical features of the students (and a few, anyway, looked almost white), but their accents, their quiet speech and respectful ways, their styles of joking and talking—these and many other traits repeatedly instructed us that we and they were alien. Equally striking was their ignorance in the scholastic field. These were not merely college students but were supposedly the outstanding young peoples of their communities, nominated by tribal or educational officials to receive a scholarship to participate in an elite workshop. Yet many spoke and wrote an English that was abysmally substandard, and they were all so provincial in their knowledge of U. S. history and so ignorant of Indian history and current events that we doubted their rank as college students.

Most likely, what transformed the bad feelings to better ones and aroused the interests of most of the students in the more academic aspects of our program was an early set of lectures by Murray on the world view and religious orientations of traditional Plains Indian peoples (M. L. Wax, 1962; Wax and Wax, 1962). When he began to quote respectfully from traditional myths, the air in the room became electric with intensity, and afterward several of the quieter and most withdrawn young men rushed forward to mention things their elders had done or said. They also remarked that never had they heard a teacher or other professional speak of Indian traditional customs in this way—that is, as vital, meaningful, and significant, rather than as superstitious, primitive, or extinct.

The result of the summer's experiences was to instill in us a strong curiosity about the nature of the schools that were serving the reservation communities. What happened within these schools that was leading to the development of the youth we were encountering at the workshop? We conceived the idea of a study of the educational system on an Indian reservation, and the state of our thinking is revealed by the hypotheses we formulated. We envisioned the school as a kind of battleground: on the one hand, the educators, flanked by the staff of the Bureau of Indian Affairs and reinforced by the mission churches and other benevolent agencies, would be struggling to pull the children out of the Indian culture, while, on the other hand, the Indian elders would be clinging desperately to their young, trying to encompass them within the traditional social sphere.

The vision was to be proven wrong, but on the first day of our initial project on the Pine Ridge Reservation a leading Agency official seemed to be confirming it when he said, "The school gets this child from a conservative home, brought up speaking the Indian language, and all he knows is Grandma. His home has no books, no magazines, radio, television, newspapers—it's empty! He comes into school and we have to teach him everything! All right. We bring him to the point where he's beginning to know something in high school, and he drops out. . . . Because at this time he has to choose between Grandma and being an educated member of the community." At the time, we were inclined to accept this agency official's view of the conflict between Grandma and the school system as well as of her triumph in luring her grandchildren "back to the blanket." What startled us, even after so brief an experience as the workshop, was his emphasis upon the Indian household as symbolically so "empty." Yet we were to find that this was the theme of much of the formal discourse of the educational planners of the reservation school system.

"The Indian child has such a *meager* experience," one school administrator said. "When he encounters words like 'elevator' or 'escalator' in his reading, he has no idea what they mean. But it's not just strange concepts like those. Take even the idea of water. When you or I think of it, well, I think of a shining stainless-steel faucet in a sink, running clean and pure, and of the plumbing that brings it, and chlorination and water purification, or of the half-million-dollar project for the Pine Ridge water supply. But the Indian child doesn't think of water as something flowing into a bathtub."

By the time we heard these opinions we had been settled for some weeks near a country Indian household on a small bluff above a creek. During the warm days, people would come to the creek to bathe and would enjoy the coolness and the vegetation. Periodically, and accompanied by a pack of yelping dogs, our host would drive his battered car perilously close to the water's edge and fill several barrels with water to be used for household purposes. The creek supported some small fish, and we surmised that it also was the locus of numerous animals; if nothing else, it was a breeding site for mosquitoes. So, hearing the words of this educational administrator, one of us replied, "I guess the Indian child would think of a creek."

But the respondent insisted upon the miserable quality of Sioux experience: "Or of a pump, broken down and hardly working."

The Vacuum Ideology

While our hypothesis about the school as a battleground was to be proven erroneous, it did predispose us to take a careful look, not only at the Indians, but at those whom we conceived to be their antagonists in the schools. We were the more disposed toward this because we regarded the reservation as a meeting ground of two different peoples, between whom on initial contact there had been and continued to be "bad feelings." Accordingly, where previous research on Indian education had focused narrowly on the children and usually restricted itself to "instruments" administered by educational personnel in the classrooms, our project (Wax, Wax, and Dumont, 1964) was organized to examine all parties to the total situation: pupils and parents, officials and educators. Quickly and emphatically, these latter made it clear that they thought Indian life was miserable and vacuous—in more formal parlance, that Indians had nothing meaningful in the way of a culture, so that the mind of the child on entering school was empty, a vacuum. Despite the powwows which were everywhere in evidence, with their distinctive dancing and singing, an educator who had worked for many years on the reservation could rise at a public meeting and declare that "Indian children have no home experiences in art or music," while others instead of correcting the speaker reinforced him by asserting that Indian children were not told stories by their parents. And these assertions were climaxed for us by an official who explained, "We must go back to the [Indian] home to find the lack of patterns that should have been learned."

For obvious reasons, we came to call this the "vacuum ideology" of the educators of the Indian reservation. In a curious way, it reminded us of the wilderness ideology of the European invaders of the American continent. Confronting a land whose every area was known to and utilized by its native inhabitants, the land-hungry whites had perceived and spoken of "a wilderness."

The White people speak of the country at this period as "a wilderness," as though it was an empty tract without human interest or history. To us Indians it was as clearly defined then as it is today; we knew the boundaries of tribal lands, those of our friends and those of our foes; we were familiar with every stream, the contour of every hill, and each peculiar feature of the landscape had its tradition. It was our home, the scene of our history, and we loved it as our country. [La Flesche,[2] 1963, p. xx.]

The parallelism is significant: just as the wilderness ideology rationalized for the invaders their seizing and occupying of Indian lands, so does the vacuum ideology rationalize for the educators their roles in the schools. First, it places upon the Indian home and the parents the responsibility for the lack of scholastic achievement of the child. Since the child is entering the school with an empty head, then surely it is a triumph if he is taught anything whatsoever. Moreover, the ideology justifies almost any activity within the school as "educational" (just as it derogates any communal activity outside the school); for if the child is presumed deficient in almost every realm of experience, then the task of the educator can properly encompass anything and everything. Finally, the ideology justifies the educators in their social and cultural isolation from the lives of the parents of their students; if the child actually had a culture including knowledge and values, then the educators ought properly to learn about these and build upon them, but if, on entering school, he is merely a vacuum, then what need to give attention to his home and community?

Before continuing with a description of the Pine Ridge scene, we should like to add that we believe that a similar constellation of attitudes and relationships currently plagues schools in urban settings (cf. Leacock, 1960). Children who come from lower-class and impoverished ethnic groups are regarded as empty and cultureless rather than as having a culture and social life of their own which educators must learn about in order to be competent in their jobs. Children from lower-class Negro homes are especially subject to this mishandling, since many "liberals" refuse on political grounds to recognize that their families participate in distinct subcultures. Among Indians such as the Sioux, who speak

[2] Born about 1857, La Flesche wrote this passage about 1900.

a distinctive language and have a distinctive ceremonial life, the investigator might have thought it would be less likely that such a misperception of their cultural life could flourish among educators and administrators, but in fact what we have classified as the vacuum ideology seems but a local variant of the ideologies of "cultural deprivation" (Riessman, 1962) and the "culture of poverty."

On the Pine Ridge Reservation—and perhaps in other reservations and urban lower-class settings—the ideology of cultural deprivation seems closely associated with the secularized version of the Protestant ethos. On the one hand, the Indian *mind* is seen as empty, and on the other hand the Indian *will* is seen as lacking. In citing materials to document and illustrate the one view, we must inevitably do the same for the other. Besides, the person who during our field research was regarded by Bureau personnel, in Pine Ridge and often elsewhere, as the intellectual authority for their educational philosophy was himself a dedicated exponent of that ethos who seems to have exhorted the Sioux and regulated his official life according to its maxims.

As principal of the Little Wound Day School in Pine Ridge during the school year 1936–37, Pedro T. Orata kept elaborate records and produced a four-volume report for the Bureau. Later he condensed this into a book, *Fundamental Education in an Amerindian Community* (1953), which was still being quoted on Pine Ridge during the 1960s. From the pages of this book there emerges so extreme a contrast between his own ethos and that of his Sioux neighbors that the effect is at first sometimes comic and then later pathetic and tragic. For example, he does not merely complain (as one might expect) that the farmer paid by the government was working hard daily while any number of able-bodied Sioux were sitting about the local store, but he assesses as "the most difficult problem" the fact that the Indians "sat there all day and seemed to enjoy doing so"! (Orata, 1953, p. 51.)

How extreme his views were can be understood from the tale in his pages about a winter crisis: South Dakota, twenty degrees below zero, knee-deep snow on poor roads; an epidemic of flu in the community that had disabled four of his six teachers and two of his bus drivers; two radiators frozen in the school and below-freezing temperatures in the classroom. Of the 140 pupils, twenty had made it to school. Undaunted, Orata exhorts his staff:

"Could we have done better today? When the boys [Indian pupils] stood around the furnace room and loafed, don't think they were not getting educated. They were. They were learning to loaf. There is no such thing as absence of education, at any time. . . . If those boys were not learning to work, they were learning to loaf. . . . If those boys repeated what they did ten times, what would happen?"

And the dutiful "straight man" on his staff answers, "They'd be sitting in the furnace room all the time." (Orata, 1953, pp. 135-37.)

From the perspective of Orata or of his contemporary disciples on Pine Ridge or in the B.I.A., Indians must adopt the Protestant ethos if they are to be morally acceptable or socially employable. Insofar as Indians do not have this ethos, it is not that they share some other value system, but that they have none.

Turning now to the contemporary versions of Cultural Deprivation on the Reservation, what we find educational administrators doing is counterposing to the Sioux child a "usual American" child who is a myth or ideal, and since this "usual American" child and his family are not real, they can be credited with countless traits, all unquestionably desirable because middle-class American; and the longer the list of these traits—and they can be made indefinite in number—the more defective the Sioux child is made to appear. The fact that the Sioux child lacks—or seems to lack—these traits is sufficient to characterize him as "empty" and "meager."

"We assume that these children have many home experiences," said one educator. "In fact, we assume that they all come to school with the same experiences. In reality we find too great a gap between the actual background the [Indian] child has and the assumed constructive home experiences, or the things that would build concepts. If this is out of balance as much as I think it is, then we must include a great many experiences normally provided by the home in the school program." She listed these experiences as "television, jet planes, rocket ships, hydrogen bombs, helicopters, polio and GG shots, supermarkets, frozen foods, hundreds of electrical appliances. The lag is terrifying!" she said.[3]

Of Power and Culture

Perhaps the best way to challenge the vacuum ideology and the ideology of cultural deprivation is to utilize an economic logic and assert that wherever children are they are learning some one thing at the cost of not learning others. So we agree with Orata's premise, but not—as we will make clear—with his conclusion. Theoretically, it would be possible to isolate children in an environment free of all stimulation, but such environments, we would surmise, are happily rare, existing perhaps only in misguided and understaffed institutions, such as the orphanages where infants succumb from lack of warmth and nurture. Given any natural environment, whether it be Harlem, Pine Ridge, or Summerhill, children will be experiencing and thereby learning. If they are part of an isolated folk society, they will be acquiring its culture; if they are part of the general U. S. middle class, they will be learning its culture, and, if this latter, they will be better fitted for early achievement in school. For example, the child reared among the middle class may acquire a larger standard (dictionary) vocabulary than one reared in the slum of the reservation; yet, while the size of standard vocabulary is predictive of early scholastic achievement, it is not a statement of linguistic or social maturity. Consider, as but one illustration, that some people of modest vocabulary can be far more eloquent than scholars whose vocabulary is huge.

What the child experiences in home and school is but a meager selection from a vast possible range, so that, in economic terms,

[3] Speech of an educator participating in the conference on a "Reservation-wide Pre-School Program," February 23, 1961, Pine Ridge Agency (minutes duplicated by the Division of Indian Education, Department of Public Instruction, Pierre, S. D.), p. 13.

if he is participating in one activity, he is not participating in another. If he is learning to sit still in class, then he is not simultaneously learning to dance powwow style. If he is learning calculus, he is not simultaneously learning how to play the *dozens*. We suggest that many intellectuals and educators are so convinced of the value of learning the calculus that they have forgotten the values of dancing and play, as well as the intimate relationships among play, art, and freedom.

It comes down to having some respect for the people themselves, and this is what has been lacking in many essays on the problems of Indians and Negroes. By labeling them as "the Indian problem" or "the Negro problem" the writers tacitly disown the fact that the whites are not only co-responsible but themselves affected by the problem (*cf.* Hughes and Hughes, 1952, pp. 18-31). The consequences are exhibited in some studies by respectable-sounding social scientists with high-sounding sponsorship. For example, in a 1960 report on the Rosebud and Pine Ridge Reservation by Drs. E. E. Hagan and Louis C. Schaw, a social psychologist and an economist, sponsored by a liberal organization, the Association on American Indian Affairs, the investigators conclude (Chap. VI, p. 8) that the Sioux are passive, apathetic, and hostilely dependent. In opposition to these terms, we must state that our own observations are that Bureau personnel are as hostile toward the Indians as the latter are toward them (and on both sides there are individuals who are not hostile); also, that Bureau personnel are utterly dependent upon the continued existence of the "backward" Indians, because, if Indians managed their own affairs, the local Indian Agency would provide no employment (this dependency is therefore especially marked among the lower and less skilled echelons of the Bureau). Our own observations again are that "apathy" is a convenient label to apply to people who don't happen to agree with the program that a government official or other reformer happens to be pushing (Wax and Wax, 1968). Frankly, when we went to Pine Ridge, we did expect to see apathetic people. Instead we saw people whose lust for life reminded us of the descriptions of Restoration England, and today we are inclined to feel that it is the urban lower middle class who are culturally deprived and whose children have such meager experiences.

But the Sioux are not the only Indians whose experiences and culture are so derogated. Under the sponsorship of the Fund for the Republic, a body with the grand title of the Commission on the Rights, Liberties, and Responsibilities of the American Indian has surveyed the scene and issued its report (Brophy and Aberle, 1966). It need scarcely be said that such a commission contained no person who was an elected representative of an Indian community or tribe, but what is perhaps more surprising is that its only "Indian" member was a millionaire oil executive, marginally of Indian ancestry, who was appointed to a "chiefdom" by President Truman. (The situation is much like a monarchical appointment to a barony or dukedom, including the fact that the impoverished Indian people have no control on the behavior of the chief who presumes to act in their name and to control their communal assets.) This committee announces on page one of its report that its goal is "making the Indian a self-respecting and useful American citizen," a phrase so patronizing and paternalistic that it could not be modified to apply to any other minority without the gravest repercussions. Then, matching its arrogance with ignorance, it asserts on the following page that "it would be unwise to dismiss all that is in the traditional Indian culture as being necessarily a barrier to change," as if the Sioux in Pine Ridge, the Navajos in Arizona, or the Cherokees in eastern Oklahoma had not changed voluntarily—and, true, involuntarily and under duress—so that today they resemble their forefathers no more than the neighboring whites and Negroes do theirs.

The situation is climaxed by the report of John Bryde, S.J., Ph.D., who, having administered large batteries of tests to Indian and white children of Pine Ridge and its environs, has concluded that the Sioux children are alienated and lack pride in themselves. As a remedy he proposes a course or courses in which the children will be instructed about their past and taught pride in it, but the course is to be taught by himself and his disciples, not by the Sioux themselves. Perhaps the significant index to the potential of his program is the fact that after scores of years of work among the

Sioux, the Jesuits are still operating a "mission," just as the Roman Catholic and many other Christian denominations do among Indian peoples generally. Thus, neither the churches nor the federal government, nor most investigators, nor most private foundations, are prepared to accept the realities of Indian experience or recognize the ability of Indians to operate their own churches or schools or teach their own history and traditions to their own children.

If the Indian child appears as "culturally deprived," it is not because he is lacking in experience or in culture, but because the educational agencies are unwilling to recognize the alienness of his culture and the realities of his social world. It is not that the child is deprived of culture, it is that the culture which is associated with his parents is derogated because they are impoverished and powerless.

BIBLIOGRAPHY

Brophy, William A., and Sophie D. Aberle, *The Indian: America's Unfinished Business,* report of the Commission on the Rights, Liberties, and Responsibilities of the American Indian. Norman, Okla.: University of Oklahoma, 1966.

Hagen, E. E., and Louis C. Schaw, *The Sioux on the Reservations: The American Colonial Problem,* mimeographed "preliminary edition." Cambridge, Mass.: MIT Center for International Studies, 1960.

Hughes, Everett C., and Helen M. Hughes, *Where Peoples Meet: Racial and Cultural Frontiers.* New York: Free Press, 1952.

LaFlesche, Francis, *The Middle Five: Indian Schoolboys of the Omaha Tribe.* Madison: University of Wisconsin Press, 1963.

Leacock, Eleanor Burke, *Comment,* Human Organization Monograph No. 2 (1960), pp. 30-32.

Orata, Pedro T., *Fundamental Education in an Amerindian Community.* Lawrence, Kans.: Haskell Press, U.S. Bureau of Indian Affairs, 1953.

Riessman, Frank, *The Culturally Deprived Child.* New York: Harper and Row, 1962.

Wax, Murray L., "The Notions of Nature, Man, and Time of a Hunting People," *Southern Folklore Quarterly,* Vol. 26 (1962), pp. 175-86.

Wax, Murray L., and Rosalie H. Wax, "The enemies of the people," in *Institutions and the Person: Essays presented to Everett C. Hughes,* ed. Howard S. Becker *et al.* Chicago: Aldine Press, 1968.

Wax, Murray L., Rosalie H. Wax, and Robert V. Dumont, *Formal Education in an American Indian Community,* Monograph No. 1, Society for the Study of Social Problems, 1964.

Wax, Rosalie H., and Murray L. Wax, "The Magical World View," *Journal for the Scientific Study of Religion,* Vol. 1 (1962), pp. 179-88.

THE INTEGRITY OF THE CHEROKEE STUDENT[1]

MILDRED DICKEMAN

Examining the structural discrimination of the school system against the lower-class pupil, Frank Riessman (1962, pp. 23-24) stated the need for two ingredients if the middle-class teacher is to succeed in his educational goals: first, a deeper understanding, particularly of cultural differences, and, second, respect for the student. Riessman indicated how the latter must grow in part from the former. Yet, since the publication of his work, little serious examination of cultural differences in behavior within the classroom has been undertaken. On the contrary, there has been increasing acceptance in both sociological and educational circles of sweeping and unverified generalities about the "culture" of the poor, in which Riessman also unfortunately indulged.[2] More recently, Fuchs (1966, p. 161) has commented that "although we give lip service to the notion that the dignity of each child should

[1] This essay is a product of research sponsored by the University of Kansas, under contract with the U. S. Department of Health, Education and Welfare, Office of Education, and directed by Dr. Murray L. Wax. First-hand data were gathered during six months' residence in a rural, predominantly Cherokee community in northeastern Oklahoma, and included one month of classroom observations in the two-room public elementary school which served it. In addition, I visited several surrounding communities and their schools, and collected through Cherokee assistants over a hundred interviews of Cherokee parents. My own data have been supplemented by those of other members of the project, especially the classroom observations and student interviews of Robert V. Dumont. All personal and place names referring to the field situation are pseudonymous.

[2] For a recent critique of these concepts, see Roach and Gursslin, 1967.

be respected, the ongoing interpersonal relations and the experiences of the youngsters do not seem to indicate that we really do this." There has been "little empirical research on the destructive role played by interpersonal relations within schools."

This discussion of the relations between Cherokee students and their teachers is an attempt at such an exploration. Focusing on only one of the many factors which combine to produce the educational failure of the school system relative to Oklahoma Cherokees, it emphasizes the need for an informed respect, resting on the recognition of deep cultural differences in values and behavior. Although dealing with an ethnic subculture markedly different from the dominant society in history and ethos and geographically isolated from many of its institutions, I believe this analysis has wider relevance to those social classes and ethnic minorities more closely incorporated into Western society which, however, share with Cherokees an unwillingness, variously expressed, to be educated on terms that involve the violation of their personal and social selves.[3] It will, I think, demonstrate as well the futility of attempts to define as a unified "culture" that diverse collection of subsocieties whose classification as an entity (by social scientists and by the society at large) rests merely on their common alienation from the seats of economic and political power.

By all the standard indices, the Cherokees of northeastern Oklahoma fall under the rubric of the economically and educationally deprived. "Fullblood"[4] Cherokees, numbering about ten thousand, live primarily in small, dispersed rural communities in the Ozark foothills of five northeastern counties. Available data indicate that they earn less than half the average family income for the counties in which they reside, and a recent survey

[3] A valuable discussion of the notion of self-concept (closely similar to the idea of integrity elaborated here) and its application to the experiences of Harlem Negro students is Fuchs, 1966, pp. 139-69.

[4] The term "fullblood" is used here sociologically, to refer to members of primarily Cherokee-speaking communities who are so identified by their co-residents. Although there is, of course, no value to the term as a biological designation, it is true that the structure of Oklahoma society has ensured a fairly close correspondence between modern Cherokee racial identity and sociocultural Cherokeeness.

(Wahrhaftig, 1965b, pp. 54-62) of communities in four of these counties revealed a median family income of $2,250–$2,300 and a per-capita income of $450–$600, with over half of the households wholly or partially dependent upon welfare. Likewise, the educational achievement of Cherokees is extremely low. The survey referred to above shows 5.5 as the median number of school years completed by adult Cherokees, an increase over the 3.3 years reported in 1933. Almost all Cherokees are educated in public schools, in what is for them a foreign language. Forty percent of adult Cherokees are functionally illiterate in English (Wahrhaftig, 1965b, pp. 33-41). While detailed data on enrollment and dropout patterns are lacking, a study of the 1965 school registers (Underwood 1966) indicated fairly constant enrollment to the eighth grade, a decline of 20 percent at the ninth grade, and a further decline to only one third of the first-grade enrollment by the twelfth grade. Only 1 or 2 percent actually graduate. (It must be cautioned that enrollment figures are difficult to evaluate where there is wide variance in the enforcement of truancy laws, and where many advantages accrue to the school district that inflates its Indian enrollment figures.)

Some Cherokee Interactional Premises[5]

Cherokees grow up in a world of restraint. Not the restraint of Anglo-Saxon American society, compounded of a high value on internalized willpower, a deep sense of individual responsibility and a respect for formal rules and regulations. Rather, they value and inculcate an emotional and behavioral restraint in dealing with others, which expresses great respect for the physical and psychic autonomy and privacy of others, and fear in the face of social intrusion, operating in a societal context of close kin and long co-residence ties. Thus, the essential tension of the Cherokee ethos is that between one's own autonomous feelings and actions

[5] My understanding of Cherokee values has been greatly aided by discussions with Robert K. Thomas and Albert Wahrhaftig of the Carnegie Cross-cultural Education Project, University of Chicago.

and the obligation to recognize the autonomy and privacy of others. The result is a deep sensitivity to the interactional responses of the community of significant others.

This restraint is manifest both verbally and gesturally. Strong emotional responses to life are displayed only rarely or by indirection. Sorrow is not openly communicated by strong verbal exclamations or by tears; Cherokees do not cry in public even if that "public" be one's immediate family. Profoundly distressing and even threatening news (such as the news of mistreatment of Cherokee children by authorities, received at a public meeting at which I was present) is received only with the softest of murmurs and by facial expressions of intense and profound sorrow. The expression of anger is placed under even greater control. Indeed, while feelings of sadness may find verbal expression in appropriately muted tones, situations which would evoke open expression of anger in Oklahoma whites produce in Cherokees verbalizations of sorrow or of fear. Thus, in discussing individuals intensely disliked by the majority of the community, or against whom the speaker has major grievances, they remark, "When I think about that man I feel sorry," or "I'm not mad at him, just afraid of him," or "I'm not mad, I just don't understand those people." (Referrents of these remarks were both Cherokee and white.) Cherokees find in the fundamentalist Cherokee Baptist Church, to which most are affiliated, additional support for this behavior. Indeed, the only fullblood whom I recall expressing anger openly ("I'm mad," regarding injustices against Cherokees) is a youth of far more than average education and experience in white society.

The disapproval of anger extends to physical violence, which is rare and extremely furtive in Cherokee communities, and condoned only as a response to a series of extreme provocations, or as a community action. Violence arising out of community consensus, and directed against individuals regarded as traitors to Cherokee society, exemplified by the political assassinations of Cherokee history, is seen as an unfortunate necessity. Indeed, Cherokees have long viewed themselves as followers of the "white path" of peace, in contrast to warlike Western tribes (*cf.* Thomas,

1954). This is in great contrast to white mores in northeast Oklahoma, where the individual defense of masculine pride by fist and gun is still common. Rather than open physical violence, Cherokees with long-term grievances are more likely to resort to other modes of personal revenge: witchcraft and house-burning. So true is this that when Cherokees learn of a house burning down their immediate response is to speculate on interpersonal enmities. And individuals of high status who die suddenly are regularly regarded as possible victims of witchcraft. Yet the disapproval of physical violence pursues one even here: when their enemies die, Cherokees fear being accused of witchcraft.

This ethos is clearly demonstrated in the initiation of social interaction. In receiving visitors at his home, a Cherokee maintains social distance by receiving strangers outside the house, standing in the yard or at the door. But once trust is established, the privilege of entry into the house without knocking is granted without any verbal invitation. Although a fearful and suspicious reception (with a minimum of verbal responses) is more often accorded to whites, it is not limited to them, and once a relation of trust has been established whites too are included in the second category. In approaching the home of another Cherokee who is not an intimate relation, or when the mission may involve rejection (as in interviewing), a Cherokee screws up his body in a tense, constrained, slow-motion walk expressing not only the defense of his own self from invasion, but hesitation over invasion of another's privacy. Cherokees visiting in automobiles will park in the drive, waiting for the resident to emerge at the sound of the car. A bold youth will honk the horn and wait. This seems rude to a white resident, because he must leave his house to answer the call, but polite to a Cherokee because it is less intrusive into the other's home and allows the latter the privilege of ignoring the visit. It is usually only younger and bolder Cherokees who knock on doors as whites do.

Restraint extends to physical contacts. Cherokees do not often shake hands. When they do, the handshake is neither firm nor prolonged. Physical contact even with close associates and kin is much less common than in white society, especially between adults. Only in joking situations are Cherokees seen openly nudging and jostling each other. In fact, joking and teasing, highly developed arts among Cherokees, serve many important interactional functions which are related to the ethos of restraint. They are used to express close personal fondness in a society which taboos public embrace or caress, and are employed to convey approval or disapproval of individuals present or absent. They are used to probe the intentions and trustworthiness of others, in contexts in which whites would engage in direct questioning. Cherokees do not indulge in direct interrogation except on the most trivial and nonthreatening matters, or where it is absolutely unavoidable. Inquiry into personal, emotion-laden opinions is very ill-mannered until trust has been established. It is another invasion of personal privacy; the census and the interview must appear to Cherokees as appalling inventions.

Not only physical contact and verbal interrogation, but even too persistent looking at another is, in the Cherokee view, intrusive. Staring, especially at strangers, is avoided, and the feeling of being stared at is deeply disturbing to adult Cherokees. Although they may in some contexts look each other directly in the eyes, this is proper only in situations defined as nonthreatening, and even then they do not do so in the prolonged and intense manner employed by some American whites while in conversation. Two Cherokees deep in conversation, feeling accord and successful communication, are more likely to incline their heads toward each other, gazing in the same direction as they focus on the same subject, with occasional glances of eye contact. Staring is in fact so penetrating that it is used by Cherokees, as by some other American Indian societies, as a powerful means of disciplining and controlling the young. Cherokee adults respond to continued staring by removing themselves from visibility or, if that is not feasible, turning their backs to the viewer.

Loud voices are similarly objectionable. The quietness of Cherokees is sometimes unnerving to Oklahoma whites, who tend to equate privacy with secrecy, and loudness with honesty. In public meetings as well as in smaller gatherings, Cherokees speak softly. They do not show marked approval at meetings or parties by loud interjections or clapping or by loud laughing. To a white observer, all is muted. Approvals are muttered or chuckled. Disapprovals are more often seen than heard. There could be no greater contrast than that between the behavior of Cherokee participants at political meetings and the "campaign manner" of the white Oklahoma politician. Expectably, the fear of intrusion extends to situations in which an individual is on public display. Cherokees are visibly reluctant and uncomfortable at standing alone to speak or perform under the scrutiny of others, and the well-mannered audience responds to this discomfort by listening with lowered heads and eyes averted, glancing rather than looking at the exposed self. Group presentations are markedly more tolerable.

These muted and restrained approaches to human interactions are in marked contrast to the behavior of Oklahoma whites, which (although showing a much greater range of variation) is often loudly and aggressively friendly and persistent. Oklahoma whites often displease, upset and frighten Cherokees by interpersonal approaches involving loud expressions of friendship and curiosity, handshaking and backslapping. Likewise, a brusque and authoritarian manner often prevents successful communication when whites must deal with Cherokees. This restraint on the expression of strong emotion, and the fear of its expression in others, may be stated in a more revelatory manner as part of a general Cherokee ethos which frowns on acts intrusive upon another's personal privacy, both physical and mental. To this society, in other words, violence, or the violation of another's self, has both a broader meaning and a stronger interdiction than it does for Oklahoma whites.

Yet the obverse of restraint is freedom, and Cherokee fear of intrusion implies a respect for the autonomy of individuals markedly greater than that found in Anglo-American society. Even within the limitations of extensive kin and community obligations, the individual retains an essential freedom in decision-making, in defining the locus, quality and degree of his commitments. Even verbal advice or suggestion is considered coercive unless indirect, and those coercive sanctions which are employed—consisting primarily of the teasing referred to above, gossip and the fear of witchcraft—are far more subtle than those of the surrounding white society. This principle of autonomy is well expressed by Wahrhaftig (1966, pp. 64-65) in his discussion of the bases of Cherokee communal action:

Action is successful when people signify agreement by participating. Disagreement is indicated by non-participation. Withdrawal is a strong sign of disapproval. When disagreement is indicated by non-participation, the matter is dropped. The process can be re-initiated at a later time if changed circumstances warrant it, but when people express disapproval by not participating, proposals are not pressed. Pressure forces people into having to choose between doing what they think right and staying "out" or violating their own will to avoid offending people who support action. Cherokees will not put other Cherokees in this position.

The emphasis on autonomy in Cherokee life is clearly expressed in attitudes regarding learning.[6] Cherokee learning begins with observation and imitation, which ensures that the process will be initiated by the learner, not the teacher. A task is begun by a novice only when he feels competent to perform the whole process; consequently, the novice learns theory and practice simultaneously. Nor will another intrude to correct the novice if he begins to err. He is allowed to complete his task and learn for himself the consequences of error (and one of these will almost surely be teasing from his associates). Guidance, when given, is offered as opinion. If the learner cares to listen he may do so; he will not be coerced by being *told* what to do.

Aside from those activities which must be learned informally in a Cherokee community, there is one formal situation in which learner—teacher relations may be observed in a fully Cherokee institution. This is the learning of literacy in the Cherokee syllabary that occurs within the Cherokee Baptist Church, which still, in most communities, relies primarily on the New Testament in syllabary as its text. Most Cherokees do not begin to acquire literacy in Cherokee until they are in their thirties, when as re-

[6] I am indebted to discussions with Albert Wahrhaftig for much of my understanding of traditional Cherokee learning.

sponsible adults they anticipate positions of leadership. Wahrhaftig's survey (1965, p. 26) revealed that 65 percent of the adults over thirty in one of the communities in which I worked were literate in Cherokee. This literacy may be acquired through the church, from another member of one's family, or autodidactically.

In the Cherokee "Sunday school," literacy is acquired through readings in the New Testament. The preacher selects a passage and calls on each member of the congregation in turn to read aloud. If an individual has difficulty reading a word or passage, he will be prompted spontaneously by other members. An individual who is totally illiterate will be prompted word for word by his neighbor, who points at the words in the text. None is ever passed over on the basis of ignorance, none is rushed. These principles of learning give to the superficial observer an impression of much greater "equality" between teacher and learner, and between learners of differing abilities. But that impression is no more than a projection of our Western equation of "equality" with "respect." Cherokees show great esteem for the elderly, the knowledgeable, the wise. They discriminate clearly between the effective and the ineffectual, but they do not impose learning from above. The essential respect for the autonomy of others decrees that the learner shall determine the quantity and quality of his education. The primary function of others involved in the same learning situation is to serve as supportive assistants and as models. It is the "inner voice" of the learner which determines and defines the relationship.

Respect for the autonomy of others and fear of violence to one's own integrity: this Cherokee interrelational ethos implies a definition of the good man which includes a subtle sensitivity to the feelings of others. Cherokees, in English conversation, use the word "trust" frequently in evaluating themselves and others. The good man is trustworthy, which connotes not only that he is reliable (as in our semantics), but that he trusts and respects others. One gains trust from Cherokees not only by reliably meeting one's obligations, but by a marked recognition of their right to carry on their own concerns with a minimum of intrusive supervision and curiosity, however friendly. The Cherokee ethos recognizes, as whites often fail to do, that even the most friendly and well-meaning personal interest can be exceedingly coercive. Conversely, the "mean" man, in Cherokee terms, is violative, intrusive, whether physically violent or not. Untrustworthy and untrusting, he is disrespectful of others' personal integrity, which he breaks in upon and destroys.

Cherokee Parent and Child

Cherokee parents, with their responsibility to inculcate respect for others in their young, often say that they are "strict" as parents, or that they approve of strictness with children. But the white who takes this statement at face value in the semantics of his own behavior will grossly misunderstand. Cherokees rarely engage in physical discipline and do not approve its constant use in others. Rather, their means are the soft voice, withdrawal, staring and other subtle intimidations. They engage in more explanation and less dogmatic assertion. This treatment is coupled with toleration for a wide latitude of childhood behavior up until about the age of seven. And Cherokee children are allowed to be present, if they choose, at all adult events, but are not coerced into attending. Someone has said that American Indians treat their children as little adults. I would say, rather, that Cherokees accord to their children, as human beings, a status and integrity which they accord to all other human beings, but which we whites, in contrast, accord only to adults and, indeed, often only to adults in our own class and caste.

How perplexing this behavior is to the local whites! A schoolteacher expressed confusion to me over the strange alternation between indifference and overindulgence in Cherokee mothers: they do not escort their children to school on the first day as do white mothers (nor do the children cry, as do white children), yet at an annual party for schoolchildren these Cherokee mothers serve the children first, then the men, and themselves last. But what appears contradictory to whites is the logical outcome of a different definition of childhood integrity. Conversely, the behavior of white parents must appear contradictory to Cherokees. Although Cherokee women are fully as concerned as whites about the well-being of their children in school, it is only white mothers who stand at the door each morning seeing their children off. Yet whipping is employed as a standard means of discipline by most white parents, and regarded by the school system as proper, to be used at the discretion of the teacher. It is certainly true that rural Oklahoma whites accord to their young some aspects of adult status much earlier than do urban middle-class American whites. Like frontier families, they involve their offspring early in the skills and responsibilities of subsistence farming and home maintenance. Yet it is precisely the delegation of greater and more complex responsibilities which marks increasing adulthood, or humanness, among whites. Cherokees, on the other hand, are less likely to delegate, more likely to wait for the child's voluntary participation in family activities.

Task responsibility is no criterion of adulthood, nor is willingness to be coerced into tasks a criterion of good behavior. Cherokees focus, rather, on the individual's social sensitivity to other members of the Cherokee community, and delay full adulthood until the psychological maturity of the thirties. The good man, after all, is by definition an adult.

A concern for justice pervades the play of Cherokee children, which appeared to me not only minimally violent, but also less querulous than that of middle-class white children. The notion, common in rural white Oklahoma, that children should settle their disputes themselves as an exercise in self-reliance is not shared by Cherokees. Consequently, a child will regularly seek the intervention of an older sibling or an adult if he feels that he or an ally has been misused.

The consequence of these Cherokee child-rearing procedures is that, up to the age of seven or eight, children are markedly trusting, although quiet. They do not demand attention, but respond openly when it is given. They engage in the playful teasing of their adult models. By their teens, however, Cherokee children are extremely shy, especially in the presence of whites. By then they have internalized the respect values of their society and have acquired an increasing awareness of the nature of Cherokee–white relations, yet lack the sense of personal security and competence which an adult Cherokee acquires through community interactions. Teenagers lower their eyes before strangers, stand so as to interpose an object between themselves and the stranger's view. Girls appear frightened, boys "cool" and withdrawn. Their behavior and feeling-tone are in marked contrast to that of the assertive white teenagers of the surrounding society.

The relevance of these behavioral modes, and the values that underlie them, to the responses of Cherokee students confronted with formal Western schooling is apparent. The more so since the public school appears to most Cherokees as a white institution, designed to enforce compulsory integration of Cherokee children with resident whites and with white society at large. It is my contention that the response of Cherokee children to public education is not only a product of such obvious burdens as the demand that they learn about a foreign society in a foreign language, but the product, as well, of a value conflict, in which they perceive as personal violations pedagogical practices which are regarded quite otherwise by most of the whites and the few assimilated half-breeds engaged in formal education.

Cherokees in School

The small rural schools of northeast Oklahoma are far less "total institutions" than most urban American public schools. Yet the quiet submissiveness of students in the predominantly Cherokee classroom is striking to the outside observer. Students from the first grade on whisper, either with the teacher's permission or without it, but do so with restraint. They are extremely obedient and cooperative in carrying out the teacher's instructions, and respond to the slightest suggestion from her regarding the next task to be undertaken. Their muted, whispered socializing, soft but not truly surreptitious, is not merely an indication that they know the white teacher will allow it. The youngest Cherokee schoolchild has already learned that such quiet interaction is the proper form of behavior around respected adults. His noise level in class is a transposition of behavior from such Cherokee contexts as the church, where he has been present during adult services from his earliest years.

Yet the persistence of this quiet submission and the interactional limitations it implies express more than an extension of Cherokee behavior to a foreign situation. They are a response to the specific nature of that situation, and to the quality of the Western interpersonal relations which are imposed within it. Only the very youngest Cherokee students seek out individual interactions with the teacher, volunteering their own creations and their own opinions. After the first two grades, Cherokees cease to volunteer anything of themselves to the teacher as teacher, unless that teacher is very unusual. I observed a first-grade Cherokee, in the process of learning English, bring to the teacher a list of words that she had independently copied from a speller, but such behavior does not usually occur in the later grades. On the other hand, white and halfblood students continue to engage in such voluntary interactions throughout their grade-school years. For example, I was present when first- and second-graders were reading a story about a rooster. In response to the teacher's question, almost all the students present raised their hands to indicate that they had roosters at home. But only two boys, both white, began to offer comments on their roosters, their other pets, how they made their dogs obey, and so forth. On another occasion, a white second-grader came to the teacher to announce that his book was torn, but that he intended to mend it with Scotch Tape. But only one Cherokee in the first four grades of the school which I observed intensively ever engaged in such behavior, volunteering, for example, news about an egg hunt at Eastertime. He was also the only Cherokee who communicated to the teacher unsolicited observations about his progress in learning, as "Miss X, I've done page fifty-six already," and "Miss X, I said 'magic' up here [in the reader]."

Cherokees do communicate with the teacher. They ask questions regarding assignments, although this practice becomes less and less frequent as they advance in grade and age. They may, again especially in the lower grades, ask the teacher for permission to engage in honored activities, as "Miss X, may I pass out the folders?" or "Miss X, may we have a board race?" (It is significant that these requests may be described as attempts to involve oneself in group activities, either as a leader or as a participant.) And Cherokee girls in the lower grades will ask to run errands for a female teacher or invite her to join them at jacks and hopscotch. But these are generally also group activities, and they are all "extracurricular." It is the desire to establish individual learner–teacher relationships which is so strikingly absent among Cherokees.

A similar contrast emerges in the kind of "tattling" engaged in by white and Cherokee students. It is whites who inform the teacher of errors in the behavior of other students: "Miss X, Soandso's got words in her folder!" or "Miss X, Soandso was on the road [at recess]." Significantly, only one Cherokee, the same third-grader referred to above, engaged in this kind of talebearing. In contrast, Cherokee "tattling" (for it is perceived as such by the teacher) consists almost exclusively of complaints regarding injustices suffered by individuals and their allies, largely as a result of rough physical treatment on the playground. Or it involves the request for assistance in childhood crises ("Miss X, Soandso wet his pants") which require adult care. Cherokee "tattles" are not designed to advance the student's standing in the teacher's eyes at the expense of other students. (They may, however, enhance one's social status in Cherokee eyes.) Rather, they are attempts to solicit teacher aid in reducing interpersonal violence and to engage her maternal attention.

But the major orientation of Cherokee students is, rather, toward their siblings, toward their extended kin and, in the age-stratified classrooms of Western schools, toward their peers. They appear much more solicitous of each other's needs than do whites of the same group: more often sharing readers than hogging them; more frequently assisting their seat mates in completing their assignments; sharpening pencils for each other; passing out blank paper to others; warning another that his fly is open; emptying the pencil sharpener; passing and sharing playthings (although there is some competition for access to scarce resources such as the crayon box). This largely cooperative and solicitous behavior is even more evident in the upper grades (fifth through eighth), where the Cherokee students' interactions with the teacher are even more reduced, and where more mature students are capable of more complex tasks. There a great deal of independent student behavior goes on with little or no reference to the teacher, much of it behavior which is essential to a well-functioning classroom. Assigned student jobs include checking books in and out of the library closet and cleaning up after school hours. More striking is the amount of cooperative effort devoted to such unassigned tasks as repairing each other's books, spraying for termites, boys assisting girls in opening windows and adjusting blinds, all without the teacher's overt recognition or approval. Observing the upper-grade classroom, I concluded that the students regard it as their own place, the locus of their own society, in which the teacher is an unwelcome intruder, introducing irrelevant demands. It is rather as though a group of mutinous sailors had agreed to the efficient manning of "their" ship, while ignoring the captain's navigational goals.

Cherokee students not only succeed in establishing within the classroom a social system exclusive of the teacher, they also attempt, in the lower grades, to restructure the social context of the learning process itself. In so doing, they substitute for the competitive emphasis of white schools a system of social learning which is peculiarly Cherokee. This is most strikingly exemplified in the reading sessions of the lower grades, in which students are asked to read aloud in turn, either seated at their desks or standing in the center of the room. It seems at first remarkable to the outside observer that students stand with great poise and self-assurance, rarely overcome with embarrassment even when scarcely able to recognize a single word on the page. But this lack of embarrassment is contingent upon a prompting practice which the other class members initiate the moment a student has been called upon to read, before he has even found his place in the book. Prompting continues throughout his turn whenever he displays the slightest hesitation over a word, so that the performance of a poor reader consists of a series of prompted words dutifully repeated after the participant "audience" (*cf.* Wolcott, 1967, p. 104).

An excerpt from my classroom observations will demonstrate the quality of these reading sessions.[7]

After lunch. "All right, let's finish reading our story. Bruce, I believe you were reading." Prompting begins immediately, while Bruce (2) looks for his place. "Go up there and show him the place, David." Wally (1) also tries to go up. "My goodness, there are a lot of Davids!" Wally gets back in his seat, grins sheepishly. Bruce reads poorly, wants to stop . . . David (W1) reads; a great prompter but a poor reader. Two stories are assigned for tomorrow; Lucille (M1) tells the name of one, with the assistance of Mike (1), who knows the word "parade," and Wally, with prompting, reads the name of the other, is proud.

A casual observer might assume that this prompting behavior is an imitation of the teacher's practice, for it is true that she too prompts the student reader. But she does so only when he is completely unable to proceed, and often she finds it necessary to intervene to restrain the prompting of the students. In fact, the occasional prompting of the teacher is merely a cover or a license under which students can proceed to carry out their own procedures. Teachers are unaware of either the roots or the meaning of this behavior. When I inquired of one lower-grade teacher, she replied, "It's something they developed by themselves, I didn't. You notice that I have to restrain them sometimes so they'll give a fellow a chance. But I feel it's good, it keeps them on their toes." Significant here is the teacher's perception of the activity as competitive, when in fact it is nothing of the sort. Clearly, this Cherokee reading session is modeled on Cherokee literacy learning in the church. The sociological meaning of these sessions has been totally redefined. They are no longer exercises in which an individual demonstrates his competence, gaining experience and

[7] In this and subsequent excerpts, the numeral following the student's name signifies his grade. White and mixed-blood students are indicated by "W" and "M" respectively; all others are fullbloods.

confidence in public presentation while the teacher evaluates and the pupil audience, sitting passively, learns by example. They are, rather, insofar as the students can make them, communal learning exercises in which individuals alternate between being supported by their peers and demonstrating their competence as efficiently supportive peer-group members. This profound modification results in a collective, rather than individual, demonstration of competence. In this Cherokee learning process, the practice of social competence in support of one's peers is of equal importance to the learning of English reading skills.

Teaching Matter and Method

Observing the phenomena described above, one is led to the conclusion that a major disruption has begun to occur in the Cherokee classroom, even in the lower grades. Students' refusal to relate to the teacher as individual learners and their attempts to restructure learning as a group activity indicate that they have already begun to view the teacher as at least irrelevant, if not actively hostile, to the schoolroom society. And this is true even of the superior teacher, who may be respected and valued as a person. As early as the third grade, Cherokee children are learning that they must abandon group prompting in the reading sessions and instead raise their hands for recognition as individuals. But the alienation of student from teacher is far more marked in the upper grades. This progressive alienation can be best understood by an examination of two aspects of their education—namely, the subject matter and the techniques of teaching employed.

In the rural public schools of northeast Oklahoma, general school operations may be flexible and informal, but subject matter is usually highly formalized, and its presentation is rigid, relying heavily on rote learning and evoking neither group nor individual creativity. As subject matter becomes more complex, its divergence from everyday life becomes more evident. Indeed, it must appear to students, and perhaps sometimes to teachers, as downright incomprehensible. This is critical in a society where neither whites nor Cherokees, other than school officials, place any value on the facts and operations learned in school. With the exception of sports, education is valued for its extrinsic rewards alone—that is, its role in obtaining adequate employment.

The following excerpts from classroom observations in the upper grades demonstrate not only the quality of the subject matter, but teaching methods as well.

"Okay, Fifth Grade, let's hustle and get this done. Were there any problems? Any of you get stuck? Let's wake up. Turn to page x. This is old stuff, but it's extremely important. How many of you think you have a pretty good grasp of the eight principal parts of speech? What you have to do is recognize them in everyday life."

"Get this in your head, conjunctions go to subordinating clauses like prepositions go to prepositional phrases," says the teacher, explaining the uses of "like" and "as" to Ruth, who got her sentence correct anyway.

Kay (8) is working on equations. She nods when the teacher speaks to her, in an embarrassed and annoyed fashion. "Some number, which we call *n*, divided by four is equal to seven. We know what the answer is, don't we? But we must be orderly about this and follow established procedure."

"The simple subject has to be a noun or a pronoun. This is a *rule*. Two and two is four, a simple subject has to be a noun or a pronoun. They're both rules."

A teacher rarely asks students for their own explanations or opinions, although he may ask them to recite "explanations" provided by the text. It is, rather, the teacher who tells, and his explanations are by no means always comprehensible to the students. Errors are wrong because they are wrong. Thus learning becomes the memorization, recitation and application of Rules, without regard to their necessity or relevance to the rest of life.

However, it should not be assumed that students have become uninterested in learning. That their curiosity and enthusiasm for many areas of formal learning have not yet been destroyed is clearly demonstrated whenever the teacher's control is withdrawn and learning becomes a voluntary process. The following is a description of the behavior of a first-grader, one of the poorest in performance, during a third-grade reading session in the same room.

Wally has gone over behind the reading circle, in front of one of the heaters (it's chilly today; teacher allows this occasional standing by the heaters). He talks to Gordon (3). . . . Now Wally comes to the teacher and asks her for something I can't hear; returns to Gordon, hangs over Mike (3), who is sitting next to Gordon. David (W1) has turned round in his seat to listen to the story. I see Wally silently lip-reading the page of the third-grade reader over Mike's shoulder! Jack (2) is over there now, too, talks a bit to Gordon. Now Jay (1) is standing behind Mike, following the reading. Jack leans on Gordon, to, with real intent interest. Gordon is laughing and joking quietly, but these two are not, they are reading. He tries to joke with Jay, but Jay too isn't interested.

On another occasion, the performance of a first-grader during an arithmetic "board race" revealed that he had learned third-grade multiplication from his older sister.

The following interaction involved one of the poorest English performers in the upper grades, operating, according to achievement tests, almost a full year behind her grade level in reading and language skills:

Recess. Rachel (7) comes over to me the minute class is dismissed and hands me a piece of paper. "Would you like to see how some Cherokee words are written?" She has neatly written them in Cherokee syllabary and in English. I show interest and ask her if she learned to write Cherokee at home or just from the primer. She says just from the primer.

After a particularly painful history lesson on the chapter "The Indians are Pushed Westward," during which the teacher repeatedly tried to evoke individual opinions from unresponding students, the teacher was called from the room.

The students talk softly. . . . No one leaves the history circle. The girls in the history circle are pointing at the map, talking Cherokee, but have developed a game, testing themselves; one of them casually writes "Louisville" on the board beside the map. One whispers loudly, "You're not supposed to tell the name of the state." The word "Gadsden" is written on the board.

Illustrative of student enthusiasm is an unusual situation regarding library books. Recent federal funds have enabled some schools to supply each classroom with an excellent library, and teachers often allow access to the library throughout the day, in addition to overnight checkout privileges. The surprising result of this free access is that the majority of students, especially beyond the third grade, are avid readers within this voluntary context, although over two-thirds of them show marked deficiencies in reading and English comprehension both in classroom performance and on standardized achievement tests. The following excerpt from my classroom observations illustrates not only the intensive library use, but the amount of intense, though exceedingly quiet, general activity characteristic of the upper-grade room. (There are eighteen students in the classroom, including one seriously retarded who is omitted from this record.)

After recess. There is a bit of whispering, but the kids settle down. Roy (M7) asks a few questions about when his papers will be graded. Ernest (M5) works in his notebook, the eighth-graders read, play with books. Jake (5) is writing the math assignment. Felix (W5) gets a book from the library. Roy stares into space, Jane (5) is reading, Kathy (5) is organizing her books. Jake and Roy read comic books [these "educational comics" are part of the library collection]; Gene (M5) and Felix are conferring over a book . . . Wayne (8) is reading a library book, his partner is playing with some cards. The girls in back are whispering. Martha (7) and Patricia (7) go to the library for books.

Now the two 8s, Wayne and Walt, have traded books; Walt is fooling with his clipboard. Walt whispers to Wayne, who is reading a green library book. The comic-book readers, Roy and Jake, are totally absorbed. Now Walt passes a note. . . . Jane and Kathy are reading, absorbed. Now Walt passes over a book. Ernest is restless. Walt now gets Wayne's attention, he's writing another note. The girls behind are writing one. Steve (5) seems to be reading, but I can't see. Rachel (7) is writing (a note?) and her neighbor is reading.

10:45. The green book is returned to the library closet via Kathy's desk: she is in charge of checkout and return. A girl from the rear gets a library book, Wayne takes out another in the green science series: *Flowers*. He and Walt look at it. They give the cards to Kathy as they pass. Walt reads a note, grins, writes, turns around and passes it. He confers with Martha. The noise level rises. Now Martha is openly talking with him, while he reads the flower book. Wayne gets another on fishes in the same series from the library. Ernest starts to read a big red library book. Beatrice (6) comes to get a piece of paper. The eighth-grade boys look at the fish book, the comic-book readers are still intent and quiet. Felix goes to the library. Roy takes his comic book to the library, sits doing nothing, talks a bit to Jake.

Martha gets some paper. Roy is now reading Jake's comic book, Jake does nothing. Kathy gets some paper. The 8s are involved in their science book. Teacher is called to the phone.

Now the teacher returns and helps Kay (8) at her desk. Wayne shows Jake some sharks in his fish book. Most of the whispering is from the rear of the room, Felix and Gene and the girls, but right now the girls are quiet. Felix and Ernest return their library books. Jake and Jane are conferring at the bulletin board. Teacher calls Steve and Felix from the library; they have been there too long. Felix is now checking out a library book. Steve is hunched over his workbook. Wayne peeks at his fish book, then returns to his math book. Roy has given up on participating in the math lesson which has just started, and is reading his comic book, but has his math book open.

This chronological segment covered about one hour. Throughout the period, except for the brief moment noted, the teacher was present in the room, working with other students. On another occasion I recorded: "Of the sixteen students in the room at the moment, nine are reading library books." After observing this phenomenon for several days, I commented in my notes:

The library usage is interesting: all the interest shown, especially in science by the boys, is completely ignored by the teacher, not capitalized upon. But then, he'd probably kill it if he touched it. These kids are using books to fill their boredom in the classroom situation. At least some of them seem to have become serious readers: perhaps this is a good way to teach kids to value books and not have the negative label of school placed upon them!

But more significant than rote learning in determining Cherokee student responses are the teacher's restructuring of the social context of learning, and his mode of interaction with individual students. Less parentally solicitous of their pupils, upper-grade teachers define them more and more as task-responsible adults and, with the exception of athletics, school activities are structured to minimize cooperative behavior among peers. Students are more often and more severely discouraged from sharing their learning problems with each other. Rather, they are expected to perform individually, publicly, without outside assistance or emotional support. They are expected, indeed, to compete and to inviduously compare, to judge and be judged not on the basis of their total personalities, nor their sensitivity to others' feelings, but on the basis of their ability to perform allotted tasks in allotted periods of time. Older students experience a loss of autonomy as the teacher assumes an ever more authoritarian role, engaging in more ordering, direct questioning and testing, all of which demand an individual response. Consequently, interactions with peers are increasingly divorced from the formal learning sanctioned by the teacher's supervision. Thus, to a seventh-grade Cherokee the teacher says:

"Now, Rachel, I want you to keep one thing straight: keep your mouth shut, but when you have a question, ask me. You don't even have to raise your hand, just ask me. But for the last six months you have to talk to Patricia. I appreciate Patricia's intelligence, but if I wanted to know something from her I'd ask her. I expect you to at least show me the respect due me as your teacher and answer the questions I ask you." Then he sends her to the board. She works rapidly, her answer is wrong, she is clearly very angry, though silent.

Not only is task responsibility the key to adulthood in the white teacher's eyes; he expects it to be engaged in with enthusiasm. A science lesson illustrates the teacher's attempt to elicit positive emotional responses from students, on the premise that learning must be fun:

He tells them to look at the thermometer at the store during study hall. Then they can convert from Fahrenheit to Centigrade. "Isn't that right? this is kind of fun, isn't it?" No answer. "Huh?" No answer. "It's gonna be a lot of fun."

Should the student fail to comply with these demands, powerful psychological and physical sanctions are employed against him. He is subjected to loud public verbal abuse, derogating not only his classroom performance but his general character, appearance and prospects. This is excessively shaming to a Cherokee. And, as a last resort, the Oklahoma teacher may employ the paddle, engaging in the final physical violation of the Cherokee child.

These negative sanctions can be seen in operation in the following extended interaction between a white male teacher and a fifth-grade fullblood boy.

A math lesson has been under way for several minutes. Jake is giving an answer: "Forty-three and six hundred tenths." "Come to the board. You sound like Gene sounded yesterday." Beatrice (6) comes to get paper out of the teacher's desk, faces me and stares at me without smiling. The room is stone quiet. Jake, at the board, can't write 43 and 6 one-hundredths. "Do you study at night?" "Sometimes." "You really study at night? How much? Let's be a little more specific." "Two hours." "Two hours a day, a month, a year, a week?" Jake nods at "week." "Would you like to know what happens to people who don't study? You really want to know? 'Cause I can't make you study. You always bring your homework in like this, and most of it's wrong." He calls Rosemary (5) to the board, making Jake stay there. She does the problem of writing the number in decimals, correctly. Jake's face is sullen. But he writes a number correctly now. "Now you've got it correct. Do you want me to tell you why? Because you watched Rosemary and your mind was thinking. That just shows you what a little study can do for you." But he is given another and can't do it.

"You may take your seat, Jake. I'm very disappointed in you. You haven't studied. No, Jake, I'll tell you what I'm going to do. [Teacher's voice becomes more markedly Southern in accent.] If you don't learn this by Friday, I'm gonna give you ten licks. Because I'm mad. I've been good to you, too good. But now the old board is gonna talk. I'll tell you why I'm mad. One of these days, I'm gonna see a boy who's going to Johnson City to get his commodities from Welfare because he's too stupid to get a job. I don't want that to happen to you. You're not stupid, you're sharp. You have a good mind. That's why I'm mad. You better shape up."

Jake is sitting pressing his fingers in his eyes to try to keep from crying. Only an occasional soft sniff is heard. No one has the discourtesy to look at him. All is silence, except for the teacher's lecture.

"I remember a little boy up at [a nearby grade school] in the third grade who was smart. And in the fifth grade, what happened to that boy? It hurts my pride, because this is the first year you've ever had me. Those tears that you're shedding, they don't mean one thing to me. You're gonna come in at noon today and at recess, and tomorrow. If Alfred and Rosemary can do it, you can, too." . . .

"Jake, I'm gonna hang with you again, because something's on my mind." He calls on him for two answers. Jake gets two right, through choked voice. They aren't decimals but some sort of math problems. "Did you have help on these?" (No.) "Then is it just decimals that are giving you problems?" Jake's hands go to his eyes again. Teacher keeps asking Jake for more answers. He gets all right, once off the decimals. "Was this just carelessness, from working too fast," asks the teacher in regard to the decimal problems, "or something you've been doing wrong and didn't know you were doing wrong?" Mumbled: "Carelessness."

"How many got all the answers right?" Alfred's hand goes up. He asks about the others. Rosemary missed six out of twenty-four. "Jake, I want you in here immediately after lunch. You can mess around until I leave the cafeteria, then I want you here." Alfred is called to the board. He is good at math, but nervous, stony-faced. "That's very good, Alfred, very good." He returns to his seat, expressionless. Felix (W5) is called. He can't write 5 and 615 ten-millionths (neither could I). He gets it finally, but the answer is wrong for the problem he had to do. "Does anyone see a mistake?" No one sees his borrowing error. Kathy (5) is called on, does the problem. Rosemary is called, gets one right.

It's lunchtime, the other students in the lower grades can be heard leaving. Roy (M7) starts to gather his books, so does Kathy. No one else makes a move. Teacher is still at the board. No one can read the answer to Rosemary's problem, including Rosemary: 5.0329875. Rosemary, called on over and over again, begins making wild guesses, shakes her head in confusion. "Can't you just say five and three hundred . . . ?" the teacher asks in desperation. She tries but can't even repeat the numbers in the right order. Shaking her head, she's completely disoriented by now. He gives her a number to write and read. She can't read that either: 643,540. Alfred is called on, reads it correctly, finally. "How many of you agree with Alfred? How would you read it, Gene?" He reads it incorrectly. Jake is pointing his finger at the places, trying to figure it out. "How many decimal places do we have? Alfred was right, wasn't he?" He makes Alfred repeat it, Rosemary repeat it (she stumbles but gets it almost right), and Jake, who reads it correctly.

The class is excused for lunch. Teacher retains Jake. He begins to talk to him. "Now, Jake, you're a good friend of mine, but . . . When your teacher can't help you, maybe the 'board of education' can. You know what the 'board of education' is? It's that little ole cherry-wood paddle, isn't it? You're a smart boy, Jake, and a friend of mine. You're got a great personality. You may not be the best-looking boy in the world, but you're a long way from being ugly. But you're so hardheaded. You're so hardheaded sometimes, I think there ain't a bull as hardheaded as you are sometimes. I'm not bawling you out now, I'm just talking to you. I know what the trouble is, I bet. Do you have some girlfriends? . . . I'll work with you twenty-four hours a day, Jake. If you come to my house at three o'clock in the morning, I'll work with you, though that shouldn't be necessary. Now, with decimals . . ." And he begins to discuss the math.

If the treatment recorded above seems unpleasant to a white student, it is excruciating for a Cherokee. Admittedly, the instance is extreme even for the particular classroom under observation.

Yet in its extremity it demonstrates some rather characteristic modes of interaction by white Oklahomans, especially in super-ordinate–subordinate relationships, and will serve to clarify the extreme responses of Cherokee students to be described later. Here the teacher has trespassed upon the Cherokee self in several ways (and in regard to several students). He has exposed and shamed the fifth-grader by derogatory remarks about his academic performance, his intelligence and his appearance. He has held him up, over an extended period, for public scrutiny by his peer group. He has insisted repeatedly on verbal responses from the boy, indeed has forced a confession from him. (Likewise, he has forced the student's embarrassed peers into competitive action against him.) And he has threatened him with physical punishment and a low-status future. Nor has he given cognizance to the meaning of the boy's tears, and a Cherokee boy of eleven does not cry easily. This coercive treatment is intolerable to a Cherokee, and everyone in the room but the teacher knows it.

Caught in a compulsory net of meaningless learning and forced response, older Cherokee students are at the same time increasingly aware of the impingement of adult values on their schoolroom life. For the community at large, school officials and even their parents agree on the necessity of a high-school diploma for successful adult life in modern American society (although parents may be more skeptical of its value than school officials). Under great pressure to achieve academic success, students find that such success is obtainable, for most, only through the sacrifice of their personal integrity. What appears, on the part of the students, to be indifference in the face of these demands is rather their continuing attempt to preserve their integrity as Cherokees.

Corporal Punishment: A Major Value Conflict

I have said that Cherokees strongly disapprove of physical violence, except under special and rare circumstances. The approved use of corporal punishment within the school systems of northeast Oklahoma constitutes, therefore, a point of extreme conflict in values between Cherokees and whites, which highlights the more subtle conflicts already outlined. It is not easy to obtain firsthand observations on this practice, as it is not a daily occurrence, and most teachers probably tend to abstain from the practice in the presence of an outside observer to whom they impute a more "progressive" attitude. Yet they do not deny engaging in it on occasion. However, complementary data on corporal punishment were obtained from another source—namely, interviews of Cherokee parents conducted in several rural communities. Most of the children of these parents have had a relatively stable history of attendance at one or more of five public schools within the districts surveyed. Three of these public schools are rural, and two are located in small towns, one of the latter being consolidated with a high school. In addition, a few have attended a local religious boarding school, public schools in neighboring counties, or federal boarding schools.

In response to the questionnaire item "Have the children ever been punished or whipped in school? Why?," few parents mentioned any other form of punishment, although some referred to such means as extra homework. This must indicate that students do not find such other means so unbearable; I believe that their parents share this view. Such punishments are more easily seen as merely additional requirements to make up learning deficits, whether they are so in fact or not. Interviews reveal a wide variance in the frequency of whipping. One small rural school did not engage in it at all; one town school had a reputation for frequent whippings. Where teaching standards are lax and little actual instruction is given, physical discipline is used little or not at all. Where there is more concern with academic standards, it is more common. Even within a given school individual teachers, of course, vary greatly, and "mean" teachers are widely known by name as whippers throughout the Cherokee community.

The most common means of physical discipline (and probably the most approved by school officials) is the wooden paddle, but other means are employed: rapping palms or knuckles with a switch or stick, and blows of the bare hand to the child's face. Among English-speaking Cherokees, "whipping" is a general term designating all such forms of corporal punishment, and it is used as such in the following discussion. Questionnaire responses were obtained covering 170 children, from Head Start preschoolers to twelfth-graders. Interviews were conducted in Cherokee by a resident Cherokee mother and recorded by her in English.[8] In quoting the statements of respondents below, I have made a few alterations, mostly in matters of number and tense, but have tried to preserve in large measure the quality of the interviewer's original transcription. The English, although largely hers rather than the respondents', is at least more accurate in tone than my retranslation would be.

It must be emphasized that these data reflect parental knowledge and parental perceptions of corporal punishment, not actual events *per se*. Admittedly, I have no certain evidence of the validity of these reports as descriptive knowledge. I am, however, inclined to accord them such validity because of the generally detailed understanding of school events displayed by Cherokee mothers, which reflects a high amount of feedback between Cherokee child and parent, and because the reports of Cherokee parents accord with what I observed and learned myself, both in school and in discussions with several teachers and Cherokees (including one fullblood teacher) with whom I established rapport. Yet it is, after all, perceptions that we are here concerned with. The fact that large numbers of Cherokee children experience corporal punishment in school is of no import except in the context of Cherokee values, as a phenomenon evoking student resentment and deep parental concern. The statements of parents are as important as the numerical data. Further, I must assume that parental statements are a reliable guide to the feelings of the children as well. Students cannot be assumed, anywhere, to report accurately at all times the causes of punishment. What we can more safely assume is that they report accurately their sense of grievance, whatever its basis in fact.

Of the total 170 students, seventy-four, or over 43 percent,

[8] I am deeply indebted to Mrs. Lucille Proctor for her gifted and dedicated interviewing in a situation of great difficulty. Without her collaboration, this study would not have been possible.

had experienced whipping in school. Of this number, half (thirty-seven) had had experiences which were perceived by the parent as to some degree unjust. Admittedly, it is not always easy to classify parental responses in this regard, and I have had to rely on the tone of recorded statements. An example is the following: "Dean has been punished and whipped before. He failed to take the book from the locker, and also he got whipped because he had worked on workbook while the recess. The teacher punished him. Just for that." About two-thirds of these whippings (twenty-two) were for failure to pass a test, or related behavior: the student couldn't get his work done on time, didn't write his name on his homework, etc. Whipping for scholastic failures occurred as early as the third grade.

Eight of these thirty-seven whippings are described as due to inability to understand the teacher. It is significant, in this bilingual context, that all but one of those for which a grade attribution is given (five) occurred in the first or second grade, the last occurring in the sixth grade. Many Cherokee mothers recognize the especially difficult position of their non-English-speaking children on entering school. Said one, "About these little children when they went in first day in school. The teacher is really getting onto these little ones. Because these little ones didn't understand any English, so the teacher whipped them and punished. They don't teach what they should. I guess because it's Cherokee Indians."

Another mother offered a solution to the problem of non-English-speaking entering students: "I would like to see the Cherokee Indian teacher to be with the white woman teacher when these primary [children] start to school, till they are not afraid around the white teacher. Why I am saying this, I have known lots time past these little ones when they started to school. The teachers are really mean to them just because these little ones don't understand what the teacher said. So when they are old enough they won't [be] afraid to be around the white teacher."

Other cases within this category are reported as the result of trivial infractions undeserving of severe discipline or vaguely referred to as the result of the teacher's meanness. Also included are an unjust accusation of theft, a student unjustly singled out for misbehavior on the school bus, a student who worked on his workbook during recess (quoted above) and a small boy who refused to wear a girl's dress in the school play. Reporting on the experience of her four-year-old daughter in a summer Head Start program, a mother said, "She quit before she finished. 'Cause she got whipped too much from the teacher. She was afraid to go back to school. The teacher don't trust her like she should. She turned around one time in her class. The teacher started [to] whip her with her hand. She slapped her face and neck. Then she was afraid to go back to school. She went just two weeks. Then she was afraid to go back to school, so she quit." This excerpt is notable for the clarity with which it expresses the Cherokee concepts of childhood autonomy and of trust. It was the child, not the mother, who made the decision not to return to school—because she was not "trusted."

Thus, 22 percent of the total student sample has received at least one whipping viewed by the parents as unjust. Leaving aside those mixed and borderline cases in which the reasons for whipping were unclear or multiple, a little over 14 percent of the students (twenty-four of 170) have received whippings which were regarded by their parents as to some degree deserved. It is surely significant that these transgressions include talking and whispering in class (seven), which may well be regarded as disrespectful by Cherokees, and mistreatment of another student (seven). These two categories comprise well over half of the cases of deserved whippings. That students may concur in the justice of their punishments under such conditions is illustrated by this statement: "Winfield has been punished and whipped . . . when he was in public school, and he said it was his own fault. He was fighting with the schoolchildren, so his teacher punished him." Also reported without parental objection were playing in class (three), running off from school (two), being late for class, and saying a nasty word.

Although corporal punishment is certainly only one of many factors discouraging the Cherokee student from high performance and long continuance in school, it is seen by both parents and students as a cause for dropping out. One mother said, "When these schoolchildren get failed [on] the test, they get whipped by the teacher. That's why there is a lot [of] Cherokees are afraid to go to school. The way the teacher treat them. That's what my brother happened when he quit [going] to school. He dropped out tenth grade. He got whipped from a teacher. He just failing a test. So he said, 'The teacher is really rough on me. I am going to quit school and I think Dad needs me more than [to] get whipping in school.' "

Another mother said of her daughter, recently dropped out after completing the eleventh grade, "She drop out because her teacher didn't like her. Her teacher fought with her. The reason is, she was late to be in her classroom, so when she come in the teacher grabbed her and she started [to] whip and slap her face with [her] hands. So she got mad and quit school. She said, 'If the teacher was good, then I guess I would be graduated, too, like my sister did.' " And a teenage girl present during an interview remarked, "I never [have been] punished or whipped in school, ever since I had to go to school. If they do, I would quit going to school. I won't go back if they do."

Two emotions emerge, I believe, from the extended statements of Cherokees regarding corporal punishment in school. One is an expression of fear, fear of the student facing the white teacher, who is known to include this practice within his pedagogical repertoire, and fear of the mother for her child. The latter fear is expressed by a mother speculating regarding the school to which her children were being transferred in the fall:

All I'm waiting [for] is what they're doing in Warrior [rural school]. Some say they don't like X's wife. One man told me they whipped a little first grade boy who didn't understand.

The other emotion marked in these interviews in which Cherokee spoke to Cherokee, but rarely expressed to whites, is one of grievance over continuing injustice. Many complain merely of the partiality or arbitrariness of teachers in meting out punishment— that is, of injustice in their choice of one student victim over another. For example: "Everett has been punished and whipped in school last year. Just because he was talking in his class with other boys, so when the teacher is ready to whip the boys he picked on just two boys, Everett and one other boy. And the rest of 'em, they didn't get whipped."

But beyond this is a more general sense of grievance over the treatment that students receive as Cherokees. Somehow the practices of white teachers seem far from the Cherokees' conception of what school ought to be, and the treatment which their children receive there merges in the minds of many parents with a broader conviction that they are victims of discrimination in a white society. Many mothers, some of whom have been quoted above, gave poignant expression to this conviction. Said one, "There are a lot [of] teachers here in school, they are really rough for these Cherokee People. And I wish I could see these teachers to love these Cherokee children just same alike they love the White children."

In summary, Cherokee parents disapprove, except in rare circumstances, of the infliction of corporal punishment upon children, as they disapprove of physical violence among adults. Because the school persists in employing this mode of discipline, it alienates Cherokee parents and induces a view of the white teacher as "untrusting" and "mean." Corporal punishment is thus representative of a number of white interactional modes which encourage the Cherokee student to withdraw from formal education, either emotionally, by the subtle means of noncooperation and feigned indifference, or, should these tactics prove inadequate for psychic self-preservation, then by physically leaving the school.

The Integrity of the Cherokee Student

How do Cherokee students maintain their self-respect and the respect of their peers, confronted as they are with the necessity of functioning, as individuals and as a peer group, within the structure of a Western institution whose goals and modes of social control are not only in conflict with their own, but compulsorily imposed? The evolution of their means is a slow process of adaptation of general Cherokee behavior patterns to the specific class-room situation. Maturing students, caught at the center of this cross-cultural conflict, are engaged simultaneously in learning on two fronts. On the one hand, they are acquiring from their own community an understanding of appropriate Cherokee conduct, which includes both an increasingly acute awareness of those social behaviors defined as violative and the means by which Cherokees avoid and defend against such intrusions. That is, they are learning to be Cherokees. On the other hand, they are discovering as they advance in the school system the degree to which that system is offensive to their Cherokee integrity. For educators are encouraged to be intrusive, as we have seen. Consequently, student responses are most marked in the higher grades and in high school, where fully socialized Cherokees engage in evolved, elaborated responses, arising out of long years of learning about themselves and the educational system, and continual attempts to resolve or adapt to the conflict between the two.

Yet it must be recognized that teachers too attempt resolutions of this cross-cultural conflict. Their behavior undergoes modifications, as does that of students. Unfortunately, an upper-grade or high-school teacher with an average amount of aggressive desire to evoke appropriate student reactions, and with a normal white threshold of discomfort in the face of disapproving silence, will usually undergo changes in the direction of greater, rather than less, violation (in Cherokee terms) as his sense of failure and rejection grows. Long-standing teacher–student confrontations thus may become classic examples of Batesonian schismogenesis. (cf, Bateson, 1935).[9]

Subjected to direct questioning by the teacher, older Cherokee students give minimal verbal replies. Answers are almost invari-

---

[9] As Fuchs (1966, p. 162) has remarked, "We may ask, 'What of the other side of the coin?' What about those teachers thrust into situations where children with difficult behavior patterns and antagonistic attitudes confront the teacher with demeanor and deference patterns that attack *their* selves? We recognize that this happens and in some cases may indeed be the precipitating factor in the kinds of negative teacher behavior our informants described." An evolution of teacher attitudes closely similar to what I observed in Oklahoma is recorded in Kendall, 1964, a firsthand account of one teacher's experiences with Los Angeles Negro pupils.

ably so mumbled that an observer sitting within a few feet of the interrogated student cannot hear his reply.

Roy (M7) is called on next; he answers with a ruler in his mouth but does well. Patricia (6), when called on, mumbles and misses several. "Martha, give us the contractions on test number four. You didn't do it? Did you try to do it? Did you have time to do it? What?" She may be mumbling, but I can't hear a word. Rachel (7) is called on; she mutters so you couldn't understand her unless you had the book to follow; but she has them all right.

But the majority of the teacher's interrogations may receive no reply whatsoever (*cf.* Wax, Wax and Dumont, 1964, Chap. 6). Two classes of events are involved. First, the least cooperative students pursue a consistent policy of nonresponse, rarely answering even those questions directly pertaining to materials on which they are prepared. These tend to be the most traditional full-bloods, least oriented toward achievement in white society. Thus:

Teacher asks Martha (7) which of the ones she missed were not covered yet. She looks down at her book and says nothing. He asks, "Did you miss any in thirteen, fourteen, fifteen?" She mutters, "Fifteen." He calls on Martha to read. She doesn't move a muscle. "Okay, Patricia."

Secondly, the majority of students employ mumbling or quiet recitation in answering questions directly concerning assignments, but refuse to answer that large class of rhetorical questions, both academic and nonacademic, with which the despairing teacher fills the silence of the classroom, but which students regard as irrelevant. Likewise, they refuse to answer questions which seem to them probings of their inner emotional privacy.

Roy (M7) is asked a question: "Do you think this is going to help you? Do you think you're going to do it the way I showed you?" He leans back in his chair and says nothing. Teacher: "All right." Roy grins at Jake.

"Kay, did you have any trouble identifying your participial phrases? Walt, did you have any trouble with this assignment? Did you catch the idea, Kay, that the whole phrase may be considered as an adjective? Do you feel that this assignment was easy?" There is no verbal response to this outpouring. He then tells them what to study. . . .

"How many of you went to the quarterly meeting yesterday? At church?" Very few raise their hands (although most were probably present). "Was there plenty to eat? Tell me what they had to eat, Patricia." No answer. "What kind of bread did they have? Did they have bean bread? Evidently you didn't eat any bread. Were you there, Walt? Beatrice? Goodness gracious!"

This sounds at times like a conspiracy, but it is not exactly that. Rather, each student has come to perceive which interrogations he must honor in order to maintain the minimal academic status acceptable to him, and to avoid open conflict with white authority. In the Cherokee classroom, in contrast to the Sioux classroom described by Wax, Wax and Dumont (1964) or the Kwakiutl classroom described by Wolcott (1967), there is very little attempt by students to control the behavior of their peers.

Nor will Cherokee students reward the teacher's attempt to solicit enthusiasm for school and learning. I was present at a dramatic demonstration of this refusal:

Jake (5) is mopping the cafeteria under the teacher's supervision. Teacher asks him if it's fun. He says, "No, it's work." But later, not long afterward, teacher has gone off, and Jake is still mopping, now in the kitchen. The white cook engages him in conversation as he works, about how different it is today, on cleanup day, than school on most days. He volunteers, "And more fun too."

Even the teacher's attempts at humor, or humorous incidents involving the teacher, draw no response from the Cherokee once he perceives that laughter would imply approval of the teacher. Humor is manipulative; laughter is the dropping of one's defenses. Yet there is much quiet humor between students throughout the school day, some of it even at the expense of the teacher.

"A fraction is like an overweight woman; it is always trying to be reduced." Kathy (5) smiles, but no one else does.

"How many told your parents of the pie supper? How many are sure your parents are coming?" Most raise their hands. He makes a joke: "How many are sure their cousins, aunts, uncles, grandparents are coming?" No one laughs.

The teacher writes a problem on the board . . . "What are you going to borrow? Borrow one? Is it hitting you now?" Gene (M5) nods. As the teacher works at the board, the "Atlas of Human Anatomy" wall chart hanging on a nail above him begins to fall on his head. Not a soul laughs.

Only in one class, led by a sensitive and gentle mixed-blood teacher, did I observe Cherokees above the fifth grade laughing at the teacher's jokes.

Another means of evading the teacher's intrusions is nodding. This appears to be a minimal recognition of the teacher's existence and the sound of his voice. But the observer feels that even this gesture is distasteful to students, being a compromise between total emotional honesty and the pressures of the situation. Thus:

The teacher discusses the seventh-graders' assignment. He looks at Martha (7) as he speaks; she nods ever so slightly. She has her workbook out.

And:

Kay (8) isn't listening to the teacher, but nods when he looks at her. To Wayne (8), the teacher says, "All you need is a little bit more confidence." The teacher looks at Kay, but she turns away and looks in her book when she doesn't want to give a sociable answer.

Thus Cherokee students refuse, beyond a certain point, to engage in that common student pretense of comprehension in order to avoid the teacher's attentions. There is a fine line drawn here: while nodding and raising hands are approved when used in moderation, verbal hypocrisy or even the too frequent use of these gestures is frowned upon. Cherokees, in other words, draw the line of permissible compromise at a different locus than do white students (whose classroom ethnography may be found in Jules Henry, 1963, and John Holt, 1964). Consequently, one of the most striking differences between white and Cherokee students is the readiness of the latter to admit that they do not know. For example:

Andrew (5) reads; he's hard to understand. He is called to the board, works a problem, gets "4 hours, 91 minutes and 6 seconds." The teacher reads it off. "Is this your answer?" Andrew shrugs his shoulders and says, "I don't know."

Walt (8), daydreaming, is called upon, looks at his book. Wayne (8) has been following, though. "Is this the way you would do it, Walt?" "I don't know," he mouths, embarrassed. "Well, that's an honest answer. Go to the board, please." Walt gets almost all the way through the problem and doesn't know what to do next. Patricia (6) is called to the board to show him what he did wrong and works efficiently, completing the problem. Walt waggles his head around when asked if he understands.

The most extreme Cherokee responses of defensive withdrawal occur when teacher intrusiveness is directed toward a single individual or a small group as he questions and examines those in close physical proximity to him. In these awkward situations, when a student stands alone at the board or at the teacher's desk, or when a small recitation group is drawn up around the teacher, the total-body responses of adult Cherokees to highly threatening interpersonal behavior are vividly enacted in the classroom. The incidence of nervous gestures, such as rocking in the chair, tapping of hands and playing with pencils, and of nervous coughs seems higher than among white students subjected to intense and persistent attentions. So is lowering of the eyes to avoid the direct gaze of the teacher.

"Okay, Beatrice, you may bring up your workbook." Teacher goes over her work at his desk. She sits on the edge of Roy's desk; when the teacher looks at her, or when he asks her to recite, she nervously strikes her palms against the edge of the desk. But when he isn't directing his attention at her, she's calm.

But even more striking is this:

"Okay, Seventh Grade. Let's bring our chairs up to the front of the room." There are four seventh-graders: Roy, a mixed-blood, Martha,

Rachel and Patricia. All except Roy are not really facing the teacher; their chairs are, *but their bodies are twisted away*. Rachel and Roy read, mumbling, halting . . . As the teacher talks, he looks at the students. Rachel bows her head before his gaze. Patricia nods at a question, turning and dropping her head. Patricia reads with her head bent, facing the blackboard, rushing through the material until asked to slow down. Martha reads now very softly; she doesn't answer a question asked her.

This behavior is observed as early as the fifth grade, and becomes near-universal by the seventh and eighth.

"Okay, Seventh Grade, take your chairs up to the front." The teacher asks Rachel for correct answers. She has a slight private smile on her face, is a bit self-conscious, sticks her tongue out, but does okay. Martha has her back turned almost fully to the teacher, though her chair is facing him.

"How many of you missed number four?" Gene's (M5) hand is up. Rosemary (5) sits with her body turned away from the teacher. She is following proceedings, though, and seems to have learned to look at the teacher to pretend interest.

Silence, mumbling, nodding, avoidance of eye contact, and turning the body away are standard adult Cherokee defensive behaviors which are employed by Cherokee young people in the classroom in an attempt to preserve their psychic privacy from the intrusions of teachers. In the short-run context of the classroom, these means appear successful. They do succeed at any given moment in reducing the amount and duration of teacher attention focused upon any one student. They do demonstrate to the student and to his peers that he is not totally submissive to the foreign authority of the school system, that he retains within him an autonomous and private core.

But these defenses are also communications. They are, indeed, very loud and persistent communications. But they are unheard. Oklahoma white teachers, by and large, do not understand what their Cherokee students are saying and do not modify their behavior accordingly. On the contrary, their increasing exasperation and helplessness more often results in more and more extreme white behavior—that is, in more extreme violations of the Cherokee self.

There is not space here to discuss why the white teacher cannot hear the Cherokee student, how the total social, economic and political context decrees that he must not, and how white society provides the teacher with a complex mythology by which to misinterpret his own perceptions. Many teachers do see Cherokee students as different from whites, but most see that difference as a Cherokee "problem" of "shyness." The conclusion must be that these Cherokee means of self-defense are, in the long run, no solution at all. Day after day, year after year, students must still subject themselves to the school's attempts at intrusion and control, must prepare and present their defenses. The psychic strain of this demand soon grows intolerable. Unable to indulge either his natural curiosity or his social desire for education as a means to advancement, the average Cherokee must feel, by the eighth grade, thoroughly exhausted. Other pressures and temptations mount: financial needs, increasing awareness of his educational handicap and his socioeconomic inferiority, increasing social, sexual and marital involvements outside the classroom. It is not surprising, then, that most Cherokees abandon the fruitless and painful experience soon after they are legally able to do so. Total withdrawal from the school system is the final act in defense of Cherokee feelings of integrity. The skepticism of these students about the value of education must be great. And their general assessment of the emotional costs of future ventures into white society is not hard to imagine.

BIBLIOGRAPHY

Bateson, Gregory, "Culture Contact and Schismogenesis," *Man,* Vol. 35 (1935), pp. 178-83.
Fuchs, Estelle, *Pickets at the Gates.* New York: Free Press, 1966.
Henry, Jules, *Culture against Man.* New York: Random House, 1963.
Holt, John, *How Children Fail.* New York: Dell, 1964.

Kendall, Robert, *White Teacher in a Black School.* Chicago: Henry Regnery, 1964.

Riessman, Frank, *The Culturally Deprived Child.* New York: Harper and Row, 1962.

Roach, Jack L., and O. R. Gursslin, "An Evaluation of the Concept 'Culture of Poverty,' " *Social Forces,* Vol. 45 (1967), pp. 383-92.

Thomas, Robert K., *The Origin and Development of the Redbird Smith Movement,* unpublished M.A. thesis, Department of Anthropology, University of Arizona, 1954.

Underwood, J. Ross, *An Investigation of Education Opportunity for the Indian in Northeastern Oklahoma,* unpublished Ph.D. dissertation, School of Education, University of Oklahoma, 1966.

Wahrhaftig, Albert, *The Tribal Cherokee Population of Eastern Oklahoma: Report of a Demographic Survey of Cherokee Settlements in the Cherokee Nation* (mimeographed). Carnegie Cross-cultural Education Project, University of Chicago, 1965.

————, *Social and Economic Characteristics of the Cherokee Population of Eastern Oklahoma: Report of a Survey of Four Cherokee Settlements in the Cherokee Nation* (mimeographed). Carnegie Cross-cultural Education Project, University of Chicago, 1965.

————, "Community and the Caretakers," *New University Thought,* Vol. 4 (1966), pp. 54-76.

Wax, Murray L., Rosalie H. Wax and Robert V. Dumont, *Formal Education in an American Indian Community,* Monograph No. 1, Society for the Study of Social Problems, 1964.

Wolcott, Harry F., *A Kwakiutl Village and Its School.* New York: Holt, Rinehart and Winston, 1967.

THE DANISH *FRISKOLER* AND COMMUNITY CONTROL

ESTELLE FUCHS

The most striking point raised by the papers in this volume is that the problems of the poor, and of the racial and ethnic minorities in America, cannot be understood without reference to the entire structure of American society. Any discussion of the poor or of a "culture of poverty" is deficient if it does not take into account the fact that the behavior of peoples is inextricably bound up with their status in American society. Therefore, any change made by minority groups must be achieved through a change in the whole social framework; it cannot be made simply by changing the poor themselves.

All Americans, rich and poor, are participants in a common culture, but they bear different relationships to one another within it. The poor share a position together with racial minorities as socially and politically powerless enclaves. They share this position in a period of history when the spread of literacy and communication via the mass media has led more and more people throughout the world actively to seek participation in the making of decisions about the institutions which affect their lives. This includes not only people who are ethnically diverse, but also those who are younger and those who have previously not held positions of power and authority. The colonial revolutions of the post–World War II era have spread the revolution for equality, the idea of progress. The vast acceleration of cultural contact and the diffusion of ideas accompanying it are rapidly dissipating remaining pockets of isolation.

The growing insistence on equality and on participation has come into conflict with deliberate efforts to impose changes on people without deferring to their choice in the matter. No longer can programs be readily instituted, whether they stem from governments, missionaries, businessmen, or teachers, if the people who are in the recipient position do not want them. Change must be accepted voluntarily. However, when changes are desired, the rate of change can accelerate rapidly, and it is common to speak of Five-Year Plans, Leaps Forward, Decades of Development, and, in the context of our own nation, "Freedom Now."

Some of the dilemmas of the schools in the inner city are related to these developments. The city public schools have become schools for the poor and, in many instances, schools for the black poor particularly.[1] The flight of the more affluent whites to the suburbs and private systems gives the city public schools the aspect of underdeveloped areas within the nation, dependent on resources and services from the outside. The separation of races and classes might by itself not be so serious except for the fact that the inner-city schools as experienced by many ghetto residents appear to reflect the dominant society which slights, rejects, and manipulates the poor and minority groups. Barriers between the school and its pupils in a poor neighborhood include staffs which are frequently alien to a local community and beholden to superiors within a large bureaucracy rather than to the parents of the children they teach; styles of interaction and discourse which are likewise alien, as discussed by Vera John and Janet Castro in their explorations of the significance of language styles in the teaching situation; and the fundamental problem of pupil failure for which parents are generally held responsible, although they hold no authority over the schools their children attend. The urban slum school has become an intrusive institution, which shuts out the parents except on the most disadvantageous terms, and which is too often the setting for a tug-of-war between teachers and pupils. Thus, the poor stand in a markedly different relationship to schools than do the more affluent.

[1] United States Commission on Civil Rights, *Racial Isolation in the Public Schools* (Washington: U. S. Government Printing Office, 1967).

In the United States, a state-controlled, compulsory education system has come to mean that those parents who are dissatisfied with the education provided for their children must move to areas where educational systems are more compatible with or responsive to parental interests, or they must turn to private, non–publicly supported schooling. However, it is mainly those in the upper-income brackets who are able to exercise these options. The very poor and the nonwhite are limited in their choice of residence, and, since the federal and state governments do not subsidize tuition for private elementary education, the costs are prohibitive to those in the lower-income brackets. Thus the vast majority of inner-city populations are totally dependent upon the public education provided for their children. A "culture of poverty," with parental disinterest as a major component, is frequently cited as explaining the lack of success which is the outcome for most of the children. As this book has documented, and as contemporary political developments make obvious, considerable evidence exists to the contrary.

This decade has witnessed enormous efforts on the part of lower-income and minority-group parents and their leaders, notably in black but also in American Indian communities, to exercise some control over the operation of their local public schools. The best known examples are in Harlem and Bedford-Stuyvesant, where members of these major black communities have been demanding direct parental control over the staffing, curriculum, and budget of the local public schools. The famous disputes over Intermediate School 201 in Harlem and the Ocean Hill–Brownsville disputes of 1968 and 1969 are examples of the challenge being thrown out to the jurisdiction of the enormous bureaucratic organizations which rule the schools from afar—a challenge to a system which separates literally millions of people from any power over the schooling of their children.[2] Indeed, the entire history of massive boycotts and complaints against schools reflects the urgent concern of many that the public schools become more responsive to community interests. They defy the oft-repeated no-

[2] See David Rogers, *110 Livingston Street* (New York: Random House, 1969), for a thorough analysis of school bureaucracy in New York.

tion that the poor are apathetic, alienated, and disinterested in education.

Several areas of concern are manifested by the growing pressures for a more direct voice in the institutions which children are required to attend in order to be educated. One concern has to do with the desire to maintain a way of life separate and distinct from that of white urban America. Among such groups may be counted the Amish, some American Indians, and some though not the majority of Afro-Americans. For such groups, compulsory public education is viewed as intrusive, and resistance to the encroachment of schools over the socialization of their children is best understood as part of an attempt to maintain a traditional and autonomous way of life rather than in terms of a culture of poverty.

A second and more widespread motivation for demanding participation in the running of the schools stems from the school's function as the means of entry to the higher-status positions in American society. Such entry is increasingly dependent upon success in elementary school and upon movement through the certification system into the universities. A child's failure in the early grades leads to his placement in a non-academic program in high school and to the denial of college entrance. (Hence the pressure upon universities to open their doors to those denied admission by present standards.) Their exclusion from involvement in the running of schools, combined with their children's educational failure, casts the schools in the light of denying to the poor equal access to economic and social success. The mutual distrust and fear between school and community which results leads at times to open hostility. In places such as New York City, where the overwhelming majority of the school staffs is white and the school population more than 50 percent black, the conflict has become inextricably interwoven with the problem of race relations.

A third concern in the attempt to achieve control over schools involves the view of these efforts as necessary in order to make bureaucratic institutions accountable to the people they serve. People who hold this view see that acquiring some control over the institutions which pervade their lives offers an opportunity to improve and reshape the educational system according to humanistic goals. Further, they question the quality of life and personality encouraged by the schools, and they see changes in the schools as contributing to the restructuring of the whole social order.

However, control over the school opens the door to allocation of funds and to positions of political power and decision-making, as well as to the opening up of job opportunities to those for whom such jobs are now difficult to obtain. Therefore, efforts by the poor to restructure their position in society around the highly visible institution of the school brings them squarely into conflict with those administrators of the system as well as many professionals who find the present power relationships more compatible with their interests. The professional establishment willingly supports programs of curriculum improvement and compensatory programs of many descriptions for the disadvantaged as long as such programs are predicated on their retaining positions of control while helping the poor. To the poor in opposition, it is precisely the restructuring of institutions which is seen as more effective in combatting poverty than those programs which seek to impose changes upon them.

Although local control over schools is deeply rooted in American educational history, to move in the direction of local, direct parental control of publicly supported city schools stands in contrast to present inner-city organizational forms. It also conflicts with trends toward national assessments, and with national standards which are being imposed on the lower schools by such forces as the universities and nationally standardized examinations, presumably in keeping with needs of a technologically oriented, mobile, urban nation.

A trend toward decentralization also stands in marked contrast to the centrally controlled educational systems of other industrial states such as the U.S.S.R. and France. Denmark, however, represents an interesting example of a nation with a fairly centralized educational system and national standards which makes provision for schooling outside the state system. Yet Denmark has been widely acclaimed for its achievement in education, and for its influence on educational thought and structure through its famous "folk high schools," which pioneered in adult education. There is no state monopoly over education in Denmark, for here there is provision for a system of state-supported, locally controlled schools, the *Friskoler* ("free schools") whose staffs are chosen by the parents and whose curriculum is largely under parental control, but whose financing is provided by public funds. A study of the Danish experience lends perspective on the strengths and weaknesses of a system wherein alternatives to the traditional state schools are made available with public financial assistance.

The Danish *Friskole* system provides a model of how a modern state can establish standards of education required for national life and the protection of the young, while at the same time providing for the freedom of minorities, whether they be religious, ethnic, economic, or pedagogic, to oversee and direct the education of their children with minimal interference by the government. It is a model of public education which is not monopolistic, but, rather, provides for flexibility in the use of alternative types of public schools from which parents can choose for their children.[3]

The Danish government permits any group of parents, or any organization, to organize a school, and provides approximately 85 percent of the cost. Standards of sanitation, and instruction in Danish and mathematics, are required, and provisions are made for inspection. Beyond that, however, each school has control over the use of funds, hiring of staff, curriculum, and all other school matters.

In 1967 there were a total of 178 *Friskoler* in Denmark offering primary schooling. These schools can be grouped into a number of different categories representing different types of schools. The largest number, 114 are *Grundtvig-Koldske Friskoler,* operating in the direct tradition of N. F. S. Grundtvig and Kristen Kold, and practicing the pedagogical and religious principles es-

[3] A detailed study of the *Friskoler* is Estelle Fuchs, *The Danish Friskoler* (New York: Project True, Hunter College, C. U. N. Y., 1968).

poused by them.[4] There are nineteen Catholic private schools (*katolske Privatskoler*), three Adventist schools (*adventist Menighedskoler*), one Reformed school (*reformert Menighedskole*), one Jewish school (*mosaisk Menighedskole*), twenty-eight German schools (*tyske Mindretalsskoler*) serving the German-speaking minority, and also several independent "little schools" (*lille Skoler*). On the whole, these schools represent differences with the state's schools in matters of religious training, language usage, pedagogical methodology, and educational aims. The atmosphere of these schools varies widely, ranging from the permissive, intimate tone of the "little schools" to the formal, highly structured traditional air of some of the others.

Discussion of the relevance of the Danish experience with the *Friskoler* for problems facing education in American cities must make note of differences between Denmark and the United States that preclude any easy or direct modeling of one system upon the other. A major difference is the fact that in Denmark the Evangelical Lutheran state religion is taught in the public schools. From the very beginning of compulsory education in that country, the existence and support of schools outside the public system was viewed as a guarantee of religious liberty. On the other hand, in the United States the separation of church and state was viewed by the founders of this nation as essential to religious liberty, and the public support of any educational system that included religious instruction has been traditionally viewed as a danger to the democratic system. Although this view has recently been modified as regards aid to universities and also by the

[4] A profoundly significant impact upon Danish education in the nineteenth century was made by these two unusual personalities. Grundtvig, though deeply religious and himself a clergyman, opposed compulsory education and especially compulsory religious education. He attacked the Latin schools of the time and called them "schools for death" and "scholastic houses of correction." Extolling folk culture and humanitarianism, he had a profound influence on all Danish life. Grundtvig's educational ideas were put into practice by Kristen Kold, who established an independent school, soon copied by parents all over Denmark, in which the pedagogical emphasis was on oral presentation, discussion, and singing, and from which rote learning and drill were absent. These practices dominate the *Grundtvig-Koldske Friskoler* today.

"child-benefit" theory of aid to education, it nonetheless remains a strong current in American thinking about the schools.

Another basic difference is the fact that the Danish nation, consisting of some five million persons, although including a German-speaking ethnic minority and several religious minorities, is nonetheless a fairly homogeneous nation which does not have racially defined and discriminated-against minorities. In the United States, on the other hand, with its multiple ethnic and religious minorities, public compulsory education has been traditionally viewed as essential to accomplish homogenization, or Americanization, of varied peoples whose differences were viewed as threatening to national unity. Although at present the schools are primarily educating Americans, not foreigners, the traditional belief that public schools act as a unifying force, a "melting pot," persists.

Still a third difference is that the Danes, although they may question the "snobbery" of certain upper-class schools or the separation of certain intellectual groups out of the public system, nonetheless do not see in the *Friskoler* a threat to their national unity or democratic way of life. In this country, on the other hand, the private school system, where it has been supported by state governments, has been seen to operate either as an intrusion upon the principle of separation of church and state or, more recently, as an effort to circumvent integration. Thus, state-supported private schools tend to be viewed as a potentially antidemocratic force.

Yet the fact remains that affluent Americans have far greater choice concerning the education of their children than do the poor of America's inner cities. Those who are confined to the ghettos either by race or by poverty or by a combination of both are completely dependent upon a monopolistic public-school system which is compulsory. Pious talk concerning the democratic nature of the public school system does not change the fact that for many it is unsatisfactory, and social class has a great deal to do with the choices open to a family to do something about the situation. Movement to the suburbs or into private school systems is not a choice available to the urban poor. At present a major alternative open to this group, when consciously dissatisfied with the schools, is to engage in social protest, a phenomenon all American inner-city school systems have seen develop in recent years.

Much of this social protest has centered on the eradication of *de jure* and *de facto* school segregation. More recent efforts have concentrated on decentralization of city school systems and the substitution of local community control. It would appear that even if local school districts were under the direct control of local parent and community groups, this form of organization would not preclude the disaffection of some groups from what would remain essentially a monopolistic, compulsory educational system. Such programs run the risk of being stillborn, strangled not only by the opposition of conservative forces supporting the traditional system, but also by internal factional dispute.

A publicly supported system which opens alternatives to all regardless of class or ethnic-group minority needs, whether it be for the teaching of Swahili, ballet, or Navajo culture, or whether it be a desire to rear children via Montessori or Neill's Summer-hillian pedagogy, would open to the poor alternatives and positions of control now available to the more affluent. That this might then remove from the school its most militant critics and leaders of reform has been observed in Denmark. Yet all agree to the difficulty of effecting change within the large bureaucratic systems that our schools have become, and alternatives outside the system are already used by those able to afford them. The widening of alternatives for the poor would open the possibility of creative use of talent and the implementation of reforms presently inhibited by the organizational needs of schools as they are presently constituted.

The Danish *Friskole* provide some lessons on the workings of such a system. Parent control through the hiring of a headmaster and the approval of the hiring and firing of teachers does not appear threatening to teachers whose pedagogical and philosophical bents coincide with those of the parents. To those who fear the fragmentation of the public education system, the Danish experience supports the view that alternative forms of schooling do not inevitably mean the demise of the larger traditional structure, for only 7 percent of the population of that country chooses to use the *Friskoler* to meet the special educational requirements of themselves and their children. On the contrary, vigorous support for public education and the maintenance of high standards draw the support of the overwhelming majority of the population to the state schools.

An advantage of such a system is that freedom from the monolithic compulsion by huge bureaucratic organization, within which the educational preferences of groups with particular needs cannot be met easily, may free the public schools of debilitating conflict. But perhaps most important is that permitting concerned and interested groups of parents and community groups to set up schools for populations that find the present system unsatisfactory may unleash creative potential and revitalization and make possible an educational renaissance.

Aspirations for participation in the institutions which control the lives of people continue to grow. To resolve the conflicts which pervade our culture, it would seem essential to broaden the choices that make it possible for people to meet their needs. Ideologies and institutional structures which seek to impose themselves upon people without regard to their wishes will be met with resistance, as will those ideologies which deny the reality and depth of concern felt by those holding subordinate positions in our society.

PART II

Theoretical and Methodological Problems with the "Culture of Poverty" Concept

THE "CULTURE OF POVERTY": ITS SCIENTIFIC SIGNIFICANCE AND ITS IMPLICATIONS FOR ACTION[1]

CHARLES A. VALENTINE

Few ideas put forward by social scientists in recent years have been so widely accepted or so influential in practical affairs as the concept of a "culture of poverty" propounded by Oscar Lewis. The importance of this notion is by no means solely attributable to Lewis' own work. Secondary interpretations, elaborations, and applications have played a great part in producing a complex of ideas, policies, and programs related in various ways to the original concept. I propose to discuss salient aspects of the entire complex, beginning with the central ideas as they are presented in some of Lewis' more recent works.

The first section of this essay presents an analysis of the principal methods and the major factual evidence used by Lewis, followed by an evaluation of the relationship between his data and

[1] This chapter was originally written in 1967, then extensively revised and completed in late 1968. Subsequently the debate between myself and Oscar Lewis (and others) was further extended in the journal *Current Anthropology* (Valentine *et al.*, 1969). Owing to overlapping publishing schedules, the exchange in *Current Anthropology* appeared first, even though it really represents a later stage in the discussion. Because of other obligations there has been no opportunity for me to rewrite the present chapter again *in toto*. I urge interested readers to avail themselves of the further discussion in *Current Anthropology*. I feel this is important because of several specific aspects of that 1969 exchange: (1) there Professor Lewis replies to many of my criticisms; (2) he clarifies several points beyond his previous statements, and (3) in the end we are closer to agreement in some respects than is indicated by the present chapter.

his theory. In the second section the scientific significance of the "culture of poverty" is explored and assessed by comparing it with alternative hypotheses. Both these first two parts of the discussion are based largely on material from Lewis' book *La Vida*. Finally, the third section examines the implications of the poverty-culture idea for public attitudes, government policies, and social action. It is mainly in the final section that the "culture of poverty" concept in its broader forms, transcending the work of Lewis and yet rooted in that work, is dealt with. Much that is presented in the first two parts of this essay has already appeared elsewhere in a different form (Valentine, 1968). The third part was newly composed for the present work.

My own position on these topics can be summarized briefly. The writings of some who have developed or applied ideas related to the "culture of poverty" are intellectually shallow or disingenuous. In contrast, the work of Oscar Lewis, particularly his earlier writings, commands scholarly and scientific respect. In the work associated with the "culture of poverty," however, the methods of research and analysis are inadequate in some important respects. The data contain numerous and substantial contradictions of the theoretical abstractions presented. The scientific status of the "culture of poverty" remains essentially a series of undemonstrated hypotheses. With respect to many or most of these hypotheses, alternative propositions are theoretically more convincing and are supported by more available evidence. The complex of conceptions, attitudes, and activities that has grown up around the "culture of poverty" has had a predominantly pernicious effect on American society. This complex has been a keystone in the crumbling arch of official policy toward the poor. The present crisis of our society will not be resolved constructively until this collection of ideas and initiatives is thoroughly refuted and replaced by radically different alternatives.

Methods, Evidence, and Abstractions

The plan of Oscar Lewis' major works on the "culture of poverty" is simple. A brief introduction dealing mainly with method and theory is followed by an enormous bulk of concrete biographical description. The principal purpose of this design is evidently to convey the impression that the biographical evidence supports and validates the theoretical abstraction which is labeled the "culture of poverty." In order to assess the value of Lewis' concepts it is necessary to reevaluate the relationship between data and theory in his work. To do this effectively requires that we also examine how the evidence was collected and how it is presented.

Let us consider first the lengthy autobiographies and short descriptions of daily behavior which make up the bulk of these volumes. Here we are confronted with a huge mass of unanalyzed and unevaluated material. It is most difficult to determine the validity of this material or even its precise relevance to Lewis' abstractions. The author suggests that the autobiographies present a subjective picture of life among the poor, while the descriptions of daily behavior constitute a more objective portrayal. He also suggests that the appearance of the same events in life stories told by several different persons make it possible to check the reliability of one informant against another. The application of these suggestions is left entirely to the reader. The author has added no commentary to the texts. Where there are internal contradictions, the reader has no basis for preferring one source over another, save whatever impressions he may have gained from the texts themselves.

Oscar Lewis' books tell the reader more about his methods of field research than do the writings of many anthropologists. It is nevertheless true that important questions remain unanswered as to how Lewis obtained his taped autobiographies. His fullest account of this process appears in one of the earlier works, *The Children of Sanchez* (Lewis, 1961, pp. xviii-xxiii). Here we learn of Lewis' feeling that he achieved a warm personal relationship with his informants and that it was their feeling of friendship that led them to recount their life stories. The clear implication is that this circumstance enhances the reliability of the informants' testimony. This is an implication which I am inclined to accept at face value on the basis of my own experience. Nevertheless, one's confidence would be increased considerably if the problem of rapport and its effects on informant testimony were discussed critically. This should include at least a few concrete examples. Lewis also tells us that most of his taping was done in the privacy of his office or his home, both of which were apparently far from the accustomed milieu of his informants. Again one misses any critical discussion of the influence these circumstances may have had.

Lewis tells us that during some parts of the interviews he employed "a directive approach" in order to get his informants to cover systematically a broad range of subject matter which he hoped would add up to "their total view of the world." He says that many of his questions stimulated informants to deal with matters which otherwise they might never have thought about or volunteered to talk about. He adds that in addition to direct questioning he encouraged free association. It seems to me that it would have been easy to go a little further and give the reader a really clear impression of just how the autobiographical material was elicited. A few sample questions and a few lines to illustrate the materials forthcoming from different interview techniques could have gone a long way toward answering our queries.

These unanswered questions assume even greater importance when one considers another issue: the nature of editorial influences on the content of the autobiographies in their published form. In this connection, several explanatory lines by Lewis deserve quotation:

> In preparing these interviews for publication, I have eliminated my questions and have selected, arranged, and organized their materials into coherent life stories. . . . These life histories have something of both art and life. I believe this in no way reduces the authenticity of the data or their usefulness for science. [*Ibid.*, p. xxi.]

This is followed by indications that the amount and kind of editing imposed varied from one informant to another. It is clear that the author often reorganized the material, selected some portions of the testimony, and eliminated others. Without more definite specification of editing criteria, it is difficult to evaluate the published autobiographies. Are they close to the raw material on the tapes, are they a body of evidence merely organized for convenience, or are they an intellectual creation fashioned by the editor from informant testimony? Without clear answers to these questions, the nature of the main body of evidence remains cloudy.

Another query about this evidence is one that has been voiced by several critical reviewers of Lewis' work. How representative are the autobiographies? In the introduction to *La Vida,* the author briefly describes the Rios family, whose life stories take up most of the volume. He tells us that "the Rios family is not presented here as a typical Puerto Rican family but rather as representative of one style of life in a Puerto Rican slum." How common this life style may be, he adds candidly, "cannot be determined until we have many comparable studies from other slums in Puerto Rico and elsewhere." Yet this leaves us unable to evaluate another statement which appears in the same paragraph: "The Rios family, their friends and neighbors, reflect many of the characteristics of the subculture of poverty, characteristics which are widespread in Puerto Rico but which are by no means exclusively Puerto Rican" (Lewis, 1966b, p. xxv). If the actual occurrence of the behavior and beliefs described by members of the Rios family is not known, what is the basis for presenting them as representatives of a "subculture of poverty"? What chain of factual evidence links the phenomena ascribed to the Rios family by their own testimony to a way of life shared by the poor in Puerto Rico and elsewhere? Lewis does not answer these questions.

In some respects it appears that the Rios family are not at all representative. They seem, rather, to manifest minority patterns even within their particular slum community. Any reader of *La Vida* will remember how important prostitution is in the lives of all the Rios women. Lewis tells us in his introduction that only one third of the families in this slum had any history of prostitution. He adds that "prostitution has certainly made a difference in the Rios family" (*ibid,* p. xxi). He lists quite a number of special features as resulting from the importance of prostitution in this family history. These include differences in income and spending patterns, childhood exposure to sex and neglect of children, a reinforced negative self-image, and a selective factor influencing the type of men who married Rios women. In spite of all this, Lewis also says, "It seems to me that the history of prostitution has not caused any major changes in the basic patterns of their family life" (*ibid.*).

There are even some indications that the subjects of *La Vida* were chosen, not because of their representativeness, but, rather, because they manifest deviant extremes. Note, for example, Lewis' statement (p. xxvi) that "the Rios family is closer to the expression of an unbridled id than any other people I have studied." Especially coming from an author who has written so much about uncontrolled rage, violence, and sexuality, this is a singular statement of uniqueness. Nevertheless, we find our author easily identifying the apparently deviant behavior of this family with a presumably widespread culture pattern. "The remarkable stability in some of the behavior patterns of the Rios family over four generations . . . suggests that we are dealing with a tenacious culture pattern. This can be seen clearly in the high incidence of early marriages, of free unions, of multiple spouses and of illegitimate children" (p. xxvii). Following closely upon these lines comes another contradictory passage (p. xxviii): "The history of the Rios family . . . suggests that the pattern of free unions and multiple spouses is not limited to the poor. It has been a widespread pattern among wealthy rural families. . . . This illustrates a general proposition . . . namely, the remarkable similarities between some aspects of the lives of the very poor and of the very rich."

So in the space of five pages we have the characters of *La Vida* presented in many different lights, each of which bears differently on the question of their representativeness. Should we see them as (1) typical of the culture of the poor, (2) following a life style of unknown frequency and distribution, (3) deeply affected by a specialized occupational pattern confined to one third of their own community, (4) characterized by an extreme deviance unique in their chronicler's experience, or (5) spanning the gap between the upper and lower classes? It is no wonder that a curious but careful reader experiences difficulty in placing these life stories in a wider context. These particular difficulties merely illustrate the broader problem of discerning clear relationships between these case histories and the abstraction of a "culture of poverty."

Turning now to direct comparisons between the abstraction of poverty culture and descriptive evidence itself, one is confronted with more serious problems. For example, when generalized conceptions of slum localities are placed against concrete descriptions of named communities, straightforward contradictions immediately arise. Consider first the following generalization by Lewis (p. xlvii).

When we look at the culture of poverty on the local community level, we find . . . above all a minimum of organization beyond the level of the . . . family. Occasionally there are informal, temporary groupings . . . the existence of neighborhood gangs . . . represents a considerable advance beyond the zero point . . . I have in mind. Indeed, it is the low level of organization which gives the culture of poverty its marginal and anachronistic quality . . . most primitive peoples have achieved a higher level of socio-cultural organization than our modern urban slum dwellers.

Now compare this with a description from a few pages earlier (p. xxxiii):

The setting for the story of the Rios family is La Esmeralda, an old and colorful slum in San Juan, built on a steep embankment between the city's ancient fort walls and the sea. Squeezed into an area not more than five city blocks long and a few hundred yards wide are 900 houses inhabited by 3,600 people. . . .

Seen from the walls above, the slum looks almost prosperous. This is because all the houses have roofs of new green tar paper, a contribution from the mayoress. . . .

Within the larger settlement are three subdivisions . . . connected with San Juan by four entrances.

Even though La Esmeralda is only ten minutes away from the heart of San Juan, it is physically and socially marginal to the city. The wall above it stands as a kind of symbol separating it from the city. La Esmeralda forms *a little community of its own* with a cemetery, a church, a small dispensary and maternity clinic, and one elementary school [italics added]. There are many small stores, bars and taverns. . . .

To the people of Greater San Juan, La Esmeralda has a bad reputation . . . today the residents of La Esmeralda think of it as a relatively elegant healthful place, with its beautiful view of the sea, its paved streets, its new roofs, the absence of mosquitoes, the low rentals and its nearness to their places of work.

These two passages simply cannot be reconciled. Taken at face value, the description of La Esmeralda as "a little community of its own" can only mean that this slum is not part of any "culture of poverty" which is defined as lacking virtually all community organization. While this interpretation is clearly at odds with Lewis' intended message, it is difficult to draw any other conclusion from the material he presents. Thus again the reader is left to wonder about the factual foundations for the concept of a "culture of poverty."

Numerous comparable inconsistencies appear when the life histories recounted in *La Vida* are examined with care. Of the many aspects of life that might be cited in this connection, I have chosen what may be called "orientation toward the wider world." This is manifested by expressions of interest in politics, class consciousness, ethnic identity, and national identification. In Lewis' account of those who live by the "culture of poverty" he pictures them as removed and alienated, ignorant and uninterested, uninvolved and apathetic toward all these dimensions of the wider world. In his words, "The lack of effective participation and integration in the major institutions of the larger society is one of the crucial characteristics of the culture of poverty. This is a complex matter and results from a variety of factors which may include . . . fear, suspicion, or apathy. . . ." And: "People with a culture of poverty . . . usually do not belong to labor unions, are not members of political parties . . ." The principal focus for group consciousness which Lewis allows is a purely local one. This is indicated by his statement that "when the population constitutes a distinct ethnic, racial or language group . . . then the sense of local community approaches that of a village community." In conclusion Lewis generalizes as follows. "People with a culture of poverty are provincial and locally oriented. . . . they know only their own troubles, their local conditions, their own neighborhood. . . . usually they do not have the knowledge, the vision or the ideology to see the similarities between their problems and those of their counterparts elsewhere. . . . they are not class-conscious. . . ." (Pp. xlv-xlviii.)

The autobiographies of the Rios women, their consorts and their kinsmen certainly do contain a great many expressions of personal, local, and other narrowly defined interests. It seems fair to suggest that this is just what we should expect from ordinary people anywhere. This seems especially so when the life stories are being elicited by a social scientist who is explicitly interested in family studies as such. What is surprising in view of Lewis' abstract description, however, is the substantial expression of wider interests by these same informants.

Consider the following sample of such expressions by six of these informants. Fernanda, the *grande dame* of the Rios family, repeatedly generalizes intelligently about the life and social position of prostitutes. One such disquisition culminates in a pithy dissertation on the relationship between whores, the police, and the system of justice (pp. 57-58). She describes the passionately argumentative allegiance which another character gives to the Popular Party, and she goes on to explain why she and all her offspring have always been Statehood Republicans (p. 95). Erasmo, who lived with Fernanda for seven years, is allotted only fourteen pages for his account of those years. Within this space, he spends some two and a half pages comparing socioeconomic opportunities within Puerto Rico and the United States, touches lightly on the politics of four other Latin-American countries, and expounds on the major political issues, parties, and personalities in Puerto Rico (p. 84).

Fernanda's eldest daughter, Soledad, gives a class-conscious, approving description of her husband Octavio's career of robbing the rich and sharing with the poor (p. 191). She draws the moral that there is no justice of the poor against the wealthy (p. 193).

Soledad describes her unavailing efforts first to find employment and then to obtain increased aid from the welfare establishment; she then relates these experiences systematically, albeit somewhat cynically, to the nature of Puerto Rican politics (pp. 194-95). Here and there Soledad offers reflections on race relations in the United States and the implications for the education and employment of Puerto Ricans and other groups (e.g., p. 211). While living in New York, Soledad even made a pilgrimage to Washington in order to attend the funeral of President Kennedy. She explains her feelings toward Kennedy in terms of his Administration's policies and programs on race relations and aid to Puerto Rico. In addition she compares her feelings about Kennedy with her evaluation of Muñoz Martín, Eisenhower, Roosevelt, and Johnson (p. 237). Soledad's autobiography ends with an earthy and passionate assertion of Puerto Rican national identity (p. 267): "I want to be buried in Puerto Rico because that's my country. Even if I do live in New York, I never forget my country. I wouldn't change it for the world. That's where I was born and that's where I want to be buried . . . but not here. Shit! I don't care what happens here, I'm only interested in what goes on in my own country, in what happens to Puerto Ricans who belong to my race. Nobody else matters to me."

The testimony of Soledad's later husband, Benedicto, fills only a few pages. Yet Benedicto delivers himself of a number of generalizations and comparisons with respect to the cultures of the United States and Puerto Rico (e.g., pp. 226-27). He also explains in considerable detail the benefits which he feels he and others receive from membership and active participation in the National Maritime Union (p. 231).

Another of Fernanda's daughters, Felicita, has a good deal to say about the ambiguities and ambivalences of Puerto Rican and American national identification (pp. 321-22, 359-60). Elsewhere Felicita produces what is in effect an informal political essay. This passage includes descriptions of attendance by several members of the Rios family at a political rally and visits by national figures to La Esmeralda. She adds her own commentary on the political process and personalities within the slum community, and she speaks about the relationship of all this to the wider political scene both in Puerto Rico and in the United States (pp. 361-63).

Fernanda's son Simplicio lives in New York and works in a clothing factory owned by a Jewish entrepreneur. Simplicio expounds at some length on the nature of the Jews as a people, their history, their culture, and their relations with other ethnic groups (pp. 444-46). Like the other informants, Simplicio has much to say in broad terms about the interrelated problems of Puerto Rican status in the United States, American race relations, Puerto Rican party politics, and social reform in Puerto Rico (pp. 450-51, 453-54). Finally, Simplicio presents an organized discussion of the domestic politics of the United States in relation to international affairs, including Cuba, Castro, and Communism (pp. 454-55). Toward the end of this discussion, Simplicio mentions that he has just reached the age of twenty-one and wishes to vote in the next election. He adds that he has been unable, in spite of some effort, to discover how or where to register as a voter.

This last detail from Simplicio's story is an appropriate point from which to turn back to the generalized picture of the "culture of poverty." This detail reminds us that Lewis stresses lack of actual participation in the wider world. He treats participation as distinct from, and not less important than, awareness or interest in wider affairs. It is quite clear that even such portions of the autobiographies as those just cited contain much verbal expression of interest and knowledge, with relatively little evidence of actual behavior outside the circle of household and kinsmen. It seems fair to suggest, however, that this is to be expected when the attention of the interviewer-editor is so focused on family life as such. Moreover, failures in participation such as Simplicio's unsuccessful attempt to translate his political orientation into action do not appear to stem from lack of motivation or intention. They seem to be due to other factors, including some that are not only external to the individual but also outside the life of the poor altogether. There can be little doubt that if those who control the political organizations of New York attached great importance to participation by the Simplicios of the city they could find them and register them as voters.

Scientific Significance

The essence of the "culture of poverty" as conceived by Oscar Lewis can be inferred from the theoretical portion of his writings. He compares the lifeways of groups he believes live by a distinctive poverty culture with those of other groups who are poor but do not possess such a subculture, together with still other groups who have gotten rid of the poverty culture as he sees it. The essence that remains to distinguish the "culture of poverty" groups from the others consists largely of negative qualities, lacks, and absences. This remains true even though Lewis himself explicitly denies that he sees poverty subcultures as merely matters of "disorganization or the absence of something" (Lewis, 1966b, p. xliii). The major qualities that finally distinguish the unregenerate poverty culture, in his own descriptions and comparisons, are group disintegration, personal disorganization, and lack of purposeful action.

Thus Lewis and, particularly, his imitators, popularizers, and interpreters have brought together a singularly unprepossessing collection of attributes under the "culture of poverty" rubric. If one could truly find a mode of existence characterized only by these traits, it might be quite like the chronic-patient population in the back wards of state mental hospitals. It would be difficult to grant such a collectivity high valuation as a human creation. Indeed, one might even be inclined to perceive this existence in terms of negative stereotypes deeply embedded in one's own subculture—and to feel threatened by it. Nevertheless, it is puzzling that Lewis and so many others have not been disabused of this caricature by the considerable amount of available contrary evidence, not the least of which is the life stories in *La Vida*. These biographies plainly portray a great deal of very sanely organized and purposeful human life. Part of the solution to this puzzle is that the notion of a "culture of poverty" has become a dogma, an orthodoxy which is simply purveyed and repeated; rather than being subjected to critical examination.

The idea that the poor maintain a self-perpetuating way of life all their own is frequently put forward as if it were an established fact. In scientific terms, however, this old idea has never been more than a hypothesis which remains to be demonstrated, disproved, or modified. We have seen that a good deal of the evidence offered by Oscar Lewis fails to support his version of the poverty-culture hypothesis. Yet the interpretation of existence among the poor as a separate design for living is seldom discussed in a way that gives systematic attention to alternative hypotheses. Let us make such an examination, briefly opposing to each of Lewis' major points a different interpretation that is consistent with the evidence already cited from *La Vida* and similar evidence from other sources.

Lewis' thesis consists of one major hypothesis plus a series of subsidiary propositions. His ruling hypothesis states that "the culture of poverty" is "a subculture of Western society with its own structure and rationale, a way of life handed down from generation to generation along family lines." He also describes it as "a culture in the traditional anthropological sense that it provides human beings with a design for living, with a ready-made set of solutions for human problems" (Lewis, 1966a, p. 19).

As a major alternative interpretation I suggest that whatever is distinctive in social life at the lowest socioeconomic levels is determined primarily by the structure of the society as a whole and forces beyond the control of poor people. In other words, the social life of low-income people is not shaped primarily by the poor teaching a separate cultural design to each generation. The major prescriptions for living received by the poor through socialization may not be significantly distinct from those of the society as a whole. Yet the actual conditions of low-income life are highly inconsistent with actualization of this cultural design.

Lewis' formulation of a poverty culture with some seventy traits can be broken down into numerous hypothetical statements subsumed under his ruling proposition. Five of these can be examined here. The first subsidiary proposition is that poor people's lack of participation in important aspects of the wider social order is an internally perpetuated characteristic of their subculture. As Lewis puts it, "The disengagement, the non-integration, of the poor with respect to the major institutions of society is a crucial element in the culture of poverty" (1966a, p. 21).

A more realistic interpretation would suggest that disadvantaged groups participate to quite different degrees in various institutional areas of the wider society. Moreover, it should be added that these differing patterns of participation are imposed by the structure—and particularly the recruitment mechanisms—of the institutions themselves. Specifically, one would expect high participation by the poor in the police–courts–prison complex, the armed services, the welfare system, and primary public education. Similarly, low participation is predictable in desirable employment, property ownership, political parties, labor unions, and higher education.

The second subsidiary proposition in Lewis' formulation is that those who live by a "culture of poverty" do not really share the standard values of society. Their knowledge of dominant values, he says, is contradicted by their actual behavior as conditioned by their subculture. "People with a culture of poverty are aware of middle-class values, talk about them, and even claim some of them as their own, but on the whole they do not live by them" (1966b, p. xlvi).

In contrast with this, it may be argued that the poor share many or most of the major values associated with the dominant strata of our society. At the same time, poor people often simultaneously accept alternative values when there are sharp contradictions between cultural ideals and the conditions of existence. (For documentation supporting these points see Rodman, 1965, 1968.) For example, values shared by the poor and others probably include the belief that educational achievement is desirable, material comfort is a worthwhile goal, self-sufficiency is an admirable quality, and competition and cooperation are appropriate in different contexts. Alternative value judgments often made by the disadvantaged may include assessments that officialdom is neither benign nor trustworthy but can be manipulated, that blue-collar crime is not always blameworthy, that conventional family life is desirable but not necessarily attainable, and that the larger society discriminates against the poor.

A third proposition that is prominent in Lewis' thinking states that local social structure is practically nonexistent outside the household or the family. "When we look at the culture of poverty on the local community level, we find . . . above all a minimum of organization beyond the level of the nuclear and extended family" (Lewis, 1966, p. xlvi).

The factual situation in the San Juan slum presented by Lewis himself, plus evidence from many similar communities, is more consistent with a quite different formulation. Low-income districts have definite local social structures. These structures commonly include groups and relationships similar or analogous to those found in communities that are not slums. Also included in various combinations may be some social elements that are specialized adaptations to conditions of disadvantage or marginality. Common analogous elements would include community councils, political ward organizations, block associations, denominational church congregations, conventional youth groups, friendship associations, personal social networks, interhousehold reciprocity, and various service institutions. More specialized elements may include civil-rights or minority-advancement groups, poverty-oriented social-change movements, storefront churches, juvenile gangs, adult blue-collar criminal associations, and other voluntary associations.

The fourth generalization put forward by Lewis is one which has been most influential. It states that in the poverty subculture families are extremely or even uniquely unstable and disorganized. "On the family level the major traits of the culture of poverty are the absence of childhood . . . early initiation into sex, free unions or consensual marriages . . . abandonment of wives and children . . . female- or mother-centered families . . . sibling rivalry, and competition for limited goods and maternal affection" (1966b, p. xlvii).

Much evidence does indicate that families among the poor are more often unconventional in form and process than among more comfortable strata. It is clear, however, that these statistically unusual family patterns can generally be traced to externally imposed conditions impinging on the poor from the society at large.

Moreover, as Lewis himself admits in part, both households and kinship among the poor are frequently organized in ways that are adaptations to these externally imposed conditions. (Strong documentation of this interpretation can be found in Liebow, 1967.)

This alternative interpretation of family life in poverty may be further clarified by some more detailed considerations. The conventional biparental family is widely preferred as an ideal among the poor. Moreover, it is the actual existing form of household organization for a substantial proportion of poor households. The early socialization of children may be shared by a wider network of kinsmen, other adults, and peers, rather than being concentrated in the nuclear family. This may well contribute to a healthy early maturity, including development of numerous supportive relationships and sources of emotional security. Early sexuality is not necessarily maladaptive except perhaps in cases of unwanted pregnancy. The latter circumstance may be partly taken care of by somewhat flexible standards of legitimacy, and is potentially resolvable through knowledge and access to reliable contraception.

Consensual unions have been widely recognized as a flexible adaptation to certain conditions of poverty. These conditions include fluctuating economic circumstances, actual or threatened incarceration, and other external circumstances which often make it advisable for mates to separate and contract alternative unions, either temporary or lasting. Many family events that are superficially described as desertion or abandonment may actually involve one or more elements that contribute positively to the health and welfare of family members. Some of these are (1) separation by mutual consent, sometimes including considerations of alternative support for mother and children; (2) informal and extralegal but effective adoption which shifts dependents to households better able to care for them; (3) mobilization of kin ties and support sources originally established through a marital union but continuing to function in the absence of the husband; (4) support of fatherless families through other lines of kinship connection; (5) reunion, planned or otherwise, after temporary separation.

Female-centered or mother-focused households may often be more positively functional than conventional patterns because of factors such as those just listed, plus others. Husbandless mothers may identify positive male models for their children among kinsmen, neighbors, and others. Children themselves may also seek and find such identifications. Identification with admired figures in young peer groups may occur earlier than is typical in higher social strata. Intrafamily competition, either for goods or for affection, may well be mitigated by the greater resources available through extended kin ties and other associations.

The final proposition to be considered here is perhaps the crux of Lewis' formulation. It may well be crucial both in terms of theory and from the practical viewpoint of teachers, social-service personnel, and antipoverty workers. This is a psychological hypothesis, according to which the "culture of poverty" produces personal identities, individual characters, and a world view which are weak, disorganized, and restricted. "On the level of the individual, major characteristics are a strong feeling of marginality, of helplessness, of dependency, and of inferiority . . . weak ego structure, confusion of sexual identification, lack of impulse control . . . little ability to defer gratification and to plan for the future . . . resignation and fatalism . . ." (Lewis, 1966b, p. xlvii). The reasoning which makes this list of psychological characteristics crucial runs essentially like this: growing up in a poverty subculture produces these personality and character traits in most individuals, thus crippling or destroying their psychological capacities for escaping from poverty through normal behavior. It is in this sense that the "culture of poverty" is said to be self-perpetuating.

An alternative formulation opposed to this must make at least two distinct points. In the first place, many of the pessimistically toned orientations catalogued by Lewis and others are no more than realistic perceptions and evaluations born not of personality disorder but of lifelong and intergenerational experience imposed by the social order. Secondly, the fact that most poor people continue to function as human beings even under conditions of extreme adversity and deprivation, far from indicating psychological weakness, is a tribute to the inner strength and flexibility of humanity. While Lewis himself gives passing notice to "the strengths" of the Rios family in *La Vida,* his overall assessment of disorganization and pathology simply ignores the hundreds of pages of evidence to the contrary in the life stories which he collected.

It is no more than common sense to recognize that feelings of marginality, helplessness, and dependency are often in accord with the objective character of life circumstances for the poor. To the extent that conflict about sex roles actually occurs, it must be seen in the context of dramatic contradictions between cultural ideals and objective practical possibilities; this hardly requires the depth interpretation of psychopathology. Impulse deferral and gratification among the poor, much as among other people, probably vary situationally and may be maximized when a future reward can be confidently predicted, which of course is not often among those who live in poverty. Planning for the future presumably occurs when people have some sense that prospective alternatives are controllable by choice, which again is relatively infrequent for the disadvantaged. Similarly, resignation and fatalism may give way to individual aspiration or group confidence when there is a change in perceived opportunities. Beyond all this, however, one need not romanticize about the poor to recognize that, especially among the more oppressed ethnic minorities in poverty, extraordinary individual capacities are often required simply to survive socially and remain intact psychologically.

To choose with scientific rigor and confidence between the theory of a "culture of poverty" and the alternatives suggested here will require ethnographic research producing cultural studies that are thorough and comprehensive beyond anything presently available. In the meantime, however, much knowledge of life in poverty is already at hand. For those who must deal with poverty in a practical sense it is vitally important to use this knowledge to evaluate critically such notions as the "culture of poverty." Activists, practitioners, and policy makers must all avoid the rigidity of uncritical orthodoxy, but at the same time they cannot afford the luxury of awaiting ultimately definitive scientific demonstration. Informed, independent judgment is obviously required. By this criterion the "culture of poverty" must be discarded as a theoretical guide. It is certainly not convincing, and it is probably seriously misleading.

Policy and Action Implications

As the national crisis of the 1960s developed, it became clear that issues related to the idea of a poverty culture were no longer merely matters for academic debate. Unresolved scientific problems suddenly became public policy issues, and scholarly questions were converted into choices for action. As it turned out, powerful advocates and supporters of the poverty-culture theory had a free hand in the formation of emerging public policies with respect to poverty. The reasons for this were, of course, political, and the relevant decisions were made and implemented by national power holders. The concepts and theories by which the policies and programs were justified and rationalized, however, came from scholars and other intellectuals.

The concept of a "culture of poverty" was first made available to wide audiences a decade ago when Oscar Lewis used the phrase in the subtitle of his book *Five Families* (1959). By three years later Michael Harrington had incorporated the concept into his influential volume *The Other America*. The idea as presented by Harrington was stripped of technicalities and considerably simplified: "Poverty in the United States is a culture . . . a culture that is radically different from the one that dominates the society" (Harrington, 1962, pp. 16-17). This was followed by a host of writings in many different media popularizing and applying the same basic idea.

It is generally understood that Harrington's work was the chief intellectual stimulus to the policy initiatives which began during the Kennedy regime and have continued through two subsequent administrations (Donovan, 1967). Thomas Gladwin, in his *Poverty, U.S.A.*, has shown that "the whole conception of the War on Poverty rests upon a definition of poverty as a way of life." This governmental approach developed in an "intellectual climate" which "was created by studies of the culture of poverty, notably those of Oscar Lewis." This is why the resulting programs were "designed very explicitly to correct the social, occupational, and psychological deficits of people born and raised to a life of poverty" (Gladwin, 1967, p. 26).

As the end of the decade neared, the chain of rationalizations had almost come full circle. It was being argued in some quarters, as a major reason for the *failures* of antipoverty programs, that the cultural deficits of poor people are just too intractable. This argument appears, for example, in Ben Seligman's highly publicized book titled, significantly, *Permanent Poverty* (1968). In his opening chapter Seligman approvingly cites Harrington and goes on to say, "The poor had become a hidden subculture of America, a culture that perpetuated itself in endless cycles, a culture beyond the reach of the contemporary welfare state" (p. 16). By the end of the book this author is quoting Lewis and advancing the "culture of poverty" as one principal reason why the "war on poverty" had not succeeded. He writes of "those traits that accompany the subculture of poverty—illiteracy and indifference. . . . And these traits will pass from generation to generation to create unseen chains that constitute a social syndrome." Thus poverty has become "ineradicable" (p. 217). Such are the ironies of dominant but unexamined ideas being used to explain too much in a political context.

The connections between Lewis' work and national policy are far too complex and tortuous to be disentangled in detail here. This is partly because there have been so many intervening secondary presentations and elaborations of the basic thesis. It is also partly because Lewis' own statements about relevant policy issues have been somewhat diverse. He has explicitly endorsed reformist programs for increased employment and income maintenance in the United States (Kennedy and Lewis, 1967), and he has recorded his "impression" that poverty culture was done away with by revolutionary socialism in Cuba (Lewis, 1966b, p. xlix). On the other hand, his theoretical ideas have carried quite different policy implications, not only as presented by Lewis himself but particularly as construed by many other commentators and users of his writings. Evidently patterns of policy and practice have been far more influenced by these implications than by explicit statements such as those just cited.

Probably Lewis' key contribution is one of his generalizations which has been most often and most widely seized upon in general discussions of the "culture of poverty":

Once it comes into existence it tends to perpetuate itself from generation to generation because of its effect on children. By the time slum children are age six or seven, they have usually absorbed the basic values and attitudes of their subculture and are not psychologically geared to take full advantage of changing conditions or increased opportunities which may occur in their lifetime. [*Ibid.*, p. xlv.]

It is this idea which more than any other has been enlarged upon and reemphasized over and over to justify programs designed to inculcate middle-class values and virtues among the poor and especially their children, rather than changing the conditions of their existence.

Lewis himself makes it clear that he regards psychological disability and social disorganization as mutually reinforcing factors inherent in the "culture of poverty." One context in which this point is made by inference is Lewis' distinction between poverty as such and a poverty culture. This becomes clear when Lewis cites groups of people who do not live by such a culture even though they are poverty-stricken. What distinguishes these groups as Lewis sees them is their personal and social integration even under conditions of deprivation.

Consistent with this, Lewis feels that organization, solidarity, and hope are the essential factors for overcoming the "culture of poverty." He apparently feels that almost any kind of organization solidifying people behind virtually any cause, with hope enlivened by any vision, may accomplish this end. Thus, he suggests that "any movement, be it religious, pacifist, or revolutionary" may do the trick and that poverty culture declines "in socialist, fascist, and in highly developed capitalist societies with a welfare state" (*ibid.*, pp. xlviii, 1).

This line of thought soon brings Lewis to a series of contradictions with confusing implications for public policy. He lists so many different kinds of society in which the "culture of poverty" is absent or unimportant that the concept seems to have little remaining relevance for most of the contemporary world. Ultimately he declares that "the culture of poverty flourishes in, and is generic to, the early free enterprise stage of capitalism and . . . is also endemic in colonialism" (*ibid.,* p. 1). Yet at the same time he persists in maintaining that poverty culture is a widespread international phenomenon and one of the principal contemporary world problems.

Elsewhere Lewis' consideration of "solutions" focuses not on eliminating *poverty* but rather on doing away with the *"culture* of poverty." He writes about the "solutions" of American "planners and social workers" as designed to influence the poor so as to "incorporate them into the middle class" by various means including "reliance on psychiatric treatment" (*ibid.,* p. liii). The one alternative mentioned is "revolution," but this is ruled out of consideration for the United States by explicitly confining it to "the underdeveloped countries" where a "social-work solution does not seem feasible," and where "because of the magnitude of the problem psychiatrists can hardly begin to cope with it."

One further point completes Lewis' position on "solutions." He states that "it is much more difficult to eliminate the culture of poverty than to eliminate poverty *per se,"* and "the elimination of physical poverty *per se* may not be enough to eliminate the culture of poverty" (*ibid.,* pp. li, lii). It appears that his reason for regarding poverty culture as a less tractable problem than poverty itself is his belief that it produces deeply ingrained self-perpetuating psychological effects. The central idea is that the most difficult and significant problems associated with poverty exist within poor people themselves.

It is but a short step from this position to a belief that the allegedly distinctive culture patterns of the poor are more important in their lives than the condition of being poor. The policy corollary of this belief is that it is more necessary and urgent for our society to abolish the special lifeways of the poor than to eradicate poverty. So in the minds of policy makers and practitioners alike we find the key assumption that the main sources of poverty lie in the internal deficiencies and disabilities of the poor as a group, so that remedial and reformist programs consistently focus on changing poor people rather than the society as a whole or any other stratum within the system.

My point is not that Lewis himself directly expresses these key assumptions about causes and priorities. Indeed, his responses to recent criticism have included insistence that his work should be understood as an indictment of society, not of the poor, and that he favors the highest priority for eliminating deprivation (Lewis *et al.,* 1967; Lewis, 1968, p. 20). The purpose here is not to question Lewis' statements of his own convictions. My contention is rather that his writings are easily and very widely understood or interpreted as providing support for the positions described.

It is not possible here to explore fully the various relationships between Lewis' own writings and the many assertions or generalizations put forward by interpreters and commentators under the rubric "culture of poverty." One instance may be noted, however, for it is a case of clear contrast between a specification by Lewis and the general use to which his concept is put. In the course of his discussion of the distribution and prevalence of poverty culture Lewis makes the following statement. "My rough guess would be that only about 20 per cent of the population below the poverty line in the United States have characteristics which would justify classifying their way of life as that of a culture of poverty" (Lewis, 1968, p. li). This passage appears to have had little or no effect on popularizers and users of Lewis' concept who have generally treated the notion of poverty culture as if it applied automatically to all or most people in America who are poor.

There is in effect today a "culture of poverty" doctrine which has emerged as one of the more influential dogmas in contemporary American society. The most immediately apparent reason for the popularity of this doctrine is that it is really an old and satisfying belief in a new guise. Blaming poverty on the poor has long appealed to comfortable and affluent groups. This is a diagnosis of persistent social problems that poses no threat to the established order which Americans, from the organized working class to the very rich, generally believe has brought them their rewards and their security. It leads to prescriptions which demand no major changes in the structure of society.

This dogma, of course, has a long line of antecedents and has been promulgated in many forms by a multitude of earlier contributors well before Lewis' conceptions were assimilated into the tradition. Analogous formulations cultivated by other social scientists have abounded and continue to flourish within the same doctrinal trend. Among the most prominent of these in recent years have been the notions of "lower-class culture" and "the culturally deprived or disadvantaged" (*cf.* Valentine, 1968).

This complex of refurbished conventional wisdom enables Americans to evade hard questions about changes in the distribution of resources and the structure of society needed to resolve the problem of inequality which is the essence of the poverty crisis. It is used not only to silence radical critiques of our social system but also to calm the doubts of liberals or others that the system may not be working as it is supposed to. Faith in the status quo can be kept intact with no more than minor adjustments in national priorities. At the same time, new slogans like "culture of poverty" confer a gratifying feeling that a fresh understanding of a lingering difficulty has been achieved. The policy lines and action programs which flow from this may, for a time at least, create a comforting sense of new and promising practical initiatives.

The cult of poverty culture fits nicely into such expressions of the middle-of-the-road national consensus as "New Frontier," "Great Society," and whatever rhetorical title the ideologues of the Nixon regime may invent. The doctrine is nicely free of any overt association with crude racism or other obviously reactionary philosophies. Its phrasing is such as to belie or disguise the fact that this dogma both reflects and reinforces ethnocentric middle-class stereotypes of the poor. It sounds scientific or academic and hence not ideologically suspect. It combines a surface neutrality in ideology with a variety of potential philosophical associations. Adherents of the doctrine may thus feel consistent with any of a considerable range of broader outlooks, ranging at least from conservative politics to welfare-state liberalism.

The cult enables the affluent to take a benevolent stance toward the dispossessed without granting them any respect. The doctrine confirms the social inferiority of those who live in poverty. It lets social superiors feel they can be patrons of the poor without losing much. It articulates well with clichés of the political center like "opportunity" and "equality," but it arouses little anxiety that these slogans will be taken literally by anyone in power.

The very names of the resulting national programs symbolize either a benevolent despotism of regimentation (Job Corps, Youth Corps) or a patronizing rededication to the myth of rewards to the worthy via upward mobility (Upward Bound, Head Start). The rhetoric fairly reeks with "opportunity"—for those assumed to be unable to take advantage of it. It continually invokes "compensation"—not reparations to the oppressed but remediation for inferiority. The official attitudes, manners, and values of the middle class are assiduously inculcated to combat the "culture" of the poor that is said to be holding them back. If all this does little to change inadequate subsistence, unemployment, exploitation, political powerlessness, police oppression, and the many other hard realities of poverty, the underlying doctrine has not really been violated.

The social-service establishments enlisted enthusiastically in the "war," their practitioners being paid handsomely for joining up. Academics found new resources at their disposal for research or teaching that had anything to do with the now fashionable subjects of "life styles" or "social characteristics" of the poor. One of the more cynical sayings of recent years, "Poverty is where the money is," became current among middle-class professionals, not among the poor. The "war on poverty" has been a small bonanza for many elements in the middle class, a windfall hardly shared by any significant number of poor people.

Apparently most Americans outside the ranks of the poor are more concerned about something they see as pernicious in the lifeways of poor people than about the suffering these people experience or the injustice of their condition. There seems to be a widespread half-admitted fear of poor people's behavior as somehow threatening to the comfort of the affluent. One manifestation of this anxiety is the national outcry about delinquency and crime, widely associated with the poor and particularly the minority poor. Closely related to this is a fear of rebellious or even revolutionary behavior by poor people seeking to change society in their interests. Not a few conservatives who would otherwise probably subscribe to the poverty-culture dogma have even opposed the "war on poverty" on the grounds that it encourages these radical tendencies.

The preponderant national support which has kept the antipoverty programs going has flowed from a similar desire to preserve the larger structure of the existing social order. These programs are conspicuously offered as a reformist alternative to radical or revolutionary initiatives. Direct observation of the "war on poverty" in operation shows that it is frequently a series of devices for managing or controlling protest and potential rebellion. Prominent among these devices is teaching official versions of middle-class manners and modes, including allegiance to middle-class institutions and authorities. In this sense too the so-called antipoverty effort is an attack on the "culture" of the poor, not on the hard realities of poverty.

Consider the possibilities of rejuvenating this whole waning effort by revising its titles and slogans to make them more straightforward. The overall campaign would be retitled the War on the Culture of the Poor. The principal federal agency could be renamed the Office of Economical Orthopsychiatry. Within OEO there would remain various divisions concerned with the "culture of unemployment," such as the Yes-man Corps and the Jobless Corps. Present projects dealing with the "culture of the dropout" would be retitled Head Shrink and Uplift Bounce. The entire campaign could then be waged with new vigor under the revised slogan "Maximum Feasible Pacification of the Poor."

While some aspects of the national "antipoverty" programs do invite ridicule, their failure cannot be dealt with lightly. They have produced no significant change in the structure of inequality which preserves poverty. As for maintaining public peace and order, everyone knows that during the past decade confrontations between established authority and oppressed groups have grown from minor, nonviolent rebellions to massive and destructive insurrections. Of course, these developments cannot be attributed solely to deficiencies in national antipoverty policies. Yet they do indicate how dramatic the failure has been and help point to the reasons for it. The diagnosis of the problem in terms of the "culture of poverty" was wrong. Consequently the prescribed therapy has not had the desired or intended effects.

Materials for a critique of the poverty-culture dogma exist in the literature of the same social sciences that spawned the doctrine. S. M. Miller and collaborators have been warning for years that lower-class life is more varied than the subculture concept can reveal, and that focusing on deficiencies of motivation allegedly peculiar to the poor may lead to serious error (Miller, 1963, 1964a, 1964b; Miller and Rein, 1965a; Miller *et al.,* 1965). Miller and others have followed this up with critiques of the "war on poverty" which are incisive though somewhat more sanguine than the present evaluation (Miller and Rein, 1965b; Miller and Roby, 1968).

Hylan Lewis has repeatedly called attention to the fundamental errors in conceptions like the poverty subculture that confuse culture with social class and fail to grasp the significance for lower-class people of values, aspirations, and other culture patterns common to the society as a whole (H. Lewis, 1965, 1967a, 1967b). Kenneth Clark discovered and denounced "the cult of cultural deprivation." He saw that this "cultural" approach all too easily serves "subtle forms of social class and racial snobbery and ignorance," thus becoming "an alibi for educational neglect" which leads to "the perpetuation of inferior education for lower-status children" (Clark, 1965, pp. 125ff.). Elliot Liebow found that black street-corner men experience their lives as devoid of success or satisfaction precisely because they do share standards and criteria of the wider society; indeed, they live in continual and painful awareness of dominant American sentiments and values (Liebow, 1967).

A number of scholars have examined the distorting effects of middle-class biases and preconceptions on studies and portrayals of the poor (e.g., Honigmann, 1965a, 1965b; Leacock, 1967;

Rodman, 1965). Several critical reviews have exposed the implicit value judgments and conceptual confusions in the "culture of poverty" and kindred notions (Beck, 1967; Gans, 1968; Roach and Gurselin, 1967). Gans in particular has attempted to develop a more sophisticated concept of culture and to suggest an experimental methodology appropriate for the study of poverty (Gans, 1968, pp. 321-46). Studies have also begun to appear on the implications and effects of poverty-culture concepts on practice in major fields of social service, such as community mental health (Geiger, 1967), education (Leacock, 1968), and family planning (Jaffe and Polgar, 1968). The last two papers in particular document the extremely pernicious consequences of applying the "culture of poverty" doctrine in traditional settings of professional practice.

The prime nexus which makes all this relevant to public policy and national action is the connection between the poverty-culture doctrine and the governmental initiatives which have been dubbed the "war on poverty." One of the most thoughtful analyses of these connections is that by Thomas Gladwin in the volume referred to earlier. Here it is shown that the essential deficiency of antipoverty policy has been the failure to generate sufficient power for poor people so that they might bring about significant social change in their own interests. As Gladwin puts it, "the poor remain as poor as ever, and the 'power structure' remains the place where the power actually lies" (Gladwin, 1967, p. 169). The author goes on to trace this failure to a basic assumption underlying the official antipoverty effort: "that both the causes and the solutions to the problems of poverty are to be found within the ranks of the unskilled, unorganized, and disheartened poor." As Gladwin indicates, this assumption "arises directly from the fashionable and plausible concept of a culture of poverty." By ignoring the actual distribution of power and doing nothing about its reallocation, the programs based upon this theory inevitably fail. Gladwin concludes: "the social reforms necessary to make poverty avoidable and remediable must embrace a larger part of society than just the poor alone, and these reforms can be implemented only by forces greater than those conceivably available to poor people, however well organized" (*ibid., p.* 176).

A meticulous review of evidence on interconnections between poverty, policy, and violence was contributed by Hyman Rodman in a 1968 article. In stating the central issue Rodman points out: "Values, or culture, may not be at the heart of the problem, and thus the argument that jobs and money are not enough may merely be a convenient rationalization" (H. Rodman, 1968, p. 759). After a number of research studies are reviewed, the following conclusion is reached. "The heart of the ghetto problem therefore does not lie in the need to change values or to raise aspirations." In keeping with the poverty-culture doctrine, most existing efforts are essentially "treatment and rehabilitation programs with the poor, and these are in large measure wasted." Rodman concludes that the necessary solution is new policies to bring about "basic changes in the fundamental areas of income and employment." And finally: "We can therefore expect further civil disorder, an increasing incidence of civil disorder, and more widespread and more violent civil disorder, unless these policies are adopted and carried out" (*ibid.,* p. 761).

So policy makers, service professionals, and opinion molders have hardly lacked sources of alternatives to the poverty-culture dogma. This doctrine has been chosen instead because it appeals to comfortable and powerful groups in terms of their own interests as they perceive them. Yet it appears that not even these interests have been well served. Although deprivation and disfranchisement continued to be perpetuated through the decade of the 1960s, movements demanding radical change also grew during the same period. Paradoxically and ironically enough in terms of the stated and implied purposes of both architects and sponsors of the official programs, the "war on poverty" probably contributed to the growth of these movements.

Great public attention has been focused on the plight of the disadvantaged and the dispossessed. This has helped embolden many groups in poverty communities to mount more forceful and radical demands. The manifest emptiness of official promises and rosy predictions by the liberal establishment have strengthened minority insistence on self-determination and basic changes in the national social structure. There is a growing recognition among poor people that they have been deceived by a long series of false hopes ranging from civil-rights legislation through the shibboleth of integration to the war against the "culture of poverty." It has become a commonplace among people of widely varying political orientations that the most obvious failure of the anti-poverty campaign has been to promise much more than it could produce.

The recent assertiveness and militance of oppressed groups embodies new qualities of anger and determination. Cries of extremism and accusations of conspiracy from the establishment, punitive expeditions and reprisals by police and military forces, and the liberals' advice that militance only hurts the cause have all begun to lose their pacifying effect. Such standard authoritarian strategies as intimidation, cooptation, and promotion of disunifying factionalism are all meeting increased resistance. Many organizations with growing constituencies of active or passive adherents and supporters are demonstrating new willingness and capacity to confront centers of power and privilege. It is being widely recognized—even by such conscious instruments of the establishment as Presidential commissions—that our society is involved in an essentially continuous state of violent internal conflict. Most concrete manifestations of this conflict are related in one way or another to the multiple forms of inequality associated with poverty. Behind many of the most active forms of rebellion stand masses of poor people as active or passive, actual or potential, participants in the struggle.

Herein lies one further lesson to be drawn from refutation of the "culture of poverty" doctrine. A major element in the stereotypes associated with this dogma pictures the poor as collectively weak and ineffective, incapable of organization, planning or sustained purposeful action, irresolute and lacking in will, dependent, helpless, and resigned. It is no doubt because Americans have been bemused by these myths that they have been so shocked by recent rebellions. Greater realism in this respect is indispensable if the society is to emerge constructively from its present convulsions. The likelihood for the future may very well be still greater, more forceful, determined and resourceful resistance to the imposition of inequality and the preservation of privilege.

Many voices among oppressed groups are now saying that the granting of human dignity and full equality to the dispossessed can be brought about only by group self-assertion and intergroup confrontation to the uttermost degree. Some are saying explicitly that even self-destruction in the cause of destroying a system which refuses dignity, respect, and equality is preferable to existing conditions. Many victims of inequality are listening to these voices with increasing attention. No one knows how many are being led by their own experience to accept these propositions.

What is clear is that these ideas have real social force, that new kinds of organizations are being formed around them, and that new forms of action are emerging in association with them. Perhaps the most important culture of the disadvantaged will turn out to be a culture of resistance and revolution. Whether the upheaval that is already in progress can be converted into a peaceful revolution, or whether it must become more violent and destructive, is a question that can perhaps still be decided within the centers of established power. It seems likely that soon no one may have much freedom of choice.

BIBLIOGRAPHY

Beck, Bernard, "Bedbugs, Stench, Dampness and Immorality: A Review Essay on Recent Literature about Poverty," *Social Problems,* Vol. 15 (1967), pp. 101-14.

Clark, Kenneth B., *Dark Ghetto: Dilemmas of Social Power*. New York: Harper and Row, 1965.

Donovan, John C., *The Politics of Poverty*. New York: Western, 1967.

Gans, Herbert J., *People and Plans: Essays on Urban Problems and Solutions*. New York: Basic Books, 1968.

Geiger, Jack, "Of the Poor, By the Poor, or For the Poor: The Mental Health Implications of Social Control of Poverty Programs," *Amer-*

ican Psychiatric Association Research Report, Vol. 21, 1967, pp. 55-65.

● Gladwin, Thomas, *Poverty U.S.A.* Boston: Little, Brown, 1967.

Harrington, Michael, *The Other America: Poverty in the United States.* New York: Macmillan, 1962.

Honigmann, John J., "The Middle-Class View of Poverty Culture," paper given at the Conference on Cross-Cultural Psychiatry, Lexington, Ky., 1965.

———, "Psychiatry and the Culture of Poverty," *Kansas Journal of Sociology,* Vol. 1 (1965), pp. 162-65.

● Jaffe, Frederick S., and Steven Polgar, "Family Planning and Public Policy: Is the 'Culture of Poverty' the New Cop-out?," *Journal of Marriage and the Family,* Vol. 30 (1968), pp. 228-35.

Kennedy, Robert, and Oscar Lewis, "A Dialogue: Robert Kennedy and Oscar Lewis," *Redbook,* September 1967.

Leacock, Eleanor Burke, "Distortions of Working-Class Reality in American Social Science," *Science and Society,* Vol. 31 (1967), pp. 1-21.

———, "The Concept of Culture and Its Significance for School Counselors," *Personnel and Guidance Journal,* May 1968, pp. 844-51.

Lewis, Hylan, "The Family: Resources for Change," Agenda Paper No. 5, planning session, White House Conference "To Fulfill These Rights," 1965.

———, "Culture, Class and Family Life among Low-Income Urban Negroes," in *Employment, Race, and Poverty,* eds. Arthur M. Ross and Herbert Hill (New York: Harcourt, Brace and World, 1967).

———, *Culture, Class and Poverty.* Washington: Cross-Tell, 1967.

Lewis, Oscar, *Five Families: Mexican Case Studies in the Culture of Poverty.* New York: Basic Books, 1959.

———, *The Children of Sanchez.* New York: Random House, 1961.

———, "The Culture of Poverty," *Scientific American,* Vol. 215 (1966), pp. 19-25.

———, *La Vida: A Puerto Rican Family in the Culture of Poverty— San Juan and New York.* New York: Random House, 1966.

———, *A Study of Slum Culture: Backgrounds for La Vida.* New York: Random House, 1968.

———, *et al.,* "The Children of Sanchez, Pedro Martinez and La Vida," *Current Anthropology,* Vol. 8 (1967) pp. 480-500.

Liebow, Elliot, *Tally's Corner: A Study of Negro Streetcorner Men.* Boston: Little, Brown, 1967.

Miller, S. M., "Poverty and Inequality in America: Implications for Social Services," *Child Welfare,* Vol. 42 (1963), pp. 442-45.

————, "The American Lower Classes: A Typological Approach," *Sociology and Social Research,* Vol. 48 (1964), pp. 1-22.

————, "Some Thoughts on Reform," in Arthur B. Shostak and William Gomberg, *Blue-Collar World: Studies of the American Worker* (Englewood Cliffs, N.J.: Prentice-Hall, 1964).

————, and Martin Rein, "Poverty and Social Change," in *Poverty in America: A Book of Readings,* ed. Louis A. Ferman *et al.* (Ann Arbor, Mich.: University of Michigan Press, 1965).

● ————, and Martin Rein, "The War on Poverty—Perspectives and Problems," in *Poverty as a Public Issue,* ed. Ben B. Seligman (New York: Free Press, 1965).

————, F. Riessman, and A. A. Seagull, "Poverty and Self-Indulgence: A Critique of the Non-deferred Gratification Pattern," in *Poverty in America,* ed. Ferman *et al.* (Ann Arbor, Mich., 1965).

————, and Pamela Roby, "The War on Poverty Reconsidered," in *Poverty: Views from the Left,* eds. Jeremy Larner and Irving Howe (New York: William Morrow, 1968).

● Roach, Jack L., and O. R. Gurselin, "An Evaluation of the 'Culture of Poverty' Thesis," *Social Forces,* Vol. 45 (1967), pp. 383-392.

Rodman, Hyman, *Marriage, Family and Society: A Reader.* New York: Random House, 1965.

————, "Family and Social Pathology in the Ghetto," *Science,* Vol. 161 (1968), pp. 756-62.

Seligman, Ben B., *Permanent Poverty: An American Syndrome.* Chicago: Quadrangle, 1968.

● Valentine, Charles A., *Culture and Poverty: Critique and Counter-Proposals.* Chicago: University of Chicago Press, 1968.

————, *et al.,* "Culture and Poverty: Critique and Counterproposals," *Current Anthropology,* Vol. 10 (1969), pp. 181-201.

THE CONCEPT OF THE "CULTURE OF POVERTY": CONCEPTUAL, LOGICAL, AND EMPIRICAL PROBLEMS, WITH PERSPECTIVES FROM BRAZIL AND PERU

ANTHONY LEEDS

The concept of the "culture of poverty" poses a number of problems for the anthropological analyst. These issues are theoretical-conceptual, methodological, substantive, and ethical-civic.

The theoretical-conceptual issues involve, first, the use of the term 'culture,' which has generally come to embrace certain common understandings among social scientists at large. Second, the question whether the traits Oscar Lewis lists (1961, pp. xv-xvii; 1963; 1964-a, pp. 152-55)[1] are, in themselves, meaningful as concepts; whether the traits conceptualized in any way refer to autonomous elements in the sense that the traits used in culture-area analysis may be considered autonomous—i.e., not determined by the culture in which they are embedded, even when they co-

---

[1] The first use of the term 'culture of poverty' appears to be in *Five Families* (1959); the explicitly stated list of traits, in effect abstracted from its statement (pp. 28-31 *passim*), appears first in *Children of Sanchez* (1961) and is then repeated in one form or another through numerous publications with minor variations and inconsistencies (see bibliography at the end of this paper). Actually, the repetitions show an evolving statement in that, apparently under the stress of critical comment, Lewis slowly begins to develop some ideas of the connection among the traits. This is most clearly worked out in his article of 1966.

occur in "complexes." Third, among several other conceptual problems, there is the important theoretical problem of the logic of relationship betwen trait and structure.

The methodological issues involve problems of sampling, and the consideration of alternative hypotheses, canons of proof, and of how observations are connected with interpretations. These will be considered in conjunction with the theoretical and substantive issues rather than separately.

The methodological issues involve sampling, consideration of alternative hypotheses, canons of proof, and how observations are connected with interpretations. These will be considered in conjunction with the theoretical and substantive issues rather than separately.

The substantive issues revolve about the question of whether the data adduced to justify the use of the concept are correctly interpreted, selective, consistent with other data, and so on. It is especially in connection with such substantive problems that I shall refer to data comparable to Lewis's from Brazil and Peru.[2]

The ethical-civic issues involve the scientist's responsibility to see to it that his concepts and data are appropriately used and not abused and to foresee, given the nature of his social ambience and his social-science understandings and adherence, possible and even probable abuses of his concepts and data. This responsibility involves attention to the proper forms and places of publication,

---

[2] I have spent about 24 months (1965-66, 1967, 1968 twice, 1969) in field work in proletarian areas of Rio de Janeiro, with brief visits to similar settlements in Belo Horizonte, Salvador, São Paulo, and Curitiba in Brazil; Bogotá, Colombia; and San Juan, Puerto Rico. I have also spent nearly two and a half months in Lima (1967, 1968, 1969) in parallel research. My wife has accompanied me throughout, sometimes working jointly with me, sometimes doing independent research on aspects of related interest (in political science). She too has visited in the places mentioned. In addition, we have both been developing a bibliography of about 1,800 items (to be published by the University of California at Los Angeles, Latin-American Center) on the sociology of urban proletarian settlement types (E. Leeds and A. Leeds, 1966ff.). Of these items, about 500–600 have so far been abstracted. I have also carried on sporadic research in proletarian sections of Austin and San Antonio, Texas (cf. Leeds, 1969a) among people who are relevant to the present discussion (see Leeds, 1966; 1967; 1968; in press; A. Leeds and E. Leeds, 1970; Leeds, ed.).

to the nature of the audiences sought, and to the manner of presentation to such audiences.

That Oscar Lewis has failed with respect to all of these issues is the subject of this paper. Since the various issues are mostly interlaced, I shall not deal with them strictly in the order presented above, though more or less following that scheme. I turn first to the conceptual problems.

Conceptual Problems: 'Culture,' 'Society,' 'Trait,' 'the Poor,' 'the Slum,' and Other Terms

Several major conceptual problems are involved in the concept of the culture of poverty.

Though there are hundreds of definitions of 'culture' (*cf.* Kroeber and Kluckhohn, 1952), all of them may be subsumed under one of two conceptions.

In the first, the term 'culture' refers to structures of values, world views, ideologies, orders of knowledge (including technology), religions, mythologies. In short, it refers to the entire *system of meanings* of some population which is delimited by possession of a unique configuration or pattern of such cultural meaning structures, by sociogeographic isolation, or by political boundaries. In particular, the British social anthropologists, especially Radcliffe-Brown who speaks of a science of social anthropology but denies the possibility of a science of culture (1957: 106-110), and most sociologists (like Parsons and his followers) use the term this way. Society is seen, in these peoples' works, as the regularities of behavior, the *structure* of social relationships, the systems of interpersonal relations, the system of social bodies and institutions. Each more or less uniquely structured society is the organizational fabric upon which the uniquely patterned culture is an appliqué and by means of which it is passed on interpersonally through time. The culture is a unique order whose transmission through time occurs by agency of (necessarily) *all* the mediating social positions and structures of the society, of which the family, be it noted, is only one.

In the second set of definitions, typical of the majority of American anthropologists until recently (the florescence of "ethnoscience" is a move away from this), the term 'culture' refers to the interwoven network not only of meanings and behaviors but also of social bodies and relationships characteristic of some population delimited by the unique configuration or pattern of such a network, by sociogeographic isolation, or by conventional political boundaries. Such a population is usually referred to as 'a culture.' It is most important to remember, in discussing Lewis's work, that, in this standard conception, *a* culture is a self-perpetuating, *structurally* autonomous ordering of human life, though the constituent elements may have been derived by diffusion or acculturation from outside). Lewis's usage of the term 'culture' is in this tradition.

Both concepts involve the conception of independent, structural transmission through time of the unique ordering of relationships which is referred to by the term 'culture.' The dynamics are internal, part of the structured system of social relations of the delimited population itself, *not* epiphenomena to both.

Any concept which purports to discuss a culture or subculture must either fall within these conceptual conventions or give a strong rationale for a new usage and for departing from the common canons and understanding current in the social sciences.

In view of Lewis's approach to poverty in terms of culture *traits,* one qualification must be made to the comments above. American anthropology, its roots in the nineteenth-century European anthropogeographic thought, so far has still failed theoretically to resolve the contradiction between the asserted distributability of culture elements and their integration into some system. Thus, there were endless studies of the diffusion of elements or traits of culture. All of these, without exception, involved the notion that the element —in the entire literature known as the 'culture trait'—had an independent existence of its own, which made it detachable from the contexts of its origin, of its causation, and transmissible almost limitlessly to other contexts, *regardless of the age and other relations of the human transmitters,* of linguistic differences, and so on. The importance of these points will be clear in the discussion of Lewis's trait treatment of the culture of poverty and his conception of its transmission, which involve internal conceptual contradictions and do not follow the standard, accepted conceptions of traits as outlined above.

On the other hand, the fact that traits cling together, that some things that look like traits, observationally, virtually do not occur separately (e.g., Kroeber's field agriculture-animal power-plow "systemic pattern"; see 1948, pp. 312-14), and that widely different traits have formal similarities in the context of their possession by a single population led American anthropologists sequentially to develop a series of concepts to deal with the systemic characteristics of "aggregates" of traits, while at the same time Austrian anthropologists were developing parallel notions, and the British structural-functionalist anthropologists were elaborating approaches to describe the systemic relationships internal to sociocultural entities, which have since spread to all sociology and anthropology in modified forms.[3]

Problems of Oscar Lewis's concept of the culture of poverty may be examined in light of the discussion above.

First, it is quite clear in Lewis's writings that he conceives the "culture of poverty" to be transmitted through a social system or subsystem. Specifically, he says it is passed down in family lines, which, as I emphasized above, are only *one* among many transmitting channels that exist concurrently for any learner and actor of a society, and which, in any case, are not intrinsically related to culture traits. At the same time, his description of the culture of poverty is in terms of traits, especially in the earlier publications (1959a, 1961, 1963, 1964a).

---

[3] For the Americans, the sequence was the 'culture complex' (Wissler, Kroeber), the 'culture climax' (Kroeber), 'core' and 'superstructure' (Steward), the 'culture pattern' (Benedict, Kroeber, Kluckhohn), the 'theme' (Opler), the 'configuration' (Kroeber), the 'basic personality pattern' (Kardiner, Linton), 'levels of sociocultural integration' (Steward), the 'social and cultural orders' (Redfield), and, finally, the 'system' in both the British functionalist senses (Radcliffe-Brown, Malinowski) and the general systems theory sense (e.g., Binford, Flannery, Leeds, Vayda, *et al.*). Independently, the Austrians spoke of the '*Kulturkreis.*' Concurrent with the American progression of holistic ordering concepts, the use and usefulness of trait analysis has steadily declined, especially sharply after World War II.

The two conceptions are contradictory because, in the former, the culture of poverty is treated as a system and, in the latter, it is treated as detachable and independent elements which, as traits, should be transmissible to anyone, of any age, at any time. The fact which Lewis asserts is that they are not so transmitted and are not so transmissible. Therefore, the analytic model of "traits" of a "culture of poverty" is confused because he asserts their autonomy from some system and their independence of each other, both of which are contradicted by Lewis' treatment of transmission and by the data themselves.

Second, Lewis is explicit in saying that the alleged culture of poverty is not restricted to either urban or rural milieux or to any particular country—it transcends all of these—although he does say that it does not apply to the "backwardness" of primitive peoples (e.g., 1965–66, p. xlvii), and also that it is a product of capitalist societies (*ibid., p.* xliv). However, he deplores the absence of studies from socialist countries (*ibid.,* p. xlii), which should be irrelevant if the culture of poverty is a product of capitalism.[4] These passages also indicate his conceptual and analytic unclarity as to what the relationship indeed *is* to the larger society, an unclarity enhanced by his emphasis on the trait approach and by his insistence that it is a *culture* (or "subculture"), presumably dis-

[4] If the culture of poverty is a *product* of capitalism, that indicates it is a product of a form of total-societal integration: a reflex and symptom caused by it. If the cause is removed, i.e., the replacement of capitalism by socialism or some other form of integration, then it follows that the symptom should disappear. If the "culture of poverty" is in fact a *culture* at all, then it should continue more or less regardless of the presence of capitalism or socialism or any particular stage of either. It should therefore be the case that all recently former capitalist and all protocapitalist countries, i.e., *all* of today's capitalist, "underdeveloped," *and* socialist countries, display a culture of poverty in varying degree. Lewis says he is "inclined to believe that the culture of poverty does not exist in socialist countries" (1966, p. 7). In fact, the Cuban slum he "recently" revisited had changed drastically; apparently the culture of poverty he observed there in 1947, carried in family lines, enculturated in children, had disappeared in the 18 or 19 years since his visit. The high situational changeability indicates, *therefore,* that a *culture* was not involved at all. His positions are thoroughly contradictory and inconsistent, and involve the absence of the resolution of structuralist vs. culturalist analyses discussed in the text. In connection with these comments, it would be interesting to know whether Lewis could or could not demonstrate a culture of poverty for National Socialist Germany of 1933–45.

tinguishable from some other culture, passed down along family lines.

If, however, standard uses of the term 'culture' are maintained, then the culture of poverty—which, according to Lewis, can occur in all kinds of different traditions and social systems —cannot be a *culture,* though it may be some other kind of system, subsystem, or trait complex. It is not unique; it is not specific to a time and place and tradition; it has no particular or unique meaning structure; it is not sociogeographically isolable.

Further, the object, culture, conceptually is always connected, in contemporary social science, with some maximal social system or major subsystem, not a family, or many families in parallel, unless the families are coterminous with the maximal social system or subsystems, as in some very simple tribal groups. Such a subsystem, which would be the carrier of the "culture of poverty," is nowhere conceptualized or postulated by Lewis other than to refer to "the poor" (and not all or even most of then; cf. 1966, p. 5) and to family lines. Such a subsystem would include the many families iteratively, their linkages through such networks as true and fictional kin ties, friendships, and neighborhood links; through associations and agencies; and by virtue of real or attributed membership in social categories based on race, ethnicity, or other criteria. All of these link certain aggregates of people and separate them as over against other aggregates, so that each has a certain degree of internal autonomy as well as some measures of independence from the other. Such a system or set of systems is neither conceptualized nor analyzed with respect to the postulated culture of poverty, so that it is impossible to determine what social framework is the carrier of the "culture of poverty" and why one is not simply dealing with, say, family neuroses. Any cultural or social system is vastly more ramified, more complex, more multifold than *only* family histories, and the histories of individuals are elaborately involved in the broad arrays of social forms outside the family. Extrapolations from family histories to an alleged "culture" simply fail to deal with the majority of institutional and social frameworks in which families are embedded (*cf.* Leeds, in press; Leeds, 1969a and 1969b).

Lewis's conception of culture, like that of other American anthropologists, involves the structured transmission through time of an order. But the unresolved contradiction in American anthropology discussed above shows up very clearly here in his conceptual unclarity about the nature of the order: as traits. In the earlier statements (e.g., 1961, pp. xxvi-xxvii) these are, on the whole, simply listed and are obviously conceived of as independent and autonomous elements. Under criticism and discussion, the elements, here and there, have by 1966 been somewhat connected with each other, but in no systemic, conceptual, analytic, or logical way, a problem I return to below. He still conceives of them as traits and reiterates them (1966, pp. 5ff.).

In short, despite the evolution of holistic conceptions in American anthropology, despite the highly sophisticated holistic structural-functionalism current in British anthropology for forty years, despite available conceptual apparatuses for the analysis of sociocultural systems in sociology, we are given no conceptual scheme nor any analysis of the social system underlying, delimiting, and carrying that cultural system which Lewis calls "the culture of poverty." In fact, we are not given any logical or empirical proofs that such a cultural system exists, other than that the facts which are to be shown to be part of it are adduced as proof of its existence, a circularity.

A further unclarity exists in that Lewis is unable conceptually to specify for the reader the distinction between those who are poor but *not* "living in the culture of poverty" and those who are poor but "living in it," let alone provide a systemic analysis of how poor people dynamically are sorted out into the one category or the other.[5] Structurally, both appear to be in the same sort of

[5] It is interesting to note that in *Five Families* (p. 16) he is still quite far from even having recognized the problem: he refers to "the culture of the poor." In other words, he has not yet fully formalized the distinction even verbally, let alone, ostensibly, substantively, which he is never able to do. The problem, as I shall note below in the text, is much wider, because he is unable not only to sort out the poor from the "culture of poverty" poor, but the poor from the middle- and upper-class people who display the same traits (e.g., 1961, p. xxvii), although he asserts that the traits in the different classes have "peculiar patterning." For example, "drinking in the middle class is a social amenity, whereas in the lower class getting drunk has

relationship to all the major institutions of the society in which they are embedded: the labor market, the bureaucratic agencies, the transportation system, and so on. The conceptual distinction between "the poor" and "those in the culture of poverty" gets fuzzier throughout Lewis's books because of the overpowering methodological emphasis on the latter in the life-history approach. Fuzziness is compounded because he cannot even account, theoretically, for truly cultural differences found among people in the supposed culture of poverty—the differences between people of two societies of Spanish background, Mexico and Puerto Rico (cf. 1965–66, pp. xxv-xxix); differences which erode the significance of his alleged "traits" of the culture of poverty.

The realities of the distinction between the poor and those in the culture of poverty become quite distorted, as is evident when one reads Lewis's own sketchy data called "Setting" or "Introduction," the brief and highly repetitive materials which were all that were given to the public between 1959 (1959a, cf. pp. 15-31), and the recent publication (in 1968) of ethnographic data on the slums (see 1961, pp. xi-xxxi; 1965, p. 500; 1965–66, pp. xxxii-xlii; 1968; some of the distortions are discussed below).[6]

---

different and multiple functions—to forget one's troubles, to prove one's ability to drink, and to build up sufficient confidence to meet difficult life situations." There is certainly enough literature on drinking habits and alcoholism among the middle classes to know that such an assertion is at least an oversimplification if not downright false, even at those sodden "social amenities" among the professional middle classes called cocktail parties, where one can more than rarely observe the middle-class gentry drowning their troubles, proving their ability to drink, and trying to build up self-confidence. The patterning must be, first, demonstrated, and, second, demonstrated to be mutually exclusive by class.

[6] The repetitiveness is exemplified, for example, by three or four paragraphs in Lewis, 1961 (pp. xxix-xxx), which are repeated word for word, or almost so, from those published in 1959a (pp. 22-23)—the two earlier and publicly most influential books. Some phrases from both these introductions reappear in La Vida (1965–66; e.g., pp. xlvff.) so that, for a period of years, the same or very similar material, with minimal conceptual and theoretical clarification, is made to carry the weight of over 1,500 pages of undigested data. Again, paragraph after paragraph of material from the 1961 introduction reappears, virtually unchanged, in the first part of the 1964a article, while the second part of that article consists entirely of extended quotations from The Children of Sanchez. I consider this use

These data clearly indicate wide ranges of income, education, behavior, and ability to cope with urban conditions among the poor, the majority of whom appear not to be in the culture of poverty at all. This fact again raises the question as to what social subsystem and what kind of locality unit is the carrier of the supposed culture of poverty (see Footnote 7).

Another conceptual unclarity concerns the housing-settlement unit used as a locus of study. For example, the *vecindad* as described on p. 23 of 1959a clearly seems to involve quite distinct kinds of settlements. The single-story row dwellings with common patio, a kind of rooming or small apartment house, are apparently equivalent to the *callejón* of Lima studied by Patch (1961) and the *cortiço* described for Rio by Azevedo (*ca.* 1899) and illustrated in numerous photos in the studies of housing conditions in eleven Mexican cities (Instituto de Seguro Social). The units Lewis describes as "on the outskirts of the city, [consisting] of wooden shacks or *jacales* and [looking] like semitropical Hoovervilles" are clearly of the type I refer to as squatments in the discussion below. The non-squatment type, the *vecindad,* itself involves significant subtypes, according to Lewis's brief notes. These include old colonial buildings which have decayed and been subdivided; the serried apartments with some sort of patio space; and the rows of rooms. Each of these may display quite distinct social situations, and, in my experience in Rio and Lima, they are in fact significantly different from each other in a variety of ways (such as indices of average family size, household composition, locality organization, and so on), but are not distinguished at all in Lewis's writings. Respectively, the equivalent types are called in Rio *casas decadentes, casas de cômodo,* or *cabeças de porco* ("pig heads") (though this category also includes rather large buildings speculatively built specifically for the purpose of

and reuse of essentially identical materials one of the failures in responsibility of an ethical-civic sort that I referred to at the beginning, since the publication of vast quantities of new data in the later books involves little or no essentially new or revised interpretations, nor any extensions of analysis in the science to which the data are purportedly related. One wonders if there were valid *scientific* reasons for publishing at least the second (1961) and third (*Pedro Martinez,* 1964) books.

renting to the poor); *vilas;* and *avenidas.* In Lima, the terms *casas subdivididas* or *decaidas, quintas,* and *callejones* are used. Each type involves a rather different process in the development of the city and very different kinds of familial and individual articulation to the respective type.

All these types are built within the framework of the formal city layout, docketed in the city registries, and presumably have a legitimate status, although this is not explicitly reported by Lewis. Occupants are invariably renters and, for any one *vecindad,* confront a single landlord who has a number of rights and powers over the lessee. The buildings themselves, and often the areas of the city in which they are found, are consistently in decay. They may have met standards once, but are increasingly in substandard conditions.

The *arrabal,* of which Lewis's "La Esmeralda" (La Perla, in San Juan) is an example, is equivalent to the *barriadas* of Perú the *favelas* of Brazil, the *barrios paracaidistas* of México with their typical *jacales,* the *callampas* of Chile, the *barrios* of Venezuela, etc. All of these usually consist of separate "family" dwellings (although, in more advanced squatments,[7] rooming and

---

[7] The term 'squatter settlement,' or 'squatment' (invented by Charles Abrams), is used here despite the fact that certain denigrative connotations tend to get attached to it in the popular mind (as in phrases like "semi-tropical Hoovervilles" [1961, p. xxx]). I use it because it is short, unlike John Turner's 'unregulated urban settlements' or 'unauthorized urban settlements,' and also because it seems to me to indicate the one feature that is most nearly universal to the entities in question—that the residents of these urban housing-settlement types do not have title to the land on which they have settled and are there, essentially, on sufferance. It is important to indicate a number of things that the word does *not* imply. It does *not* mean that:

  a. the residents are ne'er-do-wells, hobos, tramps, "marginals," etc.;
  b. the residents are criminals, dope peddlers, assassins, robbers;
  c. the residents are significantly different in income, occupation, education, etc., from other urban housing-settlement types of largely working-class composition;
  d. the residents are ruralites;
  e. the residents are transients;
  f. the residents are illiterate, ignorant, present-oriented, fun-loving, etc.;
  g. the residents live at a substantially lower standard of living than the rest of the city;

apartment houses begin to appear), owned independently by the builder or buyer. The entire array of buildings is built outside the framework of the city layout, although many squatments in Lima and a few in Bogotá have planned streets, water mains, plazas, electric systems, and the like, which attach to the municipal services. The houses are not docketed in the city registries either as individual houses or as aggregates of houses, or places, although in Lima many of the very large and well-planned squatments have recently been made into municipalities, ostensibly with full legal status. Here titles have been promised to the residents, and the houses and lots are registered with the National Housing Council (Junta Nacional de la Vivienda, now Ministerio de la Vivienda), a sign of the importance given by the present Peruvian government to resolving the problem of illegal land possession in the most expeditious way. In general, however, they are illegal places and residents have illegal occupancy, although they own the pile of materials out of which their houses are constructed.[8]

---

h. the settlements themselves are disarrayed (see comment in text above).

Individually or collectively, these things are often asserted both popularly and in the literature (cf. Lewis, 1965–66, p. xxvi, paragraph 2). In fact, significant numbers of residents, though by no means all, are involved in solidly "middle-class," sometimes even professional, jobs; are second- and even third-generation urbanites; have opted for long-term residence in squatments as a strategy of savings in order better to achieve long-term goals; enjoy reasonable standards of living and are deeply concerned with education. There is evidence that at least a large proportion of the residents are more dynamic in their upward-mobility strivings than persons in other intra-urban-settlement types of equivalent composition.

[8] Though ownership of the pile of materials they have bought out of their own funds appears to be a right defined in Brazilian private-property law, present government activity in removing favelas appears to abrogate it in practice, either in whole or in part. "In part," because, when indemnities have been given for their houses from which squatment residents have been removed, they have been far below either the replacement-construction or market values of the houses. The residents are therefore forced to take severe losses out of the savings represented by their investment over the years in housing. In other cases, removals have been made without monetary indemnities. It has often been argued that the residents are given "better" public housing, but often the housing is demonstrably inferior, less convenient, etc., and, in any event, it is never given. The residents are forced into these places without choice and must pay governmentally established amortization payments—with "monetary correction" for inflation.

Occasionally, after sufficiently long occupancy, residents can claim squatters' rights of ownership, if no one has protested their presence, or can petition the government to give formal recognition to, and legalize, the place. In general, *favelas, barriadas, barrios,* and *arrabales*—La Perla (please note!) included—are areas of urban growth and development, areas of slow improvement both of individual houses and of the neighborhood as a whole (see Mangin, 1967).

Thus, the socioeconomic processes of the two broad kinds of places Lewis lumps together without distinction, because of his focus on specific, highly selected families, are opposite; peoples' relationships to such places and their socioeconomic dynamics are also quite different. The lack of conceptual clarity in this matter leads to obscuring, if not actually hiding, some extremely important aspects of development and social process, and Lewis's biographical method compounds this obscurantism by its methodologically unjustified selectivity.

Important conceptual problems are also to be found in Lewis's manner of listing the traits of the "culture of poverty." He feels that "the culture of poverty has some universal characteristics" (1961, p. xxv), which he then proposes to elaborate "in order to present a provisional conceptual model . . . based mainly on [his] Mexican materials." In passing, one may ask how it is possible to develop a conceptual model which deals with something "which transcends regional, rural-urban, even national differences" from a single, particularistic standpoint. In any case, the paragraphs immediately following (p. 25) give what are presumably examples of these universal characteristics (see Table 1, the major part of whose entries are taken, in the order of Lewis's own order of presentation, from 1961, pp. xxvi-xxvii, and a few from 1964a, pp. 152-55). These are followed by a group of traits called "economic," another called "social and psychological," and, probably as a subgroup of the latter, "other" traits. Later, in discussing these traits, other traits appear (as listed in Table I, under appropriate respective headings), finally ending in a "residual quality." The 1964a article adds some more traits after this final one (p. 54).

TABLE I   The Traits and Categories Comprising Lewis's
"Provisional Conceptual Model"
("Based Mainly on . . . Mexican Materials")
of the Culture of Poverty*

"Universal Characteristics" (1961, p. xxvi; 1964a, p. 152, 1965, p. 500)

Relatively higher death rate.

Lower life expectancy.

A higher proportion of individuals in the younger age groups.

Child labor and working women—therefore higher proportion of gainfully employed.

Provincially and locally oriented culture.

Only partially integrated into national institutions.

Marginal people even in the heart of a great city.

Low level of education and literacy.

Do not belong to labor unions.

Not members of political parties.

Do not participate in medical care, maternity or old-age benefits, etc., of the Seguro Social.

Make little use of city's banks, hospitals, department stores, museums, galleries, airports.

"Economic Traits" (1961, p. xxvi; 1964a, p. 152; 1965, p. 500)

Constant struggle for survival.

Unemployment and underemployment.

Low wages.

Miscellany of unskilled occupations.

* Though Lewis claims (1965–66, p. xliv) to be able to "describe" the culture of poverty in terms of "some seventy" traits (*cf.* also 1966, p. 5) and then, in a footnote, cites his 1964a article, presumably as documentation of this, the 1964a article is *identical,* for the most part, with the list in 1961 and in 1965–66, and very similar to 1966, differing from 1961 only in the group listed above as "1964a Additions." In both places, the alleged traits are presented in running paragraph form—nowhere listed—so that one is unable, *anywhere,* to establish definitively what the discrete traits are as he conceives them. I have therefore listed almost the entire body of the paragraphs concerned in a telegraphic style according to his divisions by commas and periods which seemed intended to indicate different traits. In some cases this led to repetitions and restatements, or included commentary on priorly listed traits. Even with these, the list above numbers only sixty-two. I would challenge Lewis to make an unambiguous list from his own writings.

Child labor.

Absence of savings.

Chronic shortage of cash.

Absence of food reserves in the home.

Pattern of frequent buying of small quantities of food many times a day as need arises.

Pawning.

Borrowing from local moneylenders at usurious rates of interest.

Spontaneous informal credit devices organized by neighbors.

Use of secondhand clothing and furniture.

"Social and Psychological Characteristics" (1961, p. xxvi; 1964a, p. 153)

Living in crowded quarters.

Lack of privacy.

Gregariousness.

High incidence of alcoholism.

Frequent resort to violence in settling quarrels.

Frequent use of physical violence in training children.

Wife beating.

Early initiation into sex.

Free unions, consensual marriages.

Relatively high incidence of abandonment of mothers and children.

Trend toward mother-centered families.

Greater knowledge of maternal relatives.

Predominance of nuclear family.

Strong predisposition to authoritarianism.

Great emphasis on family solidarity—ideal rarely achieved.

"Other Traits Include" (1961, p. xxvi; 1964a, p. 153)

Strong present-time orientation.

Little ability to defer gratification and plan for the future.

Sense of resignation and fatalism based upon realities of difficult life situation.

Belief in male superiority; crystallized in *machismo,* the cult of masculinity.

Martyr complex among women.

High tolerance for psychological pathology of all sorts.

Local Solutions for Problems Not Met by Institutions and Agencies (1961, p. xxvii; 1964a, p. 153)

No bank credit, therefore informal credit devices.

No doctors; suspicion of hospitals, therefore reliance on herbs, home remedies, curers, and midwives.

Critical of priests, rarely go to confession or Mass, relying on prayer to images at home, and pilgrimages to popular shrines.

"Counter Quality" and Potential for Use by Political Movements contra Existing Order (1961, p. xxvii; 1964a, p. 154)

Critical attitude toward some values and institutions of dominant class.

Hatred of police.

Mistrust of government and those in high positions.

Cynicism which extends "even" to the Church.

"Residual Quality" (1961, p. xxvii; 1964a, p. 154)

"Attempt to utilize and integrate into a workable way of life the remnants of beliefs and customs of diverse origins."

1964a Additions (pp. 154-55)

Strong feeling of marginality, helplessness, dependency, not belonging, alienation.

Feeling that existing institutions do not serve their interests and needs.

Feeling of powerlessness, inferiority, personal unworthiness.

Very little sense of history.

Know only their own local conditions, neighborhood, own way of life.

Do not have knowledge, vision or ideology to see similarities with their counterparts elsewhere in the world.

Not class conscious.

Sensitive to status distinctions.

On the whole, the set of economic traits seems internally consistent and corresponds with what is ordinarily called economic, but the other sets, singly and jointly, make little sense, the more so as there is no category of traits called "cultural." One may well ask why there is no category of cultural traits. Why, for example, are such traits as "provincially and locally oriented," "non-use of city's museums and galleries," "gregariousness," "strong present-time orientation," "male superiority" or *"machismo,"* "martyr complex of women," "sense of fatalism," "reliance on herbs, curers and midwives," "critical attitudes towards dominant class," "integration of customs of diverse origin"—as just one selection out of many possible ones from the total list and Lewis's subdivisions of it —not *all* listed simply under "cultural," where, by standard definitions of 'culture' and usual treatment of the topics in question, they clearly belong, the more so as Lewis wishes to talk about a *culture* of poverty.

The classifications, or, better, the absence of classification, and the absence of a category of cultural traits in discussing the culture of poverty clearly betoken Lewis's absence of a clear conception of standard uses of the concept of culture, on one hand, and, on the other, his failure to see the underlying processes and structures which give order to the "traits." Again the confusion is strongly underlined when one asks why such traits as "low level of education and literacy" and "higher proportion of gainfully employed" are not listed, respectively, under "Social" and "Economic"? The entire ordering of traits lacks conceptualization and logical ordering. In short, it makes no theoretical sense.

Finally, conceptual problems appear in Lewis's notion of "testing the concept of poverty . . ." (1965–66, p. xliii). One does not test a concept, one tests an hypothesis. A concept is not an hypothesis, but is a tool used in formulating hypotheses. The results of testing an hypothesis may tell whether that particular tool, the concept in question, used in the formulation is useful or not, usefulness being judged by accuracy or extensiveness of prediction, range of data accounted for, and the like. What one actually tests is a *relationship* which is asserted by using concepts and stating some particular kind of connection among them which should have specific, empirically observable characteristics. The concept is defined by specifying some set of characteristics that the observer thinks interesting—because of their potential relationship to something else. There is no way of testing a concept, because one would simply refer back to the characteristics one had used in defining it in the first place. Lewis does not seem aware of these basic methodological procedures of science, anthropology included, and indeed presents us with no specifically formulated, testable hypotheses at all.

Theoretical Problems: Traits and Structure
and the Logic of Their Relationship

Although Lewis's trait listings are accompanied in the later statements by assertions that the traits occur in the context of capitalist societies, he nowhere spells out what the connection with capitalist society is. If true, the correlation is such a striking one that it demands the most intensive treatment (see Footnote 3), especially as it suggests that the *efficient causes* of poverty, if not of the culture of poverty itself, lie in capitalism. The entire web—if such it be —of connection between that structuring of society which we call capitalist and the proposed culture of poverty is left unexplained. In the absence of a treatment of this important question, we are left with a culture (or "subculture"), a more or less self-generating and autonomous process, described only by a trait list, resting on that trait treatment of culture which has so venerable a history.[9]

Lewis, of course, came of anthropological age during the time that a trait approach to culture was in its heyday. Nevertheless, even at that time, some of the issues of structural-functional analysis, of systemic approaches, were already widely current in the scientific discourse of the day in America. Structural-functionalism was represented, for example, by the trends at Chicago—the urban ecologists and the Radcliffe-Brownians (especially Redfield), both trends later being crucial to Oscar Lewis's work in rural–urban relations (1951, 1952) and the anthropology of city life. Yet neither their structuralism nor their functionalism—their systemic

[9] This approach to culture culminated in the vast surge of distributional, historical ethnology of the first half of the twentieth century in America, Austria, and partly in England. The trait treatment infused all approaches to problems of culture: developmental, evolutionary, typological, historical. For example, J. H. Steward's trial formulation of lawfulness in cultural development (1949) is based essentially on trait similarities; his typologies of South American Indian cultures are almost entirely based on trait inventories; his conception of 'superstructural' aspects of culture depends on a trait conception of culture. His, Kroeber's, Wissler's and many others' historical reconstructions grow out of trait-distribution analysis. The date of Lewis's Ph.D., 1940, falls between Kroeber's *Natural and Cultural Areas of Native North America* (1939), and Steward's *Handbook of South American Indians* (1946–49), both synthetic peaks—and dead ends—of trait analysis as a mode of interpretation of culture.

approaches—seems to have penetrated to the level of Lewis's meta-languages: his assumptions, his models, and his basic units and parameters. He persists in an essentially trait-analytic approach to understanding the empirical data of his urban people.

Fundamental to the concept of trait and its use as an analytic device in historical reconstruction and anthropological analysis is the postulate that each trait or at least each trait complex[10] is not causally related to other traits or trait complexes. They are independent, autonomous, detachable as entities. They move separately from one another in time and space. The position is epistemologically and methodologically summarized in Lowie's well-known apothegm that culture is a thing of "shreds and patches" —a sum of the accidental congeries of cultural things that have come together in the flow of history.

By giving a trait list purportedly characterizing that "culture" (see Table I), Lewis treats the culture of poverty in the same way.

What is striking in his repeated presentations of the concept of the culture of poverty is his failure to deal with the asserted "adhesiveness" of these traits, their asserted character of being a trait complex, or, in his terminology, a "culture." In other words, he fails to deal with their wholeness, their systemicness, their interrelatedness. He fails to give us either the dynamics, *in natura,* of how these traits are linked or the logic at the meta-language level, of asserting their linkage. The failure is consistent with the failure of *all* proponents of trait analysis to solve, or at least to deal with, these problems.[11]

Here I wish to deal mainly with the logical aspects of Lewis's traits, though passing attention is given to empirical questions, especially insofar as linkage among the traits is involved; below I

[10] The analog to 'trait complex,' in Tylor's language, is 'adhesions'; in Schmidt's, *'Kulturkreis'*; in Kroeber's, the concept of 'systemic pattern.'

[11] *No systematic anthropological-philosophical analysis of the status of traits, their interrelations, and their relation to sociocultural structure exists in the literature of our discipline,* although the issue is of utmost importance. Only structural-functional analysis, combined with evolutionary theory, appears to shed light on this problem, a subject that will have to be pursued elsewhere.

shall turn to some questions of the empirical validity of the observations. Starting with the economic, I shall take selected traits
more or less in the order Lewis presents them (1961, 1964a), except when convenient to deal concurrently with two or more
scattered through his list, revolving about the same issue. Using
a sizable sample, the purpose is to be illustrative rather than exhaustive.

Constant Struggle for Survival. Aside from the vagueness of
this "trait" and the question whether, in some way or another, all
members of all species, plant and animal, are not in a constant
struggle for survival, it is impossible to decide, *a priori,* what
features of human society or behavior are to be designated as
constant struggle for survival and which not. The term implies no
correspondence rules that lead one to look at specified things in
the real world. In this respect, the so-called trait has no useful
empirical content to which an observer is directed. It does not
help distinguish between a person with no income and no possibility of making one; the professional criminal; the college professor
who must publish or perish; the family farmer in competition
with capital-intensive corporate farming; the corner grocer in competition with the chain store; and the Senator trying to hold his
seat; or the New Haven Railroad in competition with the Pennsylvania Railroad.

*Unemployment and Underemployment, Low Wages, Miscel-
lany of Unskilled Occupations, Child Labor.* First, these are
largely identities. Underemployment, for example, *by definition,*
involves a miscellany of unskilled occupations, child labor, and
low wages, although the latter may also characterize a condition
of formal "full" employment. Unskilled occupations entail low
wages, by definition, and so on.

Second, Lewis himself has pointed out that not all people who
are unemployed or underemployed or who earn low wages display
the culture of poverty. This is, of course, logically confused, because (a) if the trait is *of* the culture of poverty, then anyone displaying it is by definition *in* the culture of poverty, or (b) the
trait cannot be part of the culture of poverty. In other words, it
does not distinguish those who are in from those who are outside

the said culture, and therefore cannot be a trait of the culture of poverty.

In either case, it is quite plain that neither unemployment nor underemployment nor the other "traits" are part of a *culture* or of some self-perpetuating autonomous sociocultural system. Rather, they are all characteristic of certain kinds of labor market which are structured by the condition of national technology, available capital resources, enterprise location, training institutions, relations to foreign and internal markets, balance-of-trade relations, and the nature of the profit system of capitalist societies. The form and characteristics of the labor market can be predicted from states of these variables, and with that prediction also the state and rates of un- and underemployment can be reasonably predicted. These are not independent traits of some supposed culture, but characteristics or indices of certain kinds of total economic systems, such as so-called underdeveloped economies or certain sectors of developed economies—for example, the internally colonized and "underdeveloped" labor force constituted by Negroes, Puerto Ricans, Mexicans, Cubans, Orientals, and, formerly, Irish, Italians, Poles, Jews, and other European immigrants to the United States.

These are economies of which under- and unemployment are not *merely* historically accidental traits but, rather, structural and functional reflexes. In fact, I would argue that they are essential to the operation of such societies.

In turn, under- and unemployment have consequences—e.g., depression of wages, especially for the unskilled[12]—because of the excess of labor available in capital-intensifying capitalist econ-

[12] The current wave of study of *marginalidad* in Latin America (Argentina, Chile, Colombia, and Perú, in particular) centers its entire theoretical understanding and substantive description around under- and unemployment in industrializing and capitalist societies. Much of what I am saying here is paralleled, with somewhat different theoretical interpretation, by such persons as José Nun, Aníbal Quijano, the Desal group in Chile, the Desco group in Perú, Ramiro Cardona, and others. In a way, they are trying to account for kinds of data similar to Lewis's but with much more sophisticated theory, a theory of a structural sort (see, for example, Quijano, 1966) which logically must reject conceptualization of the data in terms of a culture constituted of traits.

omies. It is to the interest of others (for example, elite classes), as employers of labor, to maintain these consequences. These reflexes are part of the total system of the society, not independent elements of a subsystem which acts autonomously as an alleged culture of poverty. Put another way, the dynamics lie in the major institutions of the society, in the macrosystem, not in the subculture or microsystem.

Thus, none of the traits of underemployment and unemployment, miscellany of unskilled occupations, child labor, or low wages has a status as a trait logically independent of the others or the larger societal system. They are identical to each other definitionally, empirically, or logically and are direct consequences of the same causes which produce them all.[13]

Absence of Savings, Chronic Shortage of Cash, Pawning, Borrowing from Usurers, Spontaneous Informal Credit Devices. These traits likewise display no logically definable discreteness and indeed appear, on one hand, to be identities either in whole or part and, on the other, clearly logically derivable as real consequences of the operation of the "traits" discussed just above.

Any usual conception of under- and unemployment, with their characteristic of low wages and consequent low incomes given by definition, necessarily implies a chronic shortage of cash. That is one major thing the term 'low wages' intrinsically means. One aspect of low wages or chronic shortage of cash is *necessarily*—i.e., logically as well as empirically—an absence of savings.[14] One cannot save where there is no surplus of cash.

[13] As Lewis himself points out (1961, p. xxvi), it follows from the fact of child labor (and also the incidence of working women) that there will be a "higher proportion of gainfully employed," which he claims as one of the universal characteristics of the culture of poverty, but obviously it is a trait of the poor and not just of those in the culture of poverty.

[14] Astonishing are the amounts actually saved, for example, in the squatments of Lima (and elsewhere). There are large numbers of home-building and civic-improvement cooperatives which depend on continuous accretion of minute sums of savings in order to pay for land and to fund house construction. Such collections of capital may go as high as millions of dollars and serve for general capitalization of the settlements, including their infrastructure, a process observable in San Juan's La Perla, studied by Lewis. Consumer cooperatives, burial funds, and a variety of other future-oriented savings and crisis-confronting procedures are widespread among squatment

Another way of putting this whole problem is to point out that the "lowness" of wages can be defined only with respect to the cumulative costs of ends to which the wages are to be applied by individuals or domiciles. There is no absolute "lowness" of wage, but a relatively lowness defined by some hypothetically irreducible set of needs and wants of individuals or groups. Thus, where the balance between wages and some set of wants is so precarious that one or another want goes begging for its fulfillment, one can clearly describe a situation of "lowness of wage."

But other things follow from this description (aside from the shortage of cash resulting from the wages' having been used to fulfill some of the wants). Where the unfilled want may be, or is perceived as, vital, it becomes necessary to mobilize cash—within a structure, a capitalist one, of money mobilization which requires security that money be loaned with minimum risk and maximum guarantees such as collateral and underwriters. Automatically, this excludes the un- and underemployed and also generally, the regularly employed who live in illegal places like squatments, because none of them can offer such guarantees. *Therefore,* formal credit agencies, banks, savings and loan associations, are necessarily outside the universe of these people in a *structural* way. Describing this exclusion or constraint system as traits of some proposed culture of poverty is entirely misleading and fallacious and obfuscates the *logic* of the system.

The necessity to mobilize cash for unfilled vital needs or at times of crisis, under these circumstances of exclusion from formal money-mobilizing institutions, permits one to deduce that either the poor themselves will devise methods outside the formal institutions for mobilizing resources or others, operating, as it were, as intermediaries between the formal institutions and the

---

residents. In one case in Rio, a *favela* incorporated itself as a cooperative so that it might buy the land on which it was located, which it now owns in condominium. This associative group recognized that in order not only to pay for the land, but to be able to make improvements on it, it would also have to invest in "human resources," so it established a plan of both academic and vocational schooling for members of the *favela*. The solution that Favela Guararapes devised is unique in Rio, but other *favelas* are constantly devising other solutions to similar problems.

poor, will invent means for affording themselves advantage by moving resources to the poor, but at the latter's expense. Thus, one is led to expect such modalities as (a) direct exchange of goods for money (e.g., pawning); (b) direct exchange of services for money (e.g., regular and odd jobs, acts of prostitution); (c) mobilization of cash or services or goods through personal ties (e.g., mobilization of kin, ritual kin, friendship and patronage networks, informal credit systems); (d) borrowing where possible (e.g., usury); (e) exchange of goods or services for services or goods (e.g., work bees). One might look at pawning, prostitution, usury, and the like as forms of structural parasitism, quite "normal" in a capitalist system. These institutions, it may be noted, are among the few semiformal courses open to the poor for moving resources and quite rational ones to use. The informal ones—social networks of family, ritual kin, friends, neighbors, and work companions—as is clear from Lewis's and many other people's data, are all used, accounting, in part, for the "trait" of "the great emphasis on family solidarity" that Lewis lists. All these specific usages are generated by the structure of un- and underemployment and, more widely, "low wages."

The various responses to cashlessness raise interesting points for consideration. For example, pawning is often empirically associated with small capital accumulations in the form of pawnable items used, in effect, as banks for storing value which can, at some future time, be converted into cash. This procedure has a special importance in inflationary economies, since the items appreciate, whereas savings depreciate, a fact Lewis does not consider. Another use is to acquire, by pawning, small amounts of capital which may be used in deals to create more capital. Thus, pawning may be attached to a form of future-oriented penny capitalism, rather than to present-orientedness (see p. 250 below). In general, it is more or less intrinsically linked with low income levels in capitalist society because it is not an effective way of moving large sums of capital.

Again, where persons, because of joblessness or extreme lowness of wages, have not been able to accumulate pawnable items or salable capital (e.g., electrodomestic equipment) or have no social networks from which to mobilize resources, as for example is the case for certain types of recent urban immigrants, then the solution is to turn to usurers. This is a structural response to needs, usually rational and problem-solving, under extremely difficult conditions, rather than a specific trait of a postulated subculture. It should be noted in this case that the *cultural* conception of a trait like this involves a distinct implication of choice or arbitrariness, whereas a *structural* interpretation means that there is no choice, there is no other way out. In my experience, people do not go to usurers because they want to but because they must.

It is interesting to observe the varied forms of "spontaneous informal credit devices" that are generated under the constraint system of low wages in capitalist society. In Mexico, Lewis says, they are organized by neighbors. Though this occurs on occasion in Brazil, typically they are organized by a group of work colleagues in what are called *vaquinhas* or *caixinhas* ("little cows," "little boxes," i.e., 'kitties'). These are, in effect and often explicitly, social-security devices for people for whom the social-security system operates but poorly.[15] I would consider such informal credit devices as forthright evidence of future-orientation under very constrained structural conditions, i.e., completely contradicting Lewis's "trait," for the same people, of "strong present-time orientation."

Absence of Food Reserves in the Home; Pattern of Buying Small Quantities of Food Many Times a Day as Need Arises; Use of Secondhand Clothing and Furniture; Living in Crowded Quarters. It seems to me fatuous to call these "cultural traits" in view

[15] The Brazilian social-service institutes—formerly twelve in number, now unified into one—appear to operate less and less effectively the further down the income scale the member is. The result is that many poor avoid using the Instituto hospitals and other services because they are so slow, inefficient, ineffective, punitive, brusque, dehumanizing. They turn, rather, to private institutions where they can get immediate and better help. Often this *saves* money in the long run, because the Instituto's medical and remedial care is so restricted that the sick person who needs immediate, intensive, full-scale care remains on sick leave, not working, for months—and, not infrequently, years—at 70 percent of his ordinary wages at a time when he needs more than his regular salary, since he is sick, to support his family and himself.

of the structural realities of "poverty." Where, given the nature of the labor market and its consequences of low wages, there is a chronic shortage of cash, *obviously* one reduces—one is *forced* to reduce—costs in all possible ways, such as buying secondhand clothing and furniture and finding the cheapest rentals one can tolerate for a given family size.

One may look at the situation another way. Where one is chronically short of cash, it *logically* follows that one does not have reserves—of cash, of food, of pawnable goods, or anything else; life is a battle to create and maintain sufficient reserves or reserve substitutes (like favors and obligations "banked" in social networks) to be able to withstand possible crises. In other words, "cash shortage" and "absence of savings" are identical to absence of reserves, including food.

It also follows, given lack of reserves, that one is constrained from reducing costs to a minimum, because one cannot afford the cash-saving or reserve-accumulating devices, for example, of buying in quantity or buying a refrigerator to save food which otherwise goes to waste. Without refrigerators, without adequate protection against vermin, without chunks of cash to buy quantities of food for reserves, and with the limited or total lack of storage space so characteristic of these very small housing units (ranging perhaps from 108 to 500 square feet), plainly there can be no food reserves in the house. Also, in passing, it should be emphasized that food storage in quantity in households has not been a characteristic urban pattern in countries like Mexico, Brazil, and Perú, which are typified by perpetually operating, fixed and circulating street fairs and central and subsidiary city markets, all selling fresh fruits, vegetables, meats, fish, and other things. At the same time, refrigeration is at best incipient.

For people living under these conditions, there is little choice but to buy daily, and often several times a day, (a) as things become available; (b) as cash becomes available; (c) as needs dictate. Daily purchases—even a number of daily purchases—as an activity are a positive value[16] and may contribute to savings by

[16] Threatened closing of Rio's street fairs elicits almost universal protest from housewives, who uniformly agree that fair produce is superior to that

taking advantage of minor price differences and fluctuations from place to place and time to time, considerations that Lewis does not bring up. It is also important that the frequent buying is local buying—not at large impersonal supermarkets—so that all-important personal ties with storekeepers and other clients of the store are maintained. This procedure has two functions: (a) maintenance of a patron relation with the storekeeper which can be mobilized at times of financial shortage or of family crisis; (b) maintenance of information chains which may be tremendously important in terms of job opportunities and other information useful when living under a severe constraint system with poorly organized job-filling procedures in the labor market.

Returning to the question of cost reduction: where rents, proportional to incomes, are high, obviously one "lives in crowded quarters" because one cannot do otherwise. Low or (as in a squatment) no rentals have some necessary correlates: the cheaper the renting unit, as a rule, the smaller the space, and, therefore, necessarily, the more crowded the living quarters, especially in areas of high urban land values, which are not mentioned in Lewis's "Settings." Furthermore, landlords build new buildings of the types of multiple renting units called *vecindades* (Mexico), *conventillos*

---

in the recently developing supermarkets; assert that they can get as good or better prices at the fairs by bargaining or by establishing long-term relations with particular sellers; appreciate the wider variety of choice. As another example, storage of baby foods in dozens of Gerber's baby-food jars has been out of the question until recently in Rio—there were no canned baby foods; even now the variety of Nutribaby foods is small, the expense relatively high. It is cheaper to buy food daily and mash baby foods in the ubiquitous blenders. Again, *favela* residents' buying at various times is also related to the marketing and transportation system: different times of arrival for different stocks; the occasional appearance of peddlers of fish, bananas, vegetables, etc.; the constant running out of stock at the stores, common to all Brazilian stores because of supply, transportation, and communication problems and because many stores operate at levels of capital so low that they cannot afford enough stock to last from one delivery to the next; and so on. We are not given reason to believe that Mexico is drastically different in all these respects, but in any case the trait is meaningless universally and does not distinguish the poor, let alone those in the culture of poverty, from other people, at least in Brazil. I might add that one wishes that Lewis would give some analysis at some time of the structure of the contexts in which his alleged traits are operating.

(Chile), *callejones* (Perú), *cortiços* (Rio and São Paulo) or break up old ones into small units (*casas divididas* in Lima, *casas de cô-modo* or *cabeças de porco* in Brazil), so that rent is more or less manageable by persons of low income. Because the units in a building are small and multiple, for example up to 80 or 100 rooms in a building, or 157 in Lewis's *vecindad*, people are constrained by low income to crowdedness. The trait has no meaning logically. Furthermore, crowdedness emphatically is not restricted to the poor or to some alleged subset of the poor who are "in the culture of poverty." Very large segments of Brazilian "middle-class" people live in great density—e.g., one section of the world-famous elite playground area of Rio, Copacabana, which has about three thousand persons per hectare, in *this* case, apparently, by cultural choice: the prestige and pleasure of living right near the sea and the beach.

In sum, all these "traits" are not autonomous culture elements but, rather, all functional adaptations to small incomes which are enjoined by the nature of the labor market and the larger economic institutional structure.

Gregariousness, Lack of Privacy. Lack of privacy is entirely a function of crowdedness; gregariousness, among the poor, a function both of crowdedness and of continually mobilized or mobilizable family, ritual kin, friend, and neighbor networks. In the context of "poverty," the latter are, as I have noted above (p. 249), themselves a functional response to low incomes, absence of savings, and the consequent need for money to pay for resources, services, and the like, some of which are provided on various exchange bases by the types of personnel constituting the networks. Part of the communication of such needs as well as the mobilization for action or to supply resources is carried out through "gregariousness," which can be seen as a structural action response to the total system of society and therefore does not imply anything about an autonomous cultural feature. Gregariousness functions to create communications networks (as in the case of the local stores mentioned above). It also necessarily reduces privacy, but privacy, as a characteristic value of American middle and upper classes engaged in competition for socioeconomic rewards in career structures involving upward mobility, may be more or less irrelevant. Privacy is not, as such, a *value* of the poor, although, in my experience, the poor quite explicitly formulate the contexts in which they like privacy. However, privacy is a positive *dis*advantage to the urban poor, as a large number of them recognized when helter-skelter urban renewal, or removal to other residential locations without regard to prior community living patterns, broke them away from their old neighborhood ties consisting of linked kin- and non-kin domiciles and friendship networks (*rapaziadas* in Brazil),which operated as mutual information and security systems.

In passing it may be noted that, at least in Brazil, where little is ever done alone, neither "trait" characterizes the poor: both gregariousness and lack of privacy are markedly common to *all* classes.

Strong Feeling of Marginality, Not Belonging, Alienation, That Institutions Do Not Serve Their Interests, Helplessness, Resignation, Fatalism, Dependency, Personal Unworthiness, Inferiority. All of these involve a *single* outlook; they are not *logically* separate, as Lewis lists them. To feel marginal means the same as to be or feel alienated, not belonging, helpless, unserved by institutions. They are all synonymous or verbalizations of the same thing, namely, the feeling about the correctly cognized and analyzed position in society in which the poor find themselves.[17]

However, the existence of reality-based feelings and cognitions does not logically entail the existence of a culture; it indicates merely, and no more, that the poor cognize and feel negatively about the fact of their real position in the social structure. Yet Lewis hypostasizes an autonomous culture from their simple recognition that their relationship to the significant institutions of the society—the labor market, financial resources, education, political institu-

---

[17] In the 1964a article, all the quotations given from both Manuel and Jesús Sanchez confirm this interpretation, especially the latter, in, for example, his description of the operation of the union, the use of force, the result of being barred from education, the repressiveness of the Mexican cupola, and so on. It is interesting that both Manuel and Jesús, exemplars, according to Lewis, of the culture of poverty, have "traits" of non–culture-of-poverty people: some international views, sharp class consciousness, and union membership for the last. The sister, Consuelo, had eight years of schooling.

tions, the bureaucracy, and all—is such as to exclude them from many kinds of rewards the society offers, by virtue not only of abuses and manipulations of these institutions at their expense by persons who control them, but also because of criteria for qualification and a series of discriminatory practices based on cues such as dress, skin color, and speech. These feelings are always discovered in the context of the society's failure to meet the vital needs of the poor, because *institutionally* a poor man is *indeed* marginalized, *unserved* by institutions (see fn. 15), *made* an alien, *made* helpless, *made* to enter into dependency relations, *told* that he is inferior and personally unworthy[18] (because he is lower-class, he is black, he is illiterate, or he is "in the culture of poverty" needing psychiatric help[19]).

[18] A publication (*Seminário interuniversitário,* 1967) issued by the six rectors of the universities in and around greater Rio de Janeiro as a result of their deliberations, as an "expert group," about "solving the *favela* problem" inspired by the disastrous rains of January 1966 describes *favelas* as "social cancers," despoliators of "one of the most beautiful landscapes of the planet," part of the national "patrimony" which "we have in custody" for humanity, filled with "rebels and gangsters," and so on (see Leeds, 1968, fn. 10), an incredible document of ideologically inspired, class-maintaining distortion, explicitly indicating and reinforcing the idea of inferiority and worthlessness and encouraging the alienation and marginalization of the *favela* resident by all persons of "higher" classes.

[19] It is not possible to read pp. 158-59 in Lewis, 1964a, without logically arriving at the conclusion that the culture of poverty is a "social problem" whose "cure," *in principle,* is of a psychiatric sort, though *in practice* in underdeveloped countries it is not, because there are not enough psychiatrists. I quote from there:

In considering what can be done about the culture of poverty, one must make a sharp distinction between those countries in which it represents a relatively small segment of the population and those in which it constitutes a very large section [e.g., as in Mexico, where Lewis claims it constitutes about one third of the population; *cf.* 1961, xxvi]. Obviously, the solutions will have to differ in these two areas. In the United States, the major solution proposed by planners, social-work agencies, and social workers in dealing with . . . the so-called hard core of poverty has been to attempt slowly to raise their level of living and incorporate them into the middle class. And, wherever possible, there has been some reliance on psychiatric treatment . . . to imbue these "shiftless, lazy, unambitious people" with higher middle-class aspirations.

To this he adds: "In the undeveloped countries, however, where great masses of people live in the culture of poverty, a social-work solution does

"Resignation" and "fatalism" follow, not only because one is forced into the marginal molds and told that one is worthless and inferior, but also because, as experience repeatedly impresses on the poor, if one does not behave resignedly and fatalistically, one suffers insults and slights, jailings, beatings, lynchings, tortures, and death. Under such circumstances, dependency relations, clientages, servilities, and the like, are necessities if one is to survive.[20] "Resignation" and "fatalism," like the rest of this list of traits, disappear rapidly when the constraints weaken or are removed.

Some examples of the disappearance or sharp lessening of these "feelings" are illuminating. Although the Brazilian poor indicate fatalism when they say, *"O pobre não tem vez* ("The poor man has no chance") or that doing something *não adianta* ("doesn't get you anywhere"), they are in fact also recognizing that they *could* have his chance if the very real barriers were not in the way (Lewis fails to recognize this positive aspect of the cognition). Thus, the moment a constraint is removed or changes, a behavior changes, too.

---

not seem feasible. Because of the magnitude of the problem, psychiatrists can hardly begin to cope with it." He admits that "it may be more important to offer the poor . . . a genuine revolutionary ideology. . . . It is conceivable that some countries can, without materially increasing the standard of living, eliminate the culture of poverty . . . by changing the value systems and attitudes of the people so they no longer feel marginal . . ." The statement about revolutionary ideology is gutted by the later phrases which reestablish the problem as being inherent in the poor, essentially a psychological problem, which would be psychiatrically treatable if only there were not so many of them. In sum, it would seem, therefore, that persons "in the culture of poverty" are disturbed persons, psychiatric cases.

[20] We have elsewhere pointed out the pragmatic use and the utility of the characteristic "paternalistic" ties (see A. Leeds and E. Leeds, 1970, fn. 20) such as are so often noted in Brazil (the *patrão–moço* relation). We also point out that these paternalistic modes of behavior are highly context sensitive—a person displays them toward those people and in those situations where they are useful and sloughs them off where he does not need to use them, as among those who structurally occupy positions similar to his. From the latter he gets his rewards through reciprocal, mutually exploitative, or other modes of relation; from the former he gets them through the favor-for-service or favor-for-prestige exchanges of the paternalistic relation (see Lewis, 1961, pp. xx-xxi).

For example, when a decree was issued (1957) which made it legal to lead electric lines into *favelas,* the entire economy of individuals and collectivities began to change rapidly. With very little change in cost over kerosene, people were able to improve family finances by using electric irons, refrigerators, and other equipment which produce income or savings, decrease the danger of fire, and generally improve the quality of life. Some *favela* dwellers had had electricity before, paying owners of electric meters at the street side exorbitant amounts for the right to run a line from the latter's drops; the rest of the population had "fatalistically" and "resignedly" opted for the somewhat cheaper and more dangerous kerosene, mostly because affording electricity cut too deeply into their incomes. The governmental lifting of constraint was followed by an almost universal change of behavior.

As another case: in 1960–62, a new and unparalleled departure was made with respect to governmental policy toward *favelas,* the attempt to make community development *in situ* possible. The Director of Social Services of the State of Guanabara (city of Rio) encouraged the formation of associations of *favela* residents and made lawyers and legal information directly available to the association presidents at weekly meetings. At the meetings I observed, the *favela* presidents drank up this information, which had theretofore been inaccessible to them. Such aid and information are even today exceedingly hard to get, for two reasons. First, the information is scattered, and lawyers who are really acquainted with all the relevant laws are most rare. More important, however, has always been, and is, the active lack of cooperation of most lawyers and other professionals who are members of the Brazilian elite and subelite classes. For the most part, rather than helping *anyone* in the proletariat, their relationship tends to be exploitative —the nonresolution of a problem accompanied by the collecting of fees—and functions to maintain class boundaries (*cf.* Naro, 1966).

Mothers and Children, Mother-Centered Families. Aside from the fact that male superiority, in some sense, has characterized all classes or strata in Western society and in most Oriental and African state societies as well, it is not at all clear how these traits are to be linked logically with a supposed culture of poverty, nor how they are *logically* (let alone psychodynamically!) to be related to each other. For instance, the trait "mother-centered families" strikes one as contradictory to "male superiority" and "women's martyr complex." Much of the literature on mother-centered families describes the women as rather commanding, as possessed of a clearer sense of identity than the men, as taking active part in decision-making,[21] and so on. If this is *not* the case in Mexico, where the traits, including the "women's martyr complex" were originally formulated, then the trait may indeed be cultural but does not belong in Lewis's list of *generic* traits, which the rest are supposed to be. If, moreover, "mother-centered families" are simply a by-product of abandonment of mothers and children, which Lewis supposed to be a trait, then it is not a culture trait at all and has no logical reason to be listed as a trait of the culture of poverty. If one were to take these traits at face value, one would expect to find families or family-households where commanding or domineering men rule womenfolk, and other families or family-households where women are commanding or domineering and rule their menfolk. If this were true, we would then have difficulty with the "women's martyr complex" because many women clearly would not be bound as martyrs, and, further, we would be led to expect a men's martyr complex. The logical contradictions in Lewis's treatment, his failure to deal with existing anthropological literature relating to the problem, and much of the substantive data itself (discussed below), including the non-exclusive distribution of these "traits" through many strata of all kinds of society, render the traits useless in the designation of a special sub-culture of some postulated sub-set of the poor.

Provincial and Local Orientation would seem deducible from the

[21] There is an exceedingly important point here, because there is a vast literature, uncited in Lewis, on the Negro, and more broadly the lower class, in the New World which has argued, still somewhat inconclusively, two positions: (a) that the mother-centered family, supposedly so frequently found among New World Negroes, is derived from Negro cultural traditions, especially from the heritage of matrilineal African societies; (b) that the mother-centered family is a result of structural conditions. The opposition is between a culturalist and a structural-functionalist model of explanation of cultural dynamics. See below, fn. 29; *cf.* R. T. Smith, 1956, 1957; M. G. Smith, 1962.

financial and work conditions of life and their social-organizational consequences; it seems to have no clear status as an independent culture trait. Most social and economic activity, especially for the poor, *must necessarily* go on at local levels, which are, therefore, of consistently direct and immediate concern, whether or not they are *valued* or form part of an autonomous, unique ethnic world view, as is implied by saying that such an orientation is an element in a culture of poverty. Given the structure of life as the poor are forced to live it, they *must necessarily* cognize local and provincial worlds.

In this connection, it is interesting to note the burgeoning of the home-town and provincial associations (Mangin, 1958; 1965, works not cited by Lewis). These operate to help orient a new migrant from the interior to the large city, help enculturate him there, and help the home town from whence he came by sending back rewards of various sorts. According to C. F. Jongkind (personal communication, 1969, when he was in Lima studying such organizations), they are organized around points of origin of various types: haciendas, villages, towns, cities, and provinces (states). This hierarchic series of units roughly corresponds to the social stratification of the immigrants once they are living in Lima—the lower the stratum, the more restricted the area of influence of the point of origin to which the home-"town" association refers itself. In passing, it should be noted that neither hierarchy has any *necessary* relationship to a rural-urban scale, since small towns and hacienda headquarters, for example, may involve very considerable city experience for residents whether workers, managers, commercial people, or owners. Rather, the hierarchy is related to differential access to the central institutions of, and bodies of information significant to, the Peruvian state. The home-"town" associations of lower level units are structurally constrained by the Peruvian socio-political system from wider or "urban" participation in the institutions of state. Thus, we find a system in which people of all strata, rich and poor alike, possess a "provincial and local orientation." Yet, first, this orientation is intimately linked with a national and societal orientation; second, the associations through which the former is expressed are agents for helping people to solve problems and to move them "forward in the national-societal system; and, third, the associations are not, as Lewis's "orientation" would imply, ends in themselves, but means towards wider ends: getting personal rewards, political activity, urban enculturation, and feeding back national rewards into the locality.

Low Level of Education and Literacy. This trait has no logically independent status as a trait, but, again, is simply a reflex of the structure which creates poor people. One cannot validly deduce or infer anything about a supposed culture or value system from the statistics on low education and literacy levels.

Education provides another example of change when constraints weaken or break. First, the indices of literacy in places like *favelas* and rooming houses vary directly with the indices of literacy of the surrounding city and area. Thus, for example, literacy indices are progressively higher as one moves from *favelas* in the more provincial cities of northeast Brazil to the larger, more metropolitan cities of that area or of the south-central zone, like Belo Horizonte, to the national metropoles like Rio and São Paulo.

Second, within cities, say Rio, indices of literacy vary according to availability of schools: the physically isolated *favelas* appear to have higher illiteracy rates, as do those in parts of the city less well supplied with schools or where the schools are less adequate.

Third, literacy varies according to the number of available places (*vagas*) in schools—always, discriminatorily, fewer places for the poor—so that, as schools are built and more places created, the literacy rate goes up.

Fourth, the literacy increases with each succeeding generation. From this it may be concluded that illiterate grandparents, a large proportion of whom are rural migrants to cities who confronted hopeless barriers to education, have made shift to give their children some minimum of education. These, in turn, are, today, making enormous efforts to move their children into and through secondary schools, which are, for the most part, private in Brazil, and must be paid for out of the poor families' meager resources. The structural fact of living in an expanding city and the politico-administrative fact that Rio, during 1960–65, made a strong effort to build schools and expand the number of places available, provided the possibilities of broadening education through weakening the constraints maintaining "low levels of literacy." One may suspect that similar processes are at work in Mexico. They certainly are in Perú, where the government installs a school in every *barriada,* and people who migrated to *barriadas* from the rural interior *consistently* state they came to Lima for educational purposes.

Relatively Higher Death Rate; Lower Life Expectancy; Higher Proportion of Young. First, these are not traits of culture at all, but measures of the state or behavior of any population, including (in principle) non-human ones. Second, empirically, they all tend to be linked aspects of a single situation. All three tend to be associated with wide-based age pyramids ("higher proportion of youth"). High birth rates, combined with relatively poor medical care—both of which characterize entire nations of the type called "underdeveloped," at all social levels—produce such pyramids, hence the "three" characteristics which, *empirically,* tend to be three phrasings of the same thing. In any society, for those for whom incomes are marginal, cash little, savings absent, and who are marginalized from security institutions, including medical care, the indices are presumably greater than for those not so marginalized. Thus, it is the larger social system which generates these characteristic population indices; it is not a sub-culture of the population allegedly displaying the characteristics that does so. Third, the logical independence of the "traits" is not even clear—for example, a lower life expectancy necessarily rests on a higher death rate.

Substantive Problems of the Culture-of-Poverty Concept. The first major substantive problem is the question whether there is a meaningful referrent to the concept of the culture of poverty. Basically this question resolves itself into the question of the relationship between the index, behavioral, and ideological traits Lewis lists indiscriminately and some definable population.

Lewis is caught in a hopeless cul-de-sac, because he defines his population by one set of index-behavioral-ideological traits, which, however, are displayed by varying sets of people who are not distinguishable from each other on a number of other sets of traits. For instance, it turns out that his population is *not* "the poor," is *not* "low-income people," is *not* "residents of *vecindades*," is *not* "persons of low prestige, unskilled occupations," etc., because many people falling into these categories do not have the requisite other traits, while, at the same time, some of these other traits are not restricted to the poor, to residents of *vecindades*, or to any other such category—e.g., authoritarianism, drinking, nondeferment of gratification, and so on. In fact, he is unable to delimit a population at all. In *La Vida*, he makes his first attempt at exclusion: people who belong to unions or who have class consciousness or an internationalist outlook are not in the culture of poverty. Aside from the arbitrariness of these traits and from the question of their relevance,[22] what does one do with, say, the labor-union member living in a *vecindad* in crowded quarters, talking of class struggle to his consensual wife—the center of a network of maternal kin—over whom he exercises authority as she takes care of the many children, one of whom works[23] and another of whom is pregnant though unwed? Many such cases can be found in the real worlds of Mexican, Peruvian, and Brazilian slums and squatments.

Basically, this is the cul-de-sac that all trait analysis confronts when it deals with specific human populations. Traits are individual cultural items and do not distribute according to delimitable human populations, which are bounded by other kinds of sociocultural things than culture traits—specifically, inclusive and exclusive

[22] The choice of labor unions, for example, seems gratuitous, since it appears to be made without reference to the character of the relationship of the unions to the society. This is an important question in Mexico and Brazil where the unions, especially in the latter, are supine instruments of the governing elites operating through the Ministry of Labor and the Labor Courts. In important ways, union membership in Brazil constitutes a subservience to elite power. In many cases, one can exercise more power outside the unions.

[23] There is an important problem with the "trait," child labor, which has not been discussed before. Aside from the fact that it is not restricted to populations that are poor—e.g., it is found widely in family-farm areas—it is, in poor areas, a response which is rational and future-oriented in the sense of (a) trying to increase family income under difficult systems of constraint (b) giving children job training, and (c) moving children into the job-acquisition channels early. This trait, too, does not stand independently.

relationships. If traits did indeed distribute according to delimited populations, the observer would have *empirically* to establish that the asserted traits or characteristics are jointly unique to the given congeries of people delimited by some characteristic independent of the traits in question. He would have to show that the specified delimitable set of people display the entire range of traits all at once, rather than some of the people having some of the traits, others, or all of the specified people having some of the traits some of the time and others at another.[24] This requirement is especially important if the characteristics are—as asserted and, for many, empirically demonstrable—not limited to those who are supposed to be "in the culture of poverty" or even to the poor as a whole or even to a given society. If the traits are not continually and collectively present as an ongoing configuration, for a unique specified group of people, they cannot characterize that group and are useless in delimiting it as, say, the carriers of a culture of poverty, as over against poor noncarriers.[25]

[24] *Cf.* Lewis, 1965–66, p. xliv, talking about just such variety. If the variation exists, as he asserts, and is responsive to external variables (such as the literacy rate of the whole society, as he claims), then it is hard to understand in what possible understanding the culture of poverty is a culture. Its variations appear consistently to co-vary with parts of an external system. If this is the case, one should be able to predict the features present and their relative importance for any given population described as "poor," differentially for the "poor" and those "in the culture of poverty" across a great number of different societal structures. This would not be the case for a culture or subculture as normally understood.

[25] See fn. 5, p. 233. Aside from the three dubious items mentioned above, Lewis continues unable to differentiate between the "culture of poverty" and the "culture of the non–culture-of-poverty poor," constantly confusing the two; e.g., in *La Vida:*

p. xlii   "I shall try to define it more precisely . . . with special emphasis on the distinction between poverty and the culture of poverty."

p. xliii   "As an anthropologist, I have tried to understand poverty and its associated traits as a culture or, more accurately, as a subculture with its own structure and rationale . . ."

p. xliv   "The culture of poverty is both an adaptation and a reaction of the poor to their marginal position . . ."

p. xliv   "The way of life which develops among some of the poor under these conditions is the culture of poverty."

In what follows I wish, on the one hand, to examine a selection of traits in Lewis's lists from the publications of 1961, 1964a, and 1965–66, which do *not* seem logically derivable from, or structural-functional consequences of, the larger sociocultural system. Their existence would seem to confirm the utility of his conception of a culture of poverty. However, I question the capacity of these traits to distinguish any delimitable social group. On the other hand, I propose to question the substantive validity of several traits by

---

p. xlv   "The most likely candidates for the culture of poverty are the people who come from the lower strata of a rapidly changing society . . . Thus landless rural workers who migrate to the cities can be expected to develop a culture of poverty much more readily than migrants from stable peasant villages . . ."

p. xlv   "The lack of effective participation and integration of the poor in the major institutions of the larger society is one of the crucial characteristics of the culture of poverty."

p. xlviii "The distinction between poverty and the culture of poverty is basic to the model described here. There are degrees of poverty and many kinds of poor people. The culture of poverty refers to one way of life shared by poor people in given historical and social contexts."

From the 1964a article, the following:

p. 149   "To those who believe that the poor have no culture, the concept of a culture of poverty may seem like a contradiction in terms."

p. 150   Poverty "is also something positive in the sense that it has a structure, a rationale, and defense mechanisms without which the poor could hardly carry on."

p. 150   "Nor is the culture of poverty synonymous with the working class, the proletariat, or the peasantry, all three of which vary a good deal in economic status throughout the world."

p. 150   "The culture of poverty would apply only to those people who are at the very bottom of the socio-economic scale, the poorest workers, the poorest peasants, plantation laborers, and that large heterogeneous mass of small artisans and tradesmen usually referred to as the lumpen proletariat."

p. 151   "It is important to distinguish between impoverishment and the culture of poverty."

p. 152   "In Mexico, the culture of poverty includes at least the lower third of the rural and urban population."

It can clearly be seen that there is no consistent usage of the terms, no consistent conceptualization, nor any consistent distinction between the poor and those in the culture of poverty in the collection of passages above.

looking at the data from comparable groups in other countries.[26] In both cases, the traits seem to fade in importance because of their non-exclusiveness, their inability, individually and collectively, to distinguish any group of persons from other groups (other than, perhaps, specific family household groups).

Strong Predisposition to Authoritarianism. This trait is empirically irrelevant for defining a culture of poverty. Often attributed to Latin Americans in a stereotypic fashion, it seems to permeate all classes of society where it demonstrably exists; certainly some forms of it are quite prevalent *throughout* Mexican and generally Spanish- and Luso-American society (see, however, Romano V., 1969). Whether one looks at the structure and procedures of the Partido Revolucionario Institucional (PRI) or at paternal controls over children, especially girls, in middle and upper classes, or at the doctrines of the Catholic Church, or at the various forms of corporativist-fascist ideology, and so on, forms of authoritarianism can be seen pervasively in Mexico and elsewhere (including the United States, where they have their own peculiar ethos). Actually, however, in my own experience in Rio's *favelas,* authoritarianism is considerably less marked among the poor than among higher- and especially middle-income people. Indeed, discipline

[26] See fn. 2 and pp. 235–37. Since Lewis asserts that the culture of poverty transcends national boundaries, it is perfectly appropriate methodologically to use housing-settlement types equivalent to his *vecindades* and *arrabales.* For this reason, in this paper I refer to my own findings in Brazil, Lima, Bogotá, and elsewhere, especially in squatments. In the entire section called "Setting" (1965-66, pp. xxiii-xlii), the only mention of the fact that La Perla is a squatment is as follows: "Unlike other slums [Lewis' lumping slums and squatments together is quite clear here] studied, in which four out of five families were illegal squatters who had built or purchased their homes on government land, in La Esmeralda only about 15 percent of the residents owned their house." The term *arrabal* does not appear in the "Setting," and the absence of the standard index does not allow us to trace out other places of possible use. It is not clear from the passage quoted whether houses are legal or illegal, whether residents are squatters or renters from squatters. In other words, some of the most basic aspects of the economy of the place have been omitted. In Rio, where people rent in *favelas* and in certain poorer parts of the city outside *favelas,* the rate of investment in house improvement and neighborhood betterment is depressed. Rents are a part of the structure of capitalist exploitation which affect physical and social characteristics of *arrabales* and rooming houses.

is rather more relaxed and there is a greater degree of at least potential equality between parents and children among low-income groups than elsewhere in Brazilian society. Further, low-income people express a value for independence and liberty, a part of whose meaning is freedom from the narrow authoritarian and hierarchical constraints of the larger society (see discussion of *machismo* and martyrdom above).

Predominance of the Nuclear Family, Emphasis on Family Solidarity (Rarely Achieved Ideal), Relatively High Incidence of Abandonment of Mothers and Children, Trend toward Mother-centered Families, Greater Knowledge of Maternal Relatives. There are several substantive problems involved with this set of traits. First, they are obscure. It appears—and in certain passages it is more or less clear but nowhere systematically stated—that Lewis is talking not about families but about household compositions. The households, he is saying, are comprised predominantly of the nuclear family group, i.e., of mother, father, and one or more children. Or, apparently, they are composed of mother-centered family groups, i.e., a mother and one or more children. All of these households, by definition, do not have other relatives living with them. In certain text passages and as a residual, non-"predominant" category, he indicates that other households have something larger than the nuclear family group, some sort of extended family group, i.e., some couple or part of a couple, its children, and an ascendant and/or collateral relative or a married child and its offspring, and so on.[27] It is also unclear as to what sort of predominance he is discussing: is it simply the composition of groups; does it concern decision-making about budgets or about child-training; and so on; or is it all of these?

A second problem is that the traits, given the meaning above, are contradictory. A mother-centered family household is not a nuclear-family household. Is the trend toward the former; is there really a predominance of the latter, or is there "a trend" toward

[27] No mention is made of nonfamily households such as are occasionally encountered in Rio's *favelas* and rooming houses—the *república,* for example, consisting of several unrelated men sharing a rent and household budget.

the extended-family household? The statistics of "predominance" offered in the sections called "Setting" (e.g., 1959a, p. 26) do not distinguish between mother-centered, fatherless nuclear-family households and nuclear-family households as such.[28] The problem is most important, because quite different processes (e.g., different articulations with the labor market) may be involved, or different stages in the trajectories of family-household histories.

A third problem involves the extended family. In the text, Lewis repeatedly refers to the fact that the *vecindad as such,* as a location, is a residential-settlement place for an *extended*-family group which divides itself *inside* the *vecindad* into various constituent elements—presumably mainly the "predominant" nuclear-family household. The data suggest, and my own experience in *favelas,* rooming houses, and *cortiços* makes indubitably clear, that these extended-family residential units are operative units for certain kinds of purposes in certain kinds of contexts. A significant datum, then, for any squatment or rooming house, is (a) how many

[28] In connection with these comments, it is curious that Lewis lists among his traits "the predominance of the nuclear or immediate family." The statistics given in one place (1959a, 27) say that among the residents of one whole *vecindad*—a poorer one—six out of thirteen households had immediate families as their social composition. This is certainly no clear predominance. It is true that in another, less poor *vecindad* he says "about 72 per cent of our sample of 71 households" were nuclear families (p. 26). There are several problems here. Which of these two houses is typical? Predominance depends on the answer. Does predominance of nuclear-family households (a more precise term than Lewis's) disappear as the population gets poorer? This is a problem of distribution related to his statements about those in the culture of poverty being among the poorest of society; if the correlation is true, it contradicts Lewis's use of this trait. What is the sample? There were 157 households in the *vecindad* in question. It is not clear what kind of a sample of 157 seventy-one households is, how they were chosen, and whether they presumably represent all 157 (i.e., whether the distributions in the other 86 households are like those in the sample 71). In the passage on p. 27, he goes on to say that a large part of the *vecindad* is a kind of extended kinship unit and, undoubtedly, support group, such as one finds in equivalent housing-settlement types in Rio and Lima. It is not stated how many of the six nuclear-family households are "in the culture of poverty" and how many of the seven which are not nuclear-family households are not, nor what the composition of the latter is. The same comment holds for the 71, because it is clear from his own statements that not all residents of a *vecindad,* who, we suppose, are all poor, are necessarily in the culture of poverty.

of the households are extended-family households, and (b) how many nuclear- or subnuclear-family households have extended-family networks in the residential-settlement unit being described? Systematic treatment of these basic data is absent in Lewis's various publications at least until 1968, which raises further doubt as to the substantive meaningfulness of his statistics on "families" or his use of "the family" as a unit of analysis.

A fourth problem is that the traits, as presented, give no indication of family dynamics but treat *households* as steady states. I am certain that Lewis's data show, as mine do overwhelmingly, that for any prolonged period of time, and especially a lifetime, any difinable household (a budgeting unit) changes composition constantly, especially among the poor who are extending emergency services, care, protection, social security, and the like to relatives. While, at the same time, the children are growing, marrying, moving out, and moving back; grandchildren or others' children (*cf. La Vida,* p. xxix, footnotes) are taken in for temporary or permanent adoption or bringing up, and so on. The entire process is not, however, random. Rather, household forms display certain regularities as the household–family unit evolves under given sets of circumstances and under specifiable crisis situations. This is a structural-dynamic process which is beclouded by Lewis's treatment in terms of culture traits, and by his failure to use the literature in which aspects of it have been discussed for other world areas (e.g., Goody, ed.).

These comments also apply to listing "high frequency of abandonment of mothers and children" as a *culture trait* (a listing which some of his own statements contradict) rather than analyzing it as a structural response to a socioeconomic constraint system. These are not mother-centered families of the Caribbean (*cf.* both R. T. and M. G. Smith), where there appears to be a genuine cultural-structural tradition involved. My own evidence suggests (a) that abandonment is almost as frequent on the mothers' part as on the fathers'; (b) that abandonments are frequently engendered by tensions in the work situation;[29] and (c) that abandonments occur

---

[29] One example from Rio: the government of the State of Guanabara (city of Rio) removed a number of *favelas* from the central-city area and put them in "embryo houses" in Vila Kennedy, a public-housing develop-

most frequently in correlation with absence of property interests, a structural situation closely allied to poverty. It is interesting that there is almost universal agreement in Brazil that, in effect, people in the middle and upper classes are going through similar procedures, separating formally (*desquite*); not separating but maintaining second family-households (obviously not a feasibility for married women with children, hence necessarily a possibility almost exclusively for men); and staying together formally, but having one or many affairs or lovers. These are all forms of abandonment short of the act itself, which is avoided largely because of property concerns and the effective legal recourse of wives.

In other words, in Brazil—and I suspect in Mexico and Puerto Rico (note Lewis's comment on Puerto Rico about the very rich and the rural wealthy, 1961, p. xxviii)—the divisive *process* is found in all classes. It is not a trait restricted to the poor or those in the culture of poverty, although it takes structurally differentiated forms. Among the poor of all types, the result is permanent separation or "abandonment," with a higher frequency of women being left with the children. Given the nature of the labor markets in these places, it is inevitable that this should be so—there are fewer jobs for women, and the jobs that are most frequently available for them, such as domestic work and clothes washing, can usually be done while accompanied by one or more of the children.

There is an interesting subsidiary substantive issue here, namely

---

ment of the State, 50 kilometers out of town. Transportation to jobs in town, close to which residents had formerly lived, took one and a half to two and a half hours, plus a half- to one-hour wait in line for the buses; return trips took about the same amount of time. Given a 48-hour work week, this meant work days, including transportation time, of about 12 to 14 hours, plus major fatigue from travel on Rio's exhausting buses and trains. Many men began to look for places to stay overnight near their work, gradually beginning to stay during the work week. Quite a few eventually simply migrated to town, abandoning their new homesites and old households together, sometimes finding new living companions in town. One should note that the constraints of this system were imposed from outside the population of the poor, the pressures increased by the policies of state agencies; ultimately the welfare loads were increased as a consquence, families were broken, and job articulation was badly distorted by the externally generated action programs. There is no need to postulate a culture of poverty for the people forced into these molds of life.

that it is not clear if it is actually the man who always or most often abandons. In *La Vida* (p. xlvi) Lewis points out that women often refuse formal marriage, wish to maintain a flexibility and freedom in the marital situation, retain the right "to leave their man," and maintain property rights in the house and other things. This clearly suggests that abandonment is frequently initiated by the women and tends to contradict the trait as stated in his lists. Lewis also points out that the Puerto Rican women who get work in New York (p. xlii) give their husbands a much harder time than those who do not. All this suggests that abandonment is initiated from either side with about equal frequency and revolves about quite clearly defined interests in specifiable structural conditions. It is also a structural fact that the women will generally (but not always) retain the children, especially where wide extensions of family for either or both spouses are absent in the locality so that children cannot be handed over to aunts or grandparents.

In short, the *interests*—which, in common uses of the term, are cultural—appear to permeate all class levels in Puerto Rico, Mexico, and Brazil and do not differentiate people within the culture of poverty from poor people outside it nor from different classes. However, the *structures* of the situation necessarily produce such differentiation and inevitable produce mother-centered household groups in the poorer layers (if not also in wealthier ones) of society, a break-down in family solidarities, and, generally, a greater linkage with relatives.[30] It is also important to note that the nuclear-family household is characteristic for all layers of Western society at least insofar as budgets, household grouping, child training, and the like, are concerned. It is irrelevant to a culture of poverty.

[30] Another feature of the situation is that the predominantly male-oriented labor market creates a condition in which men are physically mobile over wide areas of the city, while women tend to be restricted to relatively narrow geographical areas in the city. When an abandonment or separation occurs, it is more likely to be the women who stay in the original place, regardless of who initiated the break. Women remaining with children structurally need to be near their support groups. Since the men are the mobile ones, they are likely to be the neolocal ones and, when they have separated from the old, tend to attach themselves to their new women in the places to which they have moved or where they discovered the new women. The reasons, then, for the greater knowledge of maternal relatives is structural rather than cultural where it is demonstrable at all.

Finally, the traits are not logically independent of each other, several of them being different analytic phrasings of the same thing. *Free Unions,* or *Consensual Marriages,* are much more widespread than only among participants in the culture of poverty, or even than among the poor and are, therefore, questionably relevant as empirical characteristics of the culture of poverty. In Brazil, a very large number of the socially winked-at free unions exist in the middle and upper classes, some of them as secondary marriages and ménages. They are also common among socially and economically mobile working-class people. In the Caribbean, such unions are ubiquitous in early stages of the family cycle (see Goody, ed.; R. T. Smith, 1956, 1957; M. G. Smith, 1962) and do not reflect a culture of poverty. It might be pointed out that free unions are frequent when property and rights to it are of little concern—e.g., in today's United States among the university student population.[31]

Violence in Mexico has been thematic throughout the society and since pre-Hispanic times. The content of Mexican jokes has a marked tone of violence. Mexican political history and present political control system have notably violent episodes. Violence is certainly not restricted to the poor. Brazil, by contrast, is repeatedly said to be a rather nonviolent culture (although this is grossly exaggerated, I believe). However, what violence there is has always occurred at all levels, whether in the form of political assassinations, fights in the legislatures, land wars (Amado), repression of slave rebellions, banditry or its repression (Cunha), messianic sacrifices, crimes of passion, or murder and assault. The trait is irrelevant for identifying the culture of poverty.

[31] The population of university students in the United States and a number of other countries is interesting in that it displays not only a high rate of consensual unions, but also many other traits supposedly characterizing a culture-of-poverty population, such as frequent daily purchases of food, an increasing amount of violence, high incidence of alcoholism or other drug use, distrust of police and government, miscellany of unskilled occupations, under- and unemployment, low wages, critical attitudes toward the dominant classes, etc. They frequently furnish their off-campus residences with secondhand furniture and buy items of secondhand clothing because they are cheaper. They display an amazing array of informal credit devices, are known to pawn, live in crowded quarters, and lack privacy, and are notably gregarious. Are they too in the culture of poverty, or do they lack some critical trait for such membership?

Cynicism about Government, Hatred of Police, Critical Attitudes toward Dominant Classes, Mistrust of Government and People in High Positions, and Cynicism "Even" to the Church. These traits are all pandemic in Brazilian and, to all appearances, Mexican society. The history of government and "even" church in Mexico has not been such as to elicit openhearted trust and faith in large segments of middle and upper classes any more than among the poor. Brazil today is in the throes of universal "cynicism, criticism, and mistrust," and alienation of almost everyone from the government, large sections of the Church, and from other major institutions of the society. In view of the realities of the situation there—and the realities, historically, of government and church behavior to the poor—a true sense of history, which Lewis denies to people "in the culture of poverty" (see below and Romano V., 1969), suggests that cynicism and mistrust reflect a hardheaded assessment of actualities which is not restricted to the culture of poverty or even to the poor. These traits are, therefore, empirically useless to diagnose the culture of poverty or to isolate groups or social bodies carrying it.

Little Sense of History (1964a, p. 155). My own observations in Rio's *favelas* lead me to conclude that the poor remember their own history exceedingly well and especially the important parts of it: their relation to those who control resources, political office, force, influence, information, legal recourse, and the courts. Their keen remembrance of this history leads the poor to clear recognition of what they can expect from those who control the major factors of their life chances, especially jobs, credit, and social security. They are quite clear that they live under a series of stringent constraints which they call *exploração* (exploitation) and oppression; they recognize that they, *in truth,* have few chances (*não tem vez*).

In short, they recognize more sharply than anyone else the truths of the historical situation. This is reflected still further in their assessments of political trends in the nation—for example, their very negative evaluation of both the Castello Branco and Costa e Silva regimes, both of which have been antipopular and antipoor in the extreme. The poor correctly recognize their structural inability to do much about the system and the fact that participation in the electoral and candidacy-for-political-office games really provide no opportunities to break through. They therefore choose not to operate through these institutions, although in 1965, in the state of Guanabara, explicitly as an act of overt opposition to the military central government and its supporters in the state government, they voted in the one remaining opposition governor remaining in Brazil today. This act provoked a major political crisis at the top which led to ending all the old political parties and creating two new ones by decree. The poor prefer to manipulate other modes of relationship to secure some of the rewards of the society (see E. Leeds, 1966).

Again, the poor are perhaps those who most widely participate in Carnaval in Brazil. Throughout Brazil, Carnaval themes are of an historical nature and the Carnaval samba competitions and theme songs serve as intensificatory rites revolving about the celebration of national and local history, major national symbols, great personages, and cultural achievements. As an example: one of the leading samba groups, in Rio, Mangueira, focused its theme songs, floats, choreography, and costumes on Monteiro Lobato, Brazil's leading children's story writer. All mass media transmit these songs to the entire populace of Rio and much of the rest of Brazil. It is, perhaps, as if Kipling or Milne were enshrined by means of country music and rock media in the consciousness of the major part of the population of the United States. Another example of historical awareness is provided by the oft-repeated theme of the abolition of slavery whose events are carefully reviewed in strict chronology in the samba songs.

Furthermore, the poor in Rio are strikingly aware of the world historical situation, including racism in the United States, Brazil's position in the world, the existence of Communism and Communist states, the Rosenberg trial, and so on, endlessly. I do not say accurately, but cognizantly they are in history.

Finally, with individual and family exceptions, the poor of the *favelas* and perhaps somewhat fewer of the poor of Rio's rooming houses are pervasively future-oriented (Leeds, 1966, 1967; A. Leeds and E. Leeds, 1970), planning intra- and trans-generationally, attempting to build for the future through a variety of capital—perhaps penny-capital—formation techniques. This is an aspect of their sense not only of history but also of their sense of personal worth which I find—Lewis's claimed "trait" of "feelings of personal unworthiness" notwithstanding—ubiquitous among the great majority of the poor with whom I have worked. It is maintained by their awareness of self, of class (phrased in a great variety of ways), of the historical situation and their place in it, and by their long-term aims and goals.

All of what I have said contradicts, too, the alleged traits of *resignation* and *fatalism* considered here in substantive terms. As a category or aggregate of people, the poor in Rio, Lima, Bogotá, and Caracas—and La Perla in San Juan—are not resigned and fatalist, though individuals or selected families may be. They are burdened by a system of constraints despite which they construct —as Lewis himself indicates (1965–66, pp.xxxii-xxxiii)—they get roofing materials, they get the alleys paved, they improve their homes. When I visited La Perla in 1967, a number of wooden houses were being rebuilt with cinder blocks. Along the central paved street and on the street at the east end of the squatment, a number of cars were to be seen. It was plain that a good deal of capital had gone into house improvement, water piping, electric systems, indoor toilets, sewers, and the like. There were a number of stores, an office of the Small Business Administration, a political-party post, several churches, and so on. One issue of the San Juan *Star* (about Nov. 7, 1967) had an article announcing the establishment of an association for carrying out repairs and emergency services in the community, especially for the elderly and widowed (*cf*. Leeds and Leeds, 1970, Footnote 5).

What group or delimited population, then, is the empirical carrier of the culture of poverty? This question is of utmost importance, since in my own work, I could not find any bounded population which corresponds to such a culture.

I think the answer, which Lewis's peculiar methodology and his choice of a family and individual biographical procedure both hide and emphasize, is that there is no such group or population. Although popularly admired as a literary form, the biography does not involve methodologically precise procedures of structural analysis, producing the empirically validated and replicable delimitation of groups and group boundaries necessary to specify the societal carrier of any culture, hence the culture of poverty. Instead, Lewis's method assumes that the setting forth of the sociocultural history of a family will automatically reveal the sociocultural situation of the total collection of families and the entire nets of interrelations among them and the population of which they are supposedly representative by virtue of their place of residence.

None of this can be true by assumption, but must be shown by evidence. What evidence Lewis gives contradicts the assumption. For instance, the aggregate statistics given for La Perla (1965–66, pp. xxxii-xxxix) clearly indicate quite a broad range of incomes, occupations, housing, and probably household histories. They also indicate that the *arrabal* has an internal economy and an internal social order. Neither in this book nor in his articles has Lewis described either of these, although both are part of the structure of the situation that must be treated if one is to discuss the population or one of its subgroups to which the concept of the culture of poverty is to refer.

My own research in Brazil similarly had to confront the problem of locating some subsection of the society which corresponded to the carrier of the culture of poverty. I have not been able to locate such a section. I find individual families, unattached to each other and scattered here and there in the same residential enclave, which display a constellation of characteristics more or less corresponding to the one Lewis speaks of, give or take a number of traits. What strikes one, however, is the isolation and difference of these families from the rest of the local population, which, on the whole, is also poor and yet works toward its own betterment, looks to the future, is aware of its own history, has identity, plans and saves, frequently buys both movable and immovable property, and builds, often with much greater persistence and perspicacity than members of the middle class.

Perhaps these isolated families do indeed tend to pass down along family lines their particular form of adaptation to their environment—"Yea, unto the seventh generation shall the sins of the father be visited on the sons"—although some appear to be newly recruited families which have been caught in excessive stresses and fallen into a slough of despond (see A. Leeds and E. Leeds, 1970, for example). However, there are several major observations to be made in this regard.

First, one need not postulate a culture to account for this, but, rather, one can explain the continuity in terms of psycho-social states of the family, external barriers imposed on the children, their and their parents' structural isolation from learning situations, the external generation of stress, the degree and continuity of such stress, and the external constraints against resolving the stress.

Second, children do break away from the pattern, although Lewis appears to imply (1965–66, p. xliii) that they do not. What they break away to is the prevailing sociocultural patterns, or simply culture, of residential or other reference groups besides their family (Lewis, apparently as a result of his method of family biography, sees the family as the unique reference group).

Third, as I have remarked above, for many such families, the moment the constraints under which they labor are even slightly released, they immediately begin to divest themselves of the symptoms in question.

Fourth, family characteristics are carried down along family lines in populations that are *not* poor, too, but no one calls these behavioral complexes 'cultures,' such as the Darwin-Galton culture, the Bach culture, the Massachusetts Adamses culture, the Huxley culture, the Rockefeller culture, and perhaps an emerging Kennedy culture. Nor, for the poor, do we speak even of a Hatfield-McCoy culture or a Jukes-Kallikak culture, but rather of these families within the context of two different versions of American Southern subsociety and subculture. Why should we do differently theoretically or methodologically for the poor of Latin-American countries?

Fifth, a methodological-empirical point of great weight: it is not even clear what the referent of "the family" is in Lewis' family studies. In my experience, when one takes a genealogy as completely as possible, one finds a great range of incomes, life styles, occupations, etc., of the people on the family tree. To *some* ancestor, this entire tree is a "family line." It is clear, therefore, that for people on the family tree, many different "sins" are visited by fathers on sons. In other words, inheritance of behavioral complexes along family lines is not at all clear, uniform, or guaranteed, unless one carefully selects, out of all the possible descent lines of a single genealogy, that line which shows the inheritance one is trying to prove. What is such a line—a household-family group, its children, and its children's children? Are the family and the household or the family and the genealogy coterminous? What are the points of divergence when one line of inheritance splits from another possessing the same parental stock, and how is one to account for the divergence which gives rise to the observed intragenealogical difference of family-household styles?

In sum, the empirical evidence from the population Lewis considers appropriate for study, or equivalent ones elsewhere, or from particular household groups displaying some complex of behaviors approximating Lewis's culture of poverty does not support Lewis's contention of the existence of a culture of poverty. Rather, empirically, the evidence suggests that the traits he lists occur as isolated outbreaks, or alternatively as one complex in a range of as yet ill-defined response systems of poor populations to rigorously imposed constraint systems. In dealing with these constraints, the majority of the poor show great ingenuity, shrewdness, and perseverance.

The empirical evidence does not support the contention, implied by Lewis's definition and made explicit by him throughout his writings, that the culture of poverty occurs as a semiautonomous, independent, sociocultural system of norms, values, world views, and behavior patterns, but, rather, indicates specific structural reflexes of a particular kind of small group, the immediate family-household, to specific aspects of the sociocultural system in which it is embedded.

Civic Issues and Conclusions

In briefest summary, the behavioral characteristics, residential conditions, etc., that stimulated Oscar Lewis to posit a culture of poverty are largely interpretable as direct consequences of the operation of some specific aspect of capitalist societal systems (see Leeds, 1969b), especially the labor market and its control by capitalist elites, the capital flow and control system, and the structure of profit management (*cf.* also Engels, 1872). One does not have to postulate a social state of mind, or culture, carried by structured social systems by means of characteristic sociocultural processes, to account for them. The structural-functional interpretation is simpler, involves fewer assumptions, and consistently corresponds more closely to the statistical data and to the variations found in the qualitative data (*cf.* Opler, 1968).

Such a postulation raises a number of ethical-civic issues. Important civic and policy consequences, with possible ethical overtones, lie immanent in Lewis's views.[32] First, it is well to re-emphasize that the postulation of a culture of poverty asserts, essentially, that the dynamic properties of that "culture" are intrinsic to the population which carries it, rather than extrinsic. In this regard, there is an undertone of Social Darwinism or even of a sophisticated social racism, whether or not intended by the concept's author, especially exemplified by (a) the rigidity of continuity of the culture of poverty expressed in Lewis's notion that it is carried down in family lines; (b) the implied ineluctibility of suffering from the culture of poverty if one's parents were "in it"; (c) the nonrecognition of the dynamic features which at times push people into certain behaviors and, at others, cause them to shift to other behaviors; and (d) the emphasis on the psychological and psychiatric dimensions of behavior (see Valentine, pp. 68–69).

That the interpretation of the behaviors of a population called the "culture of poverty" caters to widely held views about the poor or about working classes which are, in my experience, almost universal to social workers, social scientists concerned with development, and technical personnel and administrators concerned with social policies and programs. None of these types of people is provided with guidelines as to what the concept is *not* intended to

[32] Valentine (1968) deals extensively with this problem on pp. 67-77, in a chapter which deals with many of the same problems as the present work in quite parallel ways. See also his article in the present volume.

mean, or with appropriate critical tools (*cf.* Lewis, 1963). These are problems which the social scientist dealing with data of a sort commonly associated with what are said to be "social problems" must ethically take into account. He must recall that the locus of social programs *is* the population he is studying, that the "cure" for the "ill" lies in restructuring, willy-nilly, the values, world views, attitudes, outlooks, and so on, of, say, the alleged carriers of the culture of poverty (see Lewis, 1964a, 159, where the assumption of the desirability of changing the culture of poverty is unescapably clear). Since they are "apathetic," "present-oriented," "not able to defer gratification," the sufferers from the culture of poverty, and often the poor in general, must be "retrained," "motivated," "oriented," "given incentives";[33] treated psychiatrically (see fn. 19); taught how to budget their money; taught how to dress "properly" to confront the [discriminatory] job market, and so on, endlessly. The widespread justification of certain approaches in social programs for the poor on the basis of their having a culture of poverty; the diffusion of the Social Darwinist aspects of Lewis's conception by means of semipopular or mass media (*cf.* 1963); the failure to have put new, important conceptualizations to academic test before popularizing them; the widespread translation of his books (without adequate analytical context; *cf.* Valentine, p. 51, and Opler, 1968) into foreign languages to be read by persons without access to the critical literature; and the failure to consider the effects of his publications and their translations on the field situation[34] seem to me to involve important failures in ethical-civic responsibility on Lewis's part.

[33] Brazilian social workers constantly speak of having to *motivar, orientar, incentivar,* the poor uneducated *"favelado,"* who, apparently, has no idea of what he is doing. The term *favelado* conveys the sense of permanency of condition or state—it is a state of being, not a circumstance. Oscar Lewis's conception of the culture of poverty seems closer to this outlook than to understandings conveyed by terms such as "residents of *favelas"* or *"morador de barriada"* (the usual term in Perú, whose policies toward squatments seem so much more constructive than those of Brazil).

[34] As an example of the effects of Lewis's books on the field situation in Mexico, I cite Graham, 1968, p. 10:

. . . those who had a knowledge of local issues, more often than not, were reluctant to discuss them in much detail with an outsider, par-

The view of the behaviors under discussion as structural and functional responses to the societal system and the constraints it exerts on the population segments in question leads to a radically different understanding—namely, that the institutional system of those constraints must be changed, if one genuinely wants to get rid of the symptoms. This is a drastically different policy position; in some societies today it is, in fact, a revolutionary one.

That this is not a mere theoretical or rhetorical statement appears borne out by the glimpses, exiguous as they are, of the changes that have taken place where the system of pressures and constraints discussed has been fundamentally broken (though entirely other and new constraint systems, with quite different effects, may, indeed, have replaced it). I refer to the socialist countries where forms of labor market, capital circulation, and distributional system represent radical departures from those in Mexico, Puerto Rico, Brazil, or the United States. Though there are people who do not have much—who, by some standards, even their own, might possibly be considered "poor"—there appears to be no poverty; that is, real and basic exclusion from the reasonable fulfillment of basic wants and needs such as adequate food and satisfactory health facilities. There are institutional support structures, separate from wages and salaries, which permeate life even where cash is low and consumer goods scarce, so that the stress—or, in plain English, the anxiety and terror—which so widely prevails, say in our own society, with respect to such matters appears to be largely absent.[35]

---

ticularly a North American. More than once the fear was expressed that the project would be another *Children of Sanchez* . . . and would unfavorably reflect the political life of the city as they felt *Children of Sanchez* did on the social behavior of the Mexican people. The initial contact in many cases became something of an attempt to sell a bill of goods, to convince the individuals that the interviewer represented no threat.

[35] With respect to this anxiety or fear, I was struck, in a conversation with a Russian friend in Moscow, 1964, that she did not know what I meant by the phrase, familiar to Americans of almost any station of life, "Well, I don't know what I'd do if I were to get *really* sick!" She did not understand the conception of being "*really* sick," which means 'unable to meet financial obligations, like rent or payments on the house mortgage, to

In sum, Lewis's very widespread, novelistic publication of un-interpreted material, exposing his still poorly thought out concept to popular and professional misuse; his use of provocative terms—given the nature of ideological and social conditions in our own and related societies—like the term 'culture of poverty' which he himself calls "catchy" (1965–66: xlii; 1966: 3); his repeated use of the same conceptual material to bear the weight of huge amounts of data without a continuing development of analysis; his failure to cite literature which gives contrary data or indicates alternative ex-planations (see Opler, 1968); and his disregard for the effects of his publications on the field situation for later workers, together testify to the ethical-civic failure of Oscar Lewis.

BIBLIOGRAPHY

Abbreviation: ICA — International Congress of Americanists, Mar del Pluta.

Amado, Jorge, *Terras do sem fim*. São Paulo: Livraria Martins Ed., 1942. Transl. as *The Violent Land* (New York: Knopf, 1945).

Azevedo, Aluísio, *O cortiço* (*ca.* 1890). Trans. as *The Tenement* (New York: McBryde, 1926).

Cunha, Euclides da, *Os sertões* (1903). Transl. as *Rebellion in the Backlands* (Chicago: University of Chicago Press, 1962).

Engels, Frederick, *The Housing Question* (1872). New York: International Publishers, *ca.* 1937.

Goody, Jack, ed., *The Developmental Cycle in Domestic Groups*, Cambridge Papers in Social Anthropology, No. 1. Cambridge: The University Press, 1958.

Graham, Laurence S., *Politics in a Mexican Community*. Social Science Monographs, No. 35. Gainesville: University of Florida, 1968.

Instituto Mexicano de Serguro Sociàl, *Investigación de Vivienda en 11 Ciudades del País,* 3 vols. Mexico City: IMSS, 1965-1967.

Kroeber, A. L., *Natural and Cultural Areas of Native North America,*

---

solve housing, food, clothing, or health problems, to take care of the children and dependent adults, especially the old.' There appears to be no doubt that these are not matters of economic and structural concern in the Soviet Union and other East European states nor in Cuba, however much personal emotional feeling may be involved.

University of California Publications in Anthropology and Ethnology. Berkeley: University of California Press, 1939.

————, *Anthropology*. New York: Harcourt, Brace, 1948.

————, and Clyde Kluckhohn, *Culture: A Critical Review of Concepts and Definitions*. Cambridge, Mass.: Peabody Museum, 1952.

Leeds, Anthony, "Future Orientation—The Investment Climate in Rio's Favelas," paper read at the 37th ICA, 1966; to be published in Leeds, ed.

————, "The Entrepreneur in Rio's Favelas," paper read at Annual Meeting, American Association for the Advancement of Science, Dec. 29, 1967.

————, "The Anthropology of Cities: Some Methodological Considerations," in *Urban Anthropology,* ed. E. Eddy (Athens, Ga.: University of Georgia, 1968), pp. 31-47.

————, "The Adaptation of Mexican-Texans to External Constraints; San Antonio and Other Cases," paper read at Annual Meeting, Rocky Mountains Social Science Association, May 3, 1969a.

————, "The Significant Variables Determining the Character of Squatter Settlements," *América Latina,* 12(3): 44-86, 1969b.

————, "Locality Power in Relation to Supra-Local Power Institutions," in *Urban Anthropology,* ed. A. Southall (New York: Oxford University Press, in press).

————, ed., *Rio's Favelas* (Ms.) To be published by the University of Texas, Institute of Latin-American Studies.

————, and Elizabeth Leeds, "Brazil and the Myth of Urban Rurality: Urban Experiences and Work in Squatments of Rio de Janeiro and Lima," in *City and Country in the Third World,* ed. A. J. Field (Cambridge, Mass.: Schenkman, 1970), pp. 229-272, 277-285.

Leeds, Elizabeth, "Political Complementarity of Favelas and the Larger Society of Rio de Janeiro," paper read at the 37th ICA, 1966; to be published in Leeds, ed.

————, and Anthony Leeds, *Bibliography of the Sociology of Proletarian Housing Settlement Types,* 1966ff. To be published by the University of California at Los Angeles, Latin-American Center.

Lewis, Oscar, *Life in a Mexican Village: Tepoztlán Restudied*. Urbana: University of Illinois, 1951.

————, "Urbanization without Breakdown," *Scientific American,* Vol. 75 (1952), pp. 31-41.

————, *Five Families: Mexican Case Studies in the Culture of Poverty*. New York: Basic Books, 1959a.

————, "La cultura de la vecindad en la ciudad de México," Documento Informativo No. 1. Santiago: Seminario Sobre Problemas de Urbanización en América Latina, 1959a.

————, "The Culture of the Vecindad in Mexico City," in *Actas del 33° Congresso Internacional de Americanistas* (San José, Costa Rica: ICA, 1959c), Vol. 1, pp. 387-402.

————, "The Culture of Poverty in Mexico City—Two Case Studies," *The Economic Weekly of Bombay,* June 1960, pp. 965-72.

————, *The Children of Sanchez: Autobiography of a Mexican Family.* New York: Random House, 1961.

————, "The Culture of Poverty," *Transaction,* Vol. 1 (1963), No. 1, pp. 17-19.

————, "The Culture of Poverty," in *Explosive Forces in Latin America,* ed. J. J. TePaske and S. N. Fisher (Columbia, O.: Ohio State University, 1964a), pp. 149-174.

————, *Pedro Martinez.* New York: Random House, 1964b.

————, "Some Perspectives on Urbanization with Special Reference to Mexico City," Paper prepared for Symposium on Cross-cultural Similarities in the Urbanization Process. Burg Wartenstein: Wenner-Gren Foundation, 1964c.

————, *La Vida: A Puerto Rican Family in the Culture of Poverty, San Juan and New York.* New York: Random House, 1965–66.

————, "The Culture of Poverty," *Scientific American,* Vol. 215 (1966), No. 4, pp. 19-25.

————, *A Study of Slum Culture: Backgrounds for La Vida.* New York, Random House, 1968.

Mangin, William, *Clubes provincianas en Lima.* Lima: Instituto de Etnología y Arqueología, 1958.

————, "The Role of Regional Associations in the Adaptation of Rural Migrants to Cities in Perú," in *Contemporary Cultures and Societies of Latin America,* ed. D. Heath and R. N. Adams (New York: Random House, 1965), pp. 311-23.

————, "Squatter Settlements," *Scientific American,* Vol. 217 (1967), No. 4, pp. 21-29.

Naro, Nancy Smith, "Eviction! Land Tenure, Law, Power, and the Favela," paper read at the 37th ICA, 1966; to be published in Leeds, ed.

Opler, Marvin K., "On Lewis's Culture of Poverty," *Current Anthropology,* Vol. 9 (1968), No. 5, pp. 451-52.

Patch, Richard, "Life in a Callejón: A Study of Urban Disorganization," *Reports Service,* American Universities Field Staff, New York, June 1961.

Quijano, Anibal, *Notas sobre el concepto de marginalidad social* (mimeographed). Santiago: CEPAL, Divisíon de Asuntos Sociales, 1966.

Radcliffe-Brown, A. R., *A National Science of Society.* Glencoe, Ill.: Free Press, 1957.

Romano V., "The Anthropology and Sociology of Mexican-Americans: The Distortion of Mexican-American History. A Review Article," *El Grito* 2(1) : 13-26, 1968.

Seminário interuniversitário para o exame das conseqûencias das chuvas e enchentes de Janeiro de 1966 na região da Guanabara e áreas vizinhas. Rio: Universidade Federal do Rio de Janeiro, 1967.

Smith, M. G., *West Indian Family Structure.* Seattle: University of Washington, 1962.

Smith, R. T., *The Negro Family in British Guiana: Family Structure and Social Status in the Villages.* London: Cambridge University Press, 1956.

————, "The Family in the Caribbean," in *Caribbean Studies, A Symposium,* ed. V. Rubin (Jamaica, BWI: Institute of Social and Economic Research, 1957), pp. 67-75.

Steward, Julian H., "Cultural Causality and Law: A Trail Formulation of the Development of Early Civilization," *American Anthropologist,* Vol. 51 (1949), No. 1, pp. 1-27.

———— (ed.,) *The Handbook of South American Indians,* 7 vols., Bureau of American Ethnology Bull. 143. Washington: U.S. Government Printing Office, 1946–49.

Valentine, Charles A., *Culture and Poverty: Critique and Counter-Proposals.* Chicago: Univerity of Chicago Press, 1968.

THE STRUCTURAL PARAMETERS
OF EMERGING LIFE STYLES
IN VENEZUELA

LISA R. PEATTIE

Forms of thought are developed to serve the requirements of understanding particular kinds of situations. As new problems arise,
or different sorts of situations must be understood, news ways of
thinking may be required. I believe that anthropologists are at a
point where we must rethink our language and our concepts.

Field-work anthropology got its start in a series of short-term
plunges into various exotic societies without written history. Lack
of background information and the limited time span of "field
work" presented these societies to the ethnographer as isolated
from their immediate history. Real social isolation of primitive
groups was exaggerated in the field worker's perception by the
limited reach of the single researcher's ears and legs. Thus, although anthropologists have always looked at cultures as systems
of coping with specific real situations, and as developing their
systematic quality within the limits set by their situations, the nature of the societies anthropologists studied and the context within
which they studied them has made for a focus on internal organization, rather than on the relationship of small systems to larger-
scale forces.

The societies anthropologists studied, being generally small,
isolated and homogeneous, did not present within themselves
strongly varying conceptions of the good life or alternative programs of social action. The field worker, present as an outsider,

was unlikely to raise issues of change. Where questions were raised in the anthropological setting, they tended to arise in the context of the press of the Western industrialized powers on the world of the primitive or peasant; in this context the anthropologist naturally tended to react against changes which he saw as intrusive or forcibly imposed.

Thus the anthropologists have made a professional specialty out of calling attention to the way in which human beings tend to develop internally consistent patterns of thought and belief, and the tendency of such systems to perpetuate themselves over time and through altered circumstances. "Culture" has been their theme, and they have tended to stress in cultures their internal content, and the transmittal of this through time and social space.

We anthropologists have frequently carried over this pattern of thought to study situations quite different from these early ones, to social groups by no means isolated, and ones where we have a strong policy interest. For example, the anthropologist invited to look at a social issue such as juvenile delinquency still easily "comes on" talking about "lower-class culture."

But there is another recurrent experience of anthropologists involved in social action programs. The experience is marked by a shift in language. The anthropologist finds himself talking less about "culture," in the sense of "tradition," and more about "situation." He finds it less relevant to look at the content of culture as transmitted through time and space, and he finds it more relevant to focus on the patterns of behavior and of belief and affect directly or indirectly generated by the social situation at the given time of study.

An example of this shift is afforded by the research of Alexander Leighton in the camps in which Japanese Americans were placed during the Second World War. I believe that the agency in charge of the camps hired a staff of anthropologists because they recognized that the incarcerated Japanese Americans had a "different culture," and they thought that it would be useful to have anthropologists to report on that culture. The early research reports of the anthropological staff centered on the "culture" of the Japanese Americans. Leighton may at the outset have worked in that framework, but as he came to try to understand a large social disorder in one of the camps, the framework changed. The study that emerged, *The Governing of Men,* deals only to a limited extent with the differences in the way that Japanese Americans and other Americans see and deal with the world; it is primarily a book about the difference between how the incarcerated and the incarcerators see and deal with the world, and about the processes of government.

I had a similar experience when from 1962 to 1964 I went to work for a team of American planners in Venezuela. The planners, gathered together by the MIT–Harvard Joint Center for Urban Studies, were to act as consultants to a development corporation of the Venezuelan government in planning a new industrial urban center near the Orinoco River in the interior of Venezuela. A nucleus of the projected city already existed; near a small commercial town by the river, two American mining companies had established themselves in the forties and fifties, a nationally owned steel mill was already building, and the population, roughly fifty thousand when the planners arrived, was expanding rapidly. I was hired as staff anthropologist to provide counsel on "social problems" connected with the development process, and information on the "customs and values" of the people relevant to planning.

Almost from the start, I found myself unable to use the sort of intellectual framework suggested by a phrase like "the customs and values of the people." The city in which I was a participant observer was growing rapidly; its institutions were continually changing; the other residents had come from many places, and were of widely varying social characteristics. Furthermore, in trying to be relevant to the planners, I found myself noting the consequences of what the planners were doing to the people of the developing city; I tended to see behavior as representing not so much "customs and values" as a reaction to force and circumstance. Even when I turned my attention from the particular policy issues raised by planning, to describe the situation in the developing city, my observations tended to organize themselves in terms of "situation" rather than in terms of cultural "tradition."

I found myself seeing the life which surrounded me and my

family in the "squatter settlement" where we lived not so much as specifically Venezuelan, but as generically proletarian, or, more precisely, as representing a couple of emerging life styles tied in their emergence to economic change. There seemed to be a life-style much like that described by Oscar Lewis in his writings on the "culture of poverty," and by others describing the life ways of unskilled wage workers in situations of considerable unemployment. There seemed also to be a number of family groups with a way of living more like what we think of as stable working-class or lower-middle-class. Both seemed to be in a real sense "new," although incorporating within them elements of the old.

In Venezuela the apparent relationship of life style to economic situation presents itself with especial vividness because the social and economic processes involved there are so recent and so rapid. Thirty-odd years of oil boom transformed Venezuela from a nation two-thirds rural to one two-thirds urban and still urbanizing rapidly. The population of the capital tripled in a single decade. The death rate dropped, and Venezuela's population became one of the youngest and the fastest-growing in the world. Oil money spread new goods—city clothing, machine-made dishes, urban-style stuffed furniture, phonographs, radios. Oil money supported new communications—roads, newspapers, radios, general free public schools. Oil money attracted to Venezuela a vast in-migration of Europeans, a source of new skills and models. Oil money opened up new jobs and new careers. All these changes are within the memory of the generation over forty and are something of which they are intensely conscious.

The recent history of Venezuela is then, one of very rapid economic development. But this development has been lopsided in a way which is probably characteristic of the histories of the developing nations and which is particularly conspicuous in Venezuela because of the richness and dynamism of the developed sector. The immediate, although perhaps not the proximate, result of a development focused on modern capital-intensive industry can be described as a general raising of the economic level only if one uses national figures of production and per-capita income which lump together disparates at both ends of a bimodal curve.

It may be more accurately described as the separation of society into two economic sectors, one characterized by capital intensive industry, high wages and high skill levels, and the other employing (or "underemploying") people in "marginal" occupations with low levels of skill at low incomes.

This pattern of development is sometimes called a "dual economy." But it seems to me more useful to reserve that term for the areas which, even after undergoing economic development, perpetuate ways of life in which traditional economic practices are embedded in traditional social forms and cultural practices, like those of village subsistence agriculture. In such areas a part of the society may be said to be industrialized or urbanized, while alongside this sector the traditional world of the "peasants" continues.

But there are economies which seem less aptly described as dual than as bipolar. These are societies in which the drawing power of the developed sector is so great, or the holding power of the traditional sector so slight, that the whole society becomes permeated by the development process and nearly the entire population comes to focus on the developed sector. The situation in which I was working in Venezuela was one of these. Eastern Venezuela has never had the closely knit community life characteristic of the Andes or of highland Middle America. It was a thinly populated region of ranches, mines, and small farmers practicing shifting cultivation. When the oil boom came, there was nothing to stay their rush to the cities and into the commercial economy.

Around the city where I worked there was, it is true, a scant ring of still rather rural people—people who cultivated their little patches of corn and cassava and raised chickens, and from time to time got some days of work as laborers. These people might almost be said to be living in a different economy from that represented by the families whose men ride the bus every day in "hard hats." But to a considerable extent the people of the area, the poorest as well as the well-to-do and the rural as well as the urban, have definitely thrown in their lot with the city and with the cash economy. They follow urban styles in dress and in consumption patterns, to the degree that their economic resources permit. It is especially true of those who have moved to the city that the living room will stand bare until they can buy plastic-upholstered furniture on time payments. Some city dwellers may keep a few chickens, but they do not hope to live by farming, and they focus their hopes on getting "a job with the company." Their orientation is toward the modern world of mass-produced consumption goods, and if unable—as many of them are—to play directly the game which gives them the goods, they will hover about on the fringes of the rich modern economy, hoping somehow to get a toehold on it and meanwhile living on what trickles down.

In such a society as this, somewhat as in New York City, everyone in the society from top to bottom is, in effect, part of the same cash economy. The difference between those at the top and those at the bottom is not so much in the economy to which they direct their efforts, as it is in their greatly varying ability to cope with and to participate in it. At the top of the system are a group of people with technical and managerial skills who are able to use the opportunities provided in order to live well, consuming the goods which the economy provides, and training their children in the skills needed to continue this style of life. At the bottom is a large pool of unemployed, underemployed or marginally employed people who would like to imitate, superficially at least, the style of the successful, but who are unable to command an income either high enough or regular enough to make possible more than a very limited approximation of that. My *barrio* contained many people in this situation. As a distinctively working-class neighborhood, it contained none of the people at the really established level of the upper- or upper-middle-class *gente buena*. But it did have people who had, in effect, made for themselves small platforms of security within the developed sector, on which they were evolving patterns of life appropriate to that situation.

The *barrio* in which I was living began to grow up in the early 1940s just outside the fenced-in area where the Iron Mines Company of Venezuela, a subsidiary of Bethlehem Steel, was constructing installations for shipping iron ore down the Orinoco. The *barrio* now has just under five hundred people. Of the two hundred adults there at the time of study, about 22 percent had been there less than a year, and another quarter had been living there between one and five years. Still in the *barrio* was, however, a core of long-term residents; 15 percent of the *barrio*'s adults had lived there almost from its inception and another 22 percent over ten years. The very first settlers were still there.

As in other parts of the very rapidly growing city, almost everyone came from somewhere else. As in other parts of the city inhabited by working-class people, no one came from the Andean, more densely populated, and traditionally more "developed" parts of Venezuela. This is a city in which much of the commercial elite comes from Europe or the Middle East; in which technical and managerial people came from Caracas or the Andes (if not from the United States or Europe) and the lower class are drawn from the rural areas of eastern Venezuela. The people of my *barrio* were from the Orinoco delta, the poor agricultural northern coasts, the cattle-raising and oil-mining plains, or the West Indies. Their background was, in the main, scattered-settlement agricultural, but most had had some town experience, and many had gone through the great educational experience of the oil camps. My *barrio* was definitely agreed (by both upper- and lower-class people) to be a *barrio bajo*, a lower-class community, inhabited mainly by *los pobres*, the poor.

Although in 1962 the *barrio* still had a number of men employed by the Iron Mines Company, the largest single employer for people of the *barrio* was the new steel mill across the river, where twenty-one of the *barrio*'s men were working. Eighteen had jobs with either Iron Mines or the more recently established mining subsidiary of U. S. Steel. Eleven were in commerce, either as owners of small grocery stores and refreshment businesses or as ambulant salesmen. A good deal of the commercial activity reflected by these figures took place in the *barrio* itself, for at the time of my census the *barrio* had six small businesses, or roughly one for every twelve households—one a bar and the others small shops selling groceries, soft drinks and beer, and serving as social as well as shopping centers. Twelve women worked as domestic servants or washerwomen, almost all of them in one or the other of the two company "camps"—what we would call "company towns." Nineteen persons were in a variety of other jobs, from schoolteacher to cab driver. The most conspicuous economic success was an accountant who drove his new car every day to a job at a big construction plant. The worst-off household was that composed of two old ladies, one of whom got occasional help from a married daughter, the other of whom, having no kin, went out begging.

Wage labor and commerce are the economic base of the *barrio*. But they are a rather slim base. At the time of my census, the *barrio* had 490 inhabitants, living in eighty household groups. But more than half were juveniles. Thus, even with very few very old people, adults in the most work-productive years were only 34 percent of the population. Of these, furthermore, a very large number were unemployed. Of the grown males between nineteen and sixty years of age over a third were unemployed, with the rate of unemployed highest (about 40 percent) among the young men of nineteen to thirty and those in their fifties. Thus, with only eighty-one persons in the *barrio* having more or less regular sources of earned income, each employed person was on the average supporting five others, children or unemployed adults. In the absence of any system of public-welfare assistance, this large dependent population lived off the developed sector, the money trickling down through intermittent low-wage employment opportunities—like laundry work or occasional construction labor—or through assistance mediated by a kinship relation to one of those people in the *barrio* who had achieved a more stable economic situation.

The coming of the oil boom in Venezuela must have provided a set of almost unprecedented mobility possibilities. The heavily capitalized American companies which began to take oil out of Venezuela, as well as those which were involved in shipping iron ore to the steel mills of North America, presented a set of instant economic institutions providing incomes and job training. Although the boom drew to Venezuela a flood of European immigrants—largely Italians and Spaniards—who fitted themselves into many of the proffered slots, there were other jobs left over for the

Venezuelans. The shortage of persons with developed skills was so great that entry requirements were minimal. "It was just like a school," said one of my neighbors of the early days with Iron Mines; almost everyone was learning on the job.

However, the transition from construction to production and from an era of boom to one of deflation or slower growth presented a problem of consolidation. Informants saw this as a problem and were able to articulate it as such. The situation in my *barrio* suggests that the people at the working-class level who had managed to consolidate the entry experience into some kind of relatively permanent base of security had done so in two general ways. One was by investment, either in housing, for living in and for renting, or in a small business. Neither provided more than minimal income possibilities, but they did ensure some stability of income and social position. The other mode of consolidation was by acquiring, on the job, a degree of skill which could ensure steady employment at reasonably good wages. These could, of course, be combined; the owner of the bar, for example, was a man with very little formal education who had become a skilled electrician through work "in the company" and was now investing his earnings as an electrician at the steel mill in building up the business.

It is the people at the bottom who do not have any such foothold in the developed sector whose style of life suggests so strongly the writings of Oscar Lewis and others on "the culture of poverty." The sense of disengagement and alienation often reported among such urban proletariat is moderated here by an overriding national optimism derived from the recent burst of development, but it is present along with the optimistic focus on "the future of the worker." Preoccupation with *machismo* among men is a traditional Latin theme, but as I saw men in my *barrio* "acting *macho*" I thought of Harlem. Oscar Lewis speaks also of such characteristics as "high incidence of weak ego structure," "orality," "strong present-time orientation" and "high tolerance for psychological pathology" (Lewis, "The Culture of Poverty," *Scientific American,* October 1956). These seemed to me areas where it was difficult to measure, operationalize and make comparisons; certainly in my *barrio* the people at the bottom, involved in a day-to-day finagling to get fed, did not speak of plans for a long-term future and might be described as having a "strong present-time orientation." The proletarian situation, in my *barrio* as in Harlem, tends to produce a number of matrifocal and female-headed family groups. For people in this situation, there is almost nothing to hold a marriage together. There is no need to manage property in common; property, aside from personal clothing and effects, will consist at best of ownership of a house and furniture, perhaps crucial to a woman with children to care for but not to the husband. It is not held together by the pressure of interested and involved family groups; the bilateral extension of kinship ties is likely to be a dispersive factor, if anything, as kinfolk of husband and wife make their claims for aid which conflict with the claims of the nuclear family. Both men and women can earn money, and although jobs for women are very scarce, jobs for unskilled men are not to be counted on, either; thus neither spouse is a secure economic base for the other. Nor is there a necessary division of labor; women can work for wages, and men can buy their food prepared for them. Nor does the social order of the *barrio* provide, as does the social order of some highland Indian communities of Latin America, or that of the established middle class, a system of ordered statuses as a kind of game best played in partners. This social order is individualistic, and the worlds of men and of women are separate, the women to the house, to children and to their female kin, the men to "the street" and the bars. Both men and women are active and individualistic in sex, quick to form new sexual alliances. It thus happens that in such families if there is a man in the household he is there at the margins, and he may easily slip off altogether. In this situation, it seems to me remarkable that so many couples stayed together.

About a fifth of the households in my *barrio* at the time of study were headed by women. The tendency to focus on the tie between mother and children resulted in a number of household groups which were, in effect, small matrilineal lineages. Such households are in a particularly vulnerable position economically. The way in which people in my *barrio* developed networks of personal relationships through the bilateral extension of kinship and through fictive kinship in the *compadre* system may be partly understood in the context of economic insecurity, for the kinship and quasi-kinship network is a source of assistance and a basis of security. It is not a very solid basis, especially when those to whom one is related are themselves shaky, but for the people with neither economic nor social capital it is, in effect, the only basis that is available.

The kinship networks of people at the bottom in my *barrio* also—although not always—included people who had "made it," who had acquired some sort of capital, either in the form of invested savings—for example, the man with a house and small pool hall in the *barrio* and three rented houses in the center of town— or in the form of skill, like a hospital nurse or an electrician. The processes of mobility which have produced these varying levels within what upper-class Venezuelans still see as an undifferentiated "*clase obrero*" are so recent that both kinds of people may be represented within the same group of immediate kin. The hospital nurse, a very intelligent, charming woman with high educational aspirations for her children, had not only illiterate parents and cousins but an illiterate and not at all ambitious husband.

However, there are factors in the situation which should tend to separate these two kinds of people from each other. One is the fact that if the group at the bottom may be said to be consolidating a "culture of poverty," it seems equally true that their successful kin are consolidating a way of life which reveals elements of what we think of as solid working-class or lower-middle class. They save and invest. They plan for the future. They control their children, teach them to be orderly and obedient and to keep clean, and see that they get to school and go on in school.

In this strategy they are given an added advantage through the fact that the big companies in Venezuela not only pay better wages than prevail outside, but provide a large number of fringe benefits. These include not only housing and medical care, but schools, school busing and free school books and supplies. The company schools may or may not be better than those which the government has been developing—they are better than the one-room local schools, in any case—but it is clear that the child who goes to public school and who must (as he does in Venezuela) pay for books and transportation constitutes a financial burden which some families have great difficulty in carrying.

While I was there, the city, partly through the agency of planning, began to develop neighborhoods which were not so mixed as my *barrio*—which were, in fact, neighborhoods composed of the people who had this kind of small-scale security. The accountant and the nurse (who had just separated from her less mobile husband) were trying very hard to move into one of these neighborhoods. If the successful move out, they will become not only physically but socially inaccessible to their less established kin, for these sorts of loose kinship ties are extremely vulnerable to distance. Furthermore, as schooling becomes more available, educational entry requirements become continually more important in the job market. Those who fail to get the right start in life now will be at much more of a relative disadvantage than they would have been thirty years ago. Families headed by people with established niches in the company system are in a far better position to provide that right start than those outside it.

Looking at this situation for some kind of social leverage which might alter the trends which seem to emerge in this analysis leads to a look at the political structure of Venezuela. Here again there is much that widens the gap between the people at the bottom and those who have gotten into the system. The burst of economic development centering around oil—large foreign corporations operating in a context of rising nationalist aspirations—not only established the pattern of provision of social services through the private companies, but also focused the emerging labor movement. This labor movement ran very rapidly through a formative organizational period and established itself as a powerful political force with strong ties to the establishment and a minimal interest in organizing the still considerable mass of unorganized people.

It seemed to me, therefore, that I was looking at an emerging class differentiation of life styles which will tend to become even more clearly established as time goes on. The factors which should tend to set these life styles as styles and to perpetuate them through time are both internal ones (modes of behavior, focuses of interest, values, family structure) and external (national patterns of investment, especially as these relate to patterning of the job market, systems of education, patterns of urban development, political structure). These factors are interrelated in a quite complex way.

If the hypothesis of emerging class differentiation should be borne out by future trends, there would still be two styles of causal interpretation. The situation could be described as one of the consolidation of a "culture of poverty," or it could be described as one in which people are developing stylized adaptations to a particular situation of continuing institutional press. These differing points of view have obvious consequences for policy.

Is one way of describing reality more "true"? I find it hard to say so. I find the situational description both more useful and more enlightening, and find it hard to distinguish between utility and enlightment.

To describe the process of class differentiation in terms of institutional press does not mean that the life of the poor is only problematic behavior, not a "style of life." Anthropologists who study the life of the poor are quite aware that the poor develop value systems which have to do with their life situations, that here, as elsewhere, human intolerance for psychological dissonance means that people adjust their values and aspirations to the limits of the possible. The anthropologist's concern and respect for human values in any situation operate here too. A student I know recently wrote me of a summer's field work on Skid Row, that he had found on the Row a way of life with a certain validity. It is, he said, "a niche, a way of life, a life that is roughly like an extended stay within the 'Kiva'—both natural and desirable." At the same time, when we also define the situation to which people adjust as problematic, we may look at the style of adjustment in a different way, as a case of "been down so long it looks like up to me."

When we focus on the situational parameters of cultures, rather than on their internally systematic features, I think we tend also to see cultural perpetuation less in terms of internal mechanisms of transmission and of internal consistencies than in terms of the stability of relevant external factors. In describing the fact that children of the poor grow up like their parents, we might focus less on the child-rearing practices than on the institutional structures which provide the poor with crowded housing, which weaken the father's role, which inform the children of the poor that they should not expect too much or try too hard. In looking at the Negro family, we would be less interested in a continuity with the kind of family structure produced under conditions of slavery, and more interested in the current forces which tend to emasculate the Negro male.

I believe that if we are to live with the concept of a "culture of poverty" and with ourselves in our world, it will be with a concept of culture rebalanced in this way.

"GOWSTER," "IVY-LEAGUER," "HUSTLER," "CONSERVATIVE," "MACKMAN," AND "CONTINENTAL": A FUNCTIONAL ANALYSIS OF SIX GHETTO ROLES

HERBERT C. ELLIS AND
STANLEY M. NEWMAN

A lot of feeling exists in the literature and elsewhere that black ghettos are homogeneous and monolithic places.[1] This is especially the case concerning teenagers and young adults. Generally, the emphasis is on so-called gang delinquency and on pathological, antisocial, and antischool behavior. Usually stressed is the single role of the delinquent as a constant source of trouble to society. This oversimplification is compounded further by facile psychological explanations that often locate the source of the "delinquent's problem" in his intractable and recidivous nature.

While a much smaller reaction to this position has attempted to balance the research picture, very little, in our opinion, has been done by way of presenting a normative description of *all* the varied roles available to black ghetto youth.[2]

---

[1] A classic example of this syndrome is the recent so-called "Moynihan Report," *The Negro Family*. Suggestions and models for dealing with the problem of homogenizing the ghetto are dealt with in the recent work of Valentine (1968).

[2] See Kvaraceus, Miller *et al.*, 1959; Short and Strodtbeck, 1965. It should be noted that even in these cases very little is said about specific *individual roles;* rather, the emphasis is on the attributed "values" or "sub-culture" of "delinquent youth."

The purpose of this paper is to offer new data in an effort to redress the situation. This paper treats six roles played in combination and to varying degrees by some black youth residing in low-income ghettos in Chicago. The six roles are: gowster, ivy-leaguer, hustler, conservative, mackman, and continental. The motivation behind the research on these roles had its most recent origins in a paper treating one specific role, that of the "gowster."[3] At the time, we were aware that other roles existed, but we did not have the data to allow us to do more than impressionistically and briefly speculate about them.

The data were collected by the authors through the use of a questionnaire, participant observation and other techniques.[4] The questionnaire consisted of ninety items, eighty of which were used in the final analysis because of their statistical significance. The questionnaire was designed, pretested, and administered to twenty-five black teenagers ranging in age from fourteen to sixteen and representative of eighty percent of the predominantly black high schools in Chicago. The administrator of the questionnaire is black.[5]

The questionnaire items are divided into four categories that permit role description and differentiation to emerge: (1) asocial aggression, (2) sexual prowess and dominance, (3) social and economic prestige, and (4) style of dress. "Asocial aggression" refers to attitude, behavior, and demeanor. Specifically, it denotes thoughts, feelings, and acts that are viewed as negative according to the standards of the larger society. "Sexual prowess and dominance" refers to the ability to control, dominate, and manipulate women for one's own financial and sexual gain; dominance, *per se,* has to do with the extent that an individual can influence and

[3] Originally given by the second author under the title "The Gowster: A Functional Analysis of a Ghetto Personality," at the annual meeting of the American Anthropology Association in Pittsburgh, November 1966.

[4] The authors make none of the usual claims for "scientific reliability and validity." Instead, five years of varied "research" in the form of participant and nonparticipant observations, impressions, and ordinary and everyday contact (a lifetime's worth for one of the authors) seem to us to both strengthen and weaken what we are trying to say.

[5] For a full statistical treatment and elaboration of the research design, see Ellis, 1969.

control the thoughts, feelings, and actions of others. "Social and economic prestige" refers to the ability to enhance one's self-esteem by achieving high status within the peer group; economic prestige, narrowly defined, refers to the individual's skill in obtaining money, irrespective of the means used. "Style of dress" refers to a mode of dress and hair form that generally is associated with a particular role; included here are characteristics such as peculiar postures, stances, and dancing and walking styles.

Role Description

Our findings show that the six roles are overlapping and interdependent, with one role usually dominating an individual's personality style at a given time.

The Gowster. Of the six roles, one is clearly distinct—the role of the gowster.[6] Our respondents made it clear that the gowster's appearance ("style of dress") is his most obvious feature.[7] They stressed his characteristic style of dress in commenting, "He looks like a raggedy-gowster." Their ideal description reveals baggy pants[8] with deep pleats, long-tip-collar shirts, loose Italian knit sweaters with cuffs turned under, brand-name "Stacy-Adams" pointed shoes, black leather jacket or coat, and a hat worn "ace-deuce"—i.e., low to one side—and sometimes over a "do-rag" or

[6] The exact etymology of the word "gowster" is unknown to us. As a guess, "gowster" may be a derivative of *gaucho,* the Spanish word for the cowboy of the Argentine pampas.

[7] Styles of dress are important because they often signal an individual's role and thereby serve as an aid to expected behavior. The importance of dress as a correlate of role can be seen in the following passage from the autobiography of Malcolm X (1964), in which he describes his first purchase of a particular style of clothing which signals his role change from "country" to "hip" and "city": ". . . the salesman picked off the rack a zoot suit that was just wild: sky-blue pants thirty inches in the knee and angle-narrowed down to twelve inches at the bottom, and a long coat that pinched my waist and flowed out below my knees."

[8] The baggy pants serve as a clue that the term "gowster" may derive from the Spanish word *gaucho,* since the Argentine gaucho also wears large, baggy pants and is famous for his skill in guerrilla fighting (translate "guerrilla fighting" into category one, "asocial aggressions").

hair-process kerchief in order to protect the "conk," a special hair style.[9] Ties are not worn, but tie tacks are often worn on the collar. Handkerchiefs or large square cloths are pinned to a back pocket and allowed to hang down.

Part of the gowster's style is a particular stance[10] which entails either standing with the knees bent, so that a convex impression is formed in the knee of the trousers, or flexing the calf muscles, leg thrust backward, so as to accentuate the musculature of the leg. His wide-legged style of dancing, called the "do-whop," and his distinctive use of arms and hands also emphasize a particular posture.

Walking too lends itself to a gowster style. One of the questions we asked was, "Could you tell a gowster at the beach?" In many cases, the answer was yes, due to the special walk of the gowster called "the pimp," or "bopping."[11] This walk consists of a smooth, bobbing, up-and-down movement, with the body carried slightly to one side.

[9] Processed hair is no longer prevalent in the ghetto, being replaced by the *au naturel* style. Letting the hair grow naturally represents, of course, the Afro-American's recognition of his African heritage. Equally important, it signifies his rejection of white values and of his need to emulate white hair styles (Lorens, 1967, and Lee, 1967).

[10] Not much, to our knowledge, has been written about the various "stances," "postures," and "walks" which appear to exist along low-income blacks. The impression remains strong, however, that this is an important area of understanding; e.g., Woodie King, Jr., says in a short story (King, 1965): "Everyone attained a hip position. It consisted of pulling pants high, rolling the Hi-Lo collar, taking a silk handkerchief in hand, wetting the lips, getting the body limber, and the natural expressionless face." We are not saying that this or any other style of stance is unique to the gowster; we are saying that our respondents feel it is an important identifying aspect of the gowster role.

[11] "Bopping" as a form of (nonverbal) communication is poignantly illustrated in the excerpt below taken from David Henderson's poem "Bopping" (Henderson, 1968):

> we bopped when about to fight
> and we bopped when happy
> and in our slight variances
> known to the members of the Road
> and known to similar bops
> of the roaming hordes

The gowster's verbal communication is conducted in the idiom of the low-income black ghetto.[12] The frequency with which he resorts to his specialized vocabulary differentiates the gowster from others.

Though other Afro-Americans and even some small minority of whites might understand and indeed use some of these expressions, their conversation would not rely so heavily on them. In the idiom, for example, a car is a "short," the Cadillac a "hog." "Jam" means party and a "boss-jam" is a very good party. A "fox" is a female and a "stone fox" is a real fine female. "Bad" may mean good—e.g., "He's bad-good but not evil." "Tough" may mean pretty, as in "She's a tough broad."

The predominating characteristic of the gowster is his image as a "warrior." This image is characterized by two forms of asocial aggression—a propensity toward acts of violence and a generally defiant demeanor. An oft-repeated statement about the gowster was, "Don't mess with that cat, he's a gowster." Gowsters generally resent adults and feel that by defying them they are stealing their power and gaining control of the situation. Some animosity is felt toward parents because parents stress the importance of school and adherence to rules. School is for "squares" (those who are unenlightened and not like the group), a place to go to socialize or to relieve the loneliness of the streets, and to visit one's "partners" (close friends).

The gowster's need to establish himself as a warrior obligates him to conform to the image which others hold of him. One way he does this is in the handling of strangers. E.g., if a strange youth comes into the school or "hood" (neighborhood), it is frequently the gowster who will try to size him up by testing the alien's "heart" (courage) and "cool" (stoicism). It is here that the gowster expresses his physical prowess in "dusting" or "jacking up" (i.e., fighting) the stranger. On other occasions the gowster may act out his role by undertaking a foray into enemy territory

[12] While some formal linguistic research has been undertaken (Abrahams, 1964; Labov, 1967; Stewart, 1967; Hanners, 1967; Kochman, 1969), much remains to be done. Verbal creativity is so great that vocabularies change very often. Some of our examples are doubtless "out" or dated.

in order to "dust" or "oil" (fight) a "dude" (male) or by acting the enforcer to those disposed to deny or renounce membership in the group.

While the gowster conceives of himself as a fighter, he also has a concern for his larger image as a male. In short, gowsters feel that a man cannot call himself a man unless he can drink, smoke, gamble, stay out late, enjoy sex, and generally take care of himself.

The trait constellation for the role of the gowster significantly differentiates him from the other five roles. This is seen clearly in the category of "asocial aggression." Questions such as "Do they dust or burn a dude who does not want to join their gang?," "Do they enjoy doing wrong?," "Are they bad?" (i.e., *good* in the sense of being strong, brave, and daring) elicited responses indicating that these traits are felt to belong almost exclusively to the gowster role. This, we feel, is an important finding to be returned to.

The Ivy-Leaguer. Gowsters and ivy-leaguers represent dichotomous roles. Whereas the gowster is a rebel against middle-class society, the ivy-leaguer emulates middle-class behavior. Ivy-leaguers belong to social clubs (fraternities) rather than gangs; they abide by school laws and routines and dress well, by middle-class standards, wearing button-down collars and Brooks Brothers–style clothing to effect an Ivy League look. In comparison the gowster tends to dress in a "raggedy" way, not finish school, and be in conflict with family and authorities, whereas the ivy-leaguer is considered good by his middle-class teachers, goes to church and is well liked by family and the authorities.

The Hustler. The hustler represents (to us) the most complex, difficult, and diverse model of the six roles under consideration. All respondents agreed that the key to the hustler is his great abundance of "smarts" (intelligence). Concomitant with his "smarts" is the ability to be flexible—the hustler's skill to "come out of many different trick bags." To this extent the hustler's role requires more training, skill, and sensitivity in street life and personality psychology than any of the other roles.

The *complexity* of the hustler's role stems, in part, from its diverse nature. Hustling is a means of obtaining money, goods, and services in a variety of ways and from many sources. As the classic middleman his judgment must be flawless.[13]

The *difficulty* of the role comes from the severely limited margin of error with which the hustler must work. Contact with the wrong individuals (a police informer, a plainclothesman, a dissatisfied customer or a "square") presents constant threats to the hustler's ability to stay in business; indeed, it takes only a single mistake to effect a rapid transformation from the role of hustler to the role of convict or worse.

Recognition of the *diversity* of the hustler's role can be seen in the statements offered about him: If a situation presents itself, the hustler will "whup a game on a trick or a lame," i.e., one form of hustle consists of putting something over on the unsophisticated and unsuspecting for the eventual benefit of the hustler;[14] if necessary, the hustler is not averse to "pushing pot" (selling marijuana) or "ripping off" (e.g., snatching a purse or wallet, stealing a car or its parts); if possible, a hustler's "game" may require the putting together of a "stable of broads" who hustle, usually through prostitution, money for him.[15]

The hustler's collective style of dress differs in an important way from that of the gowster and the ivy-leaguer (and from that of the other roles) in not being clearly discernible. In other words, there is no one style that uniquely identifies the hustler. In acting out the many subroles of the hustler role, he chooses to wear primarily those styles of clothing universal to his milieu—e.g., the "black leather" (a coat or jacket), knitted shirts, dress shirts, trench coats, etc.). Careful use of these styles allows him to slip

[13] An excellent treatment of the hustler is Williamson, 1965.

[14] Not all hustles are one-sided. Some hustles are reciprocal transactions where money is given to the hustler in exchange for what is deemed an equal amount of service or goods.

[15] We are aware that the reader may have difficulty in differentiating among the types of hustle mentioned, feeling that common to all the examples is their illegal status. However, distinctions are made. For example, to snatch a purse does not (obviously?) require the skill demanded of the successful hustler-pimp. For this reason pimping as a form of hustle often is highly esteemed. An excellent description of the role of the pimp is offered in Slim, 1967.

out of one subrole and into another according to the need and occasion. The hustler, by choice, is the chameleon of the ghetto.

The Conservative.   The conservative's role in many respects is analogous to the roles of the gowster, the continental, and the ivy-leaguer. In regard to the category of "asocial aggression" he shows the gowster's propensity to get involved in personal kinds of violence such as fighting to defend the in-group and "dusting" to get what he wants.

The conservative tends to dress like the ivy-leaguer, wearing "Brooks Brothers" suits and dress shirts with button-down collars. Or, on the other hand, he may modify his dress by wearing the continental's "walking suit" (shirt and trousers of the same color), narrow-brimmed hats, and V-necked sweaters. In short, expediency dictates his fashion, so that he goes "WWIG" ("wear what I got").

Like both the continental and the ivy-leaguer, the conservative is "straight" (genuine, honest) to his "partners," abides by school regulations and routines, and is thought to be usually successful in life ("social and economic prestige").[16]

The Mackman.[17]   The mackman, like the gowster, may get into trouble by "ripping off" (stealing), "messing with jail bait" (involvement with under-age girls), and drinking "pluck" (cheap wine) to impress his friends.

The style of dress of the mackman is different from the gowster's, featuring the "walking suit," loud shirts, and a preference for suede shoes. His interest in controlling women for economic gain makes him reminiscent of the hustler and further differentiates him from the gowster. At different times, he acts the gowster and dresses the continental while aspiring to the role of the hustler, but does not yet, as a mackman, possess the finesse and maturity to take on this role.

The Continental.   The continental's efforts to manipulate and control women underlines his core concern. While his style of

[16] We note here, to be returned to later, the possible contradictions in the conservative's role that allow him to "fight" and "abide by school regulations."

[17] "To mack" in the idiom means to "rap"; hence a mackman (in Chicago) is a "heavy rapper"—a very good talker.

dress is not clearly of one type—e.g., he will wear "Brooks Brothers" clothing, as does the ivy-leaguer—he also favors the "walking suit" of the conservative and the mackman. This multi-style dress in alternation with loud shirts and suede shoes relatively distinguishes him from other role types.

The attitudes of the continental toward school, home, and work suggest a priority of behavior. School, for instance, while seen as a place for "squares," nevertheless is attended. Parents are a source of money, but in the event that they are not the continental will seek gainful employment rather than the "rip-off." Failing at that he may resort to "whupping a game" or "pushing pot."

The continental perhaps would like to be an ivy-leaguer, but his interest in women and need for short-range achievement cause him readily to act otherwise.

Analysis

In attempting to analyze the six roles, we posed three questions, aimed at establishing (1) how the six roles function for individuals within their ghetto environment, (2) what happens to the individuals who play these roles, and (3) whether other sub-groups produce similar roles.

1. How do these roles function for individuals?   An answer to this question is that all six roles function primarily as coping mechanisms that allow these youths to cope adaptively with their life situation within the context of their ghetto environment. By "coping adaptively" we mean in terms of fulfilling one's prag-matic and psychological needs. The low-income black youth in question, obviously, have the same needs as their black and white middle-class counterparts—the pragmatic needs of food, shelter, and clothing and the psychological needs of a positive self-image, personal dignity, ego enhancement, and sense of belonging and achievement.

To grasp fully how these roles function in fulfilling the above needs the reader must clearly be able to comprehend the life predicament of ghetto youth. Starting with certain givens, that being black and poor in a white racist society is to live an experience different in kind from white youth,[18] means that blacks have to be creative in different ways to survive.

A close analysis of the role of the gowster may serve to demonstrate what we are saying. The idea of the gowster as a fighter and a man is dominant in his role makeup. Gowsters are "gang-bangers" (fighters), members of what has been termed "warrior clubs." "The ideology of violence dominates the value system" (Keiser, 1969).

To understand the violence of the gowster it first is imperative to know something about the violent environment of the ghetto. Only after insights are gained into the "tortured, complex, and corrupt jungle that is the day-to-day reality" of the ghetto dweller can violence be understood in its proper context (Harlem Youth Opportunities Unlimited, Inc., 1964). Violence takes many forms in the ghetto, the corrupt political machine, the humiliation suffered in the classroom, the brutality of the cop, the bite of a rat, all represent violence of a kind. The rule is clear: gowsters didn't invent violence, they inherited it; to survive is both to commit and to avoid violence.

On the pragmatic level, the gowster's garb is highly functional. His hat, which is always worn, may cushion a blow. His "black leather" is difficult to identify, especially at night, and also serves as a protective device when wrapped around arm and hand for use in fighting. Loose-fitting clothing, in particular the baggy pants and loose-knit sweaters, allow weapons strapped to the leg or carried next to the wrist to be concealed.[19]

On the psychological level, the role of the gowster functions to meet personality needs. The gowster typically begins life with

[18] A growing number of white students now accept the proposition that two nearly distinct societies exist in America, one white and one black. The "Kerner Report" represents only the latest recognition of this. (Many, if not most, blacks accept the proposition as common factual knowledge.) Not unexpectedly, however, the report has been greeted with great disclaimers—to wit, "It isn't so!"

[19] It seems clear that dress styles are dictated by aesthetic and economic considerations as well as by functional needs.

very little and with little to look forward to. That is, his socio-economic status is low and he often suffers more than most from a negative self-image and deprivation. He is the "deviant youth, traumatized, highly sensitive, and suspicious," who can be found among young people in the ghetto (*ibid.*). One of the informants aptly stated the case in saying, "Man, the gowster is a born loser. He needs something, *anything,* to bring him up."

This type of answer suggests an important insight into the gowster's personality needs. Starting life with a number of deficits not of his own making, the impoverished individual is presented a clear role that he can achieve. His alienation from and ambivalence to mainstream America cause him to reject middle-class values (of both whites and blacks) and to develop his own code of behavior. He emphasizes his differentness, his special role, that allows him membership in an in-group. This group, be it a gang or some other form of organization, gives the gowster necessary ego support.

Our impressions indicate that the role of the gowster functions for the individual in singling him out and making him psychologically visible. The gowster starts from an unenviable position and uses the very traits (poverty, poor education, etc.) deemed undesirable by middle-class Americans to achieve a role which gives him status and being.

It is important to note that the gowster is likely to be the very individual who *does not* give in to his inauspicious beginnings. To be a successful gowster requires many of the same traits necessary to be successful in society at large. Courage ("heart"), unemotionalism (be "cool"), leadership ability and skills in interacting with people are traits deemed desirable in a variety of middle-class positions.

The gowster wants what most of us want and what in fact many of us already have. The goals of the gowster and his middle-class counterpart, it seems to us, are identical. Where the gowster runs into difficulty is in the *means* he frequently must use within his given context to achieve those goals: dignity, a sense of belonging and a positive self-image.

In sum, you cannot understand the gowster without fully understanding his predicament. When no other means are accessible the gowster often will use the only means available to him to achieve his goals.

What is true for the gowster is equally the case for the other roles. While the ivy-leaguer, the mackman, the conservative, the hustler, and the continental act out their roles in different fashions, all the roles function to allow the individual to cope with his situation. The skills and mannerisms required for each role are diverse. Taken together, the six roles represent a repertoire of choices. What is important and needs to be emphasized is the availability of role choices that allow for different levels of success for different individuals. Smarter individuals will succeed in more difficult roles. The point, however, is that every individual usually can play some role with a certain amount of success. The overlapping nature of the roles allows the conservative, for example, to act the continental if it is to his advantage. In a context where contriteness and a humble demeanor pay off, say before an authority figure, the hustler may act the ivy-leaguer. And the ivy-leaguer may play the continental in "rapping to" (talking seductively to) a female.[20]

2. *What happens to these roles through time?* This question can be answered only in a speculative manner at this writing. Ours was not a longitudinal study, so we can only extrapolate from what is known to how these roles may evolve. Some individuals, it would seem, outgrow a role and become impoverished adults or "streetcorner men" (Liebow, 1967). Some experience success in middle-class terms and leave the ghetto. Two such are Claude Brown, onetime law student and author of a best seller, *Manchild in the Promised Land* (Brown, 1965), and author, poet, painter, and film-maker Piri Thomas (Thomas, 1967, 1969). Others may obtain sufficient steady employment and become "adult ivy-leaguers"—just plain mainstream Americans.

A particular difficulty in predicting future role evolvement stems from the black revolution taking place in America. On-the-

[20] The ability of an individual to play several different roles most likely accounts for the confusion in not being able to clearly assign separate traits to each role.

scene observations indicate new roles emerging. The roles of militant, revolutionary, moderate, separatist, integrationist, and so forth suggest that what we have said here may be radically altered, particularly for the present generation of black youth.[21] For teenagers born after the start of the black revolution[22] the choice of roles has increased. All that can be said, therefore, is that the relationship of the six roles discussed to the new roles needs to be looked into.[23]

3. *Do other subgroups produce similar roles?* This final question cannot be answered until comparative research takes place.[24] Preliminary investigation of this problem suggests that a set of dichotomous roles functionally akin to the gowster–ivy-leaguer exists among white working-class teenagers. Information about the roles of the "greaser" and the "duper" sounds as though they are the white counterparts to the gowster and the ivy-leaguer.

Our hunch is that analogies exist between these two sets of roles but that differences occur to the extent that the histories and heritages differ between low-income blacks and low-income whites.[25]

Summary and Conclusions

A number of items in the questionnaire showed that certain traits are universal for all six roles. Regardless of the role played, all

[21] Malcolm X and Eldridge Cleaver are two examples of individuals who changed their roles from hustler to gowster to "black militant."

[22] More or less arbitrarily we have designated as the beginning of the current black revolution the year 1955, when Mrs. Rosa Parks refused to sit in the back of the bus in Montgomery, Alabama.

[23] For example, we know that in many cases hair style is no longer a valid criterion for identifying roles. The natural wearing of the hair simply cuts across roles. Style of dress also loses some of its reliability due to the wearing of the African-style dashiki.

[24] Since this writing the comparative research has been undertaken by the authors (see Ellis and Newman).

[25] Our research into the role of the "greaser" indicates that it is functional akin to the gowster role. In *both* cases there is a heightened effect around dress, language, and demeanor in general. There is an interesting finding in light of Suttles' work in Chicago where he "discovered" the "gowster" but not the "greaser."

of the respondents felt that a high value is placed on verbal facility. To be a "heavy rapper" and to be able to "run it down" (skill in narrative discourse) are held as *prestigious* and highly *prized* skills. This is an important finding in light of all that is being said about culturally disadvantaged youths being nonverbal, noun-oriented, nonabstract, and, finally, unintelligible and unintelligent thinkers and speakers. Our data indicate that the opposite is true. Cogently stated, we find that the value on verbal facility among black youth probably exceeds what is found among their white counterparts.

A second universal is personal stability and personnel management. All respondents agreed that it is desirable, good, and necessary to be "cool" (unemotional), have "smarts" (intelligence), possess "heart" (courage), to have many "partners" (close friends), to be able to influence others, and to be able to keep the situation "uptight," i.e., in control. Corporation executives look for these same traits in their hiring and promotion practices. It is no accident, we feel, that youth organizations (the so-called gangs) are often referred to as "street corporations."

A third universal points out that nobody respects the police and the school. Given the abovementioned universals, it is clear to us that the schools and the police fail because they do not stand for what they purport to stand. Students do not drop out of school; they are *pushed out,* because they are treated as nonverbal and dumb when in fact they evince, in many cases, a high degree of verbal virtuosity and intelligence.

A final point: our analysis of the data strongly indicates that the idea of violence as ubiquitous among black youth is incorrect. To be sure, violence exists in the ghetto. Just living through a normal day is a violent experience by any reasonable set of standards. In spite of this, it is clear to us that the use of violence as a means of solving problems most often is only a means of last resort. Of the six roles treated, only one, the gowster, includes violence in any normative sense. And the gowster is generally looked down upon (though respected) because of his quick reliance on violence as a means of problem solving.

Nevertheless, it is most often the gowster or someone like him that captures the headlines. Five years ago it was the gowster that caught our attention. A paper offered then dealt primarily with that role. The inadvertent implication, we fear, was that every, or at least many, young ghetto men were gowsters. This conception proved wrong. Our research now tells us that a number of roles exist, that the role of the gowster is different and set apart from the other roles, that to play a role demands certain skills, and that while a propensity for violence is (as always and everywhere) respected it is seen only as a behavior tactic to be utilized when individual failings prevent the playing of other more intellectual roles.

BIBLIOGRAPHY

Abrahams, Roger, *Deep Down in the Jungle*. Hatboro, Pa.: Folklore Associates, 1964.

Brown, Claude, *Manchild in the Promised Land*. New York: Macmillan, 1965.

Cleaver, Eldridge, *Soul on Ice*. New York: McGraw-Hill, 1968.

Ellis, Herbert C., *A Description and Analysis of Certain Roles and Their Relationship to the Behavior of [some] Negro Youth Residing in Low-Status Ghettos in Chicago,* master's thesis, Northeastern Illinois State College, Chicago, 1969.

Ellis, Herbert C., and Stanley M. Newman, "The 'Gowster' and 'Greaser' Compared," in *Language and Expressive Role Behavior in the Black Inner City*. Urbana, Ill., University of Illinois Press (in press).

Hannerz, Ulf, "The Rhetoric of Soul: Cognitive Dissonance and Social Change, *V Nordiske Etnografkongress,* Bergen, Norway, 1967.

Harlem Youth Opportunities Unlimited, Inc., *Youth in the Ghetto: A Study of the Consequences of Powerlessness*. New York: Orans Press, 1964.

Henderson, David, "Bopping," in *New American Review No. 4* (New York: New American Library 1968), pp. 46-47.

Kerner, Otto, *Report of the National Advisory Commission on Civil Disorders*. New York: Bantam Books, 1968.

Keiser, Lincoln R., *The Vice Lords: Warriors of the Streets.* New York: Holt, Rinehart and Winston, 1969.

King, Woodie, Jr., "The Game," *Harlem Liberator,* Vol. 8 (1965), p. 3.

Kochman, Thomas, "Rapping in the Black Ghetto," *Trans-action,* Vol. VI (1969), No. 4, pp. 26-34.

Kvaraceus, William C., Walter B. Miller, *et al., Delinquent Behavior,* Juvenile Delinquency Project, National Education Association, Washington, D.C., 1959.

Lebov, William, Paul Cohen, and Clarence Robins, "A Preliminary Study of the Structure of English Used by Negro and Puerto Rican Speakers in New York City," Cooperative Research Project No. 3091, Office of Education, U.S. Department of Health, Education and Welfare.

Lee, Don L., "Au Naturel: A Poetic Statement on Blackness," Ellis' Book Store, 6447 South Cottage Grove, Chicago, Ill., 1967.

Liebow, Elliot, *Tally's Corner: A Study of Negro Streetcorner Men.* Boston: Little, Brown, 1967.

Lorens, David L., "Natural Hair: New Symbol of Race Pride," *Ebony,* Vol. 23, Dec., 1967, 139-44.

Malcolm X, *Autobiography of Malcolm X.* New York: Grove Press, 1964.

Moynihan, Daniel P., *The Negro Family: The Case for National Action.* Washington: U.S. Department of Labor, 1965.

Short, James F., and Fred L. Strodtbeck, *Group Process and Gang Delinquency.* Chicago: University of Chicago Press, 1965.

Slim, Iceberg, *Pimp: The Story of My Life,* Los Angeles, Calif.: Holloway House, 1967.

Stewart, William R., "Sociolinguistic Factors in the History of American Negro Dialects," *The Florida FL Reporter,* Vol. 5 (1967), No. 2.

Shuttles, Gerald D., *The Social Order of the Slum.* Chicago: University of Chicago Press, 1968.

Thomas, Piri, *Down These Mean Streets,* New York: Knopf, 1967.

————, "The World of Piri Thomas," National Educational Television, 1968.

Valentine, Charles A., *Culture and Poverty.* Chicago: University of Chicago Press, 1968.

Williamson, Harry, *Hustler!* New York: Doubleday, 1965.

THE STRANGER MENTALITY AND
THE CULTURE OF POVERTY

ROLLAND H. WRIGHT

This paper suggests that the "culture of poverty" is a distortion because it is an idea conceived by one kind of man and applied to another. It consists largely of the first man trying to imagine the impact of poverty on people he assumes are like himself, without realizing it might mean something quite different to the poor themselves, because they are different men. This paper argues that they are, and that the nature of the difference goes a long way toward explaining their poverty, not the other way around. Not that this difference *in itself* accounts for the poverty. The kind of men we have in mind are not typically poor if they live in a social context of their own making. It is when they confront men of a different kind and are forced to live inside their social universe that poverty typically results. Nor do we mean to say this is the only kind of poor. Obviously, people become poor for a variety of reasons besides this, but this type of poverty is common and seems to be the one of most interest to poverty theorists.

I realize it is dangerous to speak of human beings as though they were different in kind. Most people do not consider their own society or its values as relative things, and tend to use them implicitly as standards for judging the behavior of all men. As long as they imagine that men who depart from these standards are fundamentally the same they are more apt to be tolerant of them, because there is always the chance they can become "decent"

316 THE STRANGER MENTALITY AND THE CULTURE OF POVERTY

people through education or some other corrective means. On the other hand, if they are seen as fundamentally different this is less possible, and the tendency then is to write them off through bigotry, racism or even worse. I know I run the risk of arousing these impulses with the point of view I advance here. But I assume the readers of this volume are capable of viewing their own societal values dispassionately, as scientists do, and that they can recognize differences in other men without feeling the compulsion to judge them, much less to change them into persons like themselves.

I want to be perfectly clear. To say the poor are different in kind is not to imply they are "deficient" or "inferior" individuals who have fallen to the bottom of society. Rather, the difference stems from having lived primarily in a personal world, a particular kind of social experience, in other words, which has shaped their view of the world and themselves. When such men are compelled to live in a social context which is foreign to who they are as men, they often wind up being poor. Accordingly, to judge this experience or the men who hold it as being "good" or "bad" is pointless, because it depends entirely on where they happen to be and who happens to be making the judgment.[1] Let's turn now to the first kind of experience and the first kind of man.

[1] I assume that the nature of man is relational. That is to say, I assume that radically different kinds of social relationships yield radically different kinds of men because I consider the fundamental nature of man to *be* social. Even if there were a common human nature possessed by all men regardless of differences in their societies and cultures (and there may be), it would still not interest me much as a social scientist. For such a view implies that social life is a force outside this nature, a sort of "variable" which impinges on or shapes a fixed, universal "man." The tendency, then, is to concentrate on the "force" itself and to neglect the actual definitions of the people who experience it. That is, if the social scientist holding this view can properly appreciate through his research the condition of life experienced by certain people, then it follows that he will automatically understand the people as well. Since he and they are assumed to be essentially the same, the task of understanding them depends only upon how well he can imagine himself under those same conditions of life.

If, on the other hand, one assumes, as I do, that social existence and identity are two sides of the same coin, then markedly different social backgrounds in effect produce different human "natures," or modes of being. If one makes this assumption rather than the common-human-nature one, the failure to take the definitions of groups and individuals into account *in their own terms* leads to enormous distortion.

The Urban World: A Meeting Place of Strangers

An urban world is a social context in which stranger relations predominate, and an urban man is someone capable of perceiving and acting in ways appropriate to living with strangers. We must be clear, therefore, that people who have this ability do not necessarily live in a city; nor do people who lack it necessarily live in the country. Urban men can live in rural areas, and, conversely, men who are relatively unable to understand and deal with strangers can live in the very heart of the city, and often do.

At first glance, the capacity to deal with strangers may not seem very remarkable to us, people who have been reared in or near an urban society. But when we consider that the majority of the world's population is still fairly incapable of such dealings, its significance begins to dawn on us. Tribal people, those who live in relative social isolation and most of whose relations are with kinsmen, are almost totally unable to handle strangers. The only strangers they are apt to encounter, as a friend of mine once said, are either dead or running. Peasant people have some institutional ways to include strangers, but they are few and never easily handled (*cf.* Redfield, 1953, p. 33). Then, too, there are many groups inside modern urban societies whose normal round of life is composed mostly of personal relationships with kin or friends and who tend to be uncomfortable or inept with strangers. For example, some Blacks in large American cities,[2] many American Indian tribes, segments of the European and American working class[3] and various ethnic groups are like this, I think.

The urban world, on the other hand, is one made possible precisely by the interaction of large numbers of socially and culturally heterogeneous people. It is possible for a person in the city to spend a great deal of time, even days or months, dealing with no one he knows personally or intimately, all the while receiving the necessary goods and services for survival and comfort. In many tribes one virtually doesn't eat unless he is related to someone, because even the distribution of food depends upon kinship ties.

[2] See, for example, Elliot Liebow's *Tally's Corner* (1967).
[3] See especially Hoggart, 1957, pp. 79-105.

The Categorical Nature of Urban Life

Living in a world of strangers, an individual does not interact so much with people as he does with categories, the bulk of which are institutional: waitresses, bus drivers, teachers, salesclerks and the like. Strangers may recognize that these enacted categories do not express the unique totality of the persons engaged in them, but even if they do this is largely irrelevant. What is relevant are the standardized activities which get the stranger what he wants or needs—his meals, downtown on time, an education, his necktie or whatever. Any number of people could perform the activities associated with any given category; they do not depend upon particular people, nor upon intimate knowledge of the other with whom the category deals. In fact, personal interaction can inhibit its smooth functioning. If the waitress stops to tell you about her rheumatism, you may not get your meal in time to enjoy the remainder of your lunch hour, or you may be late for work, while she will reduce her own earnings by the number of tips she does not receive.

Now, when we deal with other people as categories, it means that we too must act in terms of a category: we become customer, passenger, student and so forth as a counterpart to the first. When we do this we are often aware (though not always) that this activity is somehow external to what we are as a person, that there is much more to us than this or even the sum of all the categories we enact. Thus, an urban man is often aware of two realities about himself psychologically: the person he is in the enacted category and the whole person he is apart from that. So he is capable of experiencing himself in a double sense, as an *object* which can be manipulated in certain social situations, and as an integrated personality aside from those situations, what some of my students speak of as a "real" self. Since so much of his social life consists of acting as an object, with the real self held in abeyance, it is not surprising that an extremely urban man could come to see his own society and its institutions as external things, perhaps even things which threaten his existence as a real person. The rhetoric of some young people today and much contemporary literature seem to reflect this point of view.[4]

The necessity to handle oneself as an object implies considerable *self-awareness* on the part of urban people, too. An urban man must constantly monitor his own behavior to insure that he is acting in the category most appropriate to the social occasion or the one he wishes to convey. An extremely urban man, for example, is capable of self-consciously acting out being "sensitive," "human," "warm," "spontaneous," "real," "caring," "rebellious," "nonconforming," or any other diffuse quality he deliberately chooses to enact. He does this generally because it is related to some goal—impressing the boss, seducing a woman, being left alone, or whatever—but his chances of achieving it will depend ultimately on how well he convinces his audience that the category is genuine. This, in turn, requires him to pay close attention to the audience to see how he is coming, and to manipulate himself around so as to gain the maximum credibility, all of which involves considerable awareness. Incidentally, I think this goal-oriented awareness of the other is often mistaken for sensitivity by urban people, while the "image" presented to the audience is often taken for the real person, even by the actor sometimes, because it is the category, not the person, which produces the desired results.

Finally, and perhaps most obvious, the necessity to deal with categories produces a man who is relatively abstract. That is, he becomes adept at selecting out certain features of some particular thing (person) which allow him to assign it to a more general class of object. But there are at least two ways this process of abstraction might take place, and they should not be confused. One might, for instance, start with something, a particular thing, and in the course of trying to understand it pick out certain aspects which have counterparts in some other object, so that both objects might now be considered as belonging to the same class. This method of generating abstractions to understand the particular I would call generalization. Another way to abstract is to

---

[4] Two books that come to mind are Ken Kesey's *One Flew Over the Cuckoo's Nest* (1962) and Joseph Heller's *Catch-22* (1962).

begin with the characteristics of some general class and use these to sort out particulars to determine if they belong to the class or not. This mode of thought is most typical of urban life, I think, and is what we've been speaking of as categorization.

Notice, in passing, that categorizing implies that ideas are the most important thing, not understanding the particular, because it is through them that understanding of the particular comes. Perhaps this is why parents react so strongly when their son shows up with a beard. According to the abstract criteria of the parents this indicates he is a "radical" or some other category, and they may treat him as if this were so, despite twenty years of particular experience which might contradict it. So the tendency is for abstractions to take on a kind of reality in their own right. The anthropologist Sam Stanley once pointed out to me that Disneyland seems like a creation to demonstrate the reality of ideas, whereas he had always thought ideas were supposed to be creations that demonstrate reality. There are also some young people today who have learned the meaning of abstractions like freedom, nonviolence, equality, or the like, and who become angered when they do not appear in the political or social life of the country in the pure form they picture in their mind's eye. Perhaps the "revolution" some of the more militant ones imagine is the changing of reality straightway to fit their conception of it.

The Urban Ground Rule: Acts Are Definitive of the Self

We have said that urban life requires men to pay attention to the categories they and others enact because categories are the primary way that life functions. Accordingly, urban people are quite sensitive to any behavioral cues which allow them to locate an individual categorically, whether that cue is overt behavior or some expressive symbol, such as clothes, property, or even bumper stickers. Indeed, it is virtually impossible to say or do anything in an urban setting without some categorical meaning being attached to it. And since categories tend to be equated with people, perhaps it is in this way that urban men come to consider what they do as being who they are. In any event, this tendency to infer meaning about a man from his acts is so pervasive in urban life that I call it the "urban ground rule."

So many things are definitive. A run-down house with an uncut lawn might say something about the people who live inside, just as a beard might say something about the character of the person who wears it. More conventional cues which tend to be definitive are such things as property, credentials, education, talent, occupation, personal taste or wealth, say. Maurice Stein has remarked about suburban parents who seem more concerned with the way their children act than with who they are (Stein, 1954). And I read recently that many fourth-grade pupils in the United States are taking tranquilizer drugs because they are so worried about getting good grades in school. Such things testify to the importance of acts being definitive of the person, and to how urban our society has become when youngsters learn the urban ground rule so early in life.

Once a man begins to imagine that his acts are definitive, that he *is* relative to what he accomplishes or fails to accomplish, many definitions come into play. For one thing, this makes him something of a *self-creator,* since changing his identity is now simply a matter of changing his behavior. There is also a kind of built-in dissatisfaction that urban men have about themselves, so that they are almost constantly in the process of "becoming" something, or at least pretending that they are. I'm not sure why this is. Perhaps the very act of not trying to improve would cast a definition. That is, the act of standing still probably asserts that one is either smug (there is no need to change) or that he is a "loser" (there is no further ability to rise). In any case, since his activities are ways of coming true, so to speak, an urban man is quite active most of the time, so he makes a good worker or producer.[5] Some urban words which express the willingness of the individual to exert this kind of effort are "ambition," "initiative," "drive," and "aggressiveness."

[5] This may account for part of the fear of automation and the gradual disappearance of work in our own society. To imagine life without work for many urban men is like trying to imagine life without a self.

Then, too, this kind of man is also a rational planner. He must be able to look ahead and do what he can in the present to bring about the future he wants, because in exercising control over it he also controls the identity he is trying to bring about. One chief way to control the future is to control the self: to work hard, say, or to forgo immediate gratification in the present for the sake of the imagined future. There are many visible representations of this planning and self-restraint which are commonplace among urban people, such as retirement plans, insurance programs, budgets, regular savings and so on. Perhaps the most salient one is the career. A career is a vertically arranged series of steps or stages in an occupation, much like a narrowing ladder each rung of which is more difficult to attain than the previous one. As he proceeds up the ladder, which sometimes involves plans spanning many years, the careerist achieves not only higher increments of prestige, money or competence but a more desirable self-image as well.

Another notion related to self-creation is freedom. Freedom means that the individual maintains control over those acts which are definitive of him, that he is able to create himself according to his own inclinations. If another agency should gain control of an urban man's behavior, in effect it gains control of his identity. This is more insidious than slavery, for the slave at least has the possibility of maintaining psychological integrity even under conditions of physical bondage. I think this is one of the dilemmas posed by a bureaucratic society where occupations and careers become increasingly routinized and directed from above: since many career acts are now outside the control of the individual, they are no longer definitive of him, and his work tends to become meaningless and empty, a very serious problem for a man whose career is a major identity mechanism.

There is an opposite side to the freedom coin, another important part of the urban man's world—responsibility. If a man feels he is in control of his acts and thereby his identity, then as an individual he is accountable for what happens to him and to others as well. If he accomplishes certain desirable goals, he takes credit for the action and transforms his identity accordingly. On the other hand, if things work out badly he must by the same token accept the stigma or guilt associated with those acts. The assumption is that the individual is the determining agent and therefore the responsible agent.

Related to this is another urban notion—opportunity. This means essentially that a man should be given the tools or mechanisms by which to accomplish something, but that the accomplishing should be done by the individual himself; if he is given direct assistance rather than an opportunity, his actions are not his own and the result is either meaningless or even destructive of him as a person. This is why so many Americans are suspicious of foreign-aid and domestic-welfare programs. They feel that such programs sap individual initiative and may even become sources of resentment on the part of the recipients, because they have been denied their freedom as individuals.

Success is an urban notion implicit in all we have said so far. Essentially, it is a judgment about how well a man has managed in his self-creation, the extent to which he has accomplished what he set out to accomplish, relative to others who have also tried or relative to some goal he set for himself in advance. Accordingly, success entails a kind of ladder view of the world where men are ranked by their achievement, some on top and some at the bottom, and where they may be placed in similar strata according to how well they have done, even if it takes place in different fields of endeavor.[6] Having said this, it strikes me how remarkably similar this common-sense urban picture is to that of many social scientists when they speak of social class and stratification. Most social-class schemes include criteria, such as residence and income, which are very conventional symbols of success for urban men, and which suggest the "ladder" view of things. In any case, there

[6] And since accomplishment and thereby rank are tied to identity, it is easy for urban men to imagine that those on top are better *in kind* than those on the bottom. But not all urban men think this way. Since they also think people change by their acts, some feel that the poor can become just like them—i.e., improve—by getting work or the proper education, say. So some urban men tend to be indifferent to the poor, while others are busy giving them "opportunities." I suppose urban people can see the poor in other ways, but these are two common modalities.

seems to be little recognition, by either layman or scientist, that social class is an urban phenomenon, and even some tendency to see it as a universal human one.

Finally, any man for whom acts are definitive must be highly individuated. If individuation means the capacity to take identity from something other than people, then someone able to do so from his own behavior is an extreme instance. Moreover, since his conduct often represents categories, the identity he creates is not only independent of his fellows but categorical as well. He is capable of seeing himself as a set of standardized activities, which is equivalent to becoming a stranger to himself. Perhaps this is one of the meanings behind that once popular notion of alienation. That is, it might refer to instances of extreme urban individuation of this kind, where a man not only is separated from others psychologically but also might come to believe or fear that his primary identity is categorical in nature (*cf.* Keniston, 1965). If a child came to think of himself this way very early in life, I imagine it could lead to the kind of severe character disorder Bettelheim describes when he reports on the small boy who thought of himself as a machine (Bettelheim, 1964).

An Alternative to the Culture of Poverty

Let me pause now and review briefly the major dimensions of the urban or stranger mentality. Since an urban man lives categorically with others, a necessity in a stranger world, he begins to develop a sort of psychological split in his identity between a "real" and an "object" self, a potential one between himself and his society; he becomes very aware and deliberate in his relations with others; and he becomes very abstract. His acts tend to be definitive of him as a person, which in turn can yield the following kind of man: a self-creator; a person who "achieves" and "accomplishes" things; someone who admires ambition; a rational planner who sets goals for himself; someone capable of hard work and self-control (two ways to manipulate both the environment and oneself); a man oriented to the future who for its sake can postpone present gratification; a "responsible" man who values personal "freedom"; someone who measures his own worth according to something called "success"; and one who is highly individuated.

With this in mind, let's turn to a couple of definitions of the "culture of poverty." Oscar Lewis tells us that some of its major characteristics are ". . . a lack of impulse control, a strong present-time orientation with relatively little ability to defer gratification and to plan the future, a sense of resignation and fatalism" (Lewis, 1966, p. xlv). Again:

The culture of poverty is both an adaptation and a reaction of the poor to their marginal position in a class-stratified, highly individuated, capitalistic society. It represents an effort to cope with the feelings and hopelessness and despair which develop from the realization of the improbability of achieving success in terms of the values and goals of the larger society. [*Ibid.,* p. xliii.]

Without exception these characteristics are a series of urban definitions turned inside out, and not a very exhaustive list at that. Being negative constructs, they tend to be empty, something like saying the sea is not the land. It is true, but it doesn't say much about the nature of the ocean. In a similar way, the "culture of poverty" tells us the poor are not urban men, but it says nothing about who they are in their own terms, and little by way of explaining how they got that way.

Lewis implies an explanation in his second statement above, but it's puzzling. Part of the "culture," he says, is a response of the poor to the "marginal position" they hold in a certain kind of dominant society. I'm not certain what kind of marginality he has in mind, but I'm willing to accept the point. But then he goes on to say it also consists of the poor's frustration at being unable to *achieve success* in terms of the dominant society. Aside from being circular (i.e., the poor are the way they are in part because they are poor), the assertion rests on the shaky assumption that the poor understand what it means to "achieve" and "succeed" (not to mention the values and goals of the larger society). Since we now can recognize such notions as most appropriate to urban life, it suggests that Lewis assumes the poor are like urban men, only bent out of shape by poverty. Accordingly, it does not occur to him that the people who are now poor may have been different men *before* they were poor, and that this, together with the necessity to live in one of those dominant societies, might have made them poor in the first place.

In the pages that remain I want to suggest an alternative explanation to the culture of poverty. Rather than imagining that the poor are the way they are because they are poor, I want to advance the idea that they are poor because of the way they are, the kind of people they are.

And what makes them the way they are if it's not poverty? I think they are people who are used to living in personal worlds, worlds where identity is fashioned by other people, not by ideas or acts. And it is precisely this difference which makes them the logical opposites of urban men. This is not to say such people do not suffer when they confront and try to live in one of those "highly individuated, capitalistic" societies Lewis speaks about. They do, and doubtless that suffering affects their perceptions. But this is not what Lewis is speaking about with the culture of poverty. His version of it confuses the effects of poverty with some fundamental differences between men.

The Personal World

If the urban world is a meeting place of strangers, the personal world is a meeting place of familiar people, and the kind of men who emerge from the two worlds are almost completely antithetical to each other.

A personal relationship is based on familiarity. Each participant is well known to the other and they share considerable experience unlike strangers who know little about each other beyond the category each fills. Being familiar with another requires that we consider him as a *unique* person, for the better we know someone the more obvious it is how he differs from all others we know, even people who may be like him in many respects. Also, familiarity presupposes that we know the other more as a *whole* person, because we have been able to see him in a variety of situations, contexts and moods. So this kind of relationship must have time for the familiarity to establish itself, the kind of time children have growing up in a family, say, or lovers have during courtship, or friends have sharing life experiences.

A personal relationship is also *definitive*. That is, each participant expresses part of the identity of the other. Who I am relative to a personal other bears on who I am to myself. Not that I consider myself in the same way as my daughter, say, but what she thinks and feels about me is important in determining what I think and feel about myself. One is not the mirror image of the other in personal relations, but the identities of the two are so intertwined that the relation expresses in part who each of them is.[7] Perhaps this explains why social harmony is so important to people who live in very familiar social worlds, such as a tribe, for it would be unbearable to be in constant conflict with those upon whom your identity depends. It also suggests why the death of someone personally related to us is so painful: in effect we have died a little ourselves, because we can no longer *be* in exactly the same way as before.

By a personal world I mean a social context in which the central feature of life is personal relationships. There may be encounters with strangers, or even continuing relations with them, but the bulk of the person's life activities center around familiar people. A tribe is the most obvious example of a personal world, where people are not only familiar with one another but are also frequently kin. Other personal worlds might include a peasant village, an extended kin group, a family, a street-corner gang, a community, a neighborhood, a small town, and the like.

I want to suggest, too, that personal worlds are not a thing of the past, that they are not necessarily fading away, nor do they represent only small remnants left over in so-called "underdeveloped" countries or "backward" regions of developed ones. On the

---

[7] Personal relationships should not be confused with friendly ones. It is entirely possible to hate or dislike intensely someone to whom we are related personally, and, by the same token, to be friendly to total strangers.

contrary, I would guess that maybe 70 to 80 percent of the world's population today live in personal worlds. Of course, it's hard to say, because census data are not gathered according to such criteria, but when we think of the numbers of peasant and tribal peoples living in Africa, Asia, South America, the Near East and the Middle East, the estimate begins to seem less far-fetched. But if we also include the people who continue to live in personal worlds inside ostensibly urban countries, it seems even less so. In the United States, for example, there are American Indians, Mexicans, Blacks, Southern Whites, segments of the working class and some immigrant groups, many of whom live in personal worlds to a large extent, sometimes even in the very center of metropolitan areas. Every other urban country has similar groups.

Living in a personal world has consequences for a man's identity and perception, just as living with strangers does, and I want to speak now about some characteristic features of such a man. I'll call this kind of man a "folk" man, but the reader should be careful to confine its meaning to what I've said here and not equate it with Redfield's ideal type (Redfield, 1947).

To begin with, a folk man is much less individuated than an urban man. A personal relationship, remember, means we *are* the other person in a sense, because some of our identity is expressed as part of the relationship. So the more completely a man's world is personal, the less able he is to separate himself off from his fellows—the less able he is to see himself as a distinct entity. The anthropologist Dorothy Lee has pointed out that the Wintu do not even have a word which designates the individual (Lee, 1959), and we might reasonably expect this in a personal world like the tribe.[8]

Folk people do not enact categories very well either. Since they are accustomed to treating others as unique, whole persons and

[8] Consensus would be important to such a man, however, because dissent among personal others in effect calls his identity into question. Accordingly, folk people are often mistaken as being "conformists" by urban men. And if society is not experienced as external to the self, it is doubtful that a folk person could grasp much of the meaning of such urban notions as conformity or alienation.

to being treated that way in return, it is difficult for them to remember in urban situations, especially face-to-face encounters, that they and the others are categories. My mother, a working-class lady, sometimes used to embarrass me by using familiar terms when addressing salesclerks or the like, and by telling them personal and, to me, irrelevant things having to do with her or the family. I outgrew my embarrassment, but my mother never learned to act in categories very well. The inability to hold the "real" self constant and apart from the "object" self also makes for a person who cannot be very deliberate or self-aware in his dealings with others. This makes him a poor manipulator and often a gullible victim when confronted by a good one; the "sucker" label that urban people sometimes apply to folk people may have some basis in fact. Finally, such a man would not be expected to be very abstract, at least not in a categorical way, and the ones I know do gossip a great deal and in other ways stay in the realm of the particular in their conversations most of the time.

Next, and perhaps most importantly, folk people have a sense of identity which tends to be *given*. They have very little grasp that a man can "become" anything fundamentally different by the way he acts, as urban men do, but, rather, tend to look upon identity almost as though it were fixed at birth. As I remember, for example, my parents kept watching for signs as I grew up to see what kind of person I was, as though my nature were already formed and if they paid close attention it would reveal itself to them. Folk people also look to the way people act to determine who they are, as urban people do, but with the important exception that they do not consider behavior to be under the control of the individual, but, rather, look upon it as though it were ordained, given in the nature of the world. I think this is understandable if we look again at the nature of a personal relationship. If one *is* relative to his relations with others, and if these relationships are familiar and regular, as with kin for example, the person who is expressed by them is correspondingly stable. Being a nephew is not something to debate, believe in, change, pledge allegiance to or even be very aware of—it simply *is,* and the person who is relative to such relationships also simply *is.* So one does not quickly change his identity in a personal world, regardless of what dramatic events might take place in his life or learning. This state of affairs is disappointing to some young Indians I know who come home from college with the "scoop" on Indian affairs and with a pocketful of solutions. For in the context of their tribe and family they are what they always were—kin—and if they do gain a new voice in the community it depends more on the way they relate to their kinsmen or what sense they make when they're asked than it does on the fact of being educated.

Anyone with a fixed sense of self such as this would be unlikely to believe that his identity depends on how he acts or that such behavior is under his own control as an individual. So all those urban definitions we spoke of earlier, which hinge on the premise that one can create himself, would either be nonsense to such a man or take a very different character with him. For example, a folk man is likely to think that the kind of man he *is* determines what he will accomplish or achieve, not the other way around. Work for him may be fixed in nature (e.g., men do certain things, women others); or it may be tied to his personal obligations, such as providing for his family; or perhaps it is just a way to make money; but it is never a means to transform himself. For working-class people it tends much more to be a means of "getting by" rather than "getting ahead." Some men may be better than others according to folk people, but this too is because it is part of the nature of things, not because of individual achievement relative to some "success" criteria. There is a kind of freedom for such people, but it is more a lack of restraint or being interfered with than it is the ability to act so as to cast a personal definition. Responsibility is more a response to the need of another, not that the individual takes the credit or blame for his own acts because he controls them. And opportunity probably would have the meaning of a lucky break or being given help, not a springboard to self-creation.

Finally, since their identities are not tied into it, the future cannot play the same role in the lives of folk people as for urban men. And, since the world tends to be relatively unchanging, it might be that folk men do not sharply distinguish future, past or present in the first place. So the way time itself is conceived by them may be quite different. According to Murray Wax people who possess a "magical" world view, which includes tribal and peasant peoples who tend to see the ". . . interconnectedness of all things: I, you, we, plants, animals, materials, deities . . . ," have a view of time quite different from civilized men. They see life in the form of recurrent cycles (days, seasons or generations), a casual sense of time fitted to the natural environment:

Such peoples are oriented neither toward the past nor toward the future, for what is to happen, what is happening, and what has happened are not conceived as discrete and significant entities of existence but as phases of the more profound difference between an existence that is in tune with the world . . . and an existence so out of tune that man is hungry, homeless, and miserable. [M. L. Wax, 1960, p. 453.]

So we wind up with a picture of a folk man which at first glance seems similar to the one Lewis paints for the poor: he too could be seen as fatalistic, unable to defer gratification, unable to plan the future, and so on. The difference is that these attributes are artifacts of an urban point of view. Essentially they are the liabilities a folk man would possess in an urban context. To that extent they may be accurate descriptions, but they do not describe a folk man in his own terms. Surely different characteristics would have been stressed if the same man were seen from the standpoint of his own world, and it is doubtful that they would have been cast in such a negative way. Aside from this, however, the very terms themselves can take on entirely different meanings in a folk world. For example, a folk parent may go hungry so that his child can eat, as mine did sometimes during the depression, or they can make other sacrifices like putting money aside to buy the children some "good things of life." I suppose one could speak of such acts as "deferred gratification." But since his children are definitive of him as a person, the parent in effect is denying himself something in order to give himself something, a gratifying experience made possible by denying gratification, in other words. Most of the other characteristics shift their meaning this way when applied to folk people, because they rest on urban assumptions, in this case individuation, which are simply not applicable.

Some Effects of Folk and Urban Contact

Let me finish this essay with a few thoughts about what might happen when folk and urban men meet each other, especially in an urban place where urban men hold power. I know it is reckless to speak of contact between two such general social types as these without reference to particular peoples, places or times. And I confess the ideas will be tentative and incomplete, even impressionistic. I am driven to it anyway by my own impatience with the discussion carried on by so many poverty theorists. Ultimately, they are concerned with the human costs involved in the encounter of certain people with modern bureaucratic-industrial societies, whether such people live inside such societies or in countries which are dominated by them. But this concern is lost in the analysis because they insist on conceiving of the problem as though its source lay not in the encounter but in the poor themselves. So our attention is constantly directed to the mentality of the poor, to their family structure or some other attribute which obscures the nature of the contact between the people and the dominant society. We have established a framework now which might let us begin that kind of analysis.

The way folk and urban men define each other when they meet involves many distortions, because each defines the other from the standpoint of the kind of man he is himself. Folk people, for example, tend to divide people unconsciously into two camps, the "we" of the personal world and the "them" of people outside it. Any differences they manage to perceive in outsiders tends to be attributed to their being different in kind, sometimes to the point of seeing them as not quite human. This view of things would follow logically from what we've said so far. Since a folk man's identity rests with personal others, those outside this personal orbit—strangers, in other words—are nondefinitive, hence unimportant and perhaps, in the extreme, nonhuman.

Urban men distort folk men as much, but in a different way. There are some who explain human differences racially, to be sure, and it may parallel the folk man's version. But more sophisticated urban types see other men as being essentially the same on the level of human nature, and I think this view is more common by far. They account for observed differences among men on the grounds of differing life conditions, a different social background or different kinds of experience, for example. The judgment urban men will make about these differences will depend on how they estimate the value of their own society. If it is high, as it probably is for most people, then differences they observe in other men which deviate from their own behavior are seen as somehow abnormal, as "deficiencies," which might be overcome with the "proper" education, religious values, ideology or technology. Such a view is implicit in expressions like "underprivileged," "disadvantaged," "culturally deprived," "racially isolated" and, of course, "culture of poverty." On the other hand, if a man's opinion about his own society is somewhat jaded, he may come to see folk men in an opposite, but entirely stereotyped, way. He tends to romanticize folk people, in other words, so they come to embody all the qualities he feels are lacking in his own life, or to represent a state of innocence which shields them against all the dehumanizing forces in his own society. Thus, he might see them as more or less perfectly spontaneous, natural, human, warm, kind, generous, whole, simple, honest or any other desirable quality he might choose to invest them with.

These kinds of definitions come into play when folk and urban people encounter one another. But urban ones prevail in most urban situations where urban men hold the power. The representatives of urban society that a folk man faces in the classroom, in court, being interviewed for a job or applying for welfare, say, are the people whose definitions count most. He may not understand the content of those definitions, but a folk man knows that the teacher, judge, employer or social worker can affect his life for good or ill, and to that extent at least he considers them important people. Moreover, most of the definitions directed to him by these urban agents are generally negative. Since they are functionaries of the dominant society, they probably subscribe personally to its values, and if they do not they often must act as if they did anyway. Accordingly, they relate to their clients as though they were "deficient" in the way we described above, and this doubtless gets communicated to them eventually. This would not be serious in itself, perhaps, except that folk people are in dependent positions, so they are often *forced* to see themselves in this negative way in order to survive or get by in those situations. If this low self-image is internalized, it can be very destructive.

Imagine, for example, a teacher who has a folk pupil in her classroom. Remember, a folk person is someone who has a fixed sense of identity with little notion that he can change himself by his acts. Suppose the boy gets the message from the teacher that he is expected to work hard in school so that he can "improve" himself. This signals that there is something wrong with him *now,* otherwise why change? And, indeed, this is precisely what the teacher is saying in effect. But at the same time she wants to say that the badness is not permanent, and wants it to be a stimulus to "motivate" the boy to "accomplish" more than he ordinarily would in order to "be somebody" eventually. But the boy is not likely to understand the second part of the message, because he can't imagine himself "becoming" anyone different than he is now. He is left with the message that he is bad now. Moreover, if he believes the teacher, he will consider this attribute permanent because his self is permanent, fixed in nature. So he has become an inferior person to himself, a kind of "slob." Once a youngster takes on this self-definition, he is likely to become a problem to anyone around him.[9]

The process we've suggested here is subtle and complicated. Teachers communicate this message to folk people, if they do, because they are the kind of people they are. And these messages do not usually appear as explicitly stated values, but as assumptions or taken-for-granted meanings which are inferred from what

[9] This is only one possibility, however, even though a common one. That is, the pupil might never come to understand the message behind the teacher's words and behavior, or he might place another interpretation on them.

teachers say or do, whether they are aware of it or not. And what is true of teachers holds for most other agents of the urban society as well.

Let me try to illustrate some of the subtlety of this learning process by using a personal example. When I was a boy of fourteen, I had a girlfriend whose father was a minister and a former diplomat. She and her family were prototypes of urban people. I didn't know this at the time, of course, and in fact was just beginning to learn some of those definitions which I was later to call "urban," mostly from this girl and my schoolmates. One evening she and I were at a school dance when a friend of hers danced by with her date.

"I saw you and your father in a new Buick the other day," she says to my girlfriend with a big smile.

This was clearly intended as a compliment. Message: To own a new Buick, or to have a father who owns one, says something complimentary about a person. It immediately occurs to me: What kind of car does my father own? (The first time I'd ever thought to ask myself that question.) An old Chevy, the answer came back. If it's complimentary to have a new Buick, it must be terrible to have an old Chevrolet, I reason.

So a new meaning begins to emerge for me: cars are symbolic of people, I've got one that's bad, so people must think badly of me. After that, I tried to arrange it so my girl and my other friends did not see what kind of car my father owned, and when they did, it was a great embarrassment for me. Then I began keeping my family out of sight, too, for I gradually discovered that clothes, houses and all sorts of things were defined this way, not only cars, and my family seemed to have virtually none of the good ones. When a personal man turns against the people who are definitive of him, he turns against himself at the very same time. The anguish I felt during those years, the sense of being torn apart by these two forces, is difficult to recall even today.

Now, of course, I am ashamed I ever felt this way. I tell it only to indicate the process by which folk people come to learn urban definitions, and to suggest how painful it can be. And I may be exaggerating the significance of such things to my young friends of those days. After all, *I* was the one ashamed of the old car and myself, and it is likely that such things were more important to me than to them—and that girl did love me a little in spite of my bad symbols. The point is, I came to learn who I was in the eyes of urban people, a new way of looking at myself, a hard one to take, and one obtained independently of my friends' good feelings or high opinion of me. It happened this way because they were the kind of people they were and I was the kind of person I was. I suppose I'm both kinds now, and maybe a process like this is necessary in order to learn to be another kind of man. But as Huck Finn says, that's another story.[10]

BIBLIOGRAPHY

Bettelheim, Bruno, "Joey: A Mechanical Boy," in *Man Alone: Alienation in Modern Society,* ed. Eric Josephson (New York: Dell, 1964).

Heller, Joseph, *Catch-22.* New York: Simon and Schuster, 1962.

Hoggart, Richard, *The Uses of Literacy.* New York: Penguin Books, 1957.

Keniston, Kenneth, *The Uncommitted: Alienated Youth in American Society.* New York: Harcourt, Brace and World, 1965.

Kesey, Ken, *One Flew Over the Cuckoo's Nest.* New York: Viking, 1962.

Lee, Dorothy, *Freedom and Culture.* New York: Spectrum, 1959.

Lewis, Oscar, *La Vida.* New York: Random House, 1966.

[10] There is another important way urban contact can be harmful to folk people. Since urban people hold power, it is through their institutions mainly that decisions flow. If folk people happen to live in communities with indigenous institutions, as some American Indians do, for example, they begin to lose control over their own lives because their institutions are preempted by the outside power. When people lack institutional ways to deal with reality in their own terms, they are in effect unable to experience reality, so they become frozen in older patterns of behavior or begin to decay. They have few ways to grow and adapt to new life conditions, in other words. Robert K. Thomas has pointed out the nature of this process, which he calls "colonialism," in a brilliant article appearing in *New University Thought,* Vol. IV, No. 4 (Winter 1967).

Liebow, Elliot, *Tally's Corner: A Study of Negro Streetcorner Men.* Boston: Little, Brown, 1967.

Redfield, Robert, "The Folk Society," *American Journal of Sociology,* Vol. 52 (1947), No. 4.

————, *The Primitive World and Its Transformations.* Ithaca, N. Y.: Cornell University Press, 1953.

Stein, Maurice, "Suburbia—A Walk on the Mild Side," in *Voices of Dissent,* collected papers from *Dissent* magazine (New York: Grove Press, 1954).

Thomas, Robert K., "Colonialism: Domestic and Foreign," *New University Thought,* vol. IV, No. 4 (Winter, 1967).

Wax, Murray L., "Ancient Judaism and the Protestant Ethic," *American Journal of Sociology,* Vol. 65, No. 5 (March 1960).

POVERTY AND INTERDEPENDENCY

MURRAY L. WAX

"Poverty" is a folk category, which is to say it is a word or category found in natural languages—such as English—and then picked up by social scientists who endeavor to make of it something precise, so that it may be fitted into their scientific theories and reasonings. In this respect, "poverty" is like the words which have become incorporated into the natural sciences, words such as "force" or "mass" or "pressure," words that have one penumbra of meaning for the layman and another for the scientist, so that it has long been traditional that students who enter elementary courses in physics (mechanics) are told that a word such as "force" *really* means something quite different from what they had thought.

Yet the folk categories of human affairs are more tenacious than those relevant to the natural sciences, for it is these folk categories that are used to define a social problem, and without that categorical folk term the social problem would not have the form that it does. In the case of poverty, a brilliant and insightful analysis of this interrelationship was performed for us by that pioneer sociologist, Georg Simmel.

In dealing with the category of "poverty" Simmel (1908) begins with what might be called a Newtonian approach and proceeds finally toward an Einsteinian, or relativistic, approach. The Newtonian approach is to act as if there were some set of absolute standards—some fixed coordinate system of unvarying metric— which would be employed everywhere and at all times so as to label persons either as poor or as not poor. In the essay in question, Simmel has no trouble—and likely much dialectical pleasure —in disposing of that sort of Newtonian methodological orientation. With considerable skill in both writing and analysis, Simmel demonstrates to his audience that "poverty" is essentially a *relationship,* a relationship defined by the fact that the inferior is the target of gifts which he cannot and may not reciprocate (*cf.* Mauss, 1925). To be poor is to be the recipient of charity.

If poverty is indeed this kind of relationship, then the notion of dependency is built into it. Dependency is not adventitious, it is not a coincidental feature of the personality structure of the poor, it is intrinsic. For to be a candidate for charity, to be the person who receives but cannot reciprocate—this is the essence of dependency. Or, to spin the matter about, if we think charity is a virtue, then we require that there exist a category of persons as the objects upon which to release these virtuous activities; for without the existence of the poor, how can we demonstrate the existence within ourselves of the virtue of charity? But to spin the relationship about in this manner is to show that the dependency of the poor is like any other social relationship—namely, two-sided. The poor indeed are dependent; but the rich are dependent in turn, or at least interdependent, since they require the presence of the poor in order to demonstrate that they are charitable.

So far, I may seem to you to be lost in the social relationships of a half century ago and more, and hardly relevant to the urban U.S. today with its foundations and agencies for organized benevolence and its federal programs that claim to war on poverty. Yet I assure you that the applications are close to hand. When I and my associates began our studies of the Oglala Sioux of Pine Ridge, South Dakota, we encountered a considerable body of literature which characterized the Indians, including the Sioux, as "dependent," and not only as dependent but as "hostilely dependent" (Wax and Wax, 1964). The latter phrase derives, of course, from neo-Freudian parlance and was intended to characterize a relationship in which the Sioux secured most of their sustenance from programs of federal assistance, whilst in the meantime adopting an attitude of hostility toward these programs and their officers. As you may know, until recently most of the programs have been channeled through what was the Indian Service and then became the Bureau of Indian Affairs, and if an investigator talked even casually with its employees he soon learned that they had adopted a compensatory posture of injured righteousness. As they saw it, despite all the good works that they and the Bureau had been performing for the Indians, those ingrates persisted in abusing them; and in this hostile activity the Indians were reinforced by gullible White do-gooders who also joined in the sport of kicking the Bureau of Indian Affairs.

Yet, if the investigator examines (Wax, Wax and Dumont, 1964) a typical reservation system, he will find that the enterprise of administering Indians is a reasonably attractive career to persons with middle-class aspirations. The Indian Service and the Bureau of Indian Affairs have provided middle-class status and reasonably comfortable bureaucratic employment to a large cadre of people, both Indians and Whites. My own estimate is that this cadre is largely derived from rural origins within or neighboring to reservation areas, people of respectable but impoverished origins, people with the motivation and background to secure a modest education, such as a teaching certificate. I mean no derogation of the staff of the BIA, but I do mean to assert, as I have elsewhere (Wax and Wax, 1964), that if many of the Indians are hostilely dependent upon the BIA, so are the employees of the BIA in turn dependent upon the existence of the Indians, and, moreover, many of these employees are indeed very hostile toward the Indians. The hostility of these employees of the BIA is manifest even in the ideology that sustains their labors. For they think of themselves as engaged in trying to civilize—and instruct in the virtues of the American ethos—a people who are savage, idle, drunken, spendthrift, and ungrateful. So that the more the Indians resist and criticize them, the more are these employees convinced of the righteousness of their bureaucratic calling. The resistance and criticism testify to the inferiority of the Indians, their need for training.

The situation is equally graphic and dramatic in the more recent federal programs such as VISTA and the Teacher Corps. The persons who join these programs are the subject of much ritual praise, since they will dedicate themselves to work for a year or several years at minimal pay among an impoverished people. But in talking with VISTA and the Teacher Corps and watching them operate on reservations, we have been struck (Wax and Wax, 1968a) by how they fit into Simmel's paradigm of the rich and the poor. So often, these young people wish to display their moral and intellectual "richness" by giving or "helping" the Poor Indians. Conversely, they are unwilling to receive from the Indians, for if they did that they would lose their privileged status; they would admit the equality of reciprocity. They do not want to learn the native languages; they do not want to learn the logic of native traditions and native customs; or if they do expose themselves, it is as tourists to curiosities of historical interest. And, above all, they do not want to listen to the Indian and find out how he might wish to carry on a program. They feel that Indians must be pushed into entering the mainstream of American life, and I think they are puzzled and irritated by finding that Indians are well acquainted with much of that mainstream and that, like the impoverished Blacks of urban regions, Indians are quite uninterested in programs that will train and rehabilitate them or their communities. Indians want money, not programs; they are realistic enough to see that money comes from jobs, and so they want good jobs providing good money with considerable leisure and opportunity to visit and chat. From their perspective, they see such good jobs in the hands of otherwise incompetent, naïve, and ignorant people who staff the offices of federal programs, and they are too shrewd and too disenchanted to believe the moralizings about diligence, thrift, and education that are proffered by VISTA workers and others. Under the circumstances, it is not surprising that among the poor, and especially among the Indians, many of the VISTA teams fail to be viewed with the gratitude and pathos that the volunteers might otherwise have considered their proper due.

The verbal and social dynamics of poverty can be further illustrated in comparing the attitude of traditional or Country Indians toward the federal programs with that of the employees of those programs. For, as we have already noted, the employees of these programs think of themselves as performing a public and charitable service to the Poor Indians. Yet the Country Indians themselves think of these services as accruing to them because of treaties which the government signed with their forefathers. Thus, according to the Indian interpretation, the Indians are aristocrats and the Bureau of Indian Affairs is their servant; the employees of the Bureau may be incompetent and thieving, but then that is the nature of the servant class. Thus, for a half century or more, Indians and federal employees have been locked in a verbal battle as to the nature of the relationship between them. On the whole, success has gone to the federal agency, especially since the Congress has increasingly been inclined to transfer the services rendered to the Indians from special agencies designated as being for Indians to general-purpose welfare agencies; so that elderly Indians get old-age assistance just like the general poor, and unmarried and impoverished Indian mothers get AFDC just like the general poor. What this means then is that, insofar as the Indians move into closer contact with the greater society and its agencies, they find themselves defined into the category of "poor" —i.e., the objects of programs rather than the aristocrats who themselves determine activities and programs.

Indeed, it is worth noting that many middle-aged Indians have not thought of themselves as poor until recently, although they have spent most of their lives in conditions which most other Americans would judge as of appalling hardship.

The interdependency of rich and poor goes far deeper than this in the case of Indian affairs. In 1965, I and a team of fellow scientists attempted to investigate the educational problems of the Tribal Cherokee who inhabit the hills and isolated rural regions of northeastern Oklahoma. In a remarkably short period of time, we found ourselves (1968b) the object of a sustained and well-organized campaign of vilification and terrorization. To the local power structures that center about county courthouses, and especially to the regional power structure that operates under such names as the Executive Committee of the Cherokee Nation, any research that seemed sympathetically oriented toward the Tribal Cherokee was a threat. It should be explained that the Tribal Cherokee find themselves represented to federal agencies and even to national associations of Indians (such as the National Congress of American Indians) by a Principal Chief who is appointed by the President of the United States (the present Chief was appointed by Truman) and that the local associations of Tribal Cherokee have consistently been denied recognition by the federal agencies. If in Newtonian terms the poor are simply a category of people who lack wealth, and if poor Indians are simply another category of the poor, it is hard to see how any investigation of their condition is a threat to anyone. But the case in question reminds us of the truth of Simmel's analysis: a Newtonian view of poverty is not meaningful; poverty is not a condition of a group in isolation. We require an Einsteinian view of poverty in which we perceive that it is an interrelationship and an interdependency. For, in the case of the Tribal Cherokee of eastern Oklahoma, their poverty and their plight allows a wealthier stratum to secure funds in their name. Thus the regional and county establishments secure funds and positions by their abilities to present themselves as the caretakers of the Indian poor (*cf*. Spicer, 1968). On the one hand they receive merit for their virtuous and charitable concern toward these tribal folk, and on the other hand they have the custody of monies and jobs.

Of course, in previous generations the rich have been interdependent with, or simply dependent upon, the poor, since the latter constituted a source of cheap labor as well as being suitable as targets for the display of charitable virtues. But in the present age the relationship has further been transformed. The poor have become as it were a capital asset in whose name administrators and politicians may secure funds. Thus there have developed not only new occupations but also new enterprises which are devoted to the care—i.e., the exploitation—of the poor.

BIBLIOGRAPHY

Mauss, Marcel, *The Gift* (1925), transl. Ian Cunnison. Glencoe, Ill.: Free Press, 1954.

Simmel, Georg, "The Poor" (1908), transl. Claire Jacobson, *Social Problems,* Vol. 13 (1965), No. 2, pp. 140-48.

Spicer, Edward, "The Patrons of the Poor," paper delivered at the annual meeting of the American Anthropological Association, Seattle, 1968.

Wax, Murray L., and Rosalie H. Wax, "Cultural Deprivation as an Educational Ideology," *Journal of American Indian Education,* Vol. 3 (1964), No. 2, pp. 15-18.

————, "The enemies of the people," Chapter 9 of *Institutions and the Person: Essays Presented to Everett C. Hughes,* ed. Howard S. Becker *et al.* (Chicago: Aldine Press, 1968).

————, "The Protectors of the Poor," paper delivered at the annual meeting of the American Anthropological Association, Seattle, 1968.

Wax, Murray L., Rosalie H. Wax, and Robert V. Dumont, *Formal Education in an American Indian Community,* Monograph No. 1, Society for the Study of Social Problems, 1964 (Supplement to Social Problems, Vol. 11, No. 4).

CULTURE OF POVERTY?
WHAT DOES IT MATTER?[1]

HYLAN LEWIS

The title of this paper is not meant to suggest flippancy toward the idea of a culture of poverty; nor is it meant to convey despair about the people who are poor in our society.

In fact, one of my prime aims is to discuss how the culture of poverty idea does matter (1) to the behavioral-science disciplines, (2) to the images and life chances of people, the poor especially, and (3) to the structuring of relations among individuals and groups. A second aim is to discuss some of the ways in which the idea of the culture of poverty, and the research methods associated with it, fail to deal with some of the fundamental human and knowledge issues and often divert attention from them. In fairness, it is important to say that some of the reasons why the culture-of-poverty idea does not matter as much as it might, have to do more with changes in the community than with the flaws and ventures of a social-science concept.

The immediate cues for the title came from three recent observations about the characteristics of poor people. The first came from the anthropologist who coined the term, Oscar Lewis; the second came from a resident of Tarrytown, New York, in a letter to the editor of *The New York Times;* and the third was in the remarks of a black lady from the Washington community who

[1] Presented at a conference on "The Culture of Poverty" sponsored by the Department of Sociology, Temple University, Philadelphia, Oct. 10-11, 1969.

spoke to the psychologists at their recent convention in the capital.

In "A Death in the Sanchez Family" (1969, p. 3), Oscar Lewis wrote about Guadalupe, the maternal aunt and closest blood relative of the Sanchez children: "Although Guadalupe was only a minor character in my book, she played a central role in the Sanchez family. Moreover, she, her husbands, and her neighbors [in the *vecindad*] were better representatives of the 'Culture of Poverty' than were Jesus Sanchez and his children, who were more influenced by Mexican middle-class values and aspirations."

The letter writer from Tarrytown expressed the fear that the proponents of a guaranteed annual income "fail to realize the difference between a poverty income and a poverty culture." He wrote:

If the income of the culturally poor is raised, they will not suddenly accept the values of the American middle class. Instead, they will merely have more money to spend on the things they always have.

Conversely, graduate students, who must be considered as having a poverty income, are seldom included in discussions about the poor. This is because they lack a poverty culture.

Parenthetically, among other things, the letter writer does not mention the fact that the poverty of the college students is voluntary and temporary under normal circumstances—and that it is worn as a badge. The poverty of the bulk of the poor we are talking about is involuntary, and, whether it is viewed as deserved or not, it is a stigma.

The lady from the Washington ghetto told the psychologists, "You psychologists come and tell us that we're uneducable. You people shut up and come listen to us for a change. If you don't, we're going to shut you out of the ghetto. Fortunetellers, that's all you are—a bunch of fortunetellers."

These statements about the meaning and significance of the culture of poverty, differing as they do, spurred me to examine some of the ways in which the idea of a culture of poverty matters, as well as the manner in which it matters to different segments and interests in our society.

The comments of the lady from Washington led me to wonder why the idea of a culture of poverty does not seem to matter, or matters in a negative way; and especially with reference to certain kinds of problems and certain kinds of people, notably the poor themselves and blacks and Puerto Ricans.

In the broadest sense, the idea of a culture of poverty matters because its recent flowering and acceptance represent significant developments in the history of social thought, and because it has increasing significance for social structure in our times. It matters because it has become more ideological than scientific.

Like the idea of race, the idea of a culture of poverty is an idea that people believe, want to believe, and perhaps need to believe. The belief, and especially its associated assertions and inferences about the reasons why some Americans have failed and will continue to fail to make it in the system, constitute a reality that matters; scientific questions aside, this is the important reality that must be dealt with. The idea of a culture of poverty is a fundamental political fact. There are times when it seems chillingly like the idea of race.

For these reasons, the culture-of-poverty idea has significant bearing on the current issues having to do with the pressures and the proposals for political and social reorganization of American society that are based on the imperatives of class and race. It provides assumptions about the enduring characteristics of people, and therefore it gives some people important, if not necessarily new, rationales for the reordering of social relationships along both class and racial lines.

Two recent speculative proposals by social scientists, one from a psychologist at the National Institute of Mental Health and the other from a distinguished economist, are examples: they make projections about the significance for the future American social structure of certain dispositions and abilities of its citizens categorically related to poverty and to race. These intimations of a new quality of class and ethnic pluralism tend to go beyond the important point made by Glazer and Moynihan in *Beyond the Melting Pot—i.e.,* that ethnic groups tend to be political interest groups.

The psychologist in question made a recent statement at the Center for the Study of Democratic Institutions about his *belief* that there is a unique culture of the black ghetto. His statement is a good example of a kind of hat trick pulled by a person with the credentials of a behavioral scientist. It is based on ambiguous assertions about culture and race and "the black community as it is, not as it is supposed to be" (Baratz, 1969, p. 28). His view is that we should let the ghetto black be as he is. Among other things he says:

For the great masses of blacks in our inner-city, the standardized tests of our educational system measure the degree to which they have been *brought* into *our* middle-class life style. The tests reveal nothing about the knowledge and aptitudes of *blacks within their own cultural world* and *their potential or desire* for being absorbed into the mainstream.

I *believe* that a unique culture exists within the ghetto and has persisted from the shores of Africa to Watts and Hough and Harlem. *The social scientist's denial of this culture,* rather than a lack of understanding of it, has led us down a blind alley. *We have forced the Afro-American into an alien mold.* Because the Afro-American family is not organized in the same way as the idealized white family, it is considered disorganized. But it is not that the family is disorganized—it is more accurate to say it conveys different values to its members. This is the social scientist's hangup—that he continually compares two different value systems in a way that gives ascendance to one and descendance to another. . . .

The immediate goal of social science should be to determine the cultural strengths of the ghetto, to see how our own style may be in conflict with these strengths, and to develop bridges between these two distinct styles. Social science needs to make a complete re-evaluation of the assumption on which most of its literature on the Afro-American is based. It needs to return to a form of empirical observation more attuned to the black community as it is, not as it is supposed to be.

It needs to find a version of acculturation that is recognized as a two-way street between white and black and does not seek to destroy the ties that bind black Americans together. [*Ibid.*, pp. 27-28; italics added.]

For its ambiguity, its dissociation of whites from Negroes, and its doubt of the Negro's capacity and ability, this last paragraph is reminiscent of Thomas Jefferson's letter to Benjamin Banneker, the Negro mathematician and astronomer, in 1791. Almost two hundred years ago, Banneker sent Jefferson a copy of his almanac, with the suggestion that the almanac was evidence of the Negro's ability, and with added remarks on the injustice of slavery. Jefferson was a complex man who was against slavery in principle, if not in practice, but who in spite of his benign view thought Negroes were not only different but inferior. Jefferson wrote in acknowledgment:

Nobody wishes more than I do to see such proofs as you exhibit, that nature has given to our black brethren, talents equal to those of the other colors of men, and that the appearance of a want of them is owing merely to the degraded condition of their existence, both in Africa and America. I can add with truth, that nobody wishes more ardently to see a good system commenced for raising the condition both of their body and mind to what it ought to be, as fast as the imbecility of their present existence, and other circumstances which cannot be neglected, will admit. [Jordan, 1969, pp. 451-52.]

Winthrop Jordan observes wryly that Jefferson's letter "was a careful, courteous, and resoundingly ambiguous letter; the condition of the mind and body of the Negro was to be raised 'to what it ought to be' " (*ibid.,* p. 452).

It is important to call attention to the recurrence of the hackneyed plea for realism in looking at the poor and at Negroes. Ambiguous and patronizing references to "the black community as it is, not as it's supposed to be," and statements to the effect that it might be best to permit it to develop in a way different from the American way, are strangely regressive when they are mouthed by today's social scientists.

The interesting point is that, with some notable exceptions, when representatives of the poor and the blacks refer now to telling it like it is, to having control over their own institutions, and to doing their thing, they don't mean the same things that many representatives of the social sciences and of the middle classes mean when they use the terms. And certainly their versions of the way it ought to be and of taking care of business are not the same, either. And to say that some blacks are advocating the same thing that Baratz has advocated, separatism, misses the point. Negroes who are given to such positions are talking and acting as politicized blacks; theirs is the rhetoric of politics born of frustration and despair because the American system has not worked for them. And the primary reason it has not worked for them has little to do with their wishes or their ascribed unique culture, whether it is thought to stem from poverty or from racial experience. Rather, their status and behavior reflect flaws in the American culture and the American experience. The ironic truth is that blacks can neither be written out of this nor withdrawn from it in any effective way, no matter who says they want to or should. The issues are sharing and the ability to share and the uses of power to effect participation and control.

Baratz suggests the desirability of accepting and encouraging a black ghetto culture essentially because he believes that Negroes are not capable or do not want certain things because they have a unique culture. This presumption has been made about no other American citizens.

Taking a slightly different line, more in the nature of musings about the creation of new institutions, Kenneth Boulding, the economist, speculates about a kind of class pluralism that might be based upon the recognition and acceptance of a poverty substructure and subculture. In a recent book of essays (Boulding, 1970), he is reported as pointing to the problem of "milk and cream," that is, the possible cleavage within and among nations between those who "adapt through education to the world of modern technology" and those who don't make it. He suggests that "such a situation [of cleavage] could hardly persist without corrupting the cultures of both the rich and the poor," and that the situation is more serious in other parts of the world than in the United States.

Boulding suggests that major social inventions comparable to such previous ones as the socialist state, banking, insurance, the corporation, will be necessary in the near future. The problem of our times is that these new social inventions now require more rapid development than in the past. He muses that perhaps a society like the United States could afford to abandon its egalitarian, homogenizing pretenses and "invent" a mosaic society of many small subcultures (P. Seabury, 1969, p. 59).

These speculations on the future organization of our society, and our own reactions to them as students and citizens, underscore the mixture of reason, politics and emotion that marks much of our discussion of the poor and of contemporary race relations. Accounts such as these have a chilling effect because they tend to accent institutional contempt for persons; they tend to divert our attention from the demeaning effects of our institutions and from the ways in which many of them betray not only the increasingly self-conscious poor and black, but the uneasily affluent and white as well.

These observations about the serious question of alternate systems or of the drastic reorganization of existing systems underscore further the point that the question of poverty today is essentially a political one, and the complex nature of the relationships among social-science knowledge, political power, and social change. They illuminate further the political context in which the idea of a culture of poverty and the effects on social scientists must be viewed.

A report of the Special Commission on the Social Sciences of the National Science Foundation (1969, p. 19) makes two interrelated points on social science, politics, and vested interests. The first is that "social change—whether arising from social science knowledge or from some other source—threatens to erode the political power of one or another individual or group not interested in sharing or giving up the political position already held." And the second is that "whether or not the nation will use the social sciences in a given instance depends upon the outcome of the political competition among different vested interests with all their degrees of approval and disapproval toward any matter at issue."

Many groups have both political and scientific stakes in the idea of a culture of poverty. The idea matters a great deal to the behavioral-science disciplines, taken separately and together—anthropology, sociology, psychology, economics, political science, and—with added emphasis now, given the new interest in genetics—biology. The idea is a prime test of their theories, their methods, and, rightly or wrongly, their pertinence and credibility. And in comparable ways the idea matters to the applied disciplines concerned with health, education, welfare, communications, policy and planning, and the various approaches to conflict resolution. The idea is a prime test of their ability to provide and plan essential services.

The idea matters also to the groups of scholars and researchers who have invested their energies and reputations in efforts to establish the primacy and the validity of views of the culture of poverty. And similarly it matters to persons in applied fields and in policy-making positions who are shopping for ideas but are primarily interested in the usefulness of the idea.

A chief practical contribution of social-science writings and research on the culture of poverty has come from the way in which they have helped force and have facilitated a focusing on the serious problems of poverty and racism. This effect has had no necessary relationship to the scientific validity of the findings or to any social-science consensus. It may be a sign of a basic strain toward sanity and health that the concept has had its greatest circulation at the same time that the serious questioning of the relevance of the social sciences to the problems of poverty and racism has been accelerating.

This questioning of the social sciences may be related to what S. M. Miller has pointed out: that the social sciences and the general public for a long time have ignored or discounted the effects on our society of the long-time blunting of black political participation, of the failure of professional services, and of the transformations and redefinitions of power and income that are occurring in the society.

The idea of the culture of poverty is an example of a major social-science idea and preoccupation that has contributed its part to the increasing estrangement of the poor, the black, and the youth from old-line intellectuals and established men of science. The credibility, the relevance, the politics, and the humanity of scientists are being questioned by the poor, the black, and the youth. Although the idea of the culture of poverty has helped focus on the problem of the poor in our society, the effect of some of its versions and uses has been to divert energies and attention from the need for significant changes in the educational, occupational, and political structures. It has had the effect of helping to divert attention from the critical crunches in our society related to the fact that new generations of black youths—black lower- and middle-class youths—are "seeking for power [and radical change now] as against an older generation [and other ethnics] satisfied with just a little more opportunity" (N. C. Mills, 1969, p. 59).

Professor David Eaton, in his presidential address to the 1969 annual meeting of the American Political Science Association, pointed out that in recent years "the talents of political scientists have been put in the service largely of the elites in society—in government, business, the military and voluntary organizations." Further,

the professional is seen as having little communication and contact with those who characteristically benefit least from the fruits of modern industrial society—the racial and economic minorities, the unrepresented publics at home, and the colonial masses abroad. One factor is also clear. The crisis of our times spares no group, not even the social sciences. The pressures to utilize all of our resources in critically evaluating goals as well as in providing effective means are too great to be denied. For increasing numbers of us, it is no longer practical or morally tolerable to stand on the political sidelines when our expertise alerts us to disaster.[2]

Many students would agree with Bernard Pyron that "the problem of effectively reducing economic deprivation in America is in large part related to the perception of the poor by the non-poor," and that "it is also a problem involving the values which determine the perception of the poor by the non-poor. For it is the representatives of the majority of the non-poor who decide whether

[2] Quoted in *The New York Times,* Sept. 8, 1969, p. 47.

or not to make effective use of current proposals to reduce economic deprivation." (Pyron, 1967, unpublished).

The acceptance and the workings of income-maintenance programs and job-training programs as features of employment and income strategies, for example, are affected by the perceptions of the poor by the non-poor.

Giving money to the poor on a non-contingent basis or for governmental support of on-the-job training or work created by the federal government contradicts the prime American value which says that one should earn money in direct proportion to the effort he expends in working within the capitalistic labor market (exchange justice). An alternative value says that the *responsibility* for providing the necessities of life for the twenty to thirty percent of the population who are defined as poor is an obligation of society through government. The problem is whether America wants to invest $15 to $30 billion a year to reduce economic deprivation. Thus, an over-riding problem for all employment and income strategies is to change the negative perceptions of many of the non-poor toward the poor . . .

Pyron hypothesizes about the effect of perceptions of the poor:

The non-poor who hold strongly to exchange justice would . . . feel that there is an inequity in giving monetary rewards to the poor when they expend little or no effort to justify the rewards. Those who hold to the value of [societal] responsibility would be able to justify giving money to people who are below the poverty line.

The non-poor who believe in exchange justice and feel that the poor do not deserve outcomes greater than their inputs . . . tend to generate negative feeling toward the poor. Given that a middle-class person has a general negative feeling toward the poor, one way for him to maintain consistency within his perceptual and belief systems is to assume that the poor have a whole cluster of inter-related negative character traits. The non-poor person who believes in exchange justice would perceive that the poor are economically deprived because they have defective character, are lazy or lack initiative. Even professional social workers have tended to associate with economic deprivation a cluster of negative traits.

The belief in exchange justice may have also motivated some social scientists to search for basic sociological, cultural and psychological homogeneity in the poor . . .

The data on the number of families on general relief in 1961 and in 1966 also disconfirm the view that poverty is largely determined by negative personality traits which make a person unemployable. In March, 1961, at the depth of the recession period, there were 525,000 families on general relief and in January, 1966, there were less than 300,000 families on general relief. This drop indicated that many of the men on relief were employable and were willing to find work if the work existed.

There are other points that might be made in this connection about the relationship between employment and poverty and the behavior of people who are poor. One has to do with the fact that the employment level and, therefore, the number of persons who are poor at any one time are, in a basic sense, functions of federal economic policies. For example, on October 7, 1969, Secretary of the Treasury Kennedy told Congress that a four percent unemployment rate was "acceptable" to the Administration and that the Administration believed it was necessary to continue policies that might force unemployment even higher. He added, when pressed, that he could not give a figure to identify the unemployment rate the Administration would consider unacceptable.

The second set of observations about employment and poverty has to do with the earning differentials between whites and blacks, and the significance of the continuing discrimination by employers and unions.

Of the more than 25.2 million people classified as poor in the United States, only about one in seven is out of a job. Six million of the poor work full time, year round, at jobs which do not pay a living wage. The August 1969 Census Reports show further that one third of Negroes are categorized as poor; this represents a drop from 56 percent in 1951 to 33 percent in 1968. For the nation as a whole, the number which is categorized as poor is just under one in seven. This represents a drop from 22 percent in 1961 to 13 percent in 1968. It would be difficult to attribute any significant part of this decrease to the government's Poverty Program or to changes in values of the poor.

Herman Miller has shown that a gap between black and white earnings has not changed essentially over the last twenty years, despite increases in real wages for both groups, and he shows further that the gap between white and black income is relatively greater when education is controlled: the average nonwhite person with four years of college can expect to earn less over a lifetime than the white who did not go beyond the eighth grade (H. Miller, 1970). This persistent gap is an external fact which undoubtedly has some effect upon motivations. Further, there are important consequences of the type of labor-market behavior that sees people with inadequate and marginal incomes seeking to raise family income by holding more than one job, working more hours and having other family members seek employment.

A Harvard University study reported in April 1969 that blacks' returns from education are much lower than the returns for whites, even when we correct for the blacks' lower average level of learning (Harvard, 1969, p. 21).

Current programs place a great deal of stress on the need for the disadvantaged to upgrade job skills. However, there are some students, such as Ivar Berg and Shirley Gorelick, who stress that an argument can be made for the crucial role of employer policies in creating or thwarting opportunities. They charge that credentialism and educational qualifications are used for enlarging employers' and medium and top-level employees' gains at the expense of the less educated.

A part of the argument holds that (1) many jobs do not need for their performance the level of "talent" required to obtain them, and (2) the "talents" needed are not so scarce among the population as many persons have been led to believe. The argument as formulated by Shirley Gorelick, goes:

The practice of linking jobs to education levels results in the denial of higher level jobs to the less educated for these reasons:

(1) It arbitrarily lessens the number of people qualified to do the higher level jobs. By so restricting this pool the average wage or sal-

ary is made to be higher than it would otherwise be. (2) Exclusion of the less educated from these jobs arbitrarily increases the pool of people for lower jobs.

Insofar as the bulk of the wage pool comes from lower level jobs . . . the discrimination by education is profitable.

Shirley Gorelick argues that in the labor market "blatant racism has become somewhat muted and a more justifiable and seemingly neutral principle has taken the place of overt racism in keeping blacks expanding competition for the lowest level jobs. That principle has been education." She suggests:

In the tug of war over lower level wage rates the efforts of employers to keep wages low and of unions to raise them cumulate to disadvantage blacks. Employers use various exclusionary screening principles which may or may not be racist in form but whose effect is to make large numbers of blacks either unemployed or available for low level jobs. White unions, seeking to restrict the pool of labor available in order to be able to demand wage increases, seek to exclude blacks either indirectly, through nepotism rules and apprenticeship tests, or more directly and blatantly. The consequences are heavy black unemployment and heavy black concentration in lower paying jobs.

The idea of a culture of poverty matters most to the poor; because of its vogue they have had and will have labels placed on their capacities, their needs, and their preferences. These labels are used by people who make decisions that are critical with reference to the level of the economy as well as with reference to the amount and the distribution of the essential services that affect their educational and employment opportunities, their housing, and their health.

This happens and will continue to happen without any necessary relationship to the quality of research on the culture-of-poverty hypothesis; and the fact that it will occur does not mean that there should be a moratorium or cessation of research on poverty. On the contrary, the flap should signal the need for more significant studies of the nexus between poverty and affluence. There should be especially more research that seeks to get the perspectives and the participation of more of the blacks and the poor; that seeks to develop more and better systems of delivery for essential health and welfare services; that seeks to discover ways to cope with and manage the information explosion, the prodigious growth of scientific knowledge, and the increasing fragmentation of that knowledge. The following are a grim fact and a statistic that should help put in proper perspective much of the discussion about the etiology of poverty and the role of the culture of poverty.

Surely everyone can agree that science has done wonderful things for the improvement of health. But, even here, uncomfortable questions are being asked. Have our best doctors become so preoccupied with the wonders of their technology that they have become indifferent to the plight of large numbers of people who suffer from conditions just as fatal but much less interesting? Even the most earnest advocates of increased research in heart disease, cancer, and stroke must be a little bit embarrassed by the fact that the United States, which used to be a world leader in reducing infant mortality rates, has now fallen to 15th place. [R. S. Morison, 1969, p. 152.]

My own view is that the most important research in this area now should focus not on the culture of poverty but on the culture of affluence—the culture that matters more and that is far more dangerous than the culture of poverty. Jean Mayer has put the thrust and the focus succinctly:

There is a strong case to be made for a stringent population policy on exactly the reverse of the basis Malthus expounded. Malthus was concerned with the steadily more widespread poverty that indefinite population growth would inevitably create. I am concerned about the areas of the globe where people are rapidly becoming richer. For rich people occupy much more space, consume more of each natural resource, disturb the ecology more, and create more land, air, water, chemical, thermal and radioactive pollution than poor people. So it can be argued that from many viewpoints it is even more urgent to control the numbers of the rich than it is to control the numbers of the poor. [Mayer, 1969, p. 5.]

This paper has not had a primary concern for examining the scientific significance of the culture of poverty concept, for two reasons: (1) the concept has been examined and assessed by a number of students, including myself, and most thoroughly and brilliantly recently by Charles Valentine, and many others including Camille Jeffers, Elliot Liebow, Lee Rainwater, Dorothy Newman, Elizabeth Herzog, Kenneth Clark, Eleanor Leacock; and (2) as has been stressed, its scientific significance as such is only one of the things that matters mightily today.

In thinking about this paper, I thought back over some observations I made as far back as 1960 in connection with a study of low-income families in Washington, D.C. I would like to close with a paraphrase of some of my observations that appear to be still pertinent to questions raised about the way in which the culture of poverty matters to science, to public policy, and to the people who are affluent as well as poor.

1. Many of the formulations of lower-class culture, as well as of the culture of poverty with which it is frequently confused, contain within them a number of intellectual assumptions and untested hypotheses. These often beget generalizations that are not consonant with existing data. For such reasons alone, it is urgent that the versions of lower-class culture and of the culture of poverty that have filtered into pedagogical and social welfare planning and practice, and popular thinking as well, should be looked at very carefully.

2. One danger lies in the tendency to subsume under the term "lower-class culture" a medley of traits without making distinctions among the kinds of traits and among levels of abstraction. A related danger comes from the failure to separate essence from accident, the crucial from the trivial, and the persistent from the transitory in the packages of traits.

3. The behaviors observed in the bulk of poor families are not generated by or guided by an urban lower-class "cultural system in its own right—with an integrity of its own." This is not meant to suggest that there are no differences other than income between this category and the adequate-income category of the population, or that there are no modalities in the characteristics and in the behaviors of the poor.

There are several modes of styles of low income (and lower-class) living rather than a single or basic mode or style. We are impressed by the range and variability of structures and behaviors within the low-income category.

4. There are significant differences in hopes and expectations here of changes for the better, and in the estimates of resources poor parents think they have—or can find to effect changes in themselves. In other words, there are cutting points in the optimism and confidence of many parents about the futures of their families—and in the belief that their efforts alone might affect them.

5. Confidence that is continuing—even though mixed or fluctuating—distinguishes as much as anything low-income families that are not now marked by neglect or dependency from those that are "clinically" dependent or neglectful.

6. The "multiproblem" or "hard-core" cases of inadequacy, dependency, and neglect are, to use medical terminology, "clinical cases" with unknown or varying potential for rehabilitation. As in types of heart disease and cancer, when the condition becomes known or public it is frequently too late; prognosis for these relatively few cases is poor. "Clinical" dependency—that which is known to public and private agencies and health and welfare institutions—is costly and provokes concern beyond the numbers involved. And, although it is necessary and important to seek improved ways of rehabilitation or containment, the long-range dividends are likely to be greater from research and demonstration programs that seek to identify and work with the highly vulnerable families not yet publicly dependent or neglectful—to examine the "preclinical" and "subclinical" aspects of dependency and neglect.

7. The behaviors of the bulk of the low-income families appear as pragmatic adjustments to external and internal stresses and deprivations experienced in the quest for essentially common values. A seeming paradox is that affirmation of, if not demonstration of, some of America's traditional virtues and values in their purest form is found to be strong and recurrent among even the most deprived.

8. It is more fruitful to think of different types of lower-class families reacting in various ways to the facts of their position and to relative isolation rather than to think of them as reacting to the imperatives of lower-class culture.

9. It is important not to confuse basic life chances and actual behavior with basic cultural values and preferences.

10. Many of the urban poor straddle poverty and affluence. They may exhibit complex and fluctuating mixtures of the living situations and styles, possessions, and tastes of different consumption levels and classes.

11. The focus of efforts to change aspects of the behavior of people should be on background conditions and precipitants of the significantly deviant behaviors, rather than on presumably different class or cultural values.

12. The family environment of a poor family may fluctuate markedly over relatively brief periods of child-rearing time.

13. It is not likely that the way to remove the threat and to reduce the costs of deviant aspects of the behavior of poor or lower-class people—or, rather, segments of the poor and the lower class that threaten and cost most at this time—is to be found in direct efforts to change a lower-class culture or a culture of poverty that is perceived as significantly different and alien.

Significant change is not likely to come from efforts that add up to indulging, or to sealing off, or to trying to get lower-class people themselves to revamp what is presumed to be their unique culture.

There is danger that the concept will encourage the development of a spurious cultural relativism based upon race and class.

14. The concept of lower-class culture has valid but limited uses in tackling contemporary problems of dependency, delinquency, crime, and mental health. However, the fact that the concept is valid, and perhaps necessary, for research and theory purposes—and for use on certain levels—does not mean necessarily that in its present form it should be either the appropriate or the decisive guide to policy and programming. It certainly is not the most useful single tool to place in the hands of those who deal directly with poor people who have problems.

15. The lower-income male and father is a key figure in gaining an understanding of child-rearing in the poor or dependent family. Of particular importance is the man's ability to support and stand for the family—to play the economic and social roles wished of him, particularly by wives, mothers, and children. Some of the implications of this are suggested in the field document that describes a mother of

six children chiding her husband for being afraid and not showing aggressiveness in looking for a second job to increase the family income. Showing his pay stub, she said, "This looks like a receipt for a woman's paycheck instead of a man's."[3]

One of the significant differences between 1960 and today is the pervasive force of a highly politicized black consciousness. Although the responses of the Negro/black poor and nonpoor to heightened black consciousness are not to be described simplistically, the dramatic quality of affirmation, of protest, and of assertiveness—traits that have never been absent—now tends to dwarf, if not to dispute categorically, the force of a culture of poverty among Negroes.

Even before the recent surge of race and class consciousness, the evidence is that Negroes and the poor tended to react negatively to the label and the implications of the culture of poverty when they were made aware of it and felt its invidious consequences. This is only one of the prime reasons questions will be raised continually about the concept; and there will be indications that the idea of a culture of poverty matters less as a useful guide to conflict resolution based on economic deprivation and color, to positive social change, and to needed institutional alternatives in our society—whether that society is black and white integrated or not. The paradox is that the Black Power movement in interesting ways has reduced if not destroyed the power of the culture-of-poverty idea as a scientific explanatory variable at the same time that it has increased its force as a political idea—an ideology. And this is why it matters.

BIBLIOGRAPHY

Baratz, Stephen S., "The Unique Culture of the Ghetto," *The Center Magazine*, Center for the Study of Democratic Institutions, Santa Barbara, Calif., July 1969.

[3] Variously taken or adapted from Hylan Lewis, 1961a, 1961b, 1963, and 1964, the last three of which are included in Lewis, 1967.

Boulding, Kenneth, *Beyond Economics: Essays on Society, Religion and Ethics.* Ann Arbor, Mich.: University of Michigan Press, 1970.

Gorelick, Shirley, "Incentives and Obstacles to Management Hiring of the Disadvantaged," unpublished.

Harvard University Program on Regional and Urban Economics, "The Effects of Education on the Earnings of Blacks and Whites" (mimeographed), April 1969.

Jordan, Winthrop D., *White over Black: American Attitudes toward the Negro, 1550–1812.* Baltimore: Penguin Books, Pelican edition, 1969.

Lewis, Hylan, "Child Rearing Practices among Low-Income Families in the District of Columbia: A Progress Report" (mimeographed), March 1961.

———, "Child Rearing Practices among Low-Income Families in the District of Columbia," paper presented at the National Conference on Social Welfare, May 16, 1961, Minneapolis.

———, "Culture, Class and the Behavior of Low-Income Families," paper presented at the Conference on Lower-Class Culture, June 27-29, 1963, New York; revised August 1965.

———, "The Culture of Poverty Approach to Social Problems," paper delivered at the plenary session of the annual meeting of the Society for the Study of Social Problems, Aug. 29, 1964, Montreal.

———, *Culture, Class and Poverty.* Washington: Cross-Tell, 1967.

Lewis, Oscar, "A Death in the Sanchez Family: A Special Supplement," Part I, *New York Review of Books,* Sept. 11, 1969.

Mayer, Jean, "Toward a Non-Malthusian Population Policy," *Columbia Forum,* Summer 1969.

Miller, Herman, *Rich Man, Poor Man: The Distribution of Income in America.* New York: Crowell, 1970.

Miller, S. M., and Mary Morgan, " 'Max-Feas': The Evolution of a Concept." Annual meeting American Sociological Association, San Francisco, September 2, 1969 (unpublished).

Mills, Nicolaus C., "Black Youth and the NAACP," *Dissent,* July-August 1969.

Morison, Robert S., "Science and Social Attitudes," *Science,* Vol. 165, July 11, 1969.

Pyron, Bernard, "The Perception of the Poor by the Non-poor" 1967 (unpublished).

Seabury, Paul, "Expecting the Worst," *Science,* April 4, 1969.

CONTRIBUTORS

JANET CASTRO is a teacher of speech and language currently assigned to WNYE-FM, New York City's educational radio station. She writes and broadcasts language programs for use in the classroom. Mrs. Castro was formerly assigned as a language development teacher to More Effective School 307, where she worked extensively with black schoolchildren, using creative dramatics, street games, and other approaches to stimulate free verbal expression.

MILDRED DICKEMAN, chairman of the Anthropology Department at Sonoma State College, received her A.B. from the University of Michigan and a Ph.D. from the University of California at Berkeley. She has done field work in the eastern highlands of New Guinea as well as among the Oklahoma Cherokees. Her areas of interest are educational anthropology, culture change, Oceania and primate behavior.

ERNEST DRUCKER has been working for the past four years in the area of community mental health and is currently in the Divisions of Psychiatry and Social Medicine at Montefiore Hospital in New York. He was educated in the public schools of New York and received a Ph.D. in clinical psychology from the City University of New York. His professional interests include class and cultural factors in thought and social organization, developing alternatives to traditional models of psychiatric care through community programs, and the role of social structure in mental health.

HERBERT G. ELLIS is presently working as instructor and counselor at the House of Correction, a custodial institution for juvenile offenders in Chicago. For the past twelve years he has worked in the area of adjustment and rehabilitation of male youth and has conducted research among working-class youth in Chicago. He is currently pursuing a Master of Arts degree in public-school administration from De Paul University, Chicago.

ESTELLE FUCHS, associate professor of anthropology, Division of Education, Hunter College, City University of New York, has had extensive field experience studying schooling in metropolitan centers of this country, among American Indians, and in Denmark and has herself been a secondary-school teacher in New York City for a number of years. She is author of *Pickets at the Gates* and *Teachers Talk: Views from Inside City Schools*.

DR. VERA P. JOHN has a Ph.D. from the University of Chicago in psychology of language and cognition. Currently on sabbatical leave in Santa Fe, New Mexico, she is an associate professor of psychology and education at Yeshiva University. She is a co-author of *Early Childhood Bilingual Education* and of *Language Acquisition and Development in Early Childhood* and is currently working on a book on thinking.

ELEANOR BURKE LEACOCK, professor of anthropology at the Polytechnic Institute of Brooklyn, has conducted field work among the American Indians of the Labrador Peninsula and the lower Fraser River, British Columbia, as well as in Zambia and in rural Switzerland and Italy. She has also worked in the areas of social psychiatry, public health, race relations, and education. She is author of *Teaching and Learning in City Schools,* editor of a recent printing of the anthropological classic, *Ancient Society,* by Lewis Henry Morgan, and co-editor of *North American Indians in Recent History*.

ANTHONY LEEDS, professor of anthropology at the University of Texas and secretary of Section H (anthropology) of the American Association for the Advancement of Science, has carried on field work in Brazil among agricultural workers, the national elites, and the urban proletariat, as well as among the Yaruro Indians of Venezuela. He has also done comparative work on the rural proletariat of Lima, Perú, and San Antonio and Austin, Texas, and has served as evaluator and technical adviser on AID-sponsored community-development projects.

JEAN LESTER, a graduate of Brooklyn College, City University of New York, taught English in a New York City high school. Disillusioned with the teaching profession, she is presently staying at home and raising a family.

HYLAN LEWIS is professor of sociology at Brooklyn College, City University of New York, and senior vice-president of the Metropolitan Applied Research Center, Inc., of New York City. He has carried on extensive research in the areas of community studies, black culture and family life, and race relations. He is author of *Blackways of Kent*.

STANLEY M. NEWMAN is associate professor in urban anthropology at Northeastern Illinois State College, and staff anthropologist at the Mile Square Health Center of Presbyterian–St. Luke's Hospital, Chicago. He has conducted research in both black and white urban working-class neighborhoods, and, prior to attending college, himself worked as a warehouseman, a truck driver's helper, and a worker in an aircraft factory.

LISA REDFIELD PEATTIE is a social anthropologist on the faculty of the Department of Urban Studies and Planning at the Massachusetts Institute of Technology. She has done field research with American Indians, in Venezuela, in the public schools and in public housing projects. She is the author of a book based on her Venezuelan experience, *The View from the Barrio,* as well as articles on social aspects of planning, on citizen participation and planning, and on ethical and policy relations of social research.

CHARLES A. VALENTINE is associate professor of anthropology at Washington University, St. Louis. He is interested in cultural variety, structural inequality, and movements for change in complex modern societies. Following field work in New Guinea and comparative research on other ethnically stratified Pacific island societies, he has published several articles on religion, politics, and change in those areas. More recently he has been a long-term participant-observer in American minority-group advancement movements, and he has studied poverty and ethnic relations in several U. S. cities. He is the author of *Culture and Poverty: Critique and Counterproposals* (University of Chicago Press, 1968). Since mid-1968 he and his wife have been making an intensive in-residence ethnographic study of a low-income urban, predominantly Afro-American community in the Northern U. S.

MURRAY L. WAX (Ph.D., University of Chicago) and Rosalie H. Wax (Ph.D., University of Chicago) have been working with American Indians and studying their relationships to educational institutions for over ten years. Together with Robert V. Dumont, Jr., they made an intensive study of federal schools serving the Oglala Sioux of Pine Ridge, South Dakota, and the major report of their researches was published in 1964 by the Society for the Study of Social Problems. Currently, Mr. Wax is professor of sociology and Mrs. Wax professor of anthropology at the University of Kansas.

ROLLAND H. WRIGHT, an associate professor in the Division of the Science of Society at Monteith College, Wayne State University, is the author of many sociological abstracts and essays. He is presently a Ph.D. candidate at Brandeis. His main areas of interest are urban sociology and American Indians.

INDEX

INDEX

371